Financial Crises: Causes, Consequences, Policy Responses and Management

Financial Crises: Causes, Consequences, Policy Responses and Management

Frida Ross

NY RESEARCH PRESS
New York

Published by NY Research Press
118-35 Queens Blvd., Suite 400,
Forest Hills, NY 11375, USA
www.nyresearchpress.com

Financial Crises: Causes, Consequences, Policy Responses and Management
Frida Ross

International Standard Book Number: 978-1-64725-451-3 (Hardback)

Cataloging-in-Publication Data

Financial crises : causes, consequences, policy responses and
management / Frida Ross.
p. cm.
Includes bibliographical references and index.
ISBN 978-1-64725-451-3
1. Financial crises. 2. Financial crises--Effect of monetary policy on.
3. Monetary policy. 4. Currency crises. 5. Financial crises--Prevention.
6. Economic policy. I. Ross, Frida.
HB3722 .F56 2023
338.542--dc23

Contents

Preface

This book aims to highlight the current researches and provides a platform to further the scope of innovations in this area. This book is a product of the combined efforts of many researchers and scientists, after going through thorough studies and analysis from different parts of the world. The objective of this book is to provide the readers with the latest information of the field.

Financial crisis refers to a condition wherein a financial asset unexpectedly loses a significant portion of its nominal value. There are various types of financial crises including stock market crises, external debt crises, banking crises, balance of payments crises and currency crises. A financial crisis can have several causes such as an overvalued asset or institution, which can then be worsened by irrational behavior of the investors. During a financial crisis, asset values endure a sharp decrease, firms and individuals are unable to pay their dues, and financial institutions face a shortage of liquidity. Policy responses are implemented by the governments in order to prevent the banking and financial institutions from collapsing as well as mitigating the consequences of the credit crunch on the economy. This book outlines the causes, consequences, policy responses and management of financial crisis. It will prove to be immensely beneficial to students and researchers in this field.

I would like to express my sincere thanks to the authors for their dedicated efforts in the completion of this book. I acknowledge the efforts of the publisher for providing constant support. Lastly, I would like to thank my family for their support in all academic endeavors.

Frida Ross

1

Economic Policies in Europe and Latin America: A Theoretical Overview

Stephany Griffith-Jones and Bettina De Souza Guilherme

This book is the result of the 3 years comparative and multidisciplinary Jean Monnet Network, "Crisis-Equity-Democracy for Europe and Latin America", of senior academics and policy advisors from four European and three Latin American countries, including experts on the European Union and Latin American regionalism.

The rationale of the project and the common link is that both Europe and Latin America can learn from their respective experiences on "crisis", its management and the distributive and democratic implications at national and regional level. The Latin American debt crisis of the 1980s and the global financial crisis of 2008 and the following Eurozone debt crisis have much in common in regard to their economic and social impacts and the following wave of populism and polarisation. Furthermore, the research and exchange in the network clearly showed that these crises are symptoms and consequences of the same systemic flaws inherent both in the present EU and global financial, economic and governance system. Given that both regions face fairly similar global unsustainability challenges, from a macro-financial as well as an environmental point of view, their similarities should call for the joint elaboration and implementation of a bi-regional strategic alliance for addressing the roots of the global crisis.

S. Griffith-Jones
Initiative for Policy Dialogue, Columbia University, New York, USA

Institute of Development Studies, Sussex University Brighton, Brighton, UK

B. De Souza Guilherme (✉)
Founder and Co-coordinator of the Jean Monnet Network "Crisis-Equity-Democracy for Europe and Latin America", IRELAC, Rio de Janeiro, Brazil

European Parliament, Brussels, Belgium
e-mail: bettina.desouza@europarl.europa.eu

The main purposes of the project can be summarised as to (1) locate in the current global financial system one of the very major causes of the financial and debt crises in the EU and Latin America; (2) map and evaluate how both regions and individual countries within both regions have tried to manage these crises; (3) discuss the economic, political and social effects of theses crises on both regions and individual countries; (4) and, finally, to make policy suggestions on how to transition from finance capitalism to a more sustainable real capitalism, on how both regions can better manage/govern/respond to such systemic pressures and on how they can increase their cooperation.

The book begins in Chap. 1 with a theoretical introduction which includes a chapter by Stephan Schulmeister that explores the effects of the paradigm change on economic policies in Europe and in Latin America and a second chapter by Christian Ghymers, which analyses some key systemic aspects of the global crisis, i.e. climate change, macro-financial instability and the weakening of democracy and upon their inter-connections. These intertwined aspects reflect myopic prices, the non-incorporation of externalities as well as the lack of needed regulation of financial markets and are also linked by the way public decisions are biased towards the short-term, and influenced by vested interests.

The following chapters are divided in five parts. The second part explores aspects of regional governance and how the economic and financial crises were managed in Europe and Latin America. The chapters share a common diagnosis that, with the breakup of the Bretton Woods System and the following liberalisation of capital flows and deregulation of financial markets, the emerging countries have been subject to bubbles and crisis, in which they were confronted with capital flight to safe havens similar to what occurred later to the countries in the euro area most affected by the crisis and in both cases their central banks did not have the control over the currency in which their debts were denominated. Paul De Grauwe, for instance, compares the situation of a debtor country within the Eurozone to the status of the emerging countries in a debt crisis and reveals similarities because "they cease to have control over the currency in which their debt is issued. As a result, financial markets can force these countries' sovereign defaults. This makes the monetary union fragile and vulnerable to changing market sentiments" (De Grauwe 2012).

In both regions, debtor countries had at most insufficient (public) debt relief but suffered major (internal) devaluations (lowering of real wages and pensions and cuts in essential public services, especially health and education) and a prolonged period of economic stagnation, decline or low growth. The IMF adjustment programmes for Latin America and the Troika programmes for Europe's debt crisis countries bear indeed strong similarities and economic and social consequences leading to a lost decade, decline of the middle class, lowering of living standards of poorest people and fall in investment, the increase of inequality and poverty by reducing the role of the state, cuts in public services and social spending. Griffith Jones identifies the vulnerability of European creditor banks to debt reduction as a key problem in the euro area debt crisis, as it was in the Latin American debt crisis, which was managed in the interests of the creditor banks and countries: this is in one sense much more serious in the European case than in Latin America, because the main lender to Southern European countries were creditors and investors from other European countries. This and major flaws in the architecture of EMU as well as their lack of accountability played against an EMU crisis management based on the "general interest" of the European Union and are a major cause for the publicly displayed conflict between debtor and creditor countries leading to a nearly existential crisis of Economic and Monetary Union, much to the detriment to the European Union's image within the European Union, in Latin America and globally.

Comparing the crises of the 1980s, 1990s and 2010s, we can identify failures of the coordination of both macroeconomic policies and the absence of debt restructuring mechanisms at international level (both at EU and at the global level). Failures in providing these coordination efforts could entail, as was the case in the 1980s, and is again in the 2010s, a delay in implementing the required solutions making the social cost of these episodes more profound (Sanguinetti 2014).[1]

There are, however, differences in timing and sequence of events, in the strength of the "social model", and concerning the process of regionalism. Latin America has been a pre-runner or prototype of debt crises, but both the social model and regionalism are much more developed in Europe. In fact, in Europe, where both debtor and creditor countries were in the same economic area, the European Union has been both part of the problem as a trigger of the crisis and key to solutions of the crisis. In Latin America, regionalism never achieved the same level of integration, nor was there a serious ambition or project that could pair the EU. At the time of the 1980s Latin American debt crisis, there was an attempt to coordinate different Latin American debtor positions (in the ad hoc Cartagena Group), but it had limited impact, due to insufficient political commitment by the Latin American debtor governments and effective divisive tactics by the creditor governments. Furthermore, creditors were outside Latin America. Moreover, regional organisations have been much more of a political nature in Latin America. Except for the recent results of the Pacific Alliance, even the organisations, which prioritised the liberalisation of trade such as Mercosur, never achieved full free trade. Additionally, due to the increasing political polarisation in the last years, the existing regional organisations even lost the capacity to effectively intervene in the cases of (political) crisis to mediate a solution.

The volume takes account of these differences by having a strong focus on the analysis of the architectural flaws and the democratic deficit of the Economic and Monetary Union and analysing and proposing a number of reforms of EMU, ranging from Treaty reform to reforms not requiring Treaty reforms. It presents proposals on policy priorities, including development and strategic partnerships promoting the green transition, greater cooperation for SMEs and a macroeconomic cooperation between the two regions in the framework of a renewed strategic alliance. The proposals thus foresee both the reforms to fix the problems, which triggered the

[1] Sanguinetti Pablo, Comments on "The Latin American Debt Crisis in Historical Perspective" by José Antonio Ocampo in Stiglitz, Joseph E. (2014-07-23). Life After Debt: The Origins and Resolutions of Debt Crisis (International Economic Association) (Kindle Locations 2943–2944). Palgrave Macmillan. Kindle Edition.

crisis, and proposals, which lead the way out of the crisis and into a more sustainable future for both regions with the EU as a motor.

On Latin America, we address the issue of regionalism in three chapters: one on the structure of crisis management at regional level, a second one on the impact of crisis on regionalism in the region and the third on the structural lack of total factor productivity increases, which includes proposals for improving it including by a strategic alliance with the EU. The second one deals mainly with the impact of the crisis in some of the regional key players on regionalism and the effectiveness of regional organisations addressing crises. Furthermore, it is obvious that the failure of an adequate crisis management based on solidarity at European level, the application and enforcement of similar adjustment programmes as in Latin America in spite of Europe's pride in its social model and social market economy, had the consequence of undermining confidence and enthusiasm for the European Union.

The third and fourth parts explore the impact of the crisis in Europe and Latin America, at the national and regional levels, including the political polarisation and rise in populism. The crisis in Latin American countries follows a different timeline, and the developments in Latin America seem to be ahead of Europe. In the aftermath and possibly as a reaction of the lost decade of the 1980s and the intensive austerity programmes, most of the key countries in Latin America experienced a "pink wave" of more left-wing and/or populist governments, followed by a "blue wave of neoliberalism". The interesting point in common between the two regions is that after the crisis and the austerity era, political positions, parties and governments seem to be more polarised and less stable. Some of the European populist parties on the left, such as Podemos or Syriza, were to some extent taking these movements and their strategies as a model. However, in Europe, left-wing parties and other organisations were not able to benefit from the "systemic crisis of neoliberal capitalism" to use the momentum to change both European and Global governance, while the "pink wave" did lead to establishment of a number of regional organisations and the rise at least of Brazil as one of the BRICS and motor of South-South and sustainable development for a certain period, i.e. until about 2013.

During this period, in Europe, the financial crisis and the following and overlapping migration crisis with an equally "poor" crisis management and lacking solidarity by the European Union both furthered the rise of right-wing populism, xenophobia, nationalism and euro-scepticism jeopardising liberal democracy, regional integration and multilateralism. This poses an obstacle to put into place the necessary reforms in the design of the European Union to remedy the revealed flaws of EMU's architecture and keeps the inbuilt weaknesses. A re-nationalisation of political competences will rather further increase the vulnerability in a system of global financial markets without adequate political and democratic governance and regulation. The current political wave is one of a retreat into national populism and putting into question regionalism, the urgency of climate change and multilateralism.

Given the rise of nationalism, soveranism and populism, Part IV contains five articles on these topics and their impact on regionalism, including a chapter on the populism in Europe. Additionally, a number of case studies in Part III, such as

Greece, Italy, Portugal, Venezuela and Brazil, have integrated the rise of populism within the analysis.

While the starting point in both regions are financial crises caused by deregulated financial markets in the aftermath of the break-up of the Bretton Woods system, the research also analyses the governance and legitimacy crisis regarding the crisis management and economic, social and political consequences at EU level and at national level in a sample of the debtor countries. Greece was chosen for not only being a highly indebted country at the moment the crisis broke out (in fact triggering the Eurozone debt crisis) but also having been submitted to intentionally tough and punitive austerity programmes, with extremely negative effects on the economy and the majority of its people, which were clearly and repetitively rejected by its population. Additionally, the Greek sovereign debt crisis led to a nearly existential crisis of the euro area through the risk of contagion. Portugal had been suffering from a lack of competitiveness. While the first (right wing) government rather outperformed the Troika adjustment programmes to implement pro-market structural reforms, the electorate as a consequence exchanged the government for a left-wing coalition which turned the Portuguese programmes into a success story of a country undergoing adjustment programmes, with a high degree of ownership taking into account the policy choices of the population, and with a more pro-Keynesian macroeconomic policy, that yielded positive results.

Italy went through an economic and political crisis triggered by the sovereign debt crisis and amplified by the incomplete structure of the Eurozone. The ingrained causes were the long-term structural problems and high public debt levels, leaving it vulnerable to external shocks. Italy did not undergo a Troika-led adjustment programme; however such adjustment was imposed by a technocratic government implementing austerity measures and reforms to signal to markets and stop the spiral of distrust and negative self-fulfilling expectations, but in fact so far not (successfully) addressing the sources of the problems, in particular the lack of total factor productivity growth. Italy is the example for a bigger and more powerful crisis country in which the disaffected voters turned for a time to right-wing parties, which temporarily became part of the government and confronted the other European partners by putting into question the existing rules of Economic and Monetary Union.

For the case studies in the region of Latin America, we have selected a number of key players undergoing major crisis with economic and political consequences for the entire region: Brazil, which had developed into the regional leader of South America, and Venezuela, which promoted and actively supported a populist and ideological anti-market regionalism. Brazil and Venezuela are addressed in a more in-depth analysis which focuses predominantly on the contemporary (political) crisis, including the rise of polarisation and populism, although it is clear that economic development and political crisis constantly feed on each other and can never be regarded as completely independent. Another interesting aspect we address in our volume is the rise and role of new social movements and new political parties both in Latin America and in Europe. In Venezuela and Brazil, we can observe the mobilisation of major social movements and protests as a turning point of the "pink tide", the left-wing governments, with the subsequent loss of public support, leading in both cases to a regression of the democratic development. In both cases, the economic and political crisis is partly related to the "resource curse", with an over-dependence on petrol and other primary resources and major corruption scandals and the decline of the economy in line with the fall of petrol prices. In the case of Venezuela, the mixture of the economic mismanagement and even humanitarian crisis, the political crisis and the foreign political tensions with the USA led to the conversion of the government into a left-wing authoritarian regime. In Brazil, the economic slowdown was used as a window of opportunity to impeach the elected president accusing her of creative accounting and reversing the left-wing government agenda into a Washington Consensus programme. At the following elections, the most popular (left wing) candidate was impeded to stand for elections by a judicial-political intrigue, paving the way for a populist authoritarian regime from the extreme right.

The crisis has also recently led to violent events even in successful economies in Latin America, like Chile, a country which in spite of very impressive growth (till recent years) and poverty reduction achievements had not only a very unequal income distribution but also still a rather extreme version of the market economy, in aspects like pension system, health and education. Therefore, this country also faces major challenges not just to restore growth but to significantly improve income distribution, as well as make important reforms in its economic development model, especially in sectors like its pension, health and education systems away from an extreme market economy, to a more balanced model, that involves a greater role of government institutions to deliver public goods, like good health and education at reasonable cost for all, including the poorer segments of the population, as well as sufficient pensions for the relatively poorer people, via solidarity redistributive mechanisms. Moreover, we also analyse the impact of their crisis on regional institutions in Latin America and regional integration. The book furthermore has a comparative study on the economic policies of Argentina, Brazil and Mexico.

One of the main conclusions of the network and project that is both valid for Europe and for Latin America is that the current financial system provokes economic, social, ecological and political instability and urgently needs to be reformed.

The last chapters, in Part VI, present proposals of the network reaching from the transition from finance capitalism to an economically, socially and ecologically sustainable real capitalism, to reforms in both regions and at the inter-regional level of EU-LAC relations. The increase of inequality in some countries and weakening of the middle classes as well as insufficient and slowing down of income increase of the poorer segments in recent years led to the loss of trust in the traditional political parties, often captured by the financial markets, an increased polarisation and the rise of populist forces, parties and political leaders. To give an answer to these developments, and in order to introduce more "stability", "sustainability" and "equity" into the current European and global model, Europe has the potential and the responsibility to develop a European "Eco-social model" as a prototype and motor for a global "Eco-social model". The book introduces the potential of modernising and enlarging the welfare state as probably the most important fundament of a new/renewed "European identity". New labour time models as prerequisite for continuing economic growth with continuous implementation of technical progress (raising labour productivity) and sustained full employment are desirable aims. An active modern industrial policy, partly funded by public development banks, which can help redirect also private finance to key sectors, is also essential to make growth sustainable, inclusive and dynamic.

The network considers the bi-regional EU-LAC cooperation as a further stepping stone in stimulating and reviving multilateralism and improving global governance through a "macroeconomic dialogue" between academics, civil society and officials, a "public-private strategy with a view to improve the joint competitiveness and the participation in GVCs in the global markets" as well as sustainable investment projects promoted via the EIB, targeted to achieve the new "green and social deal" for Europe, Latin America and globally. A more intensive cooperation of the two regions could be not only be mutually beneficial in times of major trade tensions but especially represent a valuable contribution to overcome the current crisis of multilateralism and global governance. The COVID-19 pandemic crisis, which evolved after the end of the research conducted by the authors of this book reinforces the arguments put forward, and the necessity to deepen the cooperation between the European Union and Latin America. We have also received the good news about the renewal of the Jean Monnet Network "Crisis-Equity-Democracy for Europe and Latin America", what will enable the researchers to continue their join efforts to reflect upon the crises, and advance proposals to the regions and their political dialogue, contributing to foster EU-CELAC Strategic Alliance.

Disclaimer The opinions expressed in this introduction/volume are the sole responsibility of the authors and do not necessarily represent the official position of the European Parliament or of any other EU institution.

References

De Grauwe, P. (2012). Managing the fragility of the Eurozone. Wiley. 45:255–268. https://doi.org/10.1111/j.1467-8462.2012.00691.x

Sanguinetti, P. (2014). Comments on "The Latin American Debt Crisis in Historical Perspective" by José Antonio Ocampo in Stiglitz, Joseph E. (2014-07-23). Life After Debt: The Origins and Resolutions of Debt Crisis (International Economic Association) (Kindle Locations 2943–2944). Palgrave Macmillan. Kindle Edition.

Part I
Economic Crisis around the World

2

Contextualizing the Crisis

Stephan Schulmeister

Abstract This chapter provides an empirically founded reconstruction of the long road of (Western) societies into the present crisis as a background for the different studies carried out as part of the Jean Monnet Network "Crisis–Equity–Democracy for Europe and Latin America".

Introduction and Overview

This chapter addresses the key puzzle of post-war economic development: until the 1970s, production, trade and employment grew strongly and steadily, in the global economy as well as in the different regions; since then, however, economic growth has been declining over the long run and has become unstable over the short and medium run. At the same time, the differences in economic dynamics have been rising across continents and regions: Latin America and – to a lesser extent – Africa were hit by debt crises in the early 1980s and late 1990s and by the instability of commodities prices, whereas the economies in (East) Asia have been performing strongly, in particular in China.

The difference in economic performance between the 1950s and 1960s the subsequent crisis phase is the more puzzling as only the second phase was shaped by basic technological innovations (microelectronics, robotics, internet, biotechnology, nanotechnology) which – according to mainstream economics – should have accelerated economic growth. Market liberalization should have had the same effect as financial markets and labour markets were highly regulated in the 1950s and 1960s. In the prosperity phase, the welfare state was built up strongly, yet the public debt declined relative to GDP, whereas the opposite developments took place over the subsequent decades. All these facts stay in contrast to conventional (equilibrium) theory. An empirically founded reconstruction of the long road of (Western)

S. Schulmeister (✉)
University of Vienna, Wien, Austria
e-mail: stephan.schulmeister@wifo-pens.at

societies into the present crisis provides the background for the different studies carried out as part of the Jean Monnet Network "Crisis–Equity–Democracy for Europe and Latin America". A first sketch of the systemic causes of the long post-war cycle is as follows.

Understanding the main causes of the Great Depression – financial instability, austerity policies and protectionism – provided the economic guidelines for the prosperity phase: the incentive conditions directed the capitalist "core energy", i.e. striving for profits, to activities in the real economy. Stable dollar exchange rates, stable commodity prices, interest rates below the rate of economic growth and "sleeping" stock markets (at least in Europe) rendered financial speculation unprofitable and raised the profitability of investment, production and trade in the real economy at the same time. In addition, building up the welfare state strengthened confidence of households, reduced income inequality and fostered the steady expansion of consumption. This "real-capitalist" system was based on the theory of John M. Keynes which called not only for an economically active government but also for stabilizing financial markets. The "European Social Model" combined real-capitalist incentive conditions with a strong welfare state (also the Cold War called for a "social capitalism"): market and state, competition and cooperation, entrepreneurship and trade unionism, and individual self-interest and social coherence were regarded as complementary. The success of real capitalism laid the ground for its own decline: Over the 1960s, full employment and the expanding welfare state shifted power from business to unions. The latter enforced more employee participation as well as a redistribution in favour of wages. The leftist "Zeitgeist" strengthened social-democratic parties. In addition, the environmental movement ("Club of Rome") denounced the capitalist growth model as unsustainable. All these developments together caused (big) business to turn towards the neoliberal ideology which promised disciplining trade unions, weakening the welfare state and establishing a truly free market economy.

Friedrich A. von Hayek, the great antipode of Keynes in the debates over the world depression in the 1930s, had begun to plan a counter-movement against Keynesianism already after his "defeat" caused by the success of Keynes' *General Theory* (1936). Hayek's book *The Road to Serfdom* (1944) provided the ideological fundament of the neoliberal movement. In 1947, Hayek founded the Mont Pelerin Society as neoliberal network of outstanding economists ("original thinkers"); intellectuals, in particular journalists ("second-hand dealers in ideas"); and wealthy people as financiers of university chairs or think tanks. During the 1950s and 1960s, the "original thinkers" worked on the theoretical foundation of their vision of a "free market economy" – from Friedman's "proof" of the impossibility of destabilizing financial speculation (1953) or Buchanan's "public-choice approach" of analysing politics as a purely egoistic business of politicians to Friedman's theory of a "natural rate of unemployment" (1968) and Robert Lucas' concept of "rational expectations" (1972). These theories legitimated the offensive against the welfare state, trade unions and financial market regulations and got rising support from "industrial capitalists" (threatened by the rising power of unions) as well as from "finance capitalists" (threatened by rising inflation).

The road into the present crisis began with the breakdown of the Bretton-Woods system between 1971 and 1973: the dollar lost 25% of its value; OPEC reacted with the first oil price "shock" in 1973. This sequence repeated itself between 1976 and 1979, leading to the second oil price "shock". Both "shocks" triggered two recessions and a strong acceleration of inflation. Neoliberal "original thinkers" took the coincidence of rising unemployment and rising inflation as disprove of Keynesian macroeconomics – even though their recommendations had contributed to this coincidence ("battle over the Phillips curve"). By the late 1970s, monetary policy began to fight inflation through raising interest rates like never before, far above the rate of economic growth. As this policy was most pronounced in the USA, the dollar almost doubled its value between 1980 and 1985, thereby appreciating the burden of international dollar debts: in 1982, the debt crisis of Latin America broke out. Within a decade, the economic system in the West was transformed from "real capitalism" to "finance capitalism", guided by the neoliberal "navigation map": the volatility of exchange rates and commodities prices, booming stock prices as well as a positive interest-growth differential shifted activities of non-financial business towards financial investments, facilitated by innovations like financial derivatives. The financial sector gradually transformed itself from a sector servicing the real economy to the dominant sector in the overall economy.

Neoliberal theories also legitimized policies against trade unions and the welfare state, first adopted in Chile after the military coup in 1973 and then in the UK and the USA where Margaret Thatcher and Ronald Reagan came to power in 1979 and 1980, respectively. Over the 1980s, high dollar interest and rising dollar exchange rates dampened the real economy in the USA strongly. Hence, monetary policy gave up monetarism and has been following an anti-cyclical course since Alan Greenspan became chairman of the Fed in 1987. Since Bill Clinton became US president in 1992, also fiscal policy has been conducted in an increasingly active, counter-cyclical manner. In other words, since the early 1990s, macroeconomic policy in the USA has been following a "trivial Keynesian" course. At the same time, economic policy in the EU gave up the Keynesian target of full employment and of social security through a comprehensive welfare state and began to follow neoliberal guidelines.

The main reason for this (gradual) change was the following. Finance-capitalist incentive conditions had caused the public debt to rise stronger in Europe than in the USA since financing the welfare state necessitates full employment. In the early 1990s, policy in the EU began to fight these "twin problems" through restrictive fiscal policy based on rules (Maastricht criteria, fiscal compact) and through labour market deregulation: the number of atypical jobs rose steadily (comprising nowadays roughly one third of overall jobs in the EU), unemployment benefits and social transfers in general have been cut, and the confidence in the welfare state got weaker. At the same time, speculative activities in financial markets boomed like never before, contributing to the rise in income and wealth inequality. After the stock market crash of 2000/2002, stock prices, house prices and commodity prices boomed simultaneously. The three "bull markets" tilted in 2007/2008 into three "bear markets", causing the biggest wealth devaluation since 1929 (the last time when these asset prices declined simultaneously).

The systemic character of the financial crisis of 2008 and, hence, of the subsequent rise of unemployment and the public debt could not be recognized through the lens of "neoliberal glasses": after saving the banking sector and stimulating the economy in the crisis year 2009, austerity policy in the EU was again intensified, in particular in Southern Europe. Speculation on the bankruptcy of these states, first against Greece, then against Portugal, Spain and Italy, had caused interest rates to rise tremendously. Looking for a "save haven", investors drove up prices of government bonds of Germany and the other "good" countries. The related decline in interest rates in the "North" and rising interest in the "South" intensified the tensions within the European Monetary Union (EMU) and endangered its existence. In 2012, the ECB turned to an extremely loose monetary policy through lowering the key interest rate to zero and through buying government bonds. This policy caused bond prices to boom like never before and strengthened also the stock bull market which had already taken off in spring 2009. In addition, house prices have been rising strongly, this time not only in the USA and in the UK but also in continental Europe. Hence, the potential for a new simultaneous wealth devaluation has been built up in recent years. Austerity policies, on the one hand, and booming financial wealth, on the other hand, have increased inequality, strengthening the feelings of bitterness, uncertainty and fear of the future not only on behalf of the underprivileged but also of middle class people. Populists address both groups, promise "social warmth" within the own nation and direct their feelings against scapegoats of all types: against "the" globalisation, "the" EU, "the" system as well as "the" Greeks or "the" foreigners – in recent years in particular against refugees.

Whereas the prosperity phase had come to an end due to the success of real capitalism and the related shift in power in favour of trade unions and leftist parties, the crisis phase comes to an end due to the failure of finance capitalism and the related meltdown of wealth (in the next financial crisis) as well as the growing frustration of the "non-elites" in society. The above hypothesis about the driving forces of postwar development implies that there operates an interaction between economic theories and reality. On the one hand, theories serve as "navigation maps" thereby changing reality and leading occasionally into crises (as in the 1930s). On the other hand, new theories emerge in reaction to these crises, guiding economic development into new directions (as in the 1950s and 1960s).

Framework Conditions and Economic Performance of Western Capitalism During the 1960s and 1970s

Over the 1950s and 1960s, an active policy aiming at full employment, stable economic growth and social coherence together with stable exchange rates, commodity prices and interest rates (below the rate of economic growth) channelled striving for profits towards entrepreneurial activities in the real sphere of the economy. Under these real-capitalist incentive conditions, the economies of industrial countries grew strongly and steadily. For several reasons, this development was particularly pronounced in Western Europe. First, the reconstruction after WWII promoted investment and production. Second, building up the welfare state strengthened the confidence of households and, hence, their consumption. Third, trade liberalization and the integration process promoted trade in Europe stronger than elsewhere (the EEC and the EFTA were founded in 1957 and 1960, respectively).

Over the 1950s, the rate of unemployment had fallen steadily. In 1960, it amounted in Western Europe to only 1.8% on average and fluctuated slightly around 2% until 1974 (Fig. 2.1). The welfare state was enlarged and the infrastructure improved. Both activities strengthened and stabilized economic growth so that the public debt was declining continuously from almost 70% of GDP in the early 1950s to less than 40% in the early 1970s (Fig. 2.1).

Against the background of historical experience, this performance appeared as "economic miracle". However, it was just the result of coherent framework conditions: liberalizing goods markets and keeping financial markets regulated fostered activities in the real economy for two reasons. First, the costs of financing investment, production and trade were low and stable. Second, financial speculation was unprofitable. At the same time, building up the welfare state strengthened confidence and fairness in society. In other words, the strength of the European Social Model consisted in providing room for individual, self-interested "expansion" in the real economy through competition in liberalized goods markets, combined with strengthening social coherence through the welfare state ("institutionalized solidarity").

Promoting activities in the real economy through competition in goods markets combined with cooperative strategies in politics shaped economic development also at the global level: international trade was liberalized in several GATT rounds; transnational cooperation was strengthened through the Marshall plan, through development aid, through the activities of The World Bank and the International Monetary Fund as well as through the international monetary system. Until 1971, the dollar remained stable vis-à-vis the other reserve currencies contributing to the (relative) stability of commodity prices and to stable growth of world production – it fluctuated just between 4% and 6% per year (Fig. 2.2).

The success of the real-capitalist system, in particular when combined with a comprehensive welfare state, slowly changed the distribution of income and power in society and prepared the ground for the neoliberal "counter-offensive". Over the 1950s, a (tacit) deal between entrepreneurs and unions had prevailed: the latter accepted the dispositive power of the entrepreneurs as "bosses" and got "in exchange" more jobs. This deal came to an end once full employment was reached. Now, unions called for (more) employee participation and in particular for redistribution in favour of wages. Supported by permanent full employment, strike activities roughly tripled between 1965 and 1968 (particularly in Italy, France and the UK), enforcing to a large extent the fulfilling of the unions' demands: wages rose much faster than labour productivity; the wage share in nominal GDP increased over the 1960s like never before (Fig. 2.1).

Also ideological developments raised the concerns of industrialists about the long-term consequences of full employment and an expanding welfare state: in

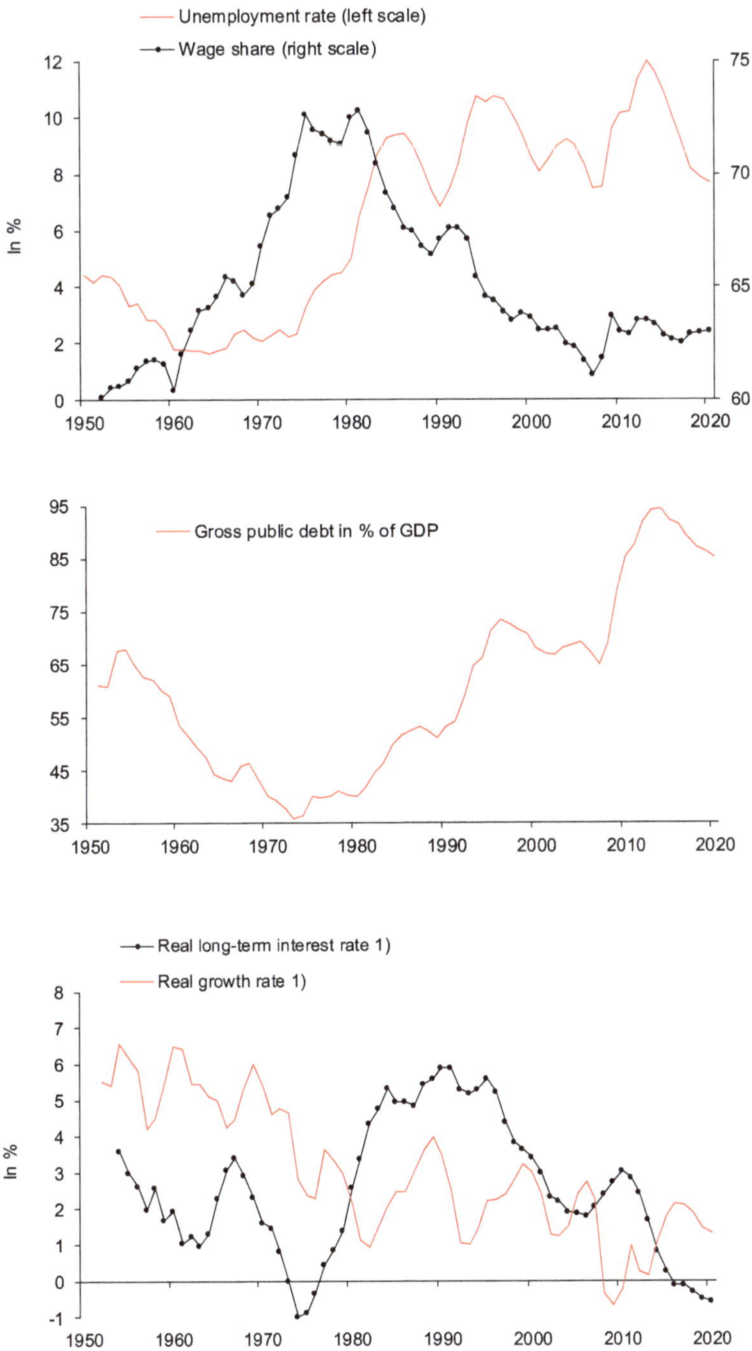

Fig. 2.1 Long-term economic development in Western Europe. 1) 3-year moving average. (Source: OECD, Eurostat, IMF)

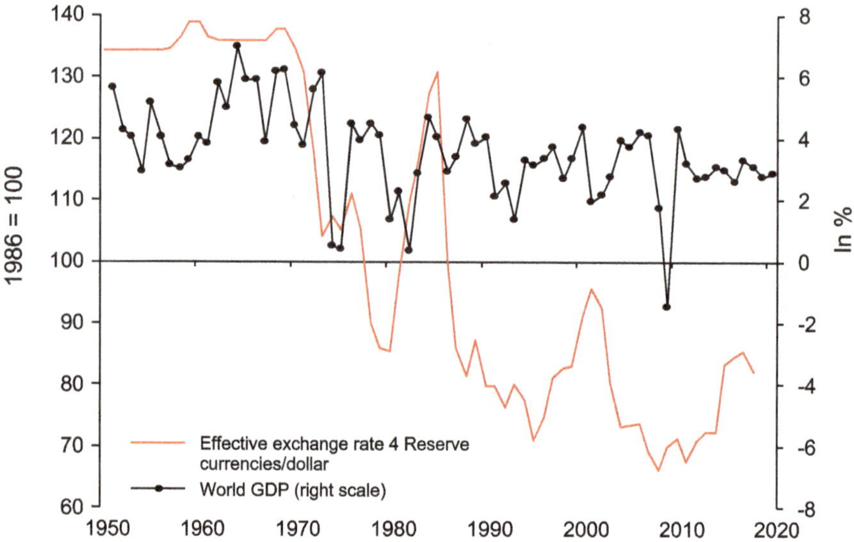

Fig. 2.2 Dollar exchange rate and the global economic growth. (Source: IMF, WIFO)

the second half of the 1960s, most intellectuals turned to the left (the students' protests in 1968 and the often sympathetic reports in the media were clear indicators of these changes). The left "Zeitgeist" strengthened social-democratic parties (Willy Brandt became chancellor in Germany in 1969, Bruno Kreisky in Austria in 1970). The "Club of Rome" criticized the resource-wasting capitalism ("The Limits to Growth", 1972) which appeared as the ultimate cause of global pollution. In the USA, industrialists became also concerned about the negative impact of the Bretton Woods system. Over the 1960s, the US economy lost almost permanently export market shares to Europe and Japan. Yet, the USA would never be able to devalue its currency due to its role as anchor of the Bretton Woods rules (the original dollar exchange rates had been "fair" due to the advantage of the US economy after WWII but became progressively overvalued due to the catching-up of other industrial countries, in particular Germany and Japan). The confidence in the exchange rate system got weaker also in the rest of the world since the USA abused its role as "world banker" through "dollar exports", in part for financing the Vietnam War. When the French president De Gaulle asked his central bank to have dollar claims converted into gold in 1967, the USA refused to do so. This decision made it clear that the USA would not stick to the gold convertibility of the dollar.[1] In addition, inflation began to rise in the 1960s, caused by persistently high economic growth and the related wage-price spiral. The acceleration of

[1] For the fundamental shortcoming of the Bretton Woods system, e.g. the double role of the dollar as standard currency of the world economy and as national currency of the USA, see Schulmeister (2000).

inflation was particularly pronounced in the USA, to a large extent due to rising expenditures for the Vietnam War.

All these developments together rendered the neoliberal ideology (mainly in the form of monetarism) progressively more attractive for wealthy people. It promised to weaken trade unions and the welfare state, to fight leftist political movements, to get rid of the system of fixed exchange rates and to reduce inflation – the latter was particularly important for owners of big financial wealth which had grown strongly during the prosperity phase. For all these promises, neoliberal "original thinkers" had produced theoretical foundations, from Hayek's "The Road to Serfdom" (1944) or Friedman's "The Case for Flexible Exchange Rates" (1953) to his "The Role of Monetary Policy" (1968) which based an attack on full employment policy on his concept of a "natural rate of unemployment" (see section "Public Finances Under Real-Capitalist and Finance-Capitalist Conditions").

Systemic Changes in Global Capitalism Since the 1970s and Their Impact

The support of "big business" alone would not have been sufficient to make neoliberalism the most influential ideology of past decades because its call for weakening the welfare state as well as trade unions was not popular, certainly not among most European citizens. Therefore, the advance of neoliberalism took place "through the backdoor" of liberalizing financial markets: letting the system of pegged exchange rates collapse with the intention to weaken the dollar, strengthened by an expansive monetary policy, produced the expectation of a dollar depreciation which was then brought about through the respective speculative transactions. Over the 1970s, two dollar depreciations triggered two oil price "shocks", followed by two recessions and a rise in inflation, unemployment and the public debt.

These problems were then "cured" through neoliberal "recipes", e.g. "structural reforms", like (further) deregulating financial markets, weakening labour protection, dampening real wages, cutting social expenditures, raising interest rates and restricting the room for manoeuvre of fiscal and monetary policy through rules. These "therapies" worsened the "disease" which in turn called for increasing the "dose". In this way, the economic regime was transformed from a real-capitalist into a finance-capitalist system. The most important steps of this process were as follows.

In August 1971, the USA let the system of fixed exchange rates collapse (Figs. 2.2 and 2.3): during the subsequent bear market, the dollar lost 25% of its value vis-à-vis the other SDR currencies (DM, franc, pound, yen). This development hit those countries most which exported exclusively crude oil, priced and paid in dollars: the OPEC countries in the Middle East. In October 1973, OPEC took advantage of the Yom Kippur War to fight back by putting through a tripling of crude oil prices (Fig. 2.3; the oil boycott served as bluff). The first "oil price shock" led into the first post-war recession in all industrial countries. As a consequence, not only inflation

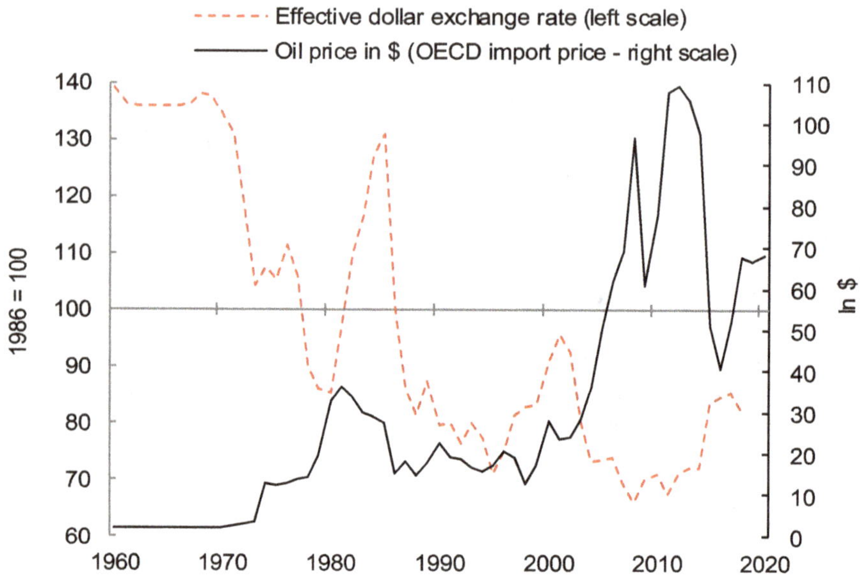

Fig. 2.3 Dollar exchange rate and oil price fluctuations. (Source: OECD, IMF)

but also unemployment rose significantly. This constellation was then taken as disprove of the Phillips curve and, hence, of Keynesian economics altogether (see below). In a second bear market, the dollar lost again 25% of its value between 1976 and 1979, leading to the second "oil price shock" in 1979 (again, OPEC took advantage of political turbulences like the coming to power of the Ayatollahs). It was again followed by a recession.

Since 1972, the oil price had risen by a factor of 11. The inflationary pressure spilled over to the prices of manufactures. As a consequence, the price level in overall world trade almost quadrupled during the 1970s (Fig. 2.4). The inverse development of the dollar exchange rate and world trade prices is, however, also due to the conversion of manufactures prices from the different national currencies into dollars. This statistical effect is of enormous economic importance: as most international debts (in particular of developing countries) are held in dollars, any persistent dollar depreciation is associated with negative real interest rates (approximated as difference between the nominal dollar rate – LIBOR – and the annual changes in world trade prices in dollar terms).

To put it concretely, exports of non-US countries to countries other than the USA earned DM, yen, etc. whose dollar value rose strongly over the 1970s. In particular, the "tiger economies" of that decade like Mexico, Argentina and Brazil took advantage of this valuation effect: they incurred more and more dollar debts to finance their import surplus (which helped industrialized countries struggling with two "oil price shocks"). This behaviour seemed rational as the falling dollar depreciated dollar debts. At the same time, the "petro dollars" of oil exporters, deposited in London, were "recycled", mainly to Latin American countries.

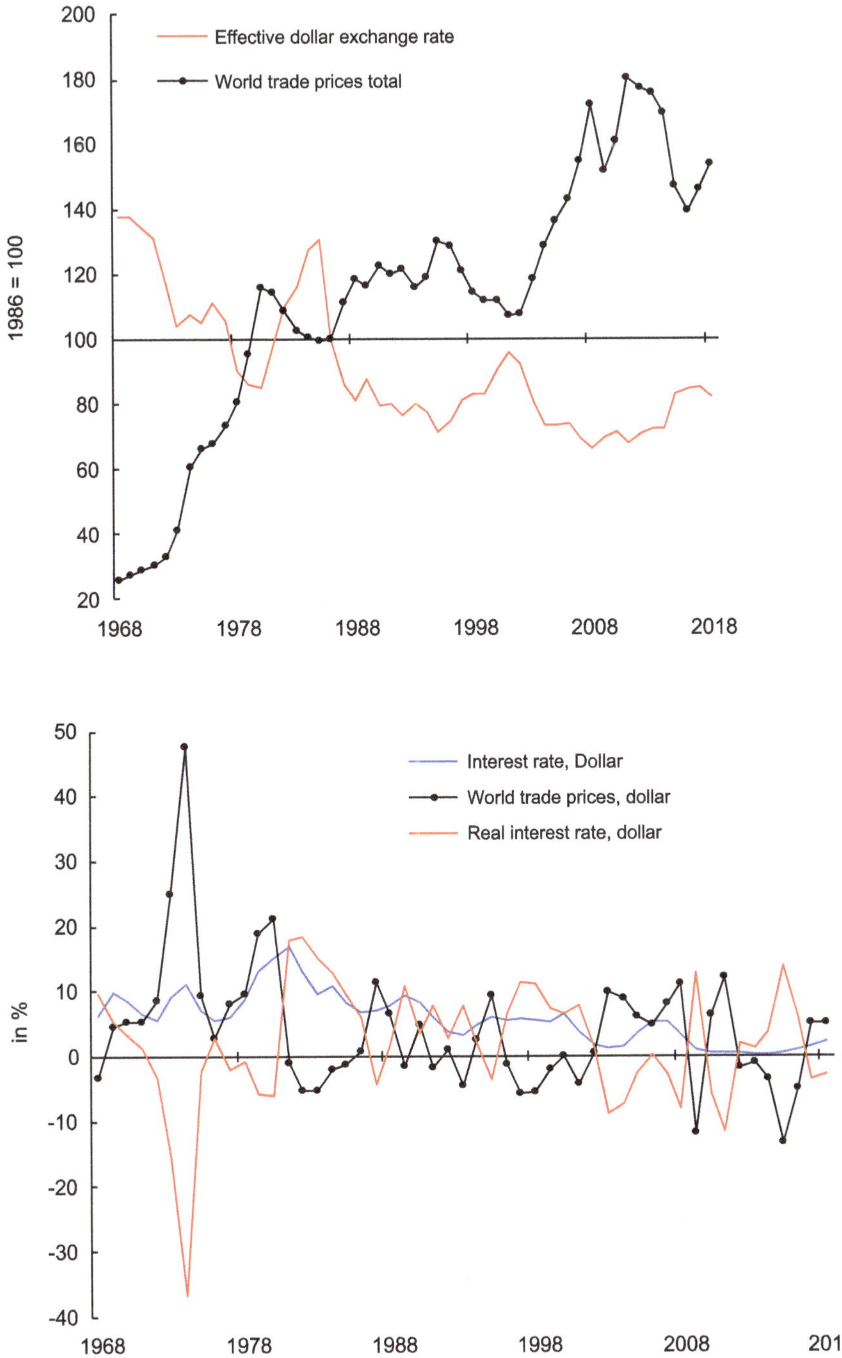

Fig. 2.4 Dollar exchange rate, world inflation and the real interest on a dollar debt. [1]Vis-a-vis DM, pound, franc, yen. (Source: IMF, WIFO)

As reaction to the acceleration of inflation in the 1970s, monetary policy increased interest rates like never before, most strongly in the USA (Fig. 2.4).[2] Hence, traders expected an appreciation of the dollar (also because it had become strongly undervalued) which finally took off when Ronald Reagan was elected president of the USA in November 1980. Over the following 5 years, the strongest dollar bull market ever took place (Fig. 2.3). It appreciated international dollar debts, which Latin American (but also African) countries had accumulated during the 1970s under completely different conditions: between 1979 and 1981, the real interest on an international dollar debt jumped from −6% to +18% (Fig. 2.4). One year later, the international debt crisis broke out, which dampened the real economy in not only in these countries but in Latin America as a whole for more than a ("lost") decade. The increasing overvaluation of the dollar caused the bull market to tilt in 1985 again into a bear market. Until 1995, the dollar lost almost 50% of its value, providing relief for international dollar debtors (Figs. 2.3 and 2.4): dollar prices in world trade picked up and, the real interest fell between 1985 and 1987 by almost 14% points.

Over the 1990s, the economic performance of the USA improved relative to Europe and Japan, due to the undervaluation of the dollar and the expansionary policy of the Clinton administration. In 1995, the second dollar bull market took off: world trade prices started to fall, the real interest on an international dollar debt jumped from −3.4% to +11.3% (Fig. 2.4). As a consequence, the booming economies in East Asia, which had financed their rising current account deficits through dollar credits, slid into a liquidity crisis in 1997/1998.[3] The crisis then spilled over to Russia and Brazil. Both countries had – partly successfully – attempted to curb inflation through fixing the exchange rate of their respective currencies vis-à-vis the dollar. As long as the inflation in these countries was significantly higher than in the USA, nominal interest rates in Russia and Brazil, respectively, exceeded dollar rates. Speculators tried to profit from this differential through short-term capital inflows in both countries. As the dollar appreciated more and more, and, hence, also the rouble and the real, confidence in the pegged exchange rate vanished, capital flew out and forced a massive depreciation of both currencies. As an indirect consequence of the depreciation of the Brazilian real by roughly 60%, also the currency board of Argentina collapsed in 2002.

Between 2002 and 2007, the dollar exchange rate again declined strongly (Fig. 2.3). This bear market induced a strong rise in world trade prices. As a consequence, interest rates on an international dollar debt became negative again,

---

[2] This policy was in line with monetarist theory and with the "trivial Keynesian" IS/LM approach. However, by raising interest rates, one does not *specifically* dampen inflation but the economy as a whole (which will then also reduce inflation). Such a strategy raises interest payments and, hence, production costs due to the interest rate accelerator: If, e.g. the interest rate rises from 5% to 8%, interest payments rise by 60% (in case of bank credits at flexible rates).

[3] The "tiger economies" ran out of dollar liquidity to service their dollar debts. As their production structure was much better than that of Latin American countries in the early 1980s, they could overcome the crisis rather fast.

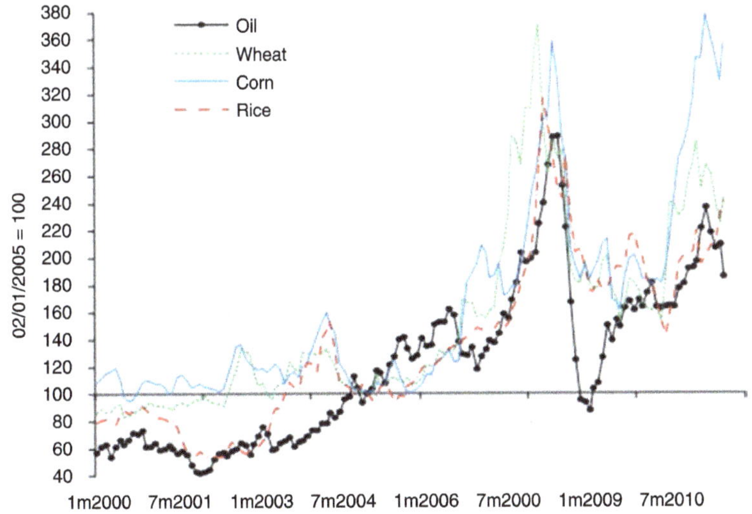

Fig. 2.5 Bull and bear markets of commodities futures prices. (Source: NYMEX, CBOT)

relaxing the financial crises of emerging market economies (Fig. 2.4). Sequences of bull and bear markets shape commodity price dynamics in general, particularly over the past 15 years when financial "investors" become increasingly active in commodity derivative trading. The parallel price movements of crude oil, wheat, corn and rice before and after 2008 indicate the importance of "bulls" and "bears" in blowing up asset values before the crisis and melting them down during the crisis (Fig. 2.5).

Under the condition of widely fluctuating exchange rates and commodity prices, and of a positive interest-growth differential (Fig. 2.1), financial and non-financial business shifted activities from the real to financial investment and short-term speculation ("finance capitalism"). This shift was fostered by financial innovations, in particular derivatives of all kinds which became the most important vehicles for speculation (Fig. 2.11). The change in incentive conditions for making profits had two effects. First, the sequence of bull and bear markets of exchange rates, commodity prices, interest rates, stock prices and house prices triggered "oil price shocks" and debt crises of developing countries and caused the great financial crisis of 2008. Second, non-financial business reduced the accumulation of real capital and, hence, the creation of "normal" jobs.

Europe was much more affected by this shift in capital accumulation from real to financial assets. First, the sustainability of the European Social Model depends much more on a high level of employment (consisting of "normal" jobs) as compared to the US model ("working-poor jobs" did – and still do – not fit to the European welfare state system). Second, economic policy in the USA emancipated itself from the concept of a rules-based fiscal and monetary policy in the late 1980s and has since then followed a (primitive) Keynesian policy. As a consequence, real capital accumulation picked up in the USA in the 1990s, whereas it declined in many European countries, in particular in Germany (Fig. 2.12).

Between the early 1970s and the late 1980s, unemployment rose strongly in (Western) Europe (in spite of the decline in the wage share (Fig. 2.1)). As unemployment is extremely costly for welfare states (due to rising social expenditures and falling receipts from taxes and social security contributions), also the public debt increased with some time lag. This rise was further strengthened by the persistently positive interest-growth differential (Fig. 2.1).

Over the 1990s and 2000s (until the financial crisis), the "twin problems" unemployment and public debt could be mitigated (Fig. 2.16), however, at the expense of damaging the European Social Model: the decline in the rate of unemployment was primarily the (statistical) result of the expansion of atypical jobs due to labour market deregulations since economic growth remained weak (fluctuating around an annual rate of 2% (Fig. 2.1)). The (small) reduction in the ratio of public debt to GDP was achieved mainly through cutting social expenditures, i.e. through weakening the welfare state. At the same time, stock prices boomed like never before (Figs. 2.8 and 2.11).

After the burst of the "internet bubble" in 2000/2002, three simultaneous bull markets developed (house prices, stock prices and commodity prices) which tilted around 2007 into three bear markets: house prices started to decline in late 2006, followed by stock prices and finally by commodity prices (Fig. 2.6). Insofar as bull markets and bear markets are the most typical feature of asset price dynamics, the financial crisis can be considered as result of "business as usual". However, a *simultaneous* devaluation of house wealth, stock wealth and commodity wealth seldom occurs; the last time this happened was in 1929.

The mutually reinforcing effects of simultaneous bear markets become evident if one compares the period 2007/2008 to that of 2000/2002 (Fig. 2.5). In the latter case, the strong devaluation of stock wealth was to a great extent compensated by the revaluation of real estate wealth (a recession followed nevertheless). The devaluation of stock wealth, housing wealth and commodity wealth contracted balance sheets, reducing the equity of all asset holders. As the share of equity in total assets was lowest in the case of banks (in order to profit from leverage), they would have collapsed had the government not refinanced them – at costs of several trillion dollars. The measures for bailing out the banks and for stimulating the economy in the Great Recession of 2009 caused budget deficits to soar to unsustainable levels, in particular in those countries like Greece where the deficit had been (much) too high already before the crisis. When the newly elected (socialist) Greek government admitted that the previous (conservative) government had reported wrong budget data to the European Commission and asked for financial support, all other EMU governments refused to grant it.

The intention of rejecting support was to "punish" Greece for the misbehaviour of its government; the effect, however, was an epidemic rise in interest rates not only in Greece but also in Ireland, Portugal, Spain and Italy. The rejection signalled financial market agents that Greece and other EMU states could in fact slide into bankruptcy since the respective national central bank cannot provide the government with credits in a monetary union. As a consequence (investment), banks and hedge funds started to speculate on the bankruptcy of EMU member states through

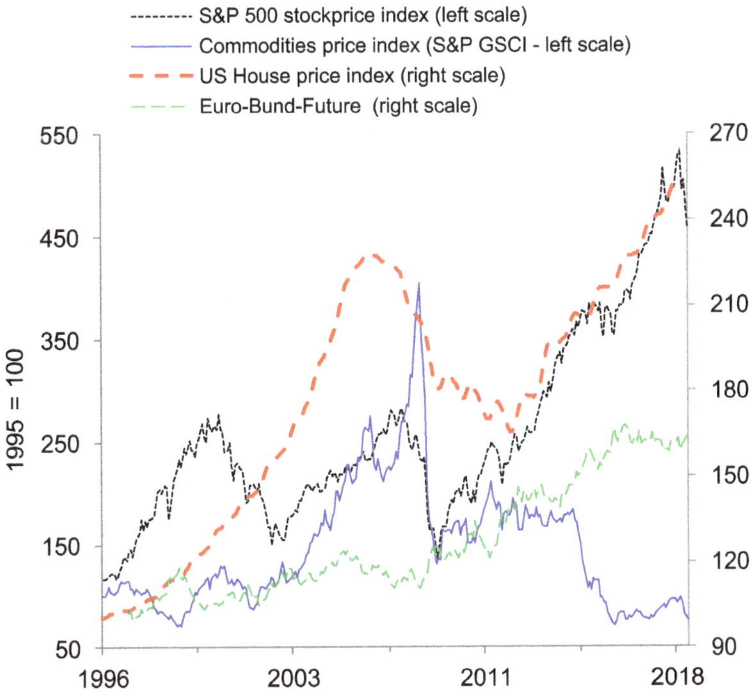

Fig. 2.6 Valuation of stock, commodity, real estate and bond wealth. (Source: Yahoo Finance, Case-Shiller, Standard & Poors, Onvista)

"credit default swaps" (CDS), first against Greece, then against Ireland, Portugal, Spain and Italy. This business turned out to be extremely profitable for the "early birds": CDS premia with respect to government bonds of Greece or Portugal rose by a factor of 10. Hence, also the value of those CDS contracts, which were concluded at an earlier stage, rose by the same factor. Interest rates on government bonds of the "targeted" states increased in tandem with the CDS premia.

At the same time, investors seeking a "save haven" drove up prices of government bonds of Germany and other "good" countries: As a consequence, interest rates declined in the "North" where the economy started to recover and soared in the "South" where the crisis deepened. The "interest split" of the euro area caused also political tensions to rise. When the interest rate "epidemic" reached Spain and Italy (causing CDS premia and the contract values to rise by a factor of 5), ECB president Mario Draghi underlined in July 2012 the determination of the ECB "to do whatever it takes to preserve the euro". This announcement together with an extremely expansionary monetary policy stopped the "game" of speculating on the bankruptcy of EMU member states. Interest rates began to fall in all EMU countries (had the ECB president Trichet adopted such a policy already 2 years earlier, the euro crisis would have been prevented).

In March 2015, the ECB intensified its loose monetary policy though "quantitative easing", i.e. asset purchases from banks to the amount of 60 bn. € per month (this sum was increased to 80 bn. € in March 2016). This policy was indispensable for saving the euro since the government of countries as big as Spain or Italy could not be (re)financed through the euro bail-out fund (European Financial Stability Facility, later European Stability Mechanism).

The developments leading into the euro crisis can be summarized as follows: the refusal of EU policy makers to give financial support to Greece in fall 2009 triggered a bear market in government bonds of Greece, Ireland, Portugal, Spain and Italy and a bull market in government bonds of Germany and the other "good" countries. The move of the ECB towards an extreme loose monetary policy in 2012 turned the bear market in government bonds of Southern European countries into a bull market and strengthened also the stock bull market which had already taken off in March 2009 – not only in Europe but on a global scale. At the same time, also house prices boomed again, this time not only in the USA and the UK but also in continental Europe. Once again, three bull markets of stock prices, house prices and bond prices have built up the potential for three bear markets (Fig. 2.6; "Euro Bund Future" indicates the development of German 10-year government bond prices).

Macroeconomic Effects of Bull Markets and Bear Markets

The long swings of asset prices impact upon the real economy through their valuation effects. Rising stock prices, for example, increase the financial wealth of their owners (also indirectly via pension and college funds, etc.). If they trust in the permanent character of the (re)valuation, gains, they will increase their expenditure as US households did during the 1990s. The expansionary effects of bull market feedback on the strength of the asset appreciation, in particular, if the latter does not increase other people's liabilities at the same time (e.g. if the bull market concerns stocks or residential buildings). By the same token, bear markets dampen the real economy. For example, a fall in the value of savings for pensions or college costs will cause households to save more (consume less) out of their current income.

In the case of exchange rates, one has also to take into account the effects of appreciation and depreciation trends on capital flows, on terms of trade and the related trade flows as well as on the re(de)valuation of international debts. These effects are strongest in the case of "bulls" and "bears" of the dollar exchange rate since commodities are priced in dollars, and most international debts, in particular of emerging countries, are held in dollars. As a consequence, any dollar appreciation (trend) improves "ceteris paribus" the terms of trade of net commodity exporters (at the expense of net importers) and appreciates dollar debts/assets.

The opposite holds in the case of a dollar depreciation (trend). The net effect of the related redistribution processes on the global economy is mostly negative as the demand of winners rises more slowly than the demand of losers falls. This is particularly true in the case of strong oil price changes. When they rise as in the 1970s (in reaction to the preceding dollar depreciations), the additional demand of oil-exporting countries falls short of the decline in the demand of industrial countries. However, when oil prices fall strongly (as 1984/1986 or 2014/2016), the net demand effect is again negative.

The strongest influence on the real economy exerts house price fluctuations: during a bull market, house owners feel richer, increase consumption and/or take up additional credits using the rising house value as collateral. In addition, real estate developers or private speculators buy and/or build houses as speculation vehicle. These activities are fettered by financial innovations which enable creditors to bundle claims against house owners in "asset-backed security" (ABS) and sell them as "collateralized debt obligation" (CDO). When the bull market tilts into a bear market, the values of houses often sink below the value of the respective credits, and the owners (have to) leave their home. As a consequence, also the ABSs and CDOs become (almost) worthless. This wealth meltdown wipes out equity and forces the losers to radically cut expenditures. By the end of the bear market, asset management firms like BlackRock or Blackstone buy houses at low prices and rent them out, partly to their former owners. When a new bull market takes off, these investors profit from the revaluation of houses (instead of their inhabitants).

In more general terms, during the upswing and downswing of asset prices, a redistribution process takes place. Who gets on the trend in its early stage makes profits at the expense of the "late-coming bandwagonists". As a group, the winners are the professional traders, and the losers are the amateurs (including many pension funds). A thought experiment clarifies the issue: If the level of stock prices at the end of the "bear" would be the same as at the beginning of the "bull", the overall value of stock wealth would be the same. However, its distribution has changed: The wealth of professionals (in the aggregate) has grown by the same amount by which the wealth of amateurs (in the aggregate) has shrunk. In accounting terms, the effects of asset price fluctuations are as follows. Any appreciation extends balance sheets, blowing up the equity of (net) asset holders and wiping out equity of (net) liability holders (e.g. of dollar debtors in the case of a dollar appreciation). The opposite holds for a depreciation process (Koo 2009). These effects of "bulls" and "bears" have become more pronounced since the 1990s due to the growing dominance of IFRS accounting standards (assets and liabilities have to be valued at their current market values).

The different channels through which the long swings of asset prices impact upon the real economy are rather neglected in macroeconomic theory. This is particularly true for the mainstream of the past decades since "New Classical Macroeconomics" and "New Keynesian Economics" exclude the possibility of "bulls" and "bears" by construction.[4] John M. Keynes had stressed the role of uncertainty, emotions and social interaction like herding as fundamental reasons for the specific instability of financial markets (particularly in Chap. 12 of his "General

[4] Equilibrium theory can take into account "bubbles" which, however, are essentially different from bull markets: A bubble represents a non-fundamental, exploding equilibrium price path (equilibrium in the sense that expectations of rising prices are fulfilled), whereas a bull market is limited by the repercussions of the overvaluation on the real economy. Agents take these feedback effects into account. Hence, they know from the very beginning that any bull market comes to an end. In addition, equilibrium theory cannot explain the persistence of bear markets.

Theory"), yet he did neither provide a theoretical elaboration of his insights nor integrate them into his general theory.[5]

Those two phenomena which have shaped economic development over the past decades and which represent characteristic features of finance capitalism have still to be theoretically explained: the tremendous rise in speed and volume of (derivatives) trading of stocks, bonds, foreign exchange and commodities, on the one hand, and the increase in the amplitude of long-term trends of these prices, on the other hand.

How Bull and Bear Markets Are Brought About

Asset prices fluctuate almost always around "underlying" trends.[6] The phenomenon of "trending" repeats itself across different time scales ("self-similarity"). For example, there occur trends based on tick or minute data (Fig. 2.10) as well as trends based on daily data (Figs. 2.7, 2.8, and 2.9). "Technical" or "algorithmic" trading aims at exploiting the trending of asset prices. In the case of *trend-following*

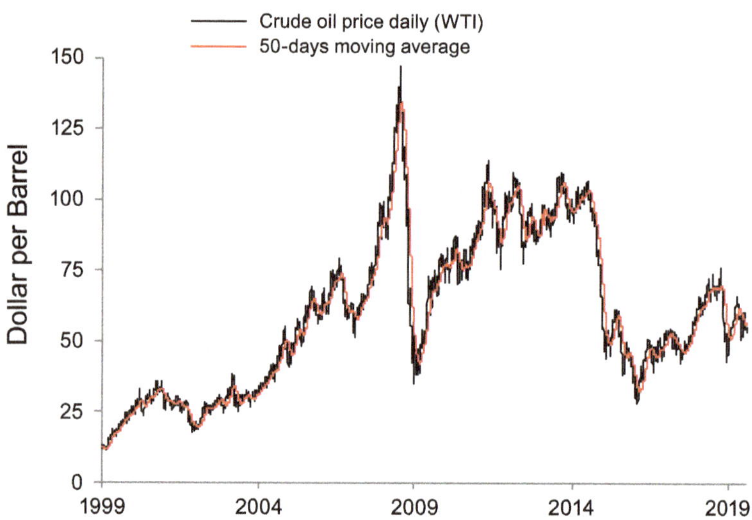

Fig. 2.7 Trending and speculation in the crude oil futures market. (Source: NYMEX)

[5] In a nutshell, these insights provided the microeconomic foundation of Keynes' macroeconomic theory ("homo humanus"). However, most "Keynesians" did not take Keynes' insights about the importance of uncertainty, emotions and social interactions serious. The main exception are "Post-Keynesians", in particular Hyman P. Minsky. However, also Minsky dealt mainly with booms in credit markets and not with everyday business in financial markets of all types, namely, self-referential "money making" through speculation (see Schulmeister 2018, Chap. 5).

[6] Empirical research on asset price dynamics is documented in Schulmeister (2008, 2018, Chap. 9).

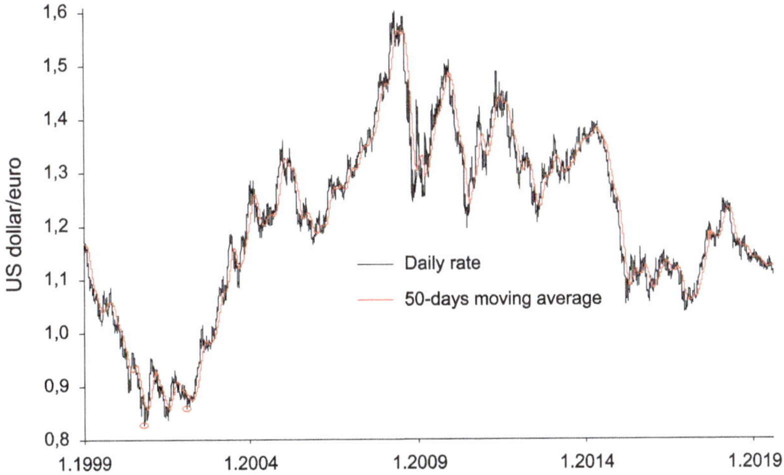

Fig. 2.8 Trending and speculation in the foreign exchange market. Daily US dollar/euro exchange rate

moving average models, a trader would open a long position (buy) when the current price crosses the MA (moving average) line from below and sells when the opposite occurs (Figs. 2.7 and 2.10). By contrast, *contrarian* models try to profit from trend reversals and, hence, change open positions when a trend "loses momentum". Technical models are applied to price data of almost any frequency (Figs. 2.7, 2.8, 2.9, and 2.10). Due to the increasing use of intraday data, "algo trading" has become the most important driver of financial transactions. They rose from 15.5 times of world GDP to 72.4 times in 2007, declined in the aftermath of the financial crisis but then picked up again, at least in Europe (Fig. 2.11).

There operates an interaction between trending of asset prices and technical trading. On the one hand, traders use different models to exploit price runs, and, on the other hand, the aggregate behaviour of all models strengthens and lengthens the price runs. Long-term price trends result from the following process. "Mini-trends" (e.g. based on minute data) add up to one trend based on 10-minute data. Several of these trends accumulate to one trend based on hourly data and so on. Over an extended period of time (often several years), upwards (downwards) trends last longer than counter-movements, causing the price to rise (fall) in a stepwise process. As a consequence, all important asset prices like exchange rates, stock and bond prices as well as commodity prices fluctuate in irregular cycles ("long swings") around their fundamental equilibrium without any tendency to converge (Figs. 2.3, 2.5, 2.6, 2.7, 2.8, and 2.9). This evidence completely contradicts equilibrium theory according to which asset prices should – in reaction to news – jump to their new fundamental equilibrium. Hence, there should be neither short-term nor long-term trending.

The pattern of asset prices can be explained as result of the following trading behaviour. Price runs are usually triggered by news. In order to reduce the complexity of trading decisions under extreme time pressure, traders form only *qualitative*

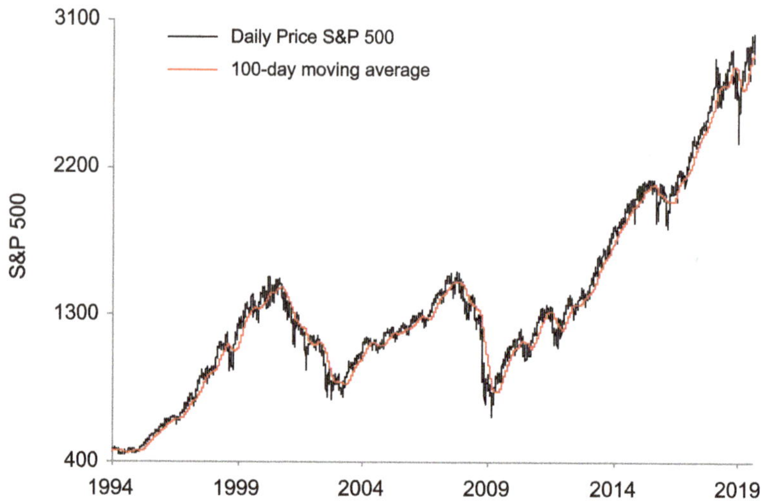

Fig. 2.9 Trending and speculation in the US stock market

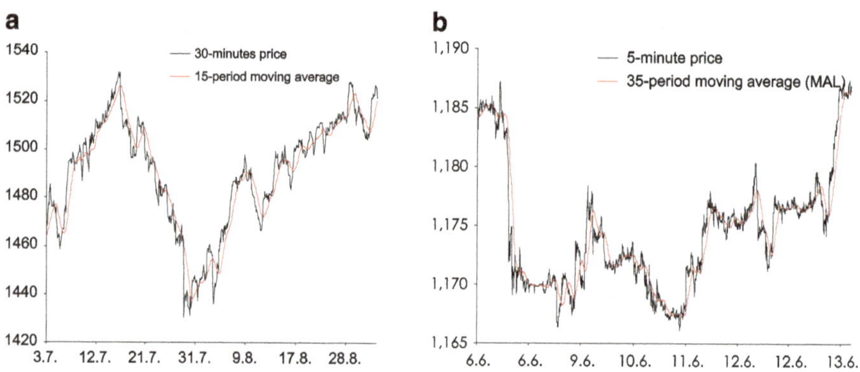

Fig. 2.10 Intraday asset price dynamics. (**a**) S&P 500 stock index futures, July and August 2000. (**b**) Exchange rate dollar/euro, June 6 to June 13, 2003

expectations in reaction to news, i.e. expectations about the *direction* of the imminent price move. Subsequent to an initial upwards (downwards) price movement triggered by news, follows a cascade of buy (sell) signals stemming from *trend-following* technical trading systems. At first, the most price-sensitive models based on high frequency data ("fast models") produce signals, at last the slowest models based on hourly or daily data. When an upwards (downwards) trend loses momentum, *contrarian* models start to open short (long) positions, thereby contributing to a trend reversal. Most of the time there prevails an "expectational bias" in the market, in favour of or against an asset. Such a bias reflects the – optimistic/bullish or pessimistic/bearish – market sentiment. News in line with the prevailing bias get

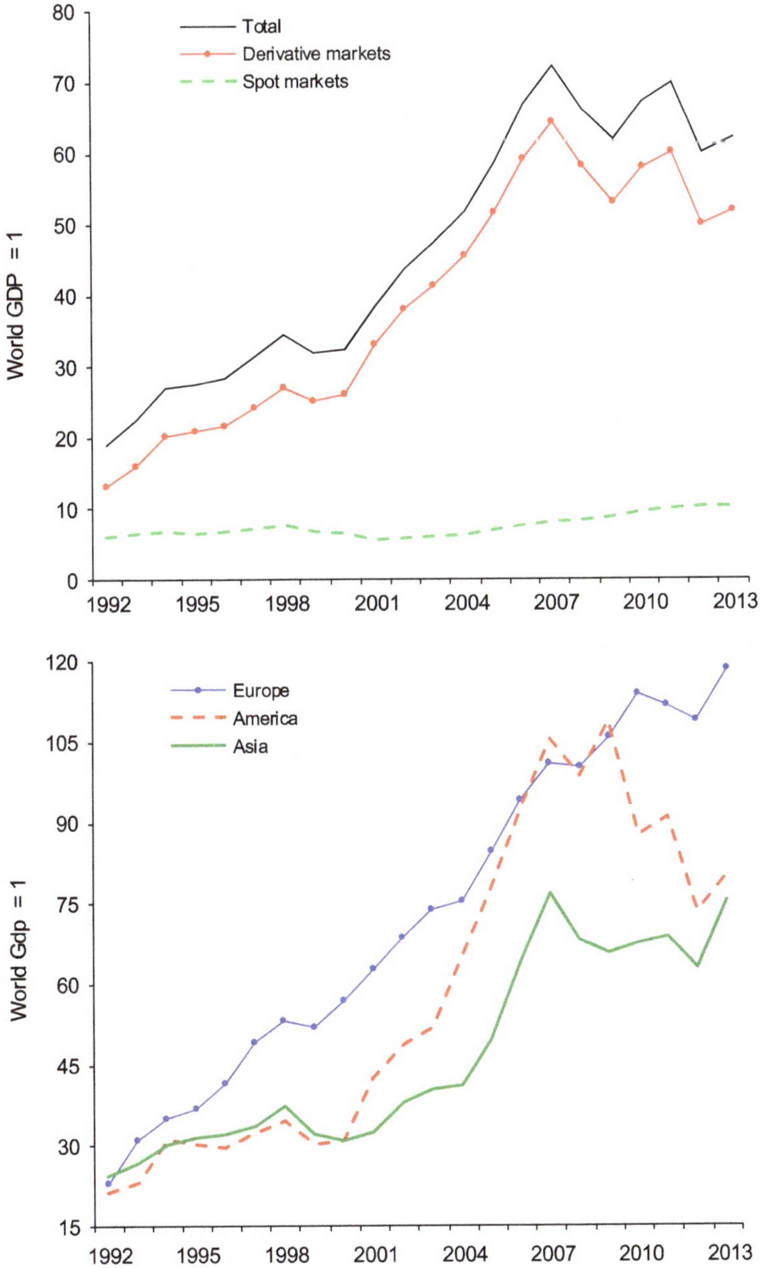

Fig. 2.11 Financial transactions in the world economy. (Source: WIFO)

higher recognition and reaction than news which contradict the market mood. This behaviour causes price runs in line with the "market mood" to last longer than counter-movements, bringing about "bulls" and "bears".

The more the asset becomes over(under)valued, the greater becomes the probability of a change in the direction of the long-term trend: first, because market participants know from experience that any bull/bear market comes to an end; second, because there operate long-term "contrarians" in the market who sell (buy) in an "overbought" ("oversold") market; and third, because the effects of an over(under) valuation on the real economy progressively strengthen corrective forces (e.g. the deterioration of the current account and the related decline in economic growth in the case of a persistently overvalued currency).

To conclude, "overshooting" is not an exception due to some "shock" but the most characteristic property of long-term asset price dynamics. Exchange rates, stock prices and commodity prices fluctuate in a sequence of "bulls" and "bears" around their fundamental equilibrium without any tendency of convergence towards this level.

A General Framework: Real Capitalism and Finance Capitalism[7]

Over the past decades, economic policy guided by the neoliberal "navigation map" has dampened economic growth through two transmission channels. First, it led into recessions as results of the "oil price shocks" in 1993 and 1979 (triggered indirectly by giving up the fixed exchange rate system) and into the big financial crises in 1982 and 2008 (caused by boom-bust cycle of asset prices). Second, the intrinsic instability of exchange rates, commodity prices, interest rates and stock prices has shifted striving for profits from the real to the financial economy. Unemployment, precarious jobs, the public debt and rising inequality are just symptoms of a dysfunctional economic system, i.e. finance capitalism. Under real-capitalist conditions (until the 1970s), non-financial business focused on the accumulation of real assets: at stable exchange rates, commodity prices and – in Europe – stagnating stock prices as well as interest rates below growth rates, financial speculation did not make sense. Since the 1970s, however, the value of financial capital rose much faster than that of real capital (at current asset prices, hence, influenced not only by real/financial investment but also by the swings of asset prices (Fig. 2.12)).

In the following, I shall sketch a theoretical framework for the distinction between a real-capitalistic and a finance-capitalistic system. There exist three types of participation in the production process, labour, real capital and finance capital, and, hence, three types of economic and political interests (Table 2.1). The economic interests of real and finance capital stay in direct conflict with one another.

---

[7]The two types of a capitalist system are discussed more in detail in Schulmeister (2018, Chap. 8). A first sketch in English is in Schulmeister (2014) (this section draws on this article).

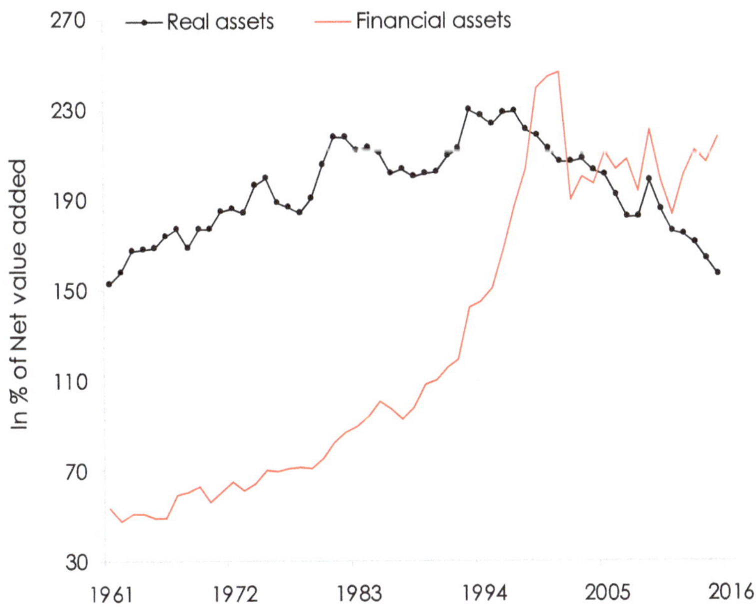

Fig. 2.12 Real and financial accumulation of non-financial business in Germany. (Source: Bundesbank, Destatis, WIFO)

Table 2.1 Labour, real capital, finance capital

	Labour	Real capital	Finance capital
Economic interests	Full employment Real wage increases	High profitability of real investments: - Low interest rates - Low exchange rates - Stable financial markets	High profitability of financial investments: - High interest rates - High exchange rates - Unstable financial markets
Conflicts of interests	Rising wages ←- - - - - - -	- - - - - - -→ ←———	———→ Rising interest rates
Potential coalition partners	Real capital	Labour or finance capital	Real capital
Economic interest in state/government	Full employment policy Social security Education Public services	Anticyclical policy Growth policy: Infrastructure Education, etc.	Strong central bank Restrictive monetary policy Privatisation of social security
Political interests	Strong welfare state Strong trade unions	Weak welfare state Weak trade unions	No welfare state No trade unions

Real investments call for low interest rates and exchange rates, and stable financial markets, whereas financial investments and speculation profit from exactly the opposite conditions. The conflict of the ("purely") economic interests between real capital and labour can be considered less pronounced than the conflict between real capital and finance capital. For example, an increase in production costs due to higher wages leads to a much higher increase in final demand and, hence, in receipts of the business sector as compared to an equivalent cost increase caused by higher interest rates. Even though the interests of real capital and labour are different as regards the distribution of income, both factors have a common interest in generating a high overall income and, hence, in a strong and stable production growth.

The interests of labour, real capital and finance capital differ markedly also with respect to the role of government. Whereas labour profits from a comprehensive welfare state, real capital is mainly interested in government activities which foster real production over the long run (e.g. through improving infrastructure and the education system) and which stabilize it over the short run (e.g. through anti-cyclical policy measures). Finance capital is mainly interested in a strong central bank, a restrictive monetary policy and the privatization of social security (Table 2.1).

Neoclassical theory cannot consider the conflicts of interest between real capital and finance capital because it assumes that there exist only utility-maximizing individuals equipped with rational expectations. However, also Keynes and his followers did not provide a general framework to analyse the interaction between entrepreneurial interests and (financial) rentier interests (even though Keynes often referred to "rentiers"). By contrast, classical economists, in particular Adam Smith and David Ricardo, did focus on the relationship between rentiers, capitalists and workers; however, their rentiers were the landlords, whereas the modern rentier is primarily owner of financial assets.

For the same reason, one cannot identify "classes" of "real capitalists" and "finance capitalists" in modern society: non-financial corporations as well as employees own financial assets and have therefore also finance capital interests. It depends on the framework/incentive conditions of the economic system whether striving for profit concentrates on investment and innovation in the real sphere or in the financial sphere of the economy. In the first case, real capitalism prevails, in the second case finance capitalism (Table 2.2). The different system conditions also affect the financial sector: In the first case, banks act as "servants" for the real economy (financing investment, production and trade); in the second case, more and more (shadow) banks engage in "finance alchemy". Real capitalism consists of many conditions which complement and reinforce each other like a (tacit) coalition between the interests of labour and real capital (against the interests of finance capital). As a consequence, industrial relations are shaped by close cooperation ("Rhine capitalism"). Market and government, competition and cooperation are regarded as complementary; there prevail many – partly conflicting – targets of economic policy, reaching from stable growth to providing social security and a "fair" income distribution.

During real-capitalist periods (as between ~1890 and 1914 and between ~1950 and the mid-1970s or in China since the early 1980s), those economic theories dominate or are at least influential which underline the crisis-prone nature of capitalism (like Keynesian theories). These theories legitimize a strong government, an active economic policy and market regulations. Stable exchange rates as well as stable and low interest rates limit the returns from financial investment and speculation and focus striving for profits on the real economy (Figs. 2.1 and 2.2). Thus, real

Table 2.2 Real capitalism and finance capitalism

	Real capitalism	Finance capitalism
Implicit coalition	Labour & real capital	Real capital & finance capital
Business/unions	Corporatism	Conflict
State/market	Complementary	Antagonistic
Targets of economic policy	Full employment, high growth, social security. "Fair" distribution of income and wealth	Price stability, "sound" public finances, regulations of policy, de-regulation of markets, declining government share. International competitiveness
"Power center" of economic policy	Government	Central bank
Economic paradigm	Keynesianism	Monetarism/neoliberalism
Diagnosis/therapy	Systemic	Symptom-oriented
Financial conditions	Interest rate < growth rate, "calm" stock markets, stable exchange rates and commodities prices	Interest rate > growth rate, boom and bust on stock markets, unstable exchange rates and commodities prices
Striving for profits focuses on	Real economy (positive-sum game)	Finance economy (zero-sum game)
Advantaged	Debitors	Creditors
Economic model	Social and regulated market economy	"Pure" market economy
Focus of globalization	Stable monetary system, regulation of financial markets, deregulation of goods markets (GATT), cooperative growth strategies (Marshall plan, development aid)	De-globalization of politics through rising competition of national economies, deregulation of financial markets, lack of global strategies to tackle global problems (e. g., climate change)

capitalism can be conceived as a positive-sum game. The theoretical/ideological basis of finance capitalism is (neo)liberal theories which call for a free market economy, especially for liberalizing financial markets, for a strong state as regards its core functions (security for citizens and their property) and for a weak state as regards welfare and labour regulations. These theories legitimate a (tacit) coalition between the interests of real and finance capital against the interests of labour because persistent full employment during a real-capitalist period shifts power in society from business to trade unions and from conservative to social-democratic parties. Therefore, entrepreneurs become (again) attracted by the (neo)liberal program. In this sense, the "excessive" success of real capitalism like full employment and the welfare state lays the ground for its fall (e.g. rising tensions in the relations between real capital and labour undermine their coalition).

Under a finance-capitalist regime, the volatility of exchange rates and commodities prices and the high level of interest rates have two effects on non-financial business. First, these conditions dampen its activities in the real sphere of the economy since they become more uncertain and more expensive. Second, these conditions make financial speculation and accumulation more attractive. This attraction is further increased by the emergence of financial innovations like derivatives which contribute to a dramatic expansion of financial markets shifting also the best human resources from real economy to "finance alchemy". At the same time, financial business becomes the dominant sector in the overall economy. The weak growth of real investment and, hence, of the overall economy causes unemployment and the public debt to rise which in turn strengthens the game "let your money work". For example, the shift in provisions for retirement from the welfare state system of "pay-as-you-go" to the (finance-capitalist) system of individual investment in financial assets lengthens stock market booms. Thus, the discrepancy between the market value of financial assets and their underlying in the real economy widens. This development leads to "corrections" in the form of financial crises (the crisis of 2008 can be seen as a particularly big correction as it concerned three bull markets at the same time). Whereas trading in asset markets represents just a zero-sum game, finance capitalism as a whole becomes a negative-sum game in its final stage: the destabilization of the most important prices for entrepreneurial activities like exchange rates, stock prices and interest rates together with the effects of financial crises progressively dampen the real economy. The system starts to implode through a series of crises, deepened by austerity policy. In this sense, the accumulation of negative outcomes of finance capitalism lays the ground for its own fall.

Employment Under Real-Capitalist and Finance-Capitalist Conditions

According to the mainstream (neoclassical) economic theory, supply and demand in the labour market determine the level of real wages and employment. When unemployment rises as a consequence of" demand shocks" such as financial crises or oil price shocks, job losses can be compensated only by real wage moderation. Higher wage flexibility is, however, hampered by unemployment benefits, labour protection, minimum wages and the power of unions (characteristic components of the European Social Model). As a matter of fact, however, labour costs are a function of real wages relative to labour productivity. In Europe, the latter has been growing even faster than wages since the late 1970s (and much faster than in the USA), exactly during that period when unemployment was rising (the wage share in national income declined noticeably (Fig. 2.1)). In addition, if the "rigidity" of European labour markets were truly important, this would have to show up in a less efficient allocation of labour and thus weaker growth of productivity as compared to the USA. Actually, however, labour productivity has been growing faster in Europe than in the USA – in tandem with the capital-labour ratio (capital intensity).

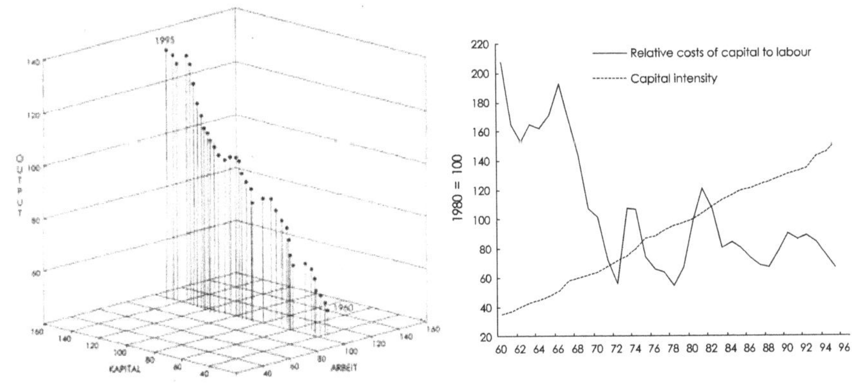

Fig. 2.13 Input, output and relative factor prices in the overall economy: Germany. (Source: OECD, WIFO)

The neoliberal explanation of labour demand rests on the (neoclassical) production function where capital input and labour input can be substituted for each other as a function of relative factor prices. However, an analysis of the observed realizations in the K-L-Y space in the USA, Germany and Japan (overall economy and 12 subsectors) between 1960 and 1995 reveals the following stylized facts:

- Capital intensity grows year after year, i.e. monotonically; the shift to ever more capital-intensive technologies is driven by technical progress and, hence, irreversible.
- The capital-labour ratio is unrelated to shifts in the factor price ratio (Fig. 2.13).
- Labour productivity grows in tandem with capital intensity: The higher and better the capital equipment of a worker becomes, the higher gets his productivity.

A linear-limitational production function with an irreversibly rising slope of the production rays fits these observations better than the neoclassical production function: in the short term, the factor input ratio is fixed; if the output is to be increased, labour and capital inputs need to be raised proportionally, and short-term demand for labour will be mostly influenced by expectations concerning demand in the goods markets; in the long term, capital intensity increases as a function of technical progress rather than of factor prices – more capital per labour is associated with a different quality of capital, meaning that labour productivity rises with capital intensity. An increase in output can be realized by either of two ways (or a mixture of both):

1. Movement along a ray with constant capital-labour ratios: capital intensity and labour productivity remain constant; the additional output is achieved by a greater input of capital and labour of the same quality.
2. Movement to a steeper production ray: the additional output is achieved by the increase and, hence, improvement of capital per labour unit and by the related learning process on the part of workers, capital intensity and labour productivity rise.

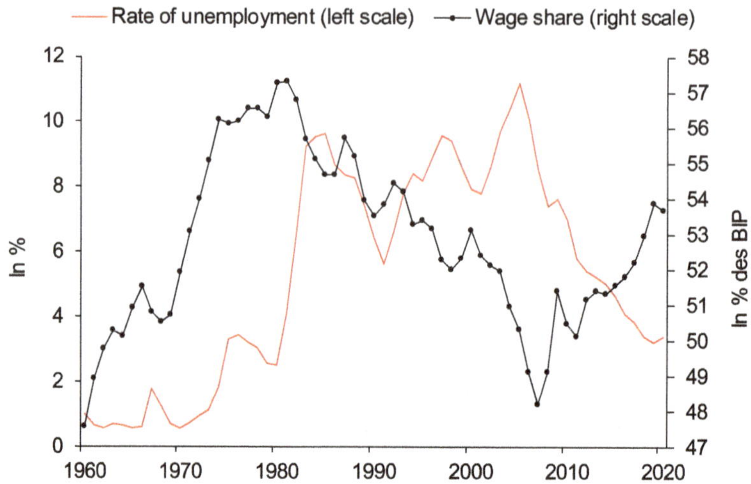

Fig. 2.14 Wage share and the rate of unemployment in Germany. (Source: Eurostat, OECD)

Under these conditions, the dynamics of job creation depends on the dynamics of real capital accumulation and of technical progress. The latter is to a large extent the result of (basic) innovations stemming from the "world of engineers" (interacting with the economic system). The dynamics of real capital accumulation depends primarily on the (expected) profitability of activities in the goods markets as compared to those in the financial markets. These observations and considerations suggest that the essence of persistent unemployment is sketched by analogy to the musical chair game: There are 100 chairs, 110 people want to get one, and those persons who do not get a chair are the least qualified. If they are (re)qualified, they might get a chair in the next rounds, yet, at the expense of others.

From this perspective, high and persistent unemployment is due to a shortage of jobs. To overcome the problem, job creation must become less risky and more profitable for entrepreneurs. This calls for real-capitalist framework conditions, not for lower wages (high/full employment in the 1960s was associated with wages rising faster than labour productivity – the opposite has been the case afterwards (Fig. 2.14)).

Public Finances Under Real-Capitalist and Finance-Capitalist Conditions

The ratio of public debt to GDP was declining in (Western) Europe for 20 years from 70% to 40% when the welfare state was built up, and it has been rising to roughly 100% since the 1970s in spite of consolidation efforts (Fig. 2.16). This development casts doubt on the belief that the government has direct control over its fiscal stance. Instead of a symptom-oriented "diagnosis", one has to take into account how the different sectors of the economy – households, business, government and the rest of the world (ROW) – behave under real-capitalist and finance-capitalist framework conditions.[8] If, e.g. the business sector reduces its deficit in a recession, then the government suffers from a rising deficit due to the operation of the automatic stabilizers (and eventually also due to discretionary measures). If the business sector increases its deficit again for financing real investments, then the government can easily improve on its balance during the recovery. The recession in Germany in 1967 and the subsequent years is a good example for the interaction of the financial balances under real-capitalist conditions (Fig. 2.15).

Over the medium and long run, real-capitalist incentive conditions ensure that the business sector takes over household saving in the form of investment credits and transforms it into real capital and jobs (Fig. 2.15). As a consequence, the government's budget remains in balance, and the debt-to-GDP ratio declines since the rate of interest lies below the rate of economic growth (Fig. 2.16). Under these conditions, the surpluses and financial assets of private households (roughly) equal the deficits and financial liabilities of the business sector.

Finance-capitalist conditions change the interaction of financial balances and the dynamics of debts/assets in three respects. First, recessions occur more frequently than in a real-capitalist regime due to turbulences like oil price "shocks", interest rate "shocks" and dollar exchange rate "shocks". Second, recoveries become progressively weaker as financial instability and the related profit opportunities from speculation dampen real investments. Third, the rate of interest is higher than the rate of economic growth.

The dynamics of public debt is driven by two factors, the accumulation of (primary) deficits and the interest-growth differential. The latter does impact upon of the development of the public debt mainly indirectly, i.e. through the adjustment of the business sector to a positive or negative interest-growth differential.[9] The reason for that is clear-cut: if the rate of interest exceeds the rate of growth (in nominal terms), any debtor (sector) has to run a primary surplus in order to stabilize its debt relative to GDP ("dynamic budget constraint"). To achieve such a surplus, non-financial business reduces real investment in favour of financial accumulation (Figs. 2.12 and 2.15). At the same time, also financial businesses and households run primary surpluses (e.g. private households – a creditor sector – save usually more than their net interest income). Under this condition, the government can achieve a primary surplus only if the rest of the world runs/accepts a primary current account deficit (the primary balances of all sectors sum up to zero). Germany, for example, was able to stabilize its fiscal stance mainly through rising surpluses vis-à-vis (and at the expense of) other countries.

---

[8] In the following, we specify only non-financial business since the financial balance of the financial sector was close to zero most of the time.

[9] When calculating the interest-growth differential, the distinction between nominal and real terms does not matter as both the interest rate and the growth rate have to be deflated with the same index of the general price level, i.e. the GDP deflator. However, in the context of analysing the interaction of financial balances of sectors, one should operate generally with nominal figures (balances cannot be deflated).

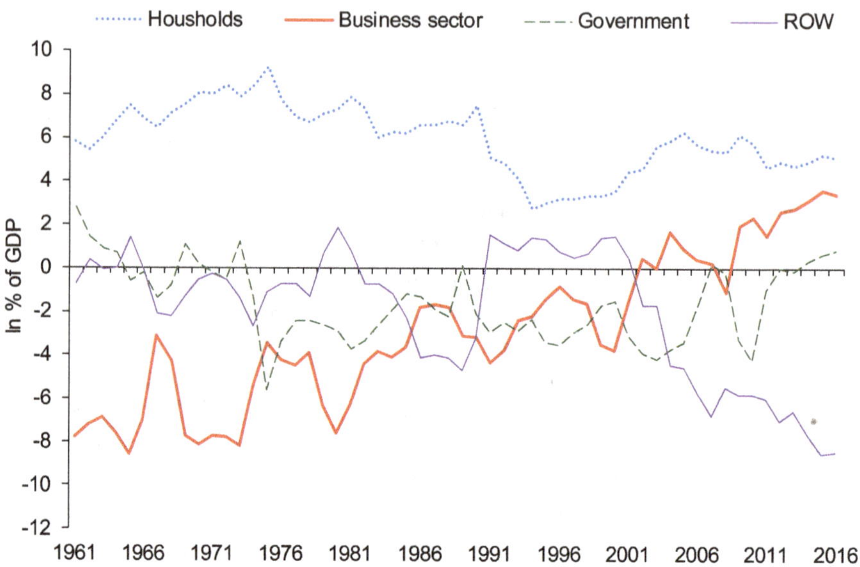

Fig. 2.15 Financial balances in Germany. (Source: Deutsche Bundesbank)

To summarize, finance-capitalist conditions in general and a positive interest-growth differential in particular inevitably lead to a rise in public indebtedness and in global imbalances (if countries compensate the decline in the deficit of non-financial business through rising current account surpluses). This conclusion is in line with the empirical evidence. Under the incentive conditions of the 1950s and 1970s, the surpluses of households were taken over by the business sector in the form of deficits (Fig. 2.15) in order to finance the accumulation of real capital and, hence, the creation of jobs (Fig. 2.13). Economic growth at full employment enabled governments to build up the welfare state and keep the budget in balance at the same time. At a negative interest-growth differential, public debt declined relative to GDP (Fig. 2.16).

Since the 1970s, the finance-capitalist framework conditions induced non-financial business to reduce its deficit und to become a surplus sector in almost all industrial countries (like Germany (Fig. 2.15)): real investments were reduced in favour of financial investments, the stock of real assets has been declining relative to financial assets (Fig. 2.12), job creation and economic growth slowed down, and unemployment rose so that most countries have been running budget deficits (even Germany (Fig. 2.15)).[10] Given the positive interest-growth differential, the public

[10] Only in recent years did Germany achieve a balanced or even a surplus budget, however, at the expense of the rest of the world: The European Monetary Union enabled Germany to fully profit from its restrictive wage and fiscal policy since the appreciations vis-à-vis Germany's euro partner countries were no longer possible. The German contribution to the development of the "euro crisis" is documented in detail in Schulmeister (2018, Chaps. 11, 12, and 13).

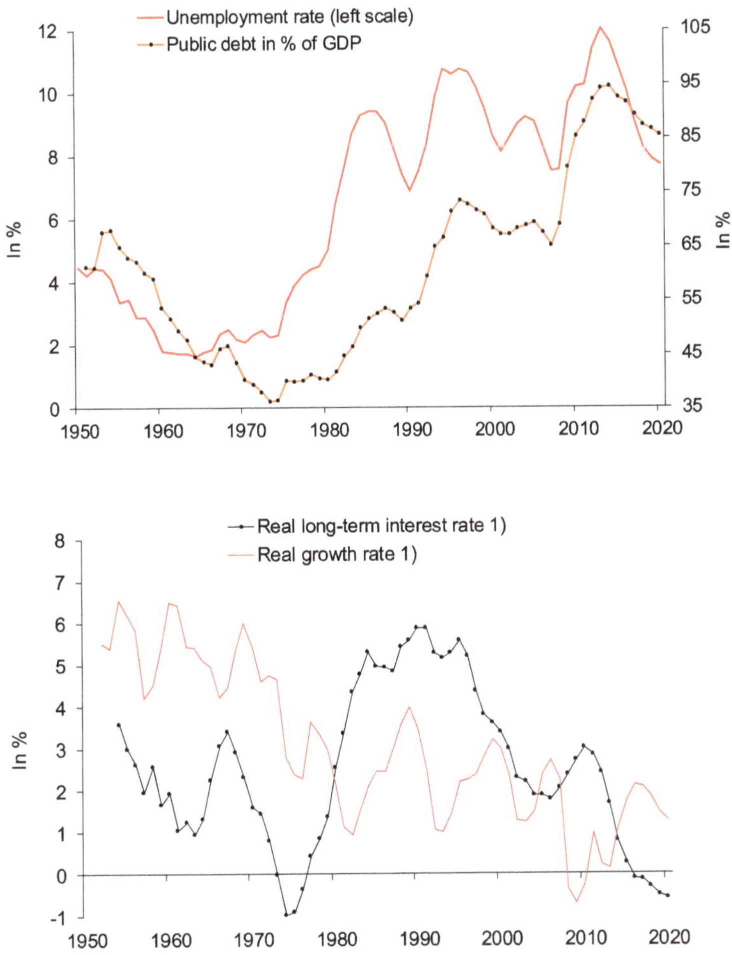

Fig. 2.16 Unemployment, public debt and the interest-growth differential in Western Europe. [1]3-years moving average. (Source: OECD, Eurostat, WIFO)

debt-to-GDP ratio has risen strongly over the long run (Fig. 2.16). The fiscal compact (signed in 2012) represents a further step in a series of attempts of EU politics to govern the fiscal stance of a country through certain rules (the first attempt consisted in the 3%-deficit rule in the Treaty of Maastricht of 1992). In addition to the 3% rule as maximum of the general budget deficit, there is a second rule for the structural budget deficit which must not exceed 0.5% of GDP. This holds for all states with a debt-to-GDP ratio exceeding 60%. According to the debt brake rule, these states have also to reduce this ratio by at least one twentieth (5%) per year of the exceeded percentage points (e.g. if a state has a debt of 100% of GDP, it should reduce this ratio by 2% points each year).

The most problematic rule concerns the structural deficit since the latter is a theoretical construction and cannot be directly calculated. Hence, the room for manoeuvre of fiscal policy can be restricted by the estimation method of structural deficits. This holds true in particular for the method used by the European Commission. These objections shall be concretized, taking the development in Spain after the crisis of 2008 as example (Fig. 2.17; all data stem from EC data bases, Fall 2013).

The financial crisis and the collapse of the real estate bubble caused a deep recession in 2009; unemployment and the budget deficit increased sharply. As unemployment did not decline afterwards, it became "natural" – by theoretical and methodological construction, the NAWRU follows the actual unemployment rate (Fig. 2.17). Since less employable people are fed into a Cobb-Douglas function, potential output started to decline. As a consequence, the output gap did not rise in spite of the deepening of the crisis but stays at roughly 4%. Therefore, most of the actual deficit became "structural" (the EC estimates the cyclical component in general as roughly 50% of the output gap). The excessive structural deficit forced the government to more austerity. In 2011, transfers stagnated (in spite of unemployment rising above 20%), and government consumption shrunk. These measures induced a further decline of GDP in 2012 (together with tax increases which however did not result in higher receipts due to the new recession). As a consequence,

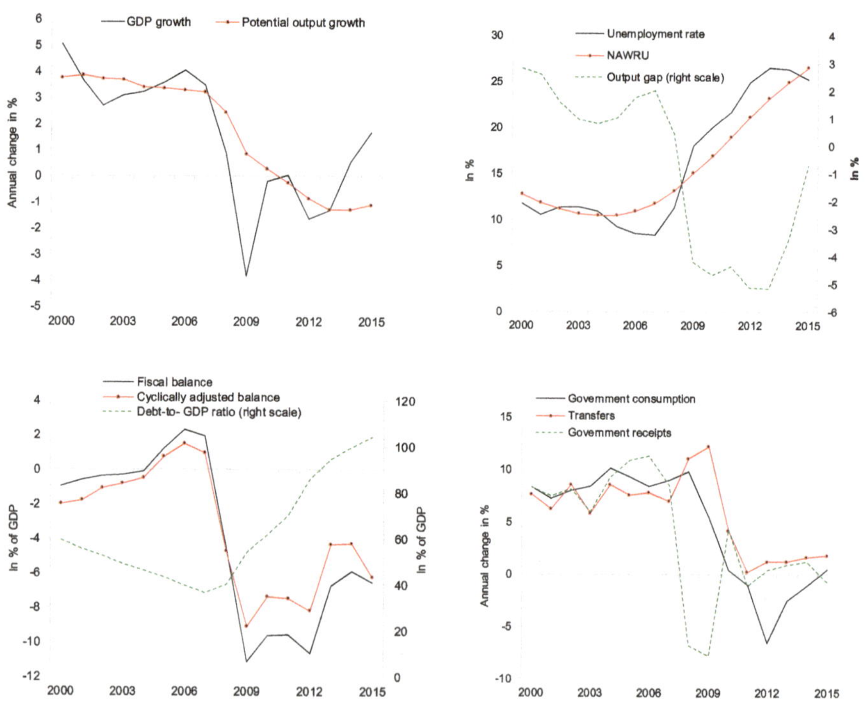

Fig. 2.17 Output, unemployment and the fiscal stance of Spain. (Source: Eurostat)

the fiscal stance improved much less than expected, calling for further austerity. In the meantime, the debt-to-GDP ratio was rising from 40% to more than 80%. If economic policy had continued to follow the fiscal rules, a downwards spiral would have developed. Fortunately, policy in Spain but also in Portugal and France deliberately (though tacitly) ignored the fiscal compact from 2013 onwards and took some expansionary measures. The structural balance of these states by far exceeded the 0.5% benchmark (whereas Italy tried to stick to this rule), yet no excessive deficit procedure was initiated by the European Commission. Together with the extremely loose monetary policy of the ECB, the moderate expansionary fiscal policy enabled the economy of these countries to recover.

Production of Economic Theories and Long-Term Economic Development

The observations presented so far cast doubts on the most fundamental propositions of neoclassical theory which has become once again the paradigm in economics (completed by "rational expectations"). Hence, this theory provided the basis of the "navigation map" of economic policy in the EU. But how could a theory remain dominant whose most fundamental propositions cannot be reconciled with the empirical evidence, in particular as regards the price dynamics in those markets which come closest to the theoretically ideal market, i.e. the financial markets? This section addresses this puzzle by reconsidering the interaction between economic developments and theory production.

The abatement of the revolution of 1848 was followed by a period of strong growth of the real economy (railways, construction), ideologically based on "laissez-faire liberalism". Marx and Engels explained the rising inequality and the misery of the working class as necessary outcome of capitalism which must be overcome on the basis of socialist theories. Together with their (real) wealth grew the temptation of "industrial capitalists" to (also) become "money capitalists" (Marx), e.g. to get even richer through speculation in the stock market, but also in real estate. By the late 1860s, stock and house prices started to rise more and more. The finance-capitalist boom ended abruptly with the crash of 1873: Both bull markets tilted into bear markets leading into the "long depression."

On the academic level, "laissez-faire theories" came under attack; instead, concepts became popular which stressed the role of economic actors as social beings and which called for an active state, be it through building up a social state ("Kathedersozialisten" like Gustav Schmoller), be it through (protectionist) industrial policy (e.g. Friedrich List). In addition, also the more radical socialist/Marxist theories influenced the economists' debates. The longer the depression lasted, the more oppressing became the social problems, and the bigger became the power of the workers' movement (in 1875, the "Sozialistische deutsche Arbeiterpartei" was founded in Gotha, unifying two socialist forerunner parties). As a reaction, the basic components of the welfare state (health and pension insurance) were introduced in Germany by chancellor Bismarck and afterwards in most other European countries.

The improved confidence in the state, new investment opportunities through implementing new technologies (electricity and chemistry), stable financial conditions through fixed exchange rates (gold standard) and low interest rates and the related wave of globalisation contributed to the real-capitalist expansion of the "belle époque" (~1890 to 1914). This was particularly true for Germany where all kinds of futures contracts were banned by law in 1896 (after a wave of wheat speculation had collapsed). Germany became the leading country in industrial production, and the capital of the UK became the leading financial centre.

On the academic level, neoclassical theory became the paradigm in economics. It had been developed since the 1870s (independently) by William Jevons, Carl Menger and Leon Walras and is strictly based on the interaction of individual agents in markets. In ideological terms, the concept of the "homo oeconomicus" and, hence, of individualism can be considered a reaction to the rising influence of socialist theories.

After World War I, the dominance of the "free-market view" facilitated the development of one of the strongest stock bull markets in history: Over only 4 years – between 1925 and 1929 – stock prices almost quadrupled in the USA, people took up more and more credits to finance buying stocks and to "let their money work". The boom then spilled over to other industrial countries. The crash of 1929 caused a recession so that budget deficits widened. Economic policy followed the advice of mainstream economists to adopt an austerity policy according to neoclassical theory. This policy paved the way into the Great Depression, together with the collapse of the gold standard, competitive devaluations and other forms of protectionism.

The consequences of the depression were so catastrophic that also the learning process enforced by this crisis was deep. It resulted in a new macroeconomic theory (provided by Keynes), in an active economic policy focusing on full employment, in stable exchange rates, deregulation of goods markets but strict regulation of financial markets. Two other developments promoted prosperity. First, confidence was strengthened through building up the welfare state. Second, there prevailed a tight coherence between the technological paradigm (Fordism) and the economic paradigm (Keynesian welfare model).

The success of the European Social Model laid the ground for its own decline: Full employment and building up the welfare state shifted power from business to unions which asked for (more) employee participation and for a redistribution in favour of wages (Fig. 2.14). The "Zeitgeist" shifted to the left (1968, etc.) and brought social-democratic parties to power as in Germany and Austria. The environmental movement took off and attacked the capitalist model as obsolescent (the "Club of Rome" was founded 1970). All these developments caused "big business" to support the neoliberal movement against full employment, Keynesianism and the welfare state.[11] The stepwise realization of the monetarists' demand for deregulation of financial markets transformed the system from a real-capitalist into a finance-capitalist regime.

All important steps on the long way from prosperity into the present crisis – from moving to "flexible" exchange rates in 1971 to the financial crisis of 2008 and the subsequent euro crisis – were guided by the recommendations of neoliberal theories.[12] Yet, this "Weltanschauung" still dominates at the academic level, in international organizations, in governmental institutions (ministries), in the media and in politics. The main reason for the persistence of neoliberalism lies in its history: never before had the enforcement of an economic paradigm so systematically been prepared, realized and anchored in the minds of the elites. This process began already during the Great Depression.

In 1931, Hayek became professor at the London School of Economics (LSE) at the age of 32 and turned soon into the most famous opponent of Keynes in the debates over the role of economic policy in the Great Depression. After the overwhelming success of Keynes' "General Theory" (1936), Hayek became an outsider within the economists' profession and began to focus on planning a movement against the foreseeable advance of the welfare state, legitimized by Keynes' theory. Hayek participated in a first meeting of like-minded economists and sociologists in Paris in August 1938 (during this "Colloque Lippmann", the term "neo-liberalism" was coined). During the war, Hayek provided the ideological fundament for the neoliberal movement with his "Road to Serfdom" (1944). As next step, Hayek founded the Mont Pelerin Society (MPS) in 1947. This network links together top scientific economists ("original thinkers" in Hayek's words – as yet, eight MPS members got the "Nobel prize"), other intellectuals working in academia, media or think tanks ("second-hand dealers in ideas"), politicians (like Ludwig Erhard) and wealthy people as financiers of MPS activities.

Hayek took the "Fabian Society" as model for the neoliberal movement. This leftist group of social reformers had successfully changed values and attitudes in the British society between the 1880s and the 1920s. In "The Intellectuals and Socialism" (1949), Hayek proposed to his combatants that also the neoliberal movement should focus on influencing the intellectuals because "once the most active part of the intellectuals has been converted to a set of beliefs, the process by which

[11] As early as 1943 did Michal Kalecki foresee the long-term political consequences of full employment policy: "Lasting full employment is not at all to their ['business leaders'] liking". The workers would "get out of hand" and the "captains of industry" would be anxious to "teach them a lesson" (…). In this situation a powerful alliance is likely to be formed between big business and *rentier* interests, and they would probably find more than one economist to declare that the situation was manifestly unsound" (Kalecki 1990, p. 355).

[12] One has to distinguish between (at least) three neoliberal schools, the Austrian school (Hayek and Co.), the Chicago (neoclassical/monetarist/New Classical) school (Friedman, Lucas and Co.) and the German ordoliberal school (one could also add the Virginia school with Buchanan as leading figure which, however, is a close "ally" of the Chicago school). These schools differ fundamentally in their assumptions and methods; however, they arrive at practically the same policy recommendations (see *Schulmeister*, Chap. 6).

these become generally accepted is almost automatic and irresistible" (quoted in Jones 2012, p. 80). Hayek was convinced that "the building of a free society" through defeating Keynesianism and weakening the welfare state could actually be achieved even though this might take "two or three generations".[13] As first step, one needed anti-Keynesian theories, produced by the "original thinkers", which would then be "translated" in the language of ordinary people by the "second-hand dealers in ideas" and promoted by think tanks.

In the 1950s and 1960s, Hayek, Friedman, Stigler, Becker, Coase and Buchanan (to name only the most prominent MPS members and – later – "Nobel laureates") produced a great variety of theories, directed against the then dominant economic paradigm, i.e. Keynesianism:

- Financial speculation is predominantly rational and, hence, stabilizing (Friedman 1953). This (tautological) "proof" legitimated later the deregulation of financial markets.
- Keynesian fiscal policy has little effect since households base their consumption on their "permanent" and not on their current income (Friedman 1957).
- In his "opus magnum", Hayek called for the restriction of any activities of the state besides protecting the individual liberty and property of its citizens (Hayek 1960).
- George Stigler (University of Chicago) developed the concept of "regulatory capture" according to which market regulations are (ab)used by lobby groups (Stigler 1971).
- At the University of Virginia, James Buchanan and Gordon Tullock built up the "public-choice school": Politicians act mainly their private interest (Buchanan and Tullock 1962).
- Gary Becker generalized the "homo oeconomicus": All human relationships such as love, marriage, parenthood, etc. are guided by rational utility maximization (Becker 1976).
- Friedman "proved" (together with Anna Schwartz) that the Great Depression was not caused by the stock market crash of 1929 and the subsequent austerity policy but by the central bank, i.e. by the state (Friedman and Schwartz 1963).

The presidential address of Milton Friedman at the meeting of the American Economic Association in 1967 signalled the start of the decisive attack (Friedman 1968): full employment policy is not only useless but detrimental because there exists a natural rate of unemployment. Any attempt to push unemployment below its level results in higher inflation. The whole argument was tautological: If one assumes that output is determined in real terms through market equilibria (vertical Phillips curve), then any monetary impulse can only have inflationary effects. The construction of Friedman's model was, however, brilliant: He took the modified

[13] Milton Friedman was more optimistic. He stated in his article "Neo-Liberalism and Its Prospects": "The stage is set for the growth of a new current of opinion to replace the old, to provide the philosophy that will guide the legislators of the next generation even though it can hardly affect those of this one". Quoted in Jones (2012, p. 85).

Phillips curve (Samuelson and Solow 1960) as point of departure, which – erroneously – implied that economic policy can choose between inflation and unemployment. Such a choice turns out to be non-sense if one takes interest rates into account: Any rise in inflation causes nominal interest rates to rise and interest payments on outstanding debts to rise even faster so that investments and employment will decline with some lag.[14] For more than a decade, monetarism became the dominant macroeconomic paradigm based on the quantity theory of money. However, being neoclassical thinkers and, hence, believing in "money does not matter", monetarists overlooked a trivial, yet fundamentally important fact: money is not only used for transactions with goods and services (PQ x Q) but also with financial assets of all kinds (PF × QF): M × V = PQ × Q + PF × QF.

Since the volume of financial transactions is many times bigger (and more unstable) than the volume of transactions with goods and services (Fig. 2.11), a stable relationship between money supply and PQ × Q is a *theoretical* impossibility (Schulmeister 2018, p. 88f and p. 157f). The collapse of the Bretton Woods system and the following dollar depreciation induced the first "oil price shock" followed by the first global recession since the 1930s. The "original thinkers" then used the coincidence of rising unemployment and rising inflation as disprove of the Phillips curve and of Keynesian theory in general. The "battle over the Phillips curve" marked the decisive defeat of Keynesian economics. As substitute, the old general equilibrium theory was restored and complemented by "rational expectations" (Lucas 1972): It is assumed that agents form their expectation according to the "true model" which is the model of the rational expectations of economists themselves (a Freudian projection). As some kind of terminological twist, Lucas and Co. called their approach "New Classical Macroeconomics" instead of "old neoclassical microeconomics".

Once any kind of non-rationality, uncertainty, social interaction and emotions were removed from the economic theorist's world, one no longer needed to account for different economic agents. Hence, the "new classical macroeconomists" constructed "dynamic general equilibrium (DSGE) models" based on "representative agents", preferably eternally living. In this world, expansionary fiscal policy is useless ("Ricardian equivalence"; Barro 1974) as is any kind of macroeconomic policy ("Lucas critique"; Lucas 1976). Business cycles can only be caused by technological shocks ("real business cycles"; Kydland and Prescott 1982). Once the "original thinkers" had produced economic theories, the intellectuals ("second-hand dealers in ideas") should sell them to the public. To this end, more and more neoliberal think tanks were founded like the "Institute for Economic Affairs" in the UK, the "Liberty Fund", the "Heritage Foundation" or the "Cato Institute" in the USA (to mention only the biggest "tanks"). Their number grew particularly fast after the

[14] To illustrate this accelerator effect, if inflation rises by 2% points causing the nominal interest rate to increase from 4% to 6%, then interest payments rise by 50% (for credits at flexible rates). Phillips himself had (plausibly) interpreted the inverse relationship between the change in wages and unemployment as reflecting just the (unidirectional) influence of the employment situation on the bargaining power of unions (Phillips 1958).

breakthrough of the neoliberal offensive in the 1970s. Since 1981 neoliberal think tanks are linked together through the "Atlas Network", it comprises today almost 500 institutions all over the world.[15]

Over several decades, the increasing dominance of the neoliberal "Weltanschauung" changed politics, values and attitudes. Slowly, "the market" became the highest (economic) being which transforms the individual egoisms into the social optimum with an "invisible hand". Therefore, men have to subordinate to market forces, even the democratically legitimized politics (see the notion "market-conform democracy" used by Chancellor Merkel). That "the market" appears to be a subject to which men have to adjust is also expressed in everyday language ("the markets discipline Greece with higher interest rates" – in its plural form, "markets" almost always means "financial markets"). Through turning the subject-object relationship between men and market upside down, neoliberalism became the most powerful ideology of anti-enlightenment and of de-politicizing politics: men cannot and/or should not organize consciously development processes in society through political coordination (e.g. by building up a comprehensive welfare state). Instead, social development should be driven by market competition of individuals, coordinated by the "invisible hand". The propagation of this ideology – massively fostered by the breakdown of "real socialism" in 1989 and thereafter – strengthened the feeling of people to be exposed to incomprehensible economic fluctuations, in particular of globalized financial markets. At the same time, austerity policies weakened the trust in the welfare state. Right-wing populists address the feelings of uncertainty, fear of the future and anger and promise to "clean up" the system.

The "Long Cycle" as Sequence of Real-Capitalist and Finance-Capitalist Regimes

The Russian economist Nikolai Kondratieff was the first to discover the phenomenon of the "long cycle" or "long wave" in economic development. In his interpretation, the upswing is caused by technological innovations like the steam engine, railways or electricity; the downswing sets in when the technology has already been widely diffused (Kondratieff 1926).

However, the post-war long cycle can hardly be explained by this model since fundamental technological innovations like microelectronics in all its manifestations, biotechnology and nanotechnology were developed primarily since the 1970s, i.e. over the downswing phase (over the 1950s and 1960s, no fundamentally new technologies had been developed). Based on the distinction between real and finance

---

[15] See www.atlasnetwork.org. For details of how the neoliberal master minds organized the advancement and diffusion of their ideology, see Walpen (2004), Burgin (2012), and Jones (2012). The essence of this literature is summarized in *Schulmeister*, Chap. 6.

capital, the long cycle might better be understood as a sequence of real-capitalist and finance-capitalist regimes.

The upwards phase of the long cycle is brought about through incentive conditions which focus profit-seeking on activities in the real economy (financial speculation is restricted). Real accumulation is booming; finance capital grows in tandem with real capital or somewhat slower due to the undervaluation of financial assets, in particular of stocks. The longer the boom lasts, the more real and financial wealth is accumulated. Their owners become increasingly interested in "let our money work" also through financial speculation. At the same time, the economic and political position of workers improve due to full/high employment. Trade unions and leftist parties go on the offensive. Liberal or neoliberal theories and political concepts become more attractive for rentiers as well entrepreneurs. In this way, the success of real capitalism, i.e. the accumulation of wealth and full employment, lays the ground for a change in the economic paradigm and in the respective "navigation map" for politics.

Under finance-capitalist incentive conditions, economic growth declines, unemployment and the public debt rise, austerity policies deepen the crisis. The "synchronization" of bull and bear markets causes asset revaluations, followed by devaluations which lead finally into a deep financial and economic crisis as in 1873, 1929 and 2008. In this way, the failure of finance capitalism lays the ground for its decline and the search for new framework conditions during the trough phase of the long cycle. The incentive structure is changed in favour of entrepreneurial activities, in particular through financial regulations and a more active economic as well as social policy.[16] The key empirical facts concerning the long cycle over the last 150 years have already been sketched in sections "Framework Conditions and Economic Performance of Western Capitalism during the 1960s and 1970s" and "Public Finances Under Real-Capitalist and Finance-Capitalist Conditions". Here, they are only shortly recapitulated. After the boom of the real economy in the 1850s and 1860s, speculation led to the great real estate, bank and stock market crash of 1873, followed by the "long depression". The tensions in society became more pronounced as did the power of the workers' movement. As a reaction, the basic components of the welfare state were introduced in the 1880s.

The related stabilization of purchasing power and, hence, of final demand, but also stable exchange rates, low interest rates and the first wave of globalisation,

---

[16] In a profound and original study in economic history, Arrighi (2010) combines a similar model of long waves with Fernand Braudel's concept of centre and periphery and the related role of the hegemon in the global economy. In Arrighi's interpretation, an economic and political system becomes the hegemon during a real-capitalist upwards phase and then moves to "high finance" and by doing so finances the upwards phase of its successor. In this way, the Republic of Genoa financed the expansion of the Dutch Republics during the sixteenth century which then financed the industrialization of Great Britain. When London moved to "high finance" in the second half of the nineteenth century, it financed the US expansion. When the Wall Street became dominant in the late 1970s, the USA started to finance the expansion of the Chinese economy through joint ventures which also provide a continuous technology transfer (it goes without saying that this note is only an extremely simplified sketch of Arrighi's concept of "systemic cycles of accumulation").

contributed to the real-capitalist expansion of the "belle époque" (~1980 to 1914). Over the "roaring 1920s", the mood of "let your money work" broadened and led to a spectacular stock-market boom which crashed in October 1929 together with real estate and commodity prices. The subsequent financial crisis and austerity policies – derived from neoclassical theory – paved the way into the Great Depression. The consequences of the depression were so catastrophic that also the learning process enforced by this crisis evolved in an in-depth manner. It resulted in a new macroeconomic theory (Keynesianism), an active economic policy focusing on stable growth and full employment, stable exchange rates ("Bretton Woods"), deregulation of goods markets (e.g. though the GATT rounds) but strict regulation of financial markets.

Whereas the Kondratieff model stresses the importance of technological innovations as driving force of the upswing, the model presented here stresses the importance of the relationship between technical and social innovations, i.e. of the coherence/incoherence between the technological paradigm and the socio-economic paradigm. The post-war prosperity phase is a good example: The "Fordistic" type of (mass) production fitted well to the Keynesian paradigm of the 1950s and 1960s which legitimates the strengthening and stabilizing of mass consumption. Expressed in more general terms: the (in)coherence between the technological paradigm and the economic and social paradigm is a key factor in the dynamics of the long cycle. When technological innovations take place, they usually cannot be fully utilized because there is a lack of accommodating social innovations. For example, Fordistic mass production was already adopted in the 1920s but could not be fully used within the "laissez-faire paradigm".

In an analogous way, one can argue that nowadays those social innovations are missing which would accommodate the technological innovations of the last decades in such a way that the society as a whole can profit from progress in technology as well as in the socio-economic relations. The contradiction between the progression in technology and regression in economics, i.e. the return to the old "laissez-faire paradigm", is one important feature of the current crisis (in natural sciences a return to an old paradigm is unconceivable).

The European Model and the US Model Under Real-Capitalist and Finance-Capitalist Conditions

Table 2.3 summarizes the main differences between the European Social Model and the US model of society in a stylized manner. These differences have developed over several centuries, whereas changes between real-capitalist and finance-capitalist framework conditions take place within few decades. The roots of the European Social Model lie in the traditionally great importance of citizens being embedded in social contexts. The respective organizations range from the feudal system or the guilds of craftsmen in medieval times to interest groups like trade unions and up to the modern welfare state. In the USA, by contrast, competition as individuals is the most important form of economic interaction – not the least because the USA has

Table 2.3 European model versus US model

	Europe	USA
Long-term development path	Citizens embedded in social contexts (feudal system, communities, interest groups, welfare state)	Citizens as (former) immigrants: Mentality of adventurers, Competition as dominant form of social interaction
Pursuit of interests	Mainly through organisations (unions, etc.)	Predominantly as individuals in markets
Fundamental values	Individual freedom *and* social justice ("Liberte, egalite, fraternite")	Individual freedom ("pursuit of happiness")
Importance of trade unions and organisations of entrepreneurs	Great	Little
Labour relations	Corporatism	No institutionalized cooperation
Labour markets	Regulated	"Hire and fire"
Insurance against illness, old-age poverty, unemployment	Provided by welfare state	Mainly private (or no) insurance, unemployment benefits modest
Education system	Primarily run by welfare state	Mainly private
Relationship market/state	Complementary	Antagonistic
Importance of the welfare state	Great	Little
Importance of the financial sector	(Traditionally) Less important	Very important
Focus of making profits	(Traditionally) Real economy	Real and financial economy
"Economic culture"	"Real capitalism" combined with welfare state	"Real and financial capitalism" ("Silicon Valley culture" combined with "Wall Street culture")

evolved from a society of immigrants in which the fight for survival and expansion is of central importance. As a consequence, organisations like trade unions or political parties as a means of pursuit of interests play a comparatively greater role in Europe. Individual freedom, social justice and solidarity can be considered the key values of European society ("liberté, egalité, fraternité"). In the USA, by contrast, individual freedom ranges by far the highest ("pursuit of happiness").

These differences are also reflected by the way how insurance against basic risks of life is provided and how the education system is organized. In both respects, the welfare state plays a much more important role in Europe as compared to the USA. As a consequence, the relationship between market and state is (traditionally) considered complementary in Europe but rather antagonistic in the USA.

Significant differences have also been prevailing as regards the relationship between the real and the financial sphere of the economy and the related "economic culture". The economies in (continental) Europe have been focused on the real economy. In the USA (and also in the UK), the "Wall Street" (and the "City") plays

Table 2.4 Europe and USA under real and finance capitalism

Institutional framework conditions	Macro-economic framework conditions: Real capitalism	Finance capitalism	Mixed (Bastard-Keynesian monetary and fiscal policy, speculation focused on stock market)
European Social Model	Europe until ~1973/1980	Europe since ~1973/1980	—
US-Model	US until ~1973/1980	US since ~1973/1980	US since ~1990

a key role in the economic system. Since the early 1990s, the practice of economic policy in the EU has been staying in an increasing contradiction to the principles of the European Social Model. This policy was shaped by the following general guidelines (Table 2.4): restrictive regulation of fiscal and monetary policy and deregulation of financial, goods and labour markets. These neoliberal guidelines have progressively weakened the European welfare state. At the same time, US economic policy has been following a "trivial Keynesian" course.

The fiscal rules were established in 1992 in the Treaty of Maastricht and have then been tightened through the Treaty of Amsterdam (1997) and 2012 through the Fiscal Compact. In the USA, by contrast, fiscal policy has been following a pronounced countercyclical course. For example, in and after recessions, the government increased the budget deficit deliberately and strongly. Afterwards it did not adopt a savings policy but let the automatic stabilizers care for a continuous improvement of the fiscal stance.[17] Monetary policy in the euro area is shaped by the statute of ECB which gives price stability the highest priority and leaves almost no room for other economic targets. By contrast, the US central bank considers growth of production and employment as important as price stability. US authorities try to support the own economy not only by means of an active fiscal and monetary policy but also by stimulating exports through an undervalued dollar exchange rate. For example, during and after the recessions in 1991 and 2001, the "talking the dollar down" on behalf of US politicians contributed to strong depreciations of the US currency. After the Great Recession of 2009, this strategy failed due to the deepening of the euro crisis which caused the euro exchange rate to decline.

To summarize, a comparison of the fiscal and monetary policy adopted by the EU, on the one hand, and by the USA, on the other, suggests that an exchange of concepts took tacitly place around 1990. The EU took over the monetarist approach of regulating fiscal and monetary policy in a restrictive manner, whereas the USA adopted a "trivial Keynesian" approach. An evaluation of the realization of the four combinations of real/finance capitalism, on the one hand, and the European/US model, on the other hand, in post-war history (plus the special case of the US

[17] This "trivial Keynesian" course was and is facilitated by the privilege of issuing the main international reserve currency, the US dollar. Since the USA can finance its external deficit in its national currency, it is much less financially constraint than all other countries. This helps also to finance the US government deficit.

strategy since the early 1990s) suggests that the best performance was realized in Europe over the 1950s and 1960s due to the coherence between the principles of the European Social Model and a real-capitalist incentive structure. The worst performance can be attributed to the (inconsistent) combination of finance-capitalist conditions and the European model, i.e. the development in the EU over the last 20 years.

References

Arrighi, G. (2010). *The long twentieth century* (2nd ed.). London: Verso.

Barro, R. (1974). Are government bonds net wealth? *Journal of Political Economy, 82*(6), 1095–1117.

Becker, G. S. (1976). *The economic approach to human behavior*. Chicago: University of Chicago Press.

Buchanan, J., & Tullock, G. (1962). *The calculus of consent – Logical foundations of constitutional democracy*. Ann Arbor: University of Michigan Press.

Burgin, A. (2012). *The great persuasion: Reinventing free markets since the depression*. Cambridge: Harvard University Press.

Friedman, M. (1953). The case for flexible exchange rates. In *Essays in positive economics*. Chicago: University of Chicago Press.

Friedman, M. (1957). A Theory of the Consumption Function, Princeton University Press.

Friedman, M. (1968). The role of monetary policy. *American Economic Review, 58*(1), 1.

Friedman, M., & Schwartz, A. J. (1963). *A monetary history of the United States 1867-1960*. Princeton: Princeton University Press.

Hayek, F. A. (1960). *The constitution of liberty*. Chicago: University of Chicago Press.

Jones, D. S. (2012). *Masters of the universe: Hayek, Friedman, and the birth of neoliberal politics*. Princeton: Princeton University Press.

Kalecki, M. (1990). Political aspects of full employment. In *Collected works of Michal Kalecki* (Vol. I). Oxford: Clarendon Press.

Kondratieff, N. D. (1926). Die langen Wellen der Konjunktur, Archiv für Sozialwissenschaft und Sozialpolitik. *Band, 56*, 573–609.

Koo, R. (2009). *The holy grail of macroeconomics: Lessons from Japans great recession*. New York: Wiley.

Kydland, F. E., & Prescott, E. C. (1982). Time to build and aggregate fluctuations. *Econometrica, 50*(6), 1345.

Lucas, R. E. (1972). Expectations and the neutrality of money. *Journal of Economic Theory, 4*(2), 103.

Lucas, R. (1976). Econometric policy evaluation: A critique. In K. Brunner & A. Meltzer (Eds.), *The Phillips curve and labor markets. Carnegie-Rochester Conference Series on Public Policy 1* (pp. 19–46). New York: American Elsevier.

Phillips, A. W. (1958). The relation between unemployment and the rate of change of money wage rates in the United Kingdom, 1861–1957. *Economica, 25*(100), 283–299.

Samuelson, P. A., & Solow, R. (1960). Analytical aspects of anti-inflation policy: Papers and proceedings. *American Economic Review, 50*, 177–194.

Schulmeister, S. (2000). Globalization without global money: The double role of the dollar as national currency and as world currency. *Journal of Post Keynesian Economics, 22*(3), 365–395.

Schulmeister, S. (2008). On the manic-depressive fluctuations of speculative prices. In E. Hein, T. Niechoj, P. Spahn, & A. Truger (Eds.), *Finance-led capitalism*. Marburg: Metropolis-Verlag.

Schulmeister, S. (2014). European Governance – Do we need a new navigation map? *Izmir Review of Social Sciences, 1*(2), 1–36.

Schulmeister, S. (2018). *Der Weg zur Prosperität*. Salzburg: Ecowin.

Stigler, G. (1971). The theory of economic regulation. *Bell Journal of Economics, 2*(1), 3–21.

Walpen, B. (2004). *Die offenen Feinde und ihre Gesellschaft: Eine hegemonietheoretische Studie zur Mont Pèlerin Society*. Hamburg: VSA Verlag.

3

The Global Crisis: Key Systemic Aspects

Christian Ghymers

Abstract This chapter argues that climate change, the global macroeconomic crisis and the weakening of democracy are all expressions of the same incoherence in the present global economic system, which operates on the basis of major 'market failures' that are characterized by the same kind of economic mechanism based on biased relative prices for fossil energies, financial returns and social cohesion. Therefore, the only practical solution is to make sustainable production profitable by first correcting these relative prices in order to re-establish a systemic convergence between private and social returns and between political and economic democracy.

A Holistic View, A Concerning Diagnostic

The crisis is systemic…

One of the important results of the comparative analysis undertaken in the Monnet Network is the awareness of systemic nature of what is commonly referred to as 'the crisis'. This result leads to a serious consideration of the hypothesis of unsustainability in the present global economic order. The emergence and persistence of the global crisis of 2008–2009, which became in the following decade (2010–2019) a global crisis of democracy in Western societies, announce a clear rupture with respect to the dominant Western models of governance and relationships among citizens. Beyond this observation, which is slowly being shared by a growing number of observers, the changes presently underway involve not only an adaptation of socioeconomic policies in Europe and Latin America to new constraints but also a more radical revision of the dominant paradigms of the world economy. Therefore, this chapter focuses on the systemic aspects of the global crisis that affects both regions and the rest of the world in order to prioritize the design of a coherent solution for particular regions.

C. Ghymers (✉)
Founder and Co-coordinator of the Jean Monnet Network "Crisis-Equity-Democracy for Europe and Latin America", IRELAC, Brussels, Belgium

...and global, characterized by unsustainability from macroeconomic policies to democracy and the environment ....

Indeed, the crisis is global, not just in the geographical sense but also in the systemic sense for being the manifestation of economic behaviours that accumulate, the costs of which are passed on to subsequent generations with an exponentially growing price. The most emblematic and fatal consequence is global warming, which should lead soon to a general unsustainability of the present economic and sociopolitical order. This unsustainability is not only limited to the environment, with climate change, but also concerns the macroeconomic aspects of our economies, with a slowdown in growth and productivity, a lack of room for manoeuvres in both monetary and fiscal policies, a concerning accumulation of debts and financial weaknesses, inefficiencies in financial globalization that increases pro-cyclical instabilities, allocation of global savings towards overconsumption and involvement of a massive waste of resources and of CO_2 emissions by the richest economies, which are not moving towards more beneficial and sustainable productive investments. Unfair income distribution and insufficient welfare expenditures increase and drive our societies towards political deadlock, exposing democracies to populist waves and ultimately to the destruction of life on the planet. Paradoxically, climate change, which is the worst global dimension of the present sustainability crisis, is not effectively prioritized either by policymakers and public opinion – except the recent wake-up call from the youth[1] – or by economists. This amazing procrastination threatens life on the planet and is dramatically increasing the costs of any solution.

...which are linked together...

The key thesis of this chapter is that climate change, the global macroeconomic crisis and the weakening of democracy are all expressions of the same incoherence in the current global economic system, which operates on the basis of the same principle, 'market failures'; i.e. those who cause damage to others do not pay for it because biased relative prices do not incorporate fatal external effects: overly low costs or no cost at all for carbon emissions, overly high relative returns for financial activities with respect to productive activities and overly high prices for safe assets in US dollars (overly low yields).

'Climate change is a result of the greatest market failure the world has seen' (Stern 2007) and the most emblematic consequence of the systemic unsustainability that results from the overwhelming short-termism of our materialist rationality, whatever be the ideological option (right or left). All these phenomena of dysfunctional behaviours share a common systemic origin and respond to the same kind of simple economic mechanisms through biased relative prices: the fact that numerous important economic decisions are biases due to being mainly taken on the basis of short-term, distorted, short-sighted price systems that amplify their damaging future effects (social, economic and political). Furthermore, both climate change and

[1]Although it is an important step for spreading awareness in public opinion, this emerging movement is still very unprepared and does not push concrete measures.

financial/macroeconomic instability are also linked to financial reasons and are a result of the same disinformation from vested interests. This short-termism and materialist rationality rely, of course, upon values, but changing them is a much more complex issue than changing relative prices and fighting against lobbies.

The reasons for such linked inefficiencies are explained below. It is a complex result from a combination of financial flows, dogmatic views, deeper mental structures that prefer short-term advantages and sociopolitical features manipulated by vested interests. In spite of these very resilient ultimate causes, these risky and costly defects could be fixed with simple technical solutions insofar as they address the same basic action mechanisms of these price distortions by using adjusted individual incentives. They all come either from market or administrated prices that do not correctly incorporate the externalities of these decentralized decisions or from a lack of collective goods or their abuse by not paying adequately for them. In both cases, relative prices are misleading. These typical situations of market failures are characterized by a systemic divergence between private and social returns, which creates a typical moral hazard that inevitably leads to unsustainability. Therefore, it is futile and even counterproductive to try to attack the effects without correcting first the systemic mechanisms. Furthermore, the different areas of unsustainability even mutually reinforce each other, which explains the unsustainability and inevitable collapse of the present regime: macroeconomic and financial architecture caveats feed global warming by diverting financial flows. The manipulation of democracy and an increasingly unfair income distribution maintain the unsustainability of these linked processes, which are a threat to democracy itself.

...and illustrated by three relevant cases of distortion...

We single out three emblematic cases of these mutually supportive price distortions or incorrect market signals that make the present system not only inefficient but also contradictory to economic efficiency and unsustainable, not only economically but also socially and therefore politically:

- The use of a national currency – the US dollar – as the main vehicle of international payments and reserves makes the public good of the international monetary system (IMS) asymmetric, impeding its management for world interests (Triffin dilemma[2]); this dollar-based IMS generates several distortions and significant spillovers upon the rest of the world: automatic financing of US external and fiscal deficits at lower interest rates (*price distortion*) by capturing the world demand for safe assets in order to allocate global savings to US overconsumption by playing the role of international banking transformation. This function biases the US policy mix towards expansionist, pro-consumption monetary policies and causes significant spillovers upon the rest of the world including mismanagement of global liquidities, accumulation of financial risks and overly low savings

[2]The Triffin dilemma expresses the simple fact that increasing international liquidity means increasing the external liabilities of the US economy, the currency of which is demanded as an international reserve; this fact leads to the logical impossibility of regulating global liquidity and managing an optimal policy mix in the USA, which provokes global liquidity cycles and global macroeconomic instability.

(public good failures). This asymmetric IMS is so dysfunctional and unsustainable that the gap between the (increasing) power of unilateral US monetary policy and the (decreasing) relative weight of the US economy has risen dramatically with the explosive increase of free international financial flows, the growing role of global banks operating in dollars and the rapid development of emerging economies resulting from the so-called globalization.

- The excessive financial globalization and deregulation promoted by the dollar-based IMS have led to another kind of moral hazard provoked by *key price distortions* and lack of regulations: the higher profitability of financial speculation with respect to production activities creates economic instability and high costs because deregulated financial systems mechanistically propagate shocks and endogenous financial crises which have amplified macroeconomic crises; financial markets are not the same as other markets because operators are dependent upon the liquidity condition, which is a public good.
- More generally regarding non-financial markets, some significant *price distortions* also result from the inadequate internalization of the externalities issued by decentralized economic actors; it is the same kind of inner near-sightedness of any decentralized (competitive) price system when prices do not incorporate all the information or do not take adequate account of spillover effects, as is the case for environmental damages and especially the very inadequate (or absent) price on carbon emission.

The parallel between the damages caused by the excessive emission of CO_2 and the excessive spillovers resulting from the conjunction of an asymmetric IMS and untamed free financial markets deserves especial attention. It is not just a similarity but an intertwined cumulative process. In concrete, positive terms, to reach the neutral carbon output required for our survival as living species, crucial changes in relative prices are urgently needed not only for the internalization of all carbon footprints but also for the IMS and financial markets in order to correct relative financial returns capable of ensuring the (very) large financial flows required for making possible and directly profitable the output changes towards a low-carbon system in the emerging economies and other LDCs. Also, the manipulation of public opinion and policymakers is very similar in these three cases, with a combination of simplistic dogmatism and rent-seeking by using financial resources to corrupt decision-makers or misinform citizens.

...which form a pyramid of systemic unsustainability...

These three global destabilizing mechanisms are related and mutually supportive both in their deeper causal origin and methods and in their functional connections for a restoration of profitable sustainability and a change in the order based upon inequality/power imbalances and the resulting lack of multilateral organization/international cooperation. Indeed, the caveats of an asymmetric IMS allow for maintaining international power for the US economy and oligarchic interests in the rest of the world on the part of financial policymakers in central banks and treasuries. This status quo combination makes global warming worse and impedes a systemic solution towards a sustainable economic order on the planet.

The lack of external constraint for the USA allows for the sustaining of a more expansionist policy mix by accelerating the cheap financial inflows necessary for feeding the global macroeconomic imbalances inherent to the (unsustainable) US consumption way-of-life. This imbalance is closely linked to the need to import external savings and to control fossil fuel markets.[3] Financial globalization through large multinational banks operating basically in dollars is a complementary part of the system based upon the free-market tale that permits an extension of unproductive financial capitalism. This extension is necessary for feeding the macroeconomic imbalances as well as for sustaining the political bias and the manipulation that are necessary to the status quo but that contribute to increases in the gap between economic and political democracy.

The result is an excessive and counterproductive financial globalization because capital movements flow in the wrong direction for sustainable economic development: from poor to rich economies and from real investments to financial ones, exposing the world to global macroeconomic disequilibrium and to the launch of negative spillovers through a pro-cyclical, global financial cycle with perverse effects upon exchange rates, capital flows, growth, savings and the environment. These three major distortions are related to – and consolidate – inequality and power abuses, thus manifesting an increasing gap between political and economic democracy. There is a total correspondence between those who benefit the most from CO_2 emissions and those who suffer the most from global warming. Rising temperatures will cause the poorest to suffer the most, even in the wealthiest nation in the world (Hsiang et al. 2017). In parallel, it is now obvious that the hypertrophy in the financial sector not only was not favourable to growth and social mobility but also increased social costs, inequality and political instability. This growing divergence between political and economic democracy is the main visible manifestation of the inner contradiction upon which the economic system has lost its rationality through fundamental relative price distortions that lead to destructive results that in turn create mistrust in democratic institutions, which feeds the rapid expansion of populism. This is a fatal paradox since materialism leads to its own contradiction by destroying the basis of material welfare and life.

...in which the unfounded belief in the efficiency of financial markets bears a very heavy responsibility...

The radical neo-liberal reaction to the Triffin dilemma was free floating and financial liberalization. Indeed, abandoning most of the regulations inhibiting capital movements appeared as the easiest and most coherent action in a binary reaction against state intervention to face imbalances developed under less liberal policies. Such a dogma was based upon the simplistic belief that financial markets would necessarily be as efficient as any product market by fixing competitive asset prices and yields as a result of their fundamental value.

This is an epistemological mistake that has triggered new mechanisms of additional macroeconomic imbalances. The paradigm of financial market efficiency

[3] Oil is traded in US dollars, like coal used to be traded in British £, when the £ was the main key currency.

plays a complementary role in the transmission of the 'built-in destabilizer' (Ghymers 1986; Triffin 1991) in the dollar system. The reason is merely that financial markets do not operate in the same way as product and service markets because the behaviours of financial operators are not independent but linked through mimetic competition to their assessment of liquidity conditions, which tends to be self-fulfilling. This absence of operator independence impedes the efficiency of financial markets and explains their inherent instability. Unlike in other markets, credit demand and supply move together with liquidity conditions, keeping yields and interest rates from playing the balancing role of 'objective' market prices. As shown by Aglietta (2018), in Minsky's (1982) line of Keynes' interpretation, financial market behaviours are not governed like other markets by the objective fundamental value of assets with a symmetry of information but by liquidity, which is mainly self-fulfilling and makes financial operators mutually dependent: liquidity intrinsically reflects this interdependency because financial markets operate under 'mimetic competition' (Orléan 1999) when forming expectations of asset values and debt sustainability: credit providers tend to expect the same kind of valuation change in asset prices as borrowers do. This link biases the credit market indicators towards a one-way bet. Therefore, credit demand and supply cannot ensure a stable equilibrium through yield changes like other markets used to do because demand and supply move together. Contrary to non-financial markets, in which the two sides of the market have opposing interests with regard to prices since demand is subject to saturation condition (i.e. the demand slope is negative), financial markets are inherently unstable and inevitably generate a succession of euphoria and panic as a result of their subjective common perceptions of liquidity, which link credit demand and supply: the credit demand slope could be positive when the expected change in asset value is higher than the costs of borrowing, but since this expectation is shared by both borrowers and credit suppliers on financial markets, the expected yields cannot have the stabilization role of normal competitive market prices. Liquidity is self-fulfilling and pro-cyclical: in the cyclical upwards phase, optimistic expectations increase the demand for credit even with interest rate increases, while lenders increase also their supply of credit since they perceive fewer business risks and since their collaterals acquire more value. Paradoxically, indebtedness tends to contract the risk premium. When the cyclical bubble bursts, the same cumulative process is in motion on the negative side: asset values decrease while debt values remain (or even increase in real terms), moving back credit supply and demand. The deterioration of debtors directly affects that of creditors and lenders, triggering a deleverage adjustment process that has macroeconomic depressing effects (balance sheet recession). Mimetic competition is necessarily biased towards pro-cyclical behaviour, impeding the self-regulation of liquidity by credit price adjustments.

Here the market price distortion comes from the fact that financial prices are self-correlated through liquidity perceptions by both sides of financial markets, which creates a destabilizing financial cycle. In the past 30 years, the size of global finance in the world economy has been moving from 280% of GDP to 430% (Artus 2019),[4] and the causality relation between the real cycle and the financial cycle has been reversed: the financial cycle explains the real cycle in the period of 1996–2018 while the contrary was true from 1980 to 1995. Except for emerging economies, the size of finance is not favourable to growth. Furthermore, Artus (2019) shows that the gravity of recession increases with the size of finance in the GDP and the 'allocative efficiency' of savings has been a concern since 1990, in the sense that savings have been oriented mainly towards inefficient uses such as real estate or public consumption and not towards productive investments. These contradictory economic results should call into question the paradigm of financial market efficiency. Facts show that market incentives are biased towards a hyper-development of financial capitalism. Distortions in market incentives have induced non-financial business to reduce its deficit (dissaving) to become a surplus (saving) sector in almost all industrial countries: real investments have been reduced in favour of financial investments, the stock of real assets has been declining relative to financial assets, job creation and economic growth have slowed, and unemployment has risen, such that even stability-oriented countries such as Germany have been running budget deficits most of the time. Given the positive interest-growth differential, the public debt-to-GDP ratio has risen strongly, leading to over-indebtedness. At the same time and as a consequence of the easiness to 'make money with money' in financial capitalism, a process of growing income inequality has started to increase the gap between political and economic power, strengthening the lobbies and amplifying the incoherence in the economic rationality. This feature is at the very centre of the political, economic and moral crisis facing humanity: economic power – ownership of financial resources in the hands of few – tends to become immune to economic democracy, in contrast to the three first decades of the post-war period, a period that showed a development of market economies oriented towards real output and quasi-full employment.

...but remains unable to answer to the threat of global warming.

On top of this macroeconomic disequilibrium leading that has led to the political crisis of the emerging populism is the unsustainability of the present Anthropocene epoch: the fact that the acceleration of the influence of human behaviour on Earth's atmosphere in recent decades is threatening the existence of humankind as a biological species. This constraint is by definition the most global ever faced, but it is also more radical than the previous ones faced by human societies insofar as – contrary to past economic constraints – the irreversibility of the damages for the planet calls into question the existence of human life itself, not to mention the costs. In the past, human societies faced many serious constraints but generally not the global life system, and the successive constraints were successfully bypassed as a result of the genetic basic instinct of our species for dominating and exploiting the Earth, especially when translated into the materialist rationalism which has been shaping our societies since the eighteenth century Enlightenment and its consequent expanding industrial revolutions.

---

[4] These numbers are based upon Natixis data: finance weight is measured as the total of outstanding loans, bonds, stock market capitalization and M2 money stock divided by world GDP at current prices.

How to Explain the Absence of a Coherent Reaction to the Present Unsustainability of the World Economy?

The procrastination of all policymakers facing the three main facets of the systemic unsustainability…

It is really amazing that the global warming which has been scientifically identified for at least half a century as an inescapable consequence of our consumption of fossil energies remains without any significant counteraction in spite of the dramatic increase of the costs of inaction. Neither the ecologists nor the economists – with minor exceptions – have formulated adequate reactions. Trying to explain this irrational behaviour affecting all political regimes is the key for understanding the global crisis and how to get out of it. Indeed, the socio-psychological mechanisms at stake are the same for climate change and for the macroeconomic deadlocks as well as for the asymmetric dollar-based IMS. The principles at work in CO_2 greenhouse effects[5]

[5] Global warming resulting from the CO_2 greenhouse effect, which was discovered by Joseph Fourier in 1824, was scientifically established in 1856 by Eunice Newton Foote, an American woman, who was not credited for her discovery due to being a female and suffragette. History attributes the discovery to John Tyndall, who 'rediscovered' it in 1859. In 1896, Svante Arrhenius (Swedish Nobel Prize winner) recalculated it. Further analysed in 1939 by Guy Stewart Calendar, it was demonstrated empirically in 1953 by Gilbert Plass and in 1957 by Roger Revelle and Hans Suess. The concept was diffused pedagogically by the magazines *Time*, *Life*, and in 1958 by the 'Bell Science Hour' and through a popular movie by Frank Capra. As of the 1950s, energy companies ordered several scientific studies, all concluding there was a causal link between the use of fossil fuels and global warming, implying therefore a questioning of their future exploitation and profits. In 1958, Revelle and Keeling started to measure a daily record of CO_2 concentration, based upon which the so-called Keeling curve shows that CO_2 emissions were accelerating and reaching a record level in 3 million years. On these bases, as of 1960, the Jason Committee (a secret group of elite scientists which advises the US government on strategic security matters of science and technology) used MacDonald's model on climate change to convince US presidents (beginning with John Kennedy in 1961) that fossil fuel burning would lead to dangerous global warming that would endanger the planet. These analyses all concluded by proving the reality of global warming due to fossil energy and the need for urgent actions and for launching international measures, including Revelle and Keeling's report in 1977 and the Charney Report in 1979 ('Carbon Dioxide and Climate: A Scientific Assessment'), from which several initiatives emerged, such as the international carbon tax proposed by William Nordhaus (Carter's economic adviser and Nobel Prize winner in 2018), Carter's 'Changing Climate' report (published in 1983) and the report by the Environment Protection Agency, both of which scientifically confirmed Charney's alarming report and warned that it was urgent (and maybe too late) to act, but all were blocked or abolished by President Reagan in the 1980s and the US press, influenced by lobbies seeking to divert the scientific conclusions through the counter-argument that market forces would take charge, thanks to the US scientific progress to come, therefore opposing any costly changes to the US economy. During the 1988 presidential campaign, G. Bush took the electoral commitment to act for curbing global warming, but the fossil energy industry and their major users organized a massive campaign of disinformation (half a billion US dollars only in 1989 and 2 billion between 2000 and 2016), throwing doubts upon the scientific basis of climate change risks and timing. In spite of a growing international consensus for an international treaty to limit CO_2 emissions with carbon taxes, the vested interests won the battle with the decisive influence of John Sununu (the head of the Bush administration), who kept the Noordwijk Conference (November 1989) from enacting an interna-

as well as those in any externality,[6] the near-sighted financial market[7] and asymmetry in the IMS,[8] have been scientifically known and explained extensively for more than half a century. In spite of all the necessary information, both the scientific community and policymakers have acknowledged that the huge gap between the causes and the effects was making it too difficult and too risky for there to be any effective action to face powerful lobbies because the value of the future was too low compared to the immediate economic advantages for citizens resulting from burning fossil fuels: all the progress in well-being since the industrial revolution has been produced by the (overly) low price of energy afforded by burning fossil combustibles. Such a generalized procrastination has also been observed in the financial and monetary fields, where the establishment strongly defends the status quo against regulations and changes in the IMS.

...helps to identify the roots of our unsustainability in our materialist rationality, with its male binary order resulting from the evolutionary process that was necessary for our past survival and economic development...

This crazy race towards human destruction is based upon much deeper aspects that analyses of economic or political economy might make clear. We are convinced that pure economic mechanisms must be viewed as reflecting our 'binary thinking' bias. The way we think and base our scientific analysis is very 'male-oriented'. This seems to be the result of millions of years of evolutionary progress based upon a primitive survival selection, combined later with the rationality built upon the post-Socratic philosophy[9] imposed by thousands of years of economic selection. Such a double natural selection has introduced fatal contradictions into our global economic system which counteract our own pretention to materialist efficiency and progress in productivity. As Sarah Myhre (2019) argues, not only is gender inequality not a 'natural law', but it is a monstrous unnatural bias destroying nature itself. In the American Andes, the 'Pachamama' – a feminist Amerindian concept that personalizes mother nature – transforms the abusive rationality of the male predator into a rape which is eventually castigated by the self-destruction of its unnatural material results, turning the expected material benefits and rationality into negative output, i.e. showing the irrational male behaviour. Therefore, the survival of not

---

tional compulsory limitation of CO_2 emissions. The doubts about the existence of global warming due to CO_2 are now scientifically discarded because, contrary to previous historic climatic changes, this time the changes are global, i.e. simultaneously observed on all continents.

[6] The inefficiencies due to externalities in market economies were explained by Alfred Marshall in 1890 and elaborated by A. Pigou in 1920 and are an indisputable part of Economics.

[7] The instability of financial markets was analysed by Keynes in the 1930s.

[8] The incoherence of the dollar-based IMS was denounced tirelessly by Triffin from the 1950s up to his death in 1993.

[9] Plato and Aristotle believed that nature ordained not only physical differences between males and female but mental differences as well, declaring that women were incapable of reasoning and as such subjected to men: 'Nature makes women inferior to men'. This long-lasting exclusion of half of humanity has had severe consequences for peace, human harmony, economic and political development and respect for life and our planet. See Whitbeck (1976) and Maloney (1991).

only our own civilization but furthermore that of humankind would depend on our ability to resolve the gender issue.

Admittedly, the cultural rationality has demonstrated its efficient supremacy. Indeed, the progressive emergence of Western societies and their temporary material superiority with the industrial revolution and its accelerated global extension are the positive results of fragmented analyses and binary belief cultures. However, these material successes are only one side of the real world. Negative spillovers and perverse effects are becoming now explicit and visible. So far, the institution of a rational materialistic science has imposed a 'dictatorship of reason and materialism'[10] in which science is not about developing human consciousness and life in a holistic approach to the planet but about power and money in a linear, fragmented, male binary hierarchical order. This order and its spectacular material results have produced a terrific illusionary bias by separating our perception of our power from our impacts on life and our planetary systems. One example is the fact that economic growth and its measure in terms of GDP have become a pathetic illusion as far as the negative output of CO_2 emissions and other depletions of natural species and resources are not taken into account in the statistics. The result is a predatory, unfair attitude on the part of the present generation against subsequent ones and of the richest against the poorest.

...but paradoxically this successful, historic evolutionary process has become a destructive natural process...

Presently, the systemic difference between this crisis and the previous ones is based upon the fact that the individual (male) genetic motor which permitted an overcoming of previous material constraints and shaped our 'way of thinking' has become itself the cause of the problem of unsustainability. According to neuroscience – which will not be developed here since it lies outside the scope of the present research[11] – the most fundamental reason for the process of destruction of life on Earth is based upon our brain structure, which has selected a segmented way of thinking necessary for ensuring our material success and the industrial revolutions. The resulting economic supremacy has pushed the world toward a male rationality based upon a binary method that has led to a dichotomist conception of life, which

---

[10] See the work of Francisco Varela and the Santiago School of Cognition, e.g. Varela et al. (2016).

[11] The deeper roots of Western societies' rationality extend far beyond the Enlightenment to the whole post-Socratic way of thinking in Western cultures. See the 'Institute of Human Conductivity', founded by Carlos Gonzalez Carrasco and based at Regent's University, London, www.humanconductivityinstitute.com: 'The old scientific narrative is practiced as an exclusive binary. The practices of scientific materialism have caused a brutal process of dehumanisation and the unprecedented destruction of our planet. Dominant "rational-logical" scientific materialistic practices have reduced life to a degraded, debased and undignified monetised commodity. It has fragmented and separated our mind from our body, our body from our spirit, human from humans and humans from nature. This is a catastrophic and collective failure of human thinking. The old fixed and rigid scientific paradigms and dogmas have decayed to the point of an irreversible collapse, a process of continuous systemic crisis of its individual parts (corporate, economic, political, social, ecological, spiritual, moral, ethical) but for HCI these individual expressions are in fact parts of a systemic crisis of the whole'. See also Ghymers and Gonzalez Carrasco (2016).

in turn has created an 'illusory commodified reality' that is engaging humankind in a dehumanized deadlock (Gonzalez Carrasco 2017) and a fictitious immediate well-being.

Such a destructive 'natural selection' seems to respond to an individual brain structure that has been shaped by millions of years of survival struggle but that has been unable, as a result of the actions of dopamine incentives, to spontaneously take into account a collective global constraint and a long-term improvement instead of an immediate satisfaction. As explained by S. Bohler (2019),the human brain balances immediate ('animal') impulses controlled by the striatum (mesencephalon) and the (human) capacity to assess and plan for the future managed by the cortex (frontostriatal fibres). The striatum was configured by the past animal fight for survival, which needed to give priority to immediate advantages when individuals were in competition in the natural selection process, while the cortex development emerged later in human societies as a result of the rational preference for the future.

...through an imbalance that is favourable to populism, which draws upon immediate impulses instead of forecasting rationality...

Nevertheless, the recent technological and economic progresses combined with the uncertain climate created by the global crisis have developed a culture biased towards instantaneity, which tends to weaken the countervailing power of our cortex upon our animal striatum through the issuance of dopamine that is neurochemically dominated by our animal nature. The result would be a trend favourable to the 'me now' of materialism and to short-term profits through individual brains in competition that prefer immediate advantages when uncertainty reigns.

This universal phenomenon, which is referred to as the psychological 'temporal loss of valorisation', is not new but has been compensated by the easy economic growth of the pre-global crisis period, during which apparently rapid productivity increases combined with social protection fed an illusionary security. The generalization of economic uncertainty with the global crisis has created a socio-psychological shock of popular fears, which weakens the collective ability to plan for the future. The popular reflex of fear gives preference to the immediacy supported by the memory of the past, 'democratically' refusing any longer-term considerations, rejecting the elites in power viewed as necessarily guilty for the current deteriorations and, opting for status quo, condemning democracy to populism. This risk was spectacularly illustrated by the recent French social revolt of the 'gilets jaunes', in which 80% of the citizens opted for the immediate purchasing power advantages of lower oil prices and deficit spending at the expense of the longer-term collective interests of financing the energy transition.[12]

...leading 'ceteris paribus' *to a civilizational collapse...*

Our current sustainability crisis is the result of all the negative human impacts on our vital planetary eco-systemic interdependencies, which the materialist-fragmented-rationality paradigm ignores by maintaining an illusory reality. As

[12] Of course, such a populist rejection of longer-term rationality was spurred and amplified by the lack of fair distribution in the government measures. However, most of their claims reflect the desire for immediacy instead of systemic improvements.

already denounced some 20 years ago by Tom Bentley and Daniel Stedman Jones (2001, p. 16), *this triumph of individualism, still superficially defensible in terms of social progress and justice, has most obviously contributed to the loss of faith in the democratic frameworks and cultures which previously underpinned common life. In every industrialised society, willingness to vote and place confidence in public institutions has steadily declined....but the collective consequences of unchecked individualism, and its primary form of agency – market exchange – present basic challenges not just to those societies in terms of their cohesiveness and quality of life, but also to the world as a whole.*

Since the method of Western thinking has led to an efficient conquest of power and impressive technical and economic performance based upon predominantly materialist cultures and apparently scientific arguments, a natural selection process has diffused it globally. With this irreversible expansion, the inner caveats of Western materialism (both capitalist and socialist) have been accumulating behaviours that are exponentially destructive for humanity and ecological systems, with counterproductive socioeconomic results that generate exponentially growing economic costs, which are leading to civilizational collapse. The reason for this threat is the difficulty for a male culture to become more aware of the interdependent and unitary nature of life as a whole when money is the main power and tends to be concentrated and used by vested interests for exploiting the animal-male determinisms in people. Regulations have been systematically reduced or inhibited by dogmatic reasoning without any scientific basis but merely driven by vested interests and rent-seeking abuses created by this imbalanced male culture.

...because the strict law of universal entropy is not counteracted by a systemic organizational progress towards a multilateral governance in the financial and environmental areas...

The most visible proof of the wrong direction of a 'simulated materialistic reality' is simply the deadlock created by our inability to wean our dependencies on fossil fuels, explained – on top of obscure manipulations from vested interests and conspiring ideologies – by our lack of vision and collective support for organizing the deeper systemic transformation urgently required to ensure an economic sustainability capable of safeguarding life and democracy through an effective multilateral governance for regulating international trade and finance.

Among the main results of the joint research of this Jean Monnet Network is the identification of a global systemic failure in the present economic order, which explains the current sustainability crisis and the impossibility of breaking the status quo in order to implement multilateral solutions. This present deadlock represents the major challenge for the survival of humankind. The window of opportunity for solving it is about to close in the midst of an amazing mood of civil reluctance or passivity that is putting the present world on the brink of our own civilizational collapse, which indicates that the systemic issue is much deeper and broader than its traditional economic and political domains. We are facing a very powerful paradigm; its roots are deeply genetic but have been transformed into cultural and philosophical features with a gender inequality bias. Its powerful resilience comes from the abuses of vested interests that exploit our genetic animal dependence upon dopamine in order to mask the growing gap between private and social returns. This abuse of power means that institutional democracy is turned into an illusion because there is no sufficient economic democracy but rather an excessive concentration of monetary power in an ethical desert. In this process, without a strong reaction in terms of 'ethical values', the emergence and achievement of '*noogenesis*'[13] (Teilhard de Chardin 1955), i.e. the inner social organizational forces of human life able to countervail the entropic forces, are dangerously inhibited.

Some Paths Towards a Solution

Tackling global warming requires tackling the caveats in the global financial architecture... the materialist bias of our societies...

The pyramid of unsustainability, with its 'moral hazard' process based upon price distortion mechanisms, is the expression of imbalances in the sociopolitical organizational process, i.e. the gap between political and economic democracy. Vested interests and increasingly unfair income distribution block the organizational responses to instability and inefficiencies, which are namely, reforms geared towards regulated markets and international cooperation. In particular, Triffin's 'built-in destabilizer' in the asymmetric dollar-based IMS, amplified by pro-cyclical financial markets, impedes an answer to financial needs and a price correction for solving the global warming challenge. Indeed, restoring climate sustainability requires restoring macroeconomic and financial sustainability, i.e. not only reversing the absorption of global savings by US consumers but also channelling financial flows from speculative investments to real ones capable of ensuring profitable green energy production everywhere, however mostly in emerging economies and LDCs. This change would also solve the lack of macroeconomic growth by correcting the biased relative yield between financial and real investments, making real output attractive again and reaching a convergence between private and public returns.

Of course, such an ideal response would ideally need a consensual, coordinated change at multilateral and national levels, which would require a radical change of relative values in order to give priority to a holistic view of life and long-term social interests, i.e. to ensure the organization of the 'Teilhardian noogenesis'. Being realistic, such a primary solution would take too much time and not prevent disasters, but economists could have a 'quick fix' at hand for helping social and private returns to converge through taxation/subsidy measures.

...by using precisely materialist incentives through market conformity measures...

If we admit this fact that the deepest origin of the problem is the generalized 'moral hazard' induced by the materialism with which we shape our thinking

---

[13]Teilhard de Chardin's concept of *noogenesis* refers to the evolutionary process by which a brighter scenario would be possible on Earth insofar as humankind could counteract the universal law of entropy by the human capacity to organize social progress and cooperation through ethical values.

through a lack of ethics that leads to the predominance of insufficiently regulated market exchanges – something difficult to change in time for saving the planet – it is fortunately possible and faster to cure the 'moral hazard' issue by merely using the same materialist market mechanisms, however after correcting relative prices in order to activate decentralized incentives through fiscal policies with a revenue-neutral carbon tax (fair distribution of the costs across society) combined with a withdrawal of the subsidies for fossil energies and an introduction of subsides for renewable energies. The first priority is to scrap the annual $87 billion of implied subsidies for fossil energies (Stefanski 2017) and to increase progressively, albeit credibly, the prices of carbon emissions (including those included in all products). This is urgent for channelling financial flows to more profitable low-carbon output. In 1979, a similar correct response was already present in Nordhaus' proposal to the Carter administration, which would have been able to stop global warming but was opposed by the Reagan administration. The alternative – an ethical change – is necessary, but it relies on education and takes too much time for ensuring durable ownership.

The same mechanism of market failure that explains climate disasters is also responsible for other sustainability challenges with regard to social cohesion, lack of key public goods and macro-financial instability. All the global issues share the same systemic bias with regard to responsibilities, i.e. moral hazard. In particular, the most influential one, due to its being macroeconomic, comes from untamed financial markets based upon an asymmetrical international monetary system (IMS) that provokes global liquidity waves and spillovers through the 'exorbitant' role of the US dollar and the capital flows moved by big multinational banks. This very systemic caveat is the origin of a pyramid of costly global disturbances characterized by the fact that those responsible for the spillovers or disturbances are not those affected by the negative impacts of these behaviours. This creates a responsibility bias ('moral hazard'): 'the polluters are not the payers', but they are the exclusively short-term beneficiaries.

Therefore, climate change risks and macroeconomic instability resulting from the asymmetrical IMS are closely linked. Those risks – which are apparently very different – not only intrinsically share the same systemic origin in their inner logic but also are linked overall by their respective solutions and by their urgency.

Both global warming and the destabilizing international monetary system share the same feature that condemns our world to unsustainability and eventual fatal destruction due to their reliance upon near-sighted free market forces. Our current sustainability crisis is the main symptom of the inability of pure free market regimes as well as centralized economic regimes to generate stability together with long-term social prosperity.

Indeed, basic economics teaches that 'liberalism' is inefficient when there are significant spillovers or clear characteristics of a public good, as is obviously the case both for the global environment and for the global monetary system and its liquidity management. Unregulated free markets and uncoordinated monetary policies impede sustainable solutions and a fair supply for ensuring sustainable stability. Opposing regimes with central planning, although theoretically able to better control externalities than market economies, present even worse failures that result from rigid management, power concentration leading to weak incentives for innovation and the negation of human rights, as demonstrated by numerous experiences.

The deterioration of the global environment comes from negative spillovers that by definition escape adequate pricing by free markets, feeding a systemic and devastating moral hazard for governments, corporations and individuals, while on the financial side, a similar unsustainable situation is provoked by the asymmetries resulting from the use of a national currency – the US dollar – as the main international reserve currency, which, combined with the untamed financial deregulation implemented for several decades, creates disturbing global monetary spillovers that explain the succession of increasingly large crises: unmanaged liquidity waves, financial asymmetries and persistent global payment disequilibrium.

...without starting with revolutionary changes but by organizing multilateral market conformity rules within existing multilateral organizations....

Although the causes of the systemic caveats are deeply rooted in our materialist cultures and will need long-term progressive changes and more ethical values, the good news is that the required urgent changes are still possible at the technical level by merely using market-conformity interventions. Indeed, they could be organized at the multilateral level by focusing on the key mechanisms that are provoking global unsustainability and without necessarily imposing centralistic regimes but rather simple consensual regulations that draw upon relative price incentives. Of course, a minimum improvement in international cooperation is required within the existing multilateral order. This necessary international consensus is bound to appear with the increasingly alarming degree of urgency combined with the growing awareness of the nonsense of nationalistic non-cooperative options: by definition, global systemic diseases require efficient global actions. The present opposition of some national leaders cannot be an excuse for no action since there are ways to exert pressure through the formation of large international coalitions that coordinate retaliation against free riders: countervailing duties on imports with high carbon paths and exclusion from multilateral financial resources, triggering heated domestic debates inside the free-rider countries. The only immediate systemic solution to the two identified key diseases is multilateral regulation and management in order to correct market-price distortions by taking externalities (both positive and negative) into account. With regard to carbon emissions, there are some simple multilateral options for pricing carbon in order to discourage its consumption while creating incentives for alternative green energies (relative price effects created by CO_2 tradable permits or UN taxation reinforced by WTO custom duties according to carbon footprint, financial green guarantees/facilities, etc.) or, in the second place, EU regional options (custom duties and subsidies) to be bargained with other regional partners or a few reluctant economies. In addition, concrete financial innovation and regulation changes are indispensable for complementing the carbon pricing positively in order to make low-carbon investment more attractive, especially in LDCs. Indeed, the magnitude of the financial resources necessary for controlling the risks of climate change seems so high (around US$ 1 trillion yearly up to 2035, 2/3 of which in emerging/LDCs) that systemic changes are simultaneously required for the financial sector.

Fortunately, these changes are necessary from both the social and the private profitability perspectives at a time of increasing financial uncertainty and inadequate sustainable investment in the real economy. According to Art. 2 of the Paris Agreement (COP21), there is a clear consensus between public and private actors for 'making finance flows consistent with a pathway towards low greenhouse gas emissions and climate-resilient development' (Dasgupta et al. 2018). This means that moving to a sustainable economy is not only a survival imperative but also a financial opportunity and therefore a decentralized incentive for financial reforms. This convergence opens an important window of opportunity for systemic changes in the international financial architecture.

...more precisely, the systemic solution to global warming requires a simultaneous systemic change in the international financial architecture...

Obviously, the public good nature of ensuring the transition to the new model of prosperity laid out in the UN Sustainable Development Goals and the implied massive shift of resources and output require collective action at the global level. Neither free market and national policy nor coercive centralization could alone ensure this successful transformation. This is precisely where a systemic change in decentralized incentives together with global financial regulation in a new multilateral monetary system is the necessary complement for ensuring global sustainability. No stability could result from free financial markets that cause damaging spillovers. Furthermore, globalized financial markets operate without multilateral agreement on an ultimate multilateral 'safe asset' issued by a genuine multilateral lender of last resort, i.e. a currency which would not be the debt of any country but of the whole system. Indeed, the IMS works with the dollar as a main international currency reserve, i.e. a debt – at sight of the US economy. This impedes a global regulation of liquidity since the US monetary policy is legitimately submitted to inwards-looking management and not to global stability.

Only international cooperation could elaborate and enact strong and better financial regulation, and this would take time. Nevertheless, the most direct and rapid way to act is by rebalancing the very asymmetrical – and thus unsustainable – international monetary system (IMS) by moving from the present dollar system to a multilateral reserve currency which is not the debt of any economy but by definition of the global system. In fact, the basis for such a systemic solution already exists; it is the special drawing right (SDR) created by the IMF in 1968 in order to become the main official reserve currency in a more symmetrical IMS. Indeed, the SDR would reduce the asymmetrical effects of the dollar and its consequent spillovers, enabling a collegial management of global liquidity as a global public good for the sake of world stability. Private financial actors are favourable to such a kind of improvement in the level playing field in order to ensure less financial turbulence. However, in order to become the primary solution, the present SDR needs to be upgraded through some adjustments in the IMF status in order to transform this currency basket of the five main international currencies (the US dollar, euro, pound, yen and renminbi) into a genuine multilateral currency issued directly by the IMF which would thus become a multilateral central bank. This quality would allow for organizing the clearing of international payments above national central banks and for the creation of a genuine multilateral lender of last resort, issuing the safest asset able to thus act upon the global monetary basis by buying or withdrawing eligible national bonds to national central banks (Ghymers 2018).

...which should make opposing interests converge in order to capitalize on profitable opportunities from a peaceful transition to a low-carbon economy...

Contrary to traditional views, it is unnecessary to rely mainly upon idealistic sponsors or massive ODA to LDCs in order to organize the financial changes because the economic crisis forces private capital to look for stable profitable investments. Sustainability – social and environmental – is becoming an attractive criterion for private returns, making it clearly feasible to establish their convergence with public (social) returns when the multilateral organization ensures a systemic correction of misleading incentives, opening the path to the 'Teilhardian noogenesis'.

An interesting observation developed by the CEPII (Aglietta and Couder) points to the effects that the move to green energy could produce upon the international financial architecture. Indeed, the hegemonic key currency of the past, the pound, was closely associated with the role of coal in the economic supremacy of the UK, while the following one, the dollar, has been closely associated with the oil markets and their crucial role in the post–Second World War period. With the urgent need for green energy markets, a massive geographical decentralization of energy production should also be able to reshuffle the key currency roles, making multi-polarization aspects essential for both financial and political stability in order to move to a multilateral key currency. Nevertheless, as clearly mentioned earlier, free financial markets are unable to ensure it due to their 'built-in destabilizer' logic. Due to the same inner reason of being a macroeconomic 'built-in destabilizer', the US dollar is unable to fulfil the role of a reliable international standard and issuer of 'safe assets'. The recent evolution towards the abuse of power, both in US macroeconomic policies (one trillion dollars of additional debt per year under Trump's presidency with visible pressures upon the FED to depreciate the reserve currency) and in other vulgar 'weaponizations' of the dollar, is accelerating the conditions for a consensus for changing the IMS in order to safeguard a financial and peaceful stability both for private and public agents. As explained, only a multilateral currency which is not the debt of any single economy can stabilize the whole system by offering the only neutral, safe asset capable of pricing all the other assets and exchange rates, preserving fully national sovereignties while collegially managing global liquidity as a public good, without any 'weaponization' or abuse.

References

Aglietta, M. (2018). Finance and macroeconomics: The preponderance of the financial cycle. *Revue de l'OFCE*, 2018/3, n° 157, 197–224.

Artus, P. (2019). *Discipliner la finance*. Paris: Odile Jacob.

Bentley, T., & Stedman, D. (2001). *The moral universe*. London: Demos.

Bohler, S. (2019). *Le Bug Humain: pourquoi notre cerveau nous pousse à détruire la planète et comment l'en empêcher*. Paris: Robert Laffont.

Dasgupta, D., et al (2018). *Did the Paris agreement plant the seeds of a climate consistent international financial regime?* https://hal.archives-ouvertes.fr/hal-01692879/document. Accessed 29 Feb 2020.

de Chardin, P. T. (1955). *Le Phénomène humain*. Paris: Seuil.

Ghymers, C. (1986). Réagir à l'emprise du dolla. In M. Aglietta (Ed.), *L'Ecu et la Vieille Dame, un levier pour l'Europe*. Paris: Economica.

Ghymers, C. (2018). Overcoming the Triffin dilemma today: A plan for a stable international financial architecture. In Reinventing Bretton Woods Committee (RBWC) and The Astana International Financial Center (AFIC) (Eds.), *10 years after: The end of the familiar... reflections on the great financial economic crisis*.

Ghymers, C., & Gonzalez Carrasco, C. (2016). Can predominant intercultural management dimensions based on the binary opposition of cultural differences bridge the cultural divide between CELAC and Europe? COLLOQUE IDA –CERALE- Centre d'Etudes et de Recherches Amérique Latine – Europe, ESCP Europe Business School, Paris 2016. Shorter and edited version available at: https://www.academia.edu/27796176/The_DeHumanizing_Binary_Machina. Accessed 29 Feb 2020.

Gonzalez Carrasco, C. (October 2017). *New science and human empowerment*, London. Accessed 29 Feb 2020.

Hsiang, S., et al. (2017). Estimating economic damage from climate change in the United States. *Science, 356*(6345), 1362–1369.

Maloney, L. M. (1991). The argument for women's difference in classical philosophy and early Christianity. In A. Carr & E. S. Fiorenza (Eds.), *The special nature of women?* (pp. 41–49). London: SCM Press.

Minsky, H. P. (1982). The financial instability hypothesis, capitalist processes and the behavior of the economy. In C. P. Kindleberger & J. P. Laffargue (Eds.), *Financial crises, theory, history and policy*. Cambridge: Cambridge University Press.

Myhre, S. (2019). *Cambio global, mujer y academia. Congreso Futuro 2019*. Santiago: Pontificia Universidad Católica de Chile, January 2019.

Orléan, A. (1999). *Le pouvoir de la finance*. Paris: Odile Jacob.

Stéfanski, R. (2017). Dirty little secrets: Inferring fossil-fuel subsidies from patterns in emission intensities. *School of economics and finance discussion paper no.* 1705. https://www.st-andrews.ac.uk/~wwwecon/repecfiles/4/1705.pdf. Accessed 29 Feb 2020.

Stern, N. (2007). Stern review: The economics of climate change – summary of conclusions. https://webarchive.nationalarchives.gov.uk/20100407163608/http://www.hm-treasury.gov.uk/d/Summary_of_Conclusions.pdf. Accessed 29 Feb 2020.

Triffin, R. (1991). The IMS (international monetary system…or scandal?) and the EMS (European monetary system…or success?). Banca Nazionale del Lavoro, quarterly review, n°179, December 1991.

Varela, F. J., Thompson, E., & Rosch, E. (2016). *The embodied mind: Cognitive science and human experience*. Cambridge, MA: MIT press.

Whitbeck, C. (1976). Theories of sex difference. In C. Gould & M. Wartofsky (Eds.), *Women and philosophy: Toward a theory of liberation* (pp. 54–80). New York: Putnam.

Part II
Management of Economic and Financial Crises and Regional Governance

4

The Sovereign Debt Crisis and EMU Crisis Management

Bettina De Souza Guilherme

Abstract This chapter will sketch how the EU has reacted to the financial crisis and in particular to the unfolding sovereign debt crisis, revealing major flaws in EMU's architecture. It will not only address these design flaws but attempt to evaluate the underlying causes, reasons and motives of the architects and decision takers by comparing the more "federalist" Werner Plan with the more "intergovernmental" blueprint of the EMU of the Maastricht Treaty, connect it with the paradigm change on economic governance discussed by Schulmeister in Chap. 2 and show the consequences for the crisis and its management in terms of efficiency, equity and democratic accountability.

Introduction

The global financial crisis of 2008, while having its origin in the US subprime crisis, quickly spread to Europe through free global capital movement and deregulated financial markets, and developed into a nearly existential crisis for the Economic and Monetary Union (EMU). The crisis exposed major flaws of the architecture of Economic and Monetary Union, leading to its failure to prevent or to protect the EU and its citizens from the crisis; to manage the crisis in a credible, equitable and democratic way; and to deliver the promises of growth, employment and wealth improvements as a result of EMU. These failures brought about the greatest deception of Europe's citizens in the European project with a loss of trust in the EU by 26% from 57% in 2006 to 31% between 2012 and 2014, and even if it improved again since then, it triggered a wave of euro-scepticism, nationalism, separatism and populism and puts the question of Europe's democratic accountability and legitimacy at the heart of future reforms of the EU.

B. De Souza Guilherme (✉)
Founder and Co-coordinator of the Jean Monnet Network "Crisis-Equity-Democracy for Europe and Latin America", IRELAC, Rio de Janeiro, Brazil

European Parliament, Brussels, Belgium
e-mail: bettina.desouza@europarl.europa.eu

This chapter will sketch how the EU has reacted to the financial crisis and in particular to the unfolding sovereign debt crisis, revealing major flaws in EMU's architecture. It will not only address these design flaws but attempt to evaluate the underlying causes, reasons and motives of the architects and decision takers by comparing the more "federalist" Werner Plan with the more "intergovernmental" blueprint of the EMU of the Maastricht Treaty, connect it with the paradigm change on economic governance discussed by Schulmeister in Chap. 2 and show the consequences for the crisis and its management in terms of efficiency, equity and democratic accountability.

EMU Crisis Management

"Bailing Out of the Banks": Yet Another Moral Hazard

As a first reaction to the shockwave triggered by the bankruptcy of the US bank Lehmann's Brothers, Member States of the EU speedily went to the rescue of the financial market and "unconditionally" bailed out the banking sector. Ironically, neoliberalism's failure and fall could only be prevented by "nationalizing" its debts and costs, which both created a "moral hazard" and jeopardized the sustainability of public finance by "ballooning" previously consolidated public debt levels and pushing EMU countries with previously high debts to the edge of sovereign default. This in turn brought about the cutting back of the welfare state and imposition of austerity and liberalization policies and accumulated in the further pushing through of neoliberal reforms and the retrenchment of countercyclical policies by the submission of governments under the control of the very same financial markets which had caused the crisis and the "Troika" for countries most hit by the crisis. According to the European Commission report on public finance 2008, public debt in 2007 was actually down to a level of 66% of GDP in the euro area and 58% in the EU, and public deficits stood at 0.6% in the Euro and 0.8% of GDP in the EU (European Commission 2008). Indeed, Greece with a level of public debt to GDP of 94.5% was an outlier among the countries later undergoing adjustment programs. Portugal with 63% was close to a public debt to GDP ceiling of 60%, Spain with 36.2% and Ireland with as low as 25.4% were by far outperforming Germany with 65%. However, when the housing and construction burst, bailing out the banks and the procyclical adjustment programmes brought about a dramatic deterioration of the debt to GDP level to 120% in Ireland in 2012 and to 101.3% in 2016 in Spain.

These figures teach us the following: firstly, decades of efforts of budget consolidation can be wiped out at once by the destabilizing effects of liberalized and deregulated financial markets in an EMU with globally free capital movement in which the EU had given up "any instruments to control credit growth or allocate credit". Second, the negligence of the destabilizing nature of deregulated financial markets and the moral hazard arising from their bailing out had been among the "original sins" of the authors of the Maastricht Treaty. Third, the risks of the macroeconomic imbalances within EMU were as well ignored. The high level of growth in Europe's peripheries in the first decade of EMU was (mis)perceived as the successful process of convergence. Benefitting from the common currency and interest rates, periphery countries enjoyed an unprecedented inflow of capital stimulating domestic demand, growth and fuelling housing and construction bubbles. The consequences of it was an increase in employment, demand and growth, but along with it wage and price increases in the periphery eroded their competitiveness, while at the same time blowing up their trade deficits and debts to the northern eurozone countries. Additionally, the housing booms proofed to be not sustainable and eventually burst in the aftermath of the US Lehmann' Bank default. Fourth, the so-called sovereign debt crisis has been a consequence of the global financial crisis. Greece with its high public debt level prior to the crisis has rather been an "outlier" within the EMU adjustment countries. There is no doubt that the previously high debt and deficit level turned unsustainable when the financial crisis erupted. Nevertheless, it clearly demonstrates that the combination of internal imbalances within the EMU and high level of current account deficits and public debts increases the liquidity risks in a situation of sudden stops.

De Grauwe (2011) observes that at the same time highly indebted countries outside of EMU such as the UK have not been threatened with sovereign default given that they kept the control of their currency and interest rates and had their national banks as lender of last resort in place. This indicates that EMU's design did not improve the crisis resilience of the eurozone countries but rather led to a weakening of it, which is a further cause for the deception of the trust in the EU.

The EERP: EMU's Only Countercyclical Fiscal Stimulus Programme – A Short-Lived Experienced

The second reaction to the financial crisis of the EU was the "European Economic Recovery Plan (EERP)" of the Member States, the EU Commission and the European Investment Bank (EIB) in the form of stimulus programme of EUR 200 billion, equivalent to 1.5% of EU GDP. The EERP has been identified by the European Fiscal Board as the only coordinated counter-cyclical fiscal policy of the EMU within its 20 years of existence. However, in comparison with the US policy response, the EU stimulus programme was rather modest (De Grauwe 2010) and short-lived, with the return to fiscal austerity already in 2010 than in 2011 (USA) (Mody 2015).

Breaking the Sovereign Banking Nexus: Banking Union

The third reaction of the EU was its engagement to regulating financial markets by establishing the legal framework to create the "Banking Union" with the ECB in charge of the supervision of major banks, which was a real stepping stone forwards and could not have been envisaged prior to the crisis and the pledge to contribute to regulating financial markets globally in all the relevant global governance institutions (UN Stiglitz Commission, G20 Summits). At the EU level, the introduction of the Financial Transaction Tax (FTT) was proposed to compensate the costs they had caused, which did not happen so far given the strong resistance and lobbying efforts of the financial markets (see Schulmeister chapter on FTT). However, up to today, the Banking Union remains incomplete without the European Deposit Insurance Scheme (EDIS). Additionally, the considerable amount of non-performing loans (NPL) and the increased number of banks "too big to fail" in the follow-up of the crisis imply that the moral hazard of the financial markets persists.

Monetary Policy

In the field of monetary policy, the ECB was initially rather cautious and reluctant to step into the role of lender of last resort while the FED's policy was earlier and from the beginning more aggressive (Kang et al. 2016). "The US Federal Reserve lowered its policy interest rate (the Fed Funds rate) from 5.25% in September 2007 to 0-0.25% in December 2008, (...) initiated quantitative easing and began 'forward guidance', making public its intention to keep interest rates low 'for some time'". "In contrast to the FED the ECB's first reaction to the Great Recession was in July 2008, with to 'raise' of the policy rate and only after the Lehman bankruptcy in September 2008, the ECB joined an internationally coordinated rate reduction on 8 October" (Kang et al. 2016).

Evaluating the first phase of the EU's reaction to the crisis and its management – before the sovereign debt crisis erupted – we can identify the Banking Union as a clearly positive reform (yet not completed: missing EDIS, prevailing risks of non-performing loans and sovereign bank nexus and an even increased number of financial institutions "too big to fail", thus implying a persistent risk of moral hazard of the financial market sector), yet costly policy errors both in the fiscal and in the monetary field due to blind adherence to the ordo-liberal paradigm and policies. While the EERP was initially largely successful, the early exit from it together with two quasi-parallel hikes of interest rates by the ECB – in April and July 2011 – lead to a double dip, aggravating the following recession of the euro area and in particular the situation of the countries entering into a sovereign debt crisis.

The Sovereign Debt Crisis: Assessing Causes

The trigger to the sovereign debt crisis was the announcement of the newly elected Greek prime minister George Papandreou in October 2009 that the public deficit, which had been communicated by the previous government, was not 6% but 12.7% (and later was corrected to more than 15% by Eurostat) of GDP. The consequence of this revelation was that Greece turned into the "scapegoat" for the crisis (Schulmeister 2018) and a systemic financial crisis was transformed into a sovereign debt crisis. De Grauwe (2010) highlighted that policymakers were using "incorrect analysis of the fundamentals" by "repeating continuously that the source of the debt crisis in the Eurozone is the profligacy of national governments". As was stressed earlier, prior to the emergence of the financial crisis, the government debt to GDP ratio in the eurozone was declining thanks to the sacrifices of the population of the countries striving to achieve the Maastricht objectives to join EMU and later to respect the rules of "Euro club". The efforts were to be rewarded by a common currency, stability, growth, convergence and increased wealth. The fact that during the same period, due to design flaws, internal imbalances occurred and led to an increase of private debt (households and financial institutions) provoked by the housing and construction bubble. These developments were however not given the necessary attention neither by the EU watchdog institutions (Commission, Eurostat) nor by the IMF.

Considering the amplitude and economic and social costs of global financial crisis, a paradigm changes, and major reforms of the global economic model and governance could have been expected, as was the case in the aftermath of the 1929 crisis – finally leading to WWII and of the energy crisis in the 1970s. Such reforms have indeed been very much at the heart of the demands of the biggest protest and social movement mobilization all over Europe and the USA (Indignados, Occupy Wall Street) and worldwide since the 1960s with the Time magazine dedicating its "Person of the Year" award to the protestor in 2012. The fact that both the neoliberal economy and world order and the ordo-liberal architecture of the EMU proved to be "unsustainable" and were on a crash course without the intervention of states and politics – the actors whose room for manoeuvre was to be much reduced according to these paradigms – and had provoked major financial, economic, social, political and human cost remained largely unanswered, despite initial resolutions of the G20, the UN and the EU. It is even more amazing that the recommendations advanced after a near meltdown of the neoliberal system and the EMU, which had actually rather worked as a transmission belt of the crisis than as a protection, were more of the same: pushing for further neoliberal reforms and strengthening the rules-based system of ordo-liberalism by increased controls and sanctions and further limiting the discretionary powers of the Member States (Schmidt 2015). Indeed, the "Greek sovereign debt crisis" came just in time to blame the guilt and responsibility of the crisis on the profligacy of countries – "spending all their money on booze and women and then asking for support" as expressed in a FAZ interview by former Eurogroup president Dijsselbloem (Dijsselbloem, 2017) – and as a consequence pushing the reform focus to increase fiscal discipline, improve the surveillance and strengthen possible sanctions for non-appliance with the adoption of the Six Pack and the Two Pack of the SGP, Fiscal Compact and the ESM.

Proposals of "risk sharing" were off the table since it seemed to be out of the question to justify a "transfer union", even more so transferring taxpayer's money to countries, which were not respecting the rules, lying to the other partners and indulging into fiscal excesses, while the bailing out of the banks had been decided within the shortest time and without much considering public opinion. Indeed, the possibility not to bail them out was never presented as an option, and the model of Iceland, where the citizens refused to go this way and had actually succeeded in a much smoother way to overcome the crisis, was largely suppressed and not promoted but rather covered up by a silence both by the political elites and the media. It is certainly correct that Greeks had not only lived above their means (as, by the way, had the Spanish, Irish, Portuguese, English, Americans, etc.) but even worse also engaged in unethical and dishonest "creative accounting measures", among which a derivative swap by Goldman Sachs to hide their true fiscal situation to the EU when joining EMU and later. On the other hand, as Bagehot indicates, "excess borrowing by fools would have been impossible without excess lending by fools: creditors and debtors are joined at the hip. A country that chooses to run current-account surpluses, indeed, one that has built its economy around generating improved competitiveness and increased external surpluses, has to finance the counterpart deficits" (Wolf 2014, p.80). Following Bagehot's logic, there is as much a responsibility of the creditor than there is of the debtor.

Furthermore, even given the case of a country, which obviously did not respect the rules (in reality, it was not the only one considering Germany and France 2003), Schauble's and even Merkel's public shaming and blaming and "punitive" approach and policies against Greece – up to the threat of expulsion from the euro area – are not only void of any spirit of European solidarity but on the contrary were awaking nationalistic and populist spirits, which were later further radicalized by the migration crisis. This reminds of Goethe's Zauberlehrling "Die ich rief, die Geister, werd ich nun nicht los" (Goethe's Sorcerer's Apprentice: "the ones I called, the spirits, I cannot get rid off"), implying and leading to a division of "Europe's demos or demoi" into Northern winners and savers against Southern losers "spending their money on women and booze", causing lasting damage to the project of the EU. How different could Europe's crisis management have been had Merkel expressed "Wir schaffen das (we can make it) – as she had done confronted by the migration crisis – and put her efforts into the elaboration of a more equitable crisis management and reform of the EMU, mobilizing the support for the European' project, by explaining the reasons of the crisis and the need to reform the shortcomings. Such a behaviour would have been more in line with Habermas "civilizational achievements". Europe managed to forge out of the ruins of the Second World War and could have propelled the EU to turn into "a place where the all the nations of Europe stand alongside each other as equals in a democratically legitimate political union as opposed to creditor and debtor member states of a dysfunctional monetary union" (Folan 2015).

Wolf interprets it as Germany's "effort of self-exculpation: as the eurozone's largest supplier of surplus capital, its private sector bore substantial responsibility for the excesses that led to the crisis". One of the most outspoken critics of the German government's position and behaviour in the Greek crisis is Jurgen Habermas, one of the most influential contemporary European intellectuals: "I fear that the German government, including its social democratic faction, have gambled away in one night all the political capital that a better Germany had accumulated in half a century," (...) by threatening Greece with an exit from the eurozone over the course of the negotiations, Germany had "unashamedly revealed itself as Europe's chief disciplinarian and for the first time openly made a claim for German hegemony in Europe" (Habermas 2015). For Habermas, the "European Council is effectively declaring itself politically bankrupt: the de facto relegation of a member state to the status of a protectorate openly contradicts the democratic principles of the European Union" and "forcing the Greek government to agree to an economically questionable, predominantly symbolic privatization fund cannot be understood as anything other than an act of punishment against a left-wing government. It's hard to see how more damage could be done" (Habermas 2015). What we were witnessing in this Greek drama at European stage was no less than the loss of national sovereignty revealing the existence of a "democratic deficit" at national level. Instead of recognizing the apparent design flaws in the architecture of EMU and assuming the co-responsibility for the faulted EMU architecture and for ignoring the risks, such as the "double moral hazard" caused by the financial market and by countries accumulating unsustainable public debt level partly also as a consequence of the neglected risks of the internal imbalances and looking jointlyfor more "equitable" solutions in the common interest of a true Economic (and Monetary) Union, creditor countries deviated the attention from the systemic failure by initiating a highly mediatized blame and shame game. Article 122 of the Treaty of the Functioning of the European Union was not invoked, which would have allowed for "financial assistance to the Member State concerned" in a situation, "where a Member State is in difficulties or is seriously threatened with severe difficulties caused by natural disasters or exceptional occurrences beyond its control". Unfortunately, Europe's political leaders chose instead to engage in humiliating public insults against the lazy South and hegemonic Northern European countries, creating division and hostility.

Additionally, the failure in the monitoring and surveillance procedures was exposed as Greece has been part of EMU, and none of "the institutions" (European Commission, IMF, Eurostat, ECB) detected that the Greek figures and finances were fraudulent, or if they did they failed to ring the alarm bells in time. Even without the "creative accounting measures", the public deficit of 6% and the public debt level of Greece above 90% of GDP were high and posed a risk. While the debt level was an official precondition for joining EMU, and M3 money supply had been monitored by the ECB until 2003, both indicators were later disregarded although they could have been very important indicators for the internal imbalances and the rising unsustainability. Instead, no safeguard measures or remedies against the risks of macroeconomic imbalances were in place, and the policies to improve competitiveness through cohesion funds to prepare for EMU membership were not sufficiently followed up once a member.

Furthermore, the publicly exposed punitive attitude with demands to expel Greece, implying and even stimulating an imminent sovereign default, and at the same time the exposed reluctance and negligent delays to assist Greece with the purpose to win regional elections in Germany, caused the yields to spread (undoing one of the major benefits of being a member of EMU), provoked the risk of contagion and the crisis to deepen and put the entire EMU at risk.

"Seen in this light Eichengreen's (2012: 132) puzzle as to "why the German government...finds it even more difficult to sell its constituents on the idea that taxpayer money should be used to recapitalise the country's own banks than to bail out Greece and Ireland"", H. Thomson argues that "If periphery bailouts have been unpopular in Germany it is because they have not been understood for what they were, which was an opportunity for Germany to 'Europeanise' the problems of its own banking sector, (…), but explaining its utility to the domestic political audience would have lessened the opportunity both to impose the costs of the banking crisis entirely on the debtor states and to change economic policies in the periphery through new institutional rules" (Thompson 2015). The imposition of the bailing out of the banks was not only in Germany's interest but as well shared by a number of other core eurozone's countries which joined efforts and policy stances to prevent that the ordo-liberal design would end up discredited and the fiscal framework and rules overhauled as a consequence. On the contrary, the Greek crisis served them well to go even further in tightening the fiscal rules and imposing "one-size-fits-all" austerity measures through the Troika and to undertake simultaneous fiscal budget consolidation not only to all the countries undergoing adjustment programmes but to furthermore impose it to the entire eurozone through the revised fiscal framework (SGP reforms: six pack and two pack, fiscal compact, ESM) resulting in the deepending and prolonging of the crisis.

Finally, the European Stability Mechanism (ESM), which was finally set up to provide financial assistance to euro area Member States threatened by financial difficulties, was set up as an intergovernmental institution governed by the Eurogroup in the form of its Board of Governors, and the Treaty on Stability, Coordination and Governance in the EMU (Fiscal Compact) requires even more stringent fiscal rules to be anchored within the national constitutions of the euro area countries. As a result, the "Fiscal Compact" succeeded in increasing credibility and incentives of fiscal consolidation but at the same time reduced the possibilities of counter-cyclical pro-growth policies and investment. A further aggravating aspect of both the ESM and the Fiscal Compact is that they are based – not on community law – but on intergovernmental treaties, thus circumventing democratic accountability to the European Parliament.

Consequences of "Governing by Rules" and "Ruling by Numbers" (Schmidt 2015)

As a consequence of this newly reinforced governance framework, Europe engaged from 2011 in coordinated simultaneous fiscal contraction across Europe, promoting austerity measures and retrenchment of the European social model and resulting in a further deepening and prolonging of the economic crisis and greater inequality and poverty in Europe. While the fiscal deficit was successfully reduced, neither the SGP nor the adjustment programmes succeeded to considerably reduce the debt level of the crisis countries (but had rather led to an increase due to the fall of GDP growth as a consequence of the adjustment programmes), which remain in some countries unsustainable in particular should another crisis erupt any time near. In 2013, the IMF revealed that "fiscal multipliers were substantially higher than implicitly assumed by forecasters" and an economic paper of the European Commission expressed concerns about the impact of simultaneous austerity policy on negative spillovers across the euro area and on output (Veld 2013), admitting that "Indeed, these negative spill-overs have made adjustment in the periphery harder, and have further exacerbated the temporary worsening of debt-to-GDP ratios in programme and vulnerable countries". The clear implication, therefore, is that countries would have grown more and would have seen their debt-to-GDP ratios fall more, if they had engaged in less austerity (Griffith-Jones 2014). The Commission's economic paper concludes "Optimal policy coordination in the euro area would have required a differentiation of consolidation efforts depending on the fiscal space to minimize the negative spillovers" (Veld 2013).

In June 2014, the European Council finally reacted: "fiscal consolidation must continue in a growth-friendly and differentiated manner. Structural reform that enhance growth and improve fiscal sustainability should be given particular attention [...] while making best use of the flexibility that is built into the existing SGP" (European Council 2014). On January 2015, the European Commission published a communication on "Making the best use of the flexibility within the existing rules of the Stability and Growth Pact" (European Commission 2015), with the purpose to provide guidance on the best possible use of the flexibility built into the existing rules of the Stability and Growth Pact (without changing the treaty) in order to strengthen the link between investment, structural reforms and fiscal responsibility. However, the European Fiscal Board's president Thygesen expressed the paradoxical conclusion that the rules allowing flexibility proved to be too rigid and limiting were applied at the wrong time and had procyclical effects and failed to protect growth enhancing investment from budget consolidation (European Fiscal Board 2019). The economic consequence for the entire eurozone was a prolonged and deepened crisis with major social and political costs that have transformed Europe and the political systems at national level. In the countries undergoing adjustment programmes, the effects were even dramatic and in some cases have even led to a humanitarian crisis.

In order to counteract these developments and to boost investment, employment and growth in the EU, Jean-Claude Juncker launched an Investment Plan for Europe, called the "Juncker Plan", which allowed the European Investment Bank to instrumentalize part of the EU budget as a guarantee to leverage private investment, which became a success story and gave rise to further proposals for investment supporting programmes such as InvestEU and the European Investment Stabilization Function (see Griffith Jones in Chap. 21).

Apart from the European Economic Recovery Programme and the Juncker Plan, an evaluation of the crisis resilience and crisis management shows thus a rather sombre picture. It is true that the total meltdown of the global financial system could be avoided as was the sovereign default of one or several of EMU's Member States and with it the risk of its implosion. On the downside, we would have to point out the deepening and prolonging of the financial and economic crisis leading to Europe's lost decade, reduced growth, serious problems of low investment (both public and private), under-target inflation and low productivity growth, the reversion of the achieved economic convergence and high social costs in the form of mass unemployment, in particular affecting Europe's South and youth (lost generation). Greece's youth unemployment hit the record with 58.2% in 2013, which left many of them no choice than to emigrate (celebrated by some economist as the necessary labour mobility, lamented by others for the economic consequences of the brain drain). Other consequences of the crisis for the entire euro area are the dismantling of the European social model and the increase in poverty and precariousness. In this way it is the European social model with strong welfare states paid the price for the failure that neoliberism caused both in regard to the design of EMU and in particularly concerning financial market's role and regulation.

Finally, the political costs of the crisis and the way it had been managed find reflection in the division of Europe in winners and losers, Northern and Southern and core and periphery EMU members, a loss of trust in the EU and EMU, but even more in mainstream political parties and systems at national level, which brought about historic mass protests and the rise of new social movements asking for a paradigm and system change and more direct democracy. After these demands had been largely ignored, began the mushrooming of new parties, increasingly polarized, first radically left and finally the rise of populist, nationalist and Eurosceptic movements and parties.

These developments have lasting impacts on the political landscape nationally and at EU level and led to an increasing polarization and destabilization of the national political systems and also at the EU level and the weakening of multilateral governance. Additionally, the prolonged crisis, the publicly exposed conflict and lack of solidarity between the member states, as well the retrenchment of the internationally appraised European social model in application of typically IMF style adjustment programmes, led to a loss of credibility, influence and international role of the Euro and the EU. As a consequence, the European model of regional integration lost in attractiveness in various regions of the world. While the worst of the financial and economic crisis might be overcome by now, its political consequences are here to stay.

Going Back in Time: A Failure of Design?

Here we come to the Gretchen Frage: Why was the EU and in particular the EMU not able to deliver appropriate and timely solutions and policies, first to avoid the crisis and second to manage the crisis? What were the flaws of the architecture of the EMU and which were the underlying reasons for them? Were the design flaws caused by too much "federalism", "European centralism" or "supranationalism" – in other words were there too many competences and decisions transferred to the EU level and were they too distant from the electorate? Or did the EU or EMU not dispose of enough and adequate competences and tools at its disposition, in other words was the crisis management too reliant on national and "intergovernmental" elements and negotiations putting national interest before the "general interests of the EU" and thus impeding a more "European and solidary" crisis response? But the reading of the crisis resilience and management requires a deeper analysis, looking into the drafting and development of EMU comparing it to its predecessor: the Werner Plan in order to assess the impact of the paradigm change from Keynesian to neoliberalism and/or ordo-liberalism for the design and functioning of EMU in particular in view of the crisis, its management and resilience. What were the motivations of and finally the reasons for the misjudgement, omissions and errors made by the authors of the Maastricht Treaty? These questions are crucial to determine the necessary reforms of EMU.

Let us start by the most obvious design flaws of EMU exposed by the crisis: by the time the financial crisis swapped over to Europe, it became clear that the architects of the Maastricht Treaty had first and foremost totally neglected the risk for financial and monetary instability stemming from the deregulated financial markets and capital market liberalization. Second, even more so, when the existence and consequences of the internal imbalances became an obvious threat and with it, third, the realistic possibility of a sovereign default of EMU member states with, fourth, the risk of contagion becoming undeniable and clashed with the, fifth, self-imposed constraints of the prohibition of bailing out a member state in balance of payment crisis.

When the architecture of the building of EMU entails a number of "fundamental" errors, its stability is jeopardized; furthermore, the misconceptions proved even worse; when the crisis broke out, EMU did not foresee any mechanism of stabilization, mutual assistance or solidarity such as a euro-area budget, a European Monetary Fund, a procedure for orderly debt restructuring. For inexplicable reasons, existing treaty provisions (Art 122, 123 of the Treaty on the Functioning of the European Union (TFEU)), which would have given a leeway for Member States in an exceptional situation, were not seized. The rules based on prohibiting risk-sharing or solidarity in order to work to counteract the risk of "moral hazard" of any Member State indulging in fiscal profligacy and free-riding of the benefits of a common currency on the other hand were considered prevailing over articles allowing for measures of solidarity and support in a situation of exceptional crisis, which was certainly the case considering the dimension of this financial crisis.

Incoherently, at the same time the "risk of moral hazard arising from deregulated financial markets destabilizing EMU" had not been previously considered and definitely not been treated the same way. Paradoxically, measures of mutual assistance still remained possible for Member States which were not part of EMU, while for the eurozone member, solidarity measures were interpreted as prohibited (no bailout) in the Maastricht Treaty leading to extremely difficult conditions for any crisis management. Institutionally, the following design failures can thus be identified. Schoeller (2017) identified the existence of the "twofold lack of institutions" with, first, no institutions regulating the mutualisation of risk (distributional problem) and, second, the institutions built to prevent moral hazard, basically the Stability and Growth Pact and the "no-bailout clause" failing. Building on the analysis of Schoeller, I would furthermore identify four key aspects: firstly, in intentional omission of institutions, tools and rules foreseen for mutual assistance for a country faced with balance of payments problems or, to be more precise, treaty articles, which could have served as a basis for measures in a situation of crisis, were intentionally disregarded. On the contrary, the rules, which explicitly prohibit any solidarity action (risk sharing) – both by Member States and by the ECB – were strictly applied until the risk of contagion threatened to blow up the euro area. Secondly, the EMU did not foresee any lender of last resort or rescue, in spite of the fact that national central banks were no longer able to play this role and the Member States had lost the tool of devaluating their currency. The ECB is forbidden to directly support EMU Member States but intervened in the secondary market and only in a later phase turned itself into a quasi-lender of last resort though "independent" (neither acting on request of a MS nor being prevented by a MS nor a national Court of Justice).

Thirdly, the treaties did not foresee any institution, decision-making process and financial tools, measures or means (euro-area budget, European Monetary Fund, Stabilization scheme or instrument) dealing with an EMU crisis. Historically, all EU countries should have been part of EMU, in which case all decisions would have taken place within its legal framework and institutions. Given that some countries, such as the UK and Denmark, had negotiated an opt-out option of EMU, and other countries have not "yet" joined EMU, the so-called Eurogroup was established as an informal discussion body, consisting of the Finance Ministers of the countries belonging to the eurozone. As a consequence, crisis management was done by the famous Merkelian way of "meddling through" – under the extreme pressure of time and financial markets – and, in a purely intergovernmental way, setting up further intergovernmental institutions (Troika, ESM) by (ab-)using the communitarian institutions (DG EcFin and the ECB) in an intergovernmental way and establishing further intergovernmental treaties (Fiscal Compact), all of this by bypassing accountability and democratic control by the European Parliament. As a consequence, crisis management under these conditions allowed the richer and more powerful northern countries to dictate the rules to follow not only during the crisis management but also to the future as a precondition for any potential assistance. Germany, which had until recently duly avoided a dominant behaviour, ended up as being regarded as Europe's authoritarian hegemon. Schoeller (2017) presents the

Fiscal Compact as perceived as the legitimate counter price for Germany joining the ESM.

Fourthly, the informal intergovernmental Eurogroup turned together with its pendant, the Euro Summit (the heads of states and governments of the euro area), into the most powerful decision-taking institutions. This development may well be considered the origin and cause of the erosion, regression and asymmetry of democracy at national level and EMU level. Whereby the decision-making process within the Eurogroup should have been consensual, which effectively allowed the strongest Member States (mostly also being the creditor countries), the strongest power, to eventually delay decisions (among others for national election purposes), to stimulate the discussion on a GREXIT and as a consequence of it speculation leading to higher yields until the risk of contagion threatened the breakup of the eurozone. The so-called consensus decision-taking gives single countries the opportunity to blackmail the others to obtain the agreement. The structure and decision-taking procedure gave rise to a hegemony, which is detrimental to the European integration process in which all countries should participate as equals. Additionally, the hegemon could then determine the creation and design of future risk management institutions such as the ESM and as a precondition the so-called fiscal compact, both negotiated outside of the EU legal framework and circumventing the co-decision of the European Parliament and the accountability to it.

Fifthly, the Eurogroup "instrumentalized" community institutions for the purpose of intergovernmental governance and implementation: the European Commission and the ECB served the Eurogroup within the so-called TROIKA, adding the IMF to elaborate and implement adjustment programmes for the debtor countries. These adjustment programmes, in particularly the one for Greece, should probably rather be described as "punitive measures" than "assistance programmes" and had little to do with any spirit of solidarity. The motive behind was to create a deterrent for the future so that no country would engage in financial profligacy and plan to be a free rider. In fact, for the same reason Germany stimulated the debate and speculation on a GREXIT.

In fact it was the lack of EMU crisis institutions, instruments, procedures and tools within the legal framework of the EU which led to the ascension of the Eurogroup to the most important player, with a totally opaque decision-taking procedure and quasi-zero democratic accountability. One of the most outspoken critics of the euro area crisis decision-taking process is the former EU Commissioner Moscovici who called it "a scandal in terms of democratic processes by deciding in this way the fate of a nation, imposing detailed decisions on pensions, the labour market" (Moscovici 2017). He also criticized the Eurogroup's extensive decisions, its structure, lack of transparency and accountability: "I am talking about the basic details of the life of a country which were decided in a body, behind closed doors, whose work is being prepared by technocrats without the minimum control of a parliament. Without the media really knowing what is being said, without stable criteria or a common guideline" (Ibid). Furthermore, Moscovici highlighted that the Eurogroup is not a place where national interests are overcome but rather that it has become the arena in which they clash so that the general European interest does not prevail. Indeed, the two institutions, which represent the community interest within the EU legal framework, one is the European Commission and the other one is the European Parliament, have largely been sidelined by the Eurogroup – an informal and deeply intergovernmental forum without any pre-established rules and regulations and without any proper accountability. Within the Troika, the European Commission seems to be rather in the role of implementing the guidelines given by the Eurogroup, than assuming its role as the guardian of the treaties. Considering the intrusive recommendations of the Troika, one also wonders to what extent the Collegium has been involved in the decision-taking or whether the Commission's DG EcFin had a dominating role without taking into account social impact assessments. The European Parliament expressed itself as "alarmed by the admission by the former President of the Eurogroup before the European Parliament that the Eurogroup endorsed the recommendations of the Troika without extensive consideration of their specific policy implications" and stressed "that, if accurate, this does not discharge euro area finance ministers from their political responsibility for the macroeconomic adjustment programmes and the MoUs". Additionally, the European Parliament's resolution on the Troika pointed out "that this admission sheds a worrying light on the blurred scope of the 'technical advising' and 'Eurogroup agency' roles devolved to both the Commission and the ECB in the framework of the design, implementation and assessment of assistance programmes." (European Parliament 2014a).

The Eurogroup's decision-taking process remains opaque due to its confidentiality and lack of democratic accountability, which has been strongly criticized by the European Parliament and by the EU's Ombudsman Emily O'Reilly – "It is obviously difficult for Europeans to understand that the Eurogroup, whose decisions can have a significant impact on their lives, [isn't] subject to the usual democratic checks and balances", both calling for reform (Smith-Meyer and Heath 2017). In particular on the subject of the crisis and its resolution, the Eurogroup had not foreseen any guidance, rules and procedures but actually works as an intergovernmental institution on the basis of "consensus" votes. On the one hand, this proved to be very detrimental in the situation of an "imminent" sovereign debt crisis requiring urgent decisions under pressure of financial market speculation. On the other hand, in the case of the Greek crisis, the existing rules were bent in two ways, there was no "consensus" attempted with Greece on the adjustment programs, but Greece was rather pressured into a "take it or leave it", with neither elections (of governments with a programme, which was clearly opposing the kind of policies imposed by the adjustment programs) nor a referendum with two thirds majority against the austerity policies making any difference and with putting pressure on the Greek government and prime minister, one being replaced by a quasi-imposed caretaker government, not even being able to negotiate the choice of measures to achieve a determined objective of the bailout programme. Given the loopholes of properly governing institutions, the entire EMU construction bears a major flaw in terms of democratic accountability and legitimacy. Neither the Eurogroup nor the Euro Summit are official institutions of the EU legal framework, but informal bodies, which allow them to circumvent democratic accountability to the European Parliament. Although as a consequence of the critiscism raised by the European Parliament, the EU Ombudsman and numerous academics, the president of the

Eurogroup engaged on a voluntary basis to participate regularly in exchange of views in the European Parliament, however this does not change the fact that the Eurogroup remains legally not democratically accountable to the European Parliament. This lack of "identifiable", in the sense to know who is really taking which decision, and "accountable" institutions provoked a severe lack of democratic accountability at national and European level. Indeed, only in a few countries there was a real accountability of the "national" finance minister to a "national" parliament on the adjustment programmes. The parliaments of the crisis countries were usually obliged to adopt a Memorandum of Understanding of the EMU with the euro area Member State in crisis as a precondition for financial assistance in the way of a "take it or leave it" deal, leaving little or virtually no choice of the measures to achieve the economic objectives to them and, at European level, by circumventing the European Parliament through an intergovernmental crisis management thus creating a "double democratic deficit". Social partners of the crisis countries were also not properly consulted on the Memorandums of Understanding (MoUs), but the recommendations of the MoUs even interfered with traditional collective bargaining structures to the detriment of labour in violation of EU's Charter of Fundamental Rights and ILO conventions.

In retrospect, it is clear that the failures and flaws of the European economic architecture had proven to be very costly economically, socially and politically with deep and long-lasting effects on the European social model and democracy, as discussed in other articles of the book. The loss of trust in the EU was historic and only outperformed by the loss of trust in national institutions and parties, which is an indicator that citizens are indeed able to identify the politicians responsible for these failures and errors. The article will now attempt to sketch the role of the architects, their ideological mindset and the impact of the paradigm change for the design of EMU by comparing it to its predecessor, the Werner Plan, looking for the causes of these major flaws, omissions, errors and neglect, which proved so costly for Europe and its citizens. As discussed in other chapters of this volume, especially Schulmeister, the negotiation of the Maastricht Treaty fell into the era of neoliberalism and shows clear traits of it as the comparison to its predecessor, which had still fallen in the era of Keynesianism. Accordingly, the single currency should eliminate transaction cost linked to currency conversion, and instabilities linked to exchange rate fluctuations in the single market, free capital flow and deregulated and globalized financial markets would lead to greater resource allocation and efficiency. Monetary policy with the primary objective of prices stability should play the predominant role and fiscal and labour policy, in the form of labour mobility, and accommodative wage policies should accommodate it. Political intervention and fiscal discretionary policy should be limited and tied into a very strict "golden straightjacket" and closely monitored. Within the EMU of Maastricht, the design foresees a "supranational monetary union", which effectively had been "delegated" to an independent European Central Bank (ECB) with a very clear and limited mandate giving primacy to "price stability", on the one hand, and a predominantly "intergovernmental economic union", which foresees a loose coordination with "disciplining" surveillance procedures by the supranational Commission and sanctions decided by the EcoFin Council, on the other hand.

When considering the dominant role and absolute independence of the ECB and the disciplining aspect of economic policy without any solidarity mechanism in the Maastricht Treaty, it comes as no surprise that the blueprint of EMU has been drafted predominantly by the governors of Europe's central banks, under the leadership of the Deutsche Bundesbank. John Singleton described EMU "as a triumph for central bankers, and proof that they had become an influential epistemic community. Predominantly central bankers and not politicians or the European central bureaucracy drew up the plans for the ECB and the Monetary Union, and they did so in accordance with the latest monetary orthodoxy" (Singleton 2011). The result is an "ordo-liberal" version of how Economic and Monetary Union should be designed and vision of the world, which stands in clear contrast to its "federalist" predecessor drafted by Pierre Werner in the 1970s.

Yves Mersch (2010) encouraged revisiting the Werner Plan: "We can call it truly visionary. Although many of the proposals of the original Werner plan have been realized, some of the original thoughts were ignored or diluted and we might with the benefit of hindsight, ask ourselves whether this has not been a mistake" (Mersch 2010). The comparison of the blueprint of the Werner Plan with the Maastricht Treaty on Economic and Monetary Union clearly demonstrates that the Werner Plan is at the same time the more European and federalist in terms of being supranational, democratic and inclusive, involving both the European Parliament and the European social partners (both sides of industry) in an institutionalized way and the far more comprehensive including a monetary, an economic, a political, a cohesion and a social dimensions. The Werner Plan was clearly a child of the Keynesian era and regarded the European social model as a vital dimension of economic integration (Danescu 2018).

Both drafts did foresee the free movement of capital, not only within the EU but globally. However, only the Werner Plan addressed concerns about the destabilizing impacts financial speculation could have for EMU and proposed financial regulation and the taxation of capital. The same is true for the occurrence of internal imbalances. The Werner Plan showed far more visionary about the risk of the destabilizing effects of imbalances, which could occur in an Economic and Monetary Union, which did not achieve sufficient convergence. This was also the reason why Werner did include economic and regional convergence into his EMU plan. The Werner Plan was more complete in terms of a symmetric construction of EMU, of institution building both in terms of clearly identifiable decision-taking institution and accountability and in terms of a stabilization function. Regarding the power balance between economic and monetary policy, the Werner Plan did include both an European Economic Union and a Community system for the central banks. For the European Economic Union the Werner plan envisaged "a gradual transfer of powers of decision-taking to the EU level and at the final stage the establishment of a "centre of decision for economic policy". In parallel, Werner planed the gradual development of a "Community system for the central banks" and a "European Fund for monetary cooperation under the control of the Governors of the central banks." The role of this fund was supposed to be to absorb the mechanisms for monetary support at short term and for financial aid at medium term, a stabilization instrument intentionally missing in the EMU blueprint. These institutions, while safeguarding their own responsibilities, were to be furnished with effective powers of decision and to work together for the realization of the same objectives. The centre of economic decision was planned to be politically responsible to a European Parliament.

TREATIES AND REFORMS INCLUDING WERNER PLAN	Treaty of ROME	Werner Plan	Maastricht Treaty	Reforms at the Crisis 2007/8 and following
Free capital movements (inside and outside of EMU, EU)	NO	✓ "	✓	
Single currency re-placing national currencies	NO	Community currencies should be completely and irreversibly convertible at permanently fixed rates of parity. Preference for a single common currency. T	✓	
ESCB or ECB in charge of Monetary Union	No	✓	✓	
ECB independent		✓	✓	
ECB, price stability as primary objective		✓	✓	
ECB in charge of Prudential super-vision of banks	NO	No	No	✓
ECB lender of last resort	NO	✓	ECB not authorized to lending to any public institution or authority (local, national, EU)	+/-

			but indirectly via secondary markets	
Reference/ to the nexus to the financial market and regulation (later banking union)	No	✓	No —·–	Banking Union regulation, supervision but missing EDIS
Multilateral assistance in payment difficulties for members of EU/ EMU	✓	✓	_NO no bailout clause or EMU for EMU members, **YES** multilateral assistance only for MS outside of EMU **YES:** **Legally possible but not applied: Article 122 TFEU**	ESM as an inter-governmental organisation outside EU legal frame-work, assistance without accountability to the EP
Reference to the Macroeconomic imbalances	✓	✓	- NO no mentioning	MIP (Macroeconomic Imbalance Procedure with a bias on deficit countries)

Comprehensive approach encompassing Monetary, Fiscal & Political governance	✓	✓ gradual and Parallel movement towards economic policy convergence and the imposition of monetary constraints with the parallel transfer of powers and corresponding development of EU institutions.	+/- + Monetary Union (suprationational) YES	
			-NO Economic Policy remained largely national and intergovernmental	Economic policy national, but coordination (Europ. semester), monitoring through Commission tand possibility of (light sanction for non-compliance) through Council (never applied)
				2020 Recovery Package Common rescue package financed by grants and loans and EU bonds, ,temporary fiscal stabilization function through increase of budget, SURE, RRF, InvestEU, TSI

Horizontal democracy social partner involvement		✓ Social Partners have an essential role in the establishment and during EMU decision taking,	As a consequence of the UK resistance, not within EMU chapter (but in annex of Maastricht is a Social Chapter with an increased role for the Social partners). For this reason the adjustment programmes and the MoU could violate the social charter without violating EU primary law.	Social partners in the crisis or crisis management not in-volved, MoUs often interfered in the national social fabric to the detriment of labour, imposing the retrenchment of collective bar-gaining to the company level and cutting of labour rights
Euro area economic decision taking body within the EU legal framework	-	✓ Centre of decision for economic policy	Only 'informal Euro Group' and informal 'Euro summit', without rules and procedures, intergovernmen tal decision-taking	Informal Euro Group and Euro Summit turned 'de facto' into the most powerful institutions, instrumentalization of the Troika and the ESM..
Accountability of fiscal policy to the European parliament	-	✓	Lack of accountability of	EP outside of decisions on crisis, its management, policies

		Under the democratic control of the EP	informal institutions	No formal accounta-bility, however EP established the CRIS (2010- 2011), TROIKA Inquiry (2014-2015) and Financial Assistance Working Group (FAWG) (2014-15) Today "exchange of views" of Eurogroup president and ESM Managing director with EP (ECON Committee) but not within legal framework of EU

Own Compilation: De Souza Guilherme B.,Jean Monnet Network'Crisis-Equity-Democracy', 2020.

The comparison between the Werner Plan and the Maastricht Treaty puts in evidence the influence and impact of the paradigm change from Keynesianism to neo- and ordo-liberalism in the construction of EMU, exchanging a "federalist" for an "intergovernmental" blueprint of EMU, which led to the elimination of crucial elements and building stones of EMU architecture, which would have been essential to make the EMU more resistant and resilient to crisis and would have allowed a more efficient, equitable and democratic crisis management. These elements which had been removed from the Werner plan and turned the Maastricht Treaty deficient reach from taking account of the risks of deregulated financial markets and internal imbalances, to political institution building and appropriate democratic accountability and to solidarity or "risk sharing" and stabilization elements such as a European Monetary Fund and an EMU budget. According to the McDougall report, which analysed the conditions necessary for the implementation of EMU from the Werner Plan, the EMU budget should have been between 2.5 and 10% of Union GNI. These intentional omissions of the Maastricht blueprint in turn proved to be the major flaws in the design of EMU when the financial crisis broke out and largely contributed to the sovereign debt crisis, became the source of policy errors in crisis management and led to a major EMU governance crisis due to publicly exposed conflicts.

The Werner Plan in contrast did foresee a two-pillar model with both a monetary union and an economic union called "centre of decisions for economic policy", and both pillars "must work together for the realization of the same objectives" (Werner 1970). In the moment of crisis, it was actually precisely the supranational pillar, the ECB, which after initial hesitations, was the one to provide support, stabilize the situation and bring resilience to the euro area, in particular from the moment on, when former ECB president M. Draghi pronounced his magic words on 12 July

2012: "within our mandate, the ECB is ready to do whatever it takes to preserve the euro. And believe me, it will be enough" (Draghi 2012). From that date on, the ECB started to take over its responsibility as a lender of last resort and became the strongest element warranting the survival of EMU. His words put a halt to financial speculation and contained the sovereign debt crisis to restore confidence through a series of extraordinary measures to support euro area's governments and banks, proof of the effectiveness of risk sharing. Had the countries of the Eurogroup behaved in similar unitary, determined and problem-solving-oriented manner, the probability of a sovereign debt crisis would have been much reduced and the crisis shorter, less profound and less painful and politically could have strengthened the EU internationally and externally. The ECB, being independent and supranational, had uncontestably made the greatest contribution to contain the crisis and had turned into one of the most powerful, and certainly the most independent central banks in the world. Powerful because, on the one hand, it turned into the real "European Central Bank," and a "quasi lender of last resort" with an additionally extended mandate to the supervision of the banks. The ECB grew and gained power with this crisis, in which it had initially been too timid to assume its role to act with countercyclical measures to contain and combat the crisis but turned into the strongest actor of crisis management in the aftermath of the financial crisis.

On the downside of the increased power, we note that the ECB started to overreach its powers by actively interfering, controlling and in some cases even sanctioning economic and fiscal policies of Member States such as Greece, Ireland and even Italy (which was not even undergoing a Troika adjustment programme). The latter role has brought the ECB considerable criticism for its "overreach" and interference and apparent "conflict of interest" between its role as central bank and lender of last resort of all the MS, including the debtor countries, and its role, interest and measures within the TROIKA and as a creditor. The ECB engaged actively in fiscal but also socioeconomic affairs of the Member States, impacting distributional aspects and the social fabric such as pushing for the transferal of collective bargaining from central or sectoral level to the enterprise level and other matters of collective bargaining and labour law, always in the direction of weakening the power and conditions of labour, which paradoxically implies that the "independent" central bank interferes in the "independent" social partner negotiations and structures in violation of the article 152 of the TFEU, which explicitly enshrines that "The Union recognises and promotes the role of the social partners at its level, taking into account the diversity of national systems. It shall facilitate dialogue between the social partners, respecting their autonomy." The consequence of this interference within the adjustment programmes is the weakening of the bargaining power of the labour side, which economically translates in the result that the recent improvement of the labour market does not have the appropriate consequences on wage growth and thus contributes directly to the lower than target inflation rate of 2%. The ECB finds itself confronted with the (self-inflicted) dilemma that while of the improved labour market trends are improving, this does not sufficiently translate into wage growth and consequently does not find reflection in inflation growth. The underlying reasons for this development are the imposed structural reforms leading to labour slack (underemployment of labour in involuntary part time and flexible and precarious jobs) and the interference in collective bargaining structures to the detriment of labour (ECB 2019).

The first institution to voice criticism about the conflict of interest, the overreach and the lack of democratic accountability given its increase in powers was the European Parliament, which had installed a Special Committee on the Financial, Economic and Social Crisis (CRIS) in 2010 and a Troika Inquiry Committee in 2014–2015. The ECB can be considered the most independent of all central banks since the ECB has only a "formal" accountability requirement to the European Parliament, which consists rather in a transparency obligation while the EP has limited possibilities to "change" the policy of the ECB, mainly through the hearings of the president and the board of the ECB and through public pressure. In contrast to the European Parliament, the FED has a "dual" mandate, price stability and employment, and has a "factual accountability". The Congress has the possibility to actually change the mandate of the FED, if it is not satisfied with the institution and its work (Hoffmann-Althelm 2017).

In Europe, a change of the mandate of the ECB would require a treaty change, which is very difficult to achieve since all MS have to agree. The result of the Maastricht Treaty in line with the objectives of neoliberalism is a shift of power to the markets by guaranteeing free capital flows and deregulated financial markets and to "limit the discretionary power of government(s)", by a framework of strict budgetary and fiscal rules and criteria and the transfer of monetary competences to an independent central bank with a restricted mandate on price stability. Neoliberalism and ordo-liberalism left a clear imprint on the Maastricht design, by basically "eliminating" the economic union pillar from the original Werner EMU blueprint: its institutions, instruments and stabilization and convergence tools and democratic accountability to the European Parliament and horizontal democracy by a stronger involvement of the social partners from the more "federalist" Werner plan. In spite of forming an "Economic and Monetary Union", any element of solidarity or risk sharing or stabilization function such as a euro area budget, a European Monetary Fund, Eurobond or an unemployment insurance scheme to assist in cases of balance of payment problems has been eliminated. According to the architects of Maastricht, the risk of a sovereign default should have been avoided by the prohibitions of "bailouts" and the "disciplining role of financial markets", imposing "own responsibility on the Member States" and with two ways of combating a sovereign default: first, by internal devaluation, in this way by the application of tough budget consolidation and rigid austerity measures, to the greatest extent by cutting wages, pensions and social benefits, thus on the back of the poorest strata of society, and, second, by bailing-in the creditors – that private creditors (banks) would take over the losses in case of sovereign default.

Although the bailing-in option had been Germany's position all the way during and after the negotiations of the Maastricht Treaty (Moody), Thompson (2015) points out that Germany found itself in the delicate situation that these private creditors, which were to shoulder the loss, were in the Greek case, mainly French and German banks. Additionally, nearly half of foreign claims on Portugal, Ireland,

Italy, Greece and Spain in the final quarter of 2009 belonged to the two countries. German banks were already vulnerable "to the prevailing problems of funding in the wholesale markets, as well as the collapse of the sub-prime mortgage-backed securities market". "The German government had already taken measure to respond to the financial crisis by establishing a €480B federal bank rescue fund, and by mid-February 2009, the cost of German financial stabilization amounted to 3.1 per cent of GDP, compared to 1.8 per cent for France and 0.9 per cent for Italy (IMF 2009: 48). Additionally, Germany also had by the same time $556B of sovereign guaranteed bank debt, which was significantly higher than that reported by the IMF for other European states except Ireland (IMF 2009: 49) (Thompson 2015). On the background of these massive interests, Germany's reaction to the Greek sovereign debt crisis becomes clearer. Germany was the country which most delayed an EU reaction and even stirred the crisis of confidence by public statements which envisaged the possibility of a GREXIT. Germany had prevented Greece turning to the IMF to request balance of payment assistance in the early phase of the Greek crisis but later was one of the strongest supporters of their involvement. The reason behind is that the IMF as a usual praxis initiates its involvement with a debt sustainability assessment and would have suggested an early debt restructuring, which had been the IMF's position throughout its involvement. At the same time, Germany refused the possibility of a "European solution" but simply threatened a Grexit and delayed the decision-taking leading to the spread of the yields until it became clear that there was a clear risk of contagion to other periphery countries among which some "too big to fail", which might put the existence of the eurozone at risk.

In the case of an early declaration of sovereign default by Greece and a later collapse of the eurozone, the burden of the debts would have fallen on the private creditors of the central or northern countries and would probably have resulted in their bailing out through their governments and figured among their public debt. It appears to be logically in the interest of Germany to support the bailout programmes to Europe's periphery under the condition that the funds would be used to bail out the private creditors: "In outcomes, the first Greek bailout and the subsequent deals for Ireland and Portugal effectively moved liability for bad loans in the periphery from German and French banks to the IMF, EU, ECB and EFSF for which Germany and France bore a share of responsibility but not the whole. Put differently, these bailouts shifted the risk of default in the periphery from German and French banks to collective European and other taxpayers, and the burden of the internal imbalances entirely to the debtor countries" (Thompson 2015).

Had the objective been an efficient and equitable bailout of Greece and avoiding the euro crisis, then "the haircut should have taken place much earlier so that private creditors would have taken the loss" (Rocholl and Stahmer 2016). The Swiss ESMT study on the Greek bailout assessed that less than 10 billion euros (9.7 billion) from Greece's first two international bailouts of the amount of 216 billion euros ended up in the hands of the Greek treasury to help the economy to kick start. The lion's share of the rescue money sent to Greece was used for debt repayments (86.9 bn), interest payments (52.3 bn), bank recapitalization (37.3 bn) and debt restructuring. Additionally, there come accusations that Germany had "massively profited from the crisis in Greece" (Rocholl and Stahmer 2016). The German Green MP, Sven-Christian Kindler, expressed his disapproval: "It cannot be the case that the German government consolidates the German budget with billions in Greek interest profits"; "Greece needs air to breath and room for manoeuvre for investments and fighting poverty in the country". Germany has received euro 3.4 billion in interest payments on Greek bonds that were both through the no-defunct bond-buying programme according to the figures that were obtained from the government on Thursday by Germany's Green Party. Germany has also received a total of euro 400 m on a loan from the KfW development bank. Germany has so far repaid euro 527 m of interest payments to Greece in 2013 and euro 387 m in 2014. But those repayments were halted after Greece's second bailout programme was agreed in 2015, leaving Germany accumulating the ongoing Greek interest payments (Allen and Chazan 2018). Eurozone countries bought 210 bn euros of government paper, including Greek bonds, from 2010 onwards in a bid to provide greater liquidity to the bloc's banks as the Greek debt crisis took hold (ibid).

Finally, debt restructuring for sovereign creditors was not achieved in the form of a haircut, as had been for private creditors after Deauville, but in a postponement of the majority of repayments on the euro 228 bin that Greece owes to the rest of the eurozone until after 2030. It also includes returning to Greece the annual profits that euro area central banks made on their holdings of the country's debt, however only from 2017 financial year onwards. Tied to it remains the closer monitoring of Greece's fiscal policy and its obligations signed in the MoUs. As Geoffrey Sachs said, "the German taxpayers believe that they have been extremely generous to Greece, giving Greece repeated financial loans. Yet this is partly a mirage. The taxpayers have been generous to their own banks, not to Greece" (Sachs 2015).

De Grauwe (2015) highlights that the eurocrisis is in reality a systemic problem of the architecture of EMU. First, EMU ripped off Member States their capacity of exchange rate devaluations and of the automatic stabilizers for the recovery without any compensating EMU stabilization function nor solidarity mechanism in place at European level. Second, he underlines the destabilizing role of the financial markets for the stability of EMU, "When entering a monetary union, member-countries change the nature of their sovereign debt in a fundamental way, i.e. they cease to have control over the currency in which their debt is issued". As a result, financial markets can force these countries' sovereigns into default. In this sense, member countries of a monetary union are downgraded to the status of emerging economies. This makes the monetary union fragile and vulnerable to changing market sentiments. De Grauwe concludes that, thus, "in a monetary union, financial markets acquire tremendous power and can force any member country on its knees, (...) This has the effect of pushing the country into a bad equilibrium, characterized by punishingly high interest rates, chronically high budget deficits, low growth and a domestic banking crisis". Third, he argues that given the degree of financial integration in the monetary union, other countries are affected by the risk of contagion. And at last, De Grauwe, after analysing the implications of this fragility for the governance of the Eurozone, concludes that additionally "some of the features of the new financial assistance are likely to increase this fragility. In addition, it is also likely to rip member-states of their ability to use the automatic stabilizers during a recession. This is surely a step backward in the long history of social progress in Europe".

Democratic Legitimacy and Accountability

After sketching the EMU crisis response and exposing the design flaws of EMU architecture and their economic, social and political consequences, and after analysing the impact of the ordo-liberal mindset of the epistemic community in charge of drafting the blueprint as well as the impact of the of the paradigm change on the design and on its more "federalist" or more "intergovernmental" features by comparing the Werner Plan versus the Maastricht Treaty, the chapter will last but not least turn to the core question of the democratic consequences and legitimacy crisis exposed by the crisis: the Double Democratic Deficit. The rapporteur of the European Parliament's Special Committee on the Financial, Economic and Social Crisis (CRIS) report, and of the EP review of the economic governance framework: stocktaking and challenges, Pervenche Beres, expressed her opinion that "there is an increasing sense of a double democratic deficit in an enhanced economic governance framework of the Union at both the EU and at national levels. There is thus a need for both the European Parliament and National Parliaments to seek ways to increase their involvement, taking into account their respective roles" (European Parliament 2014b).

The "original sin" in terms of a weakening of the democratic legitimacy and accountability started when the Eurogroup, originally foreseen as an informal and confidential coordination club among euro area finance ministers, turned with the eurocrisis into the most powerful institution in the EU and led to a "shift away from the Community method towards intergovernmental coordination. The European Council and the Eurogroup have played a dominant role throughout the process and have often interfered in the prerogatives of the European Parliament, e.g. when it unilaterally decided that the EU budget would guarantee for the EFSM loans with the margin between the Multiannual Financial Framework (MFF) ceiling and the Own Resources ceiling. In the newly created institutional setting, the European Parliament and its national counterparts only play a marginal role and have thus been largely deprived of their constitutionally granted powers as regards budgetary autonomy respectively oversight" (European Parliament 2016). This put the spotlight to the increasing erosion of democracy at EMU level, while at the same time euro area finance ministers argue that they are accountable only to national parliaments in particular since the responsibility of the budget lies with them.

One of the most outspoken critics of the euro area crisis decision-making process is the former commissioner Moscovici, when he expressed that "It is a scandal in terms of democratic processes, not because the decisions were scandalous, but because by deciding in this way the fate of a nation, imposing detailed decisions on pensions, the labour market" (Moscovici 2015). He also criticized the Eurogroup's extensive decisions, its structure, lack of transparency and accountability. "I am talking about the basic details of the life of a country which were decided in a body, behind closed doors, whose work is being prepared by technocrats without the minimum control of a parliament. Without the media really knowing what is being said, without stable criteria or a common guideline" (Moscovici 2015)

The German finance minister Scholz defended in a meeting in the Economic and Monetary Committee of the European Parliament that the national finance ministers are accountable to their national parliaments and thus democratic accountability is warranted. This argument is strengthened on the one hand by the fact that the national parliament is the one which has control on the budget foreseen and taking into account the ruling of the German Constitutional Court which anchors the role of the German national parliament for any major financial obligations or transfers. Yet his statement bears a certain weakness since the finance minister is only elected and mandated nationally to represent national interests but decides on policies of the entire euro area without being accountable to neither the European Parliament nor to the parliaments of the crisis country, while the institutions which represent the general interest of the EU were either "instrumentalized" for the purposes of intergovernmental governance and submitted under the interest of the most powerful member states or cut out of the decision-making process creating an "imbalance between the decision-taking institutions at EU level" and leading to a regression of democratic decision-taking rights. For this reason, Commissioner Moscovici expressed his doubts about the Eurogroup's capacity to negotiate a consensus in which the general European interest prevails: "The Eurogroup is not a place where national interests are overcome; it has become the arena in which they clash" (Moscovici 2015). This is even more true in the moment of an urgent crisis when considerable national interests are at stake. Interestingly, at global level, it is the debtor country, which penalizes the creditor countries and changes the rules, while at EMU level, it occurs the other way around. The common trait is that the most powerful states turn into hegemons to the detriment of a more democratic order or multilateral organization of equals. An interesting question to analyse in a future research is the correlation between democracy and supranationalism and multilateral governance with the rise of the hegemons.

Indeed, considering the EU architecture, we can identify both intergovernmental institutions, such as the Council or national parliaments and supranational institutions such as the European Commission, the European Parliament, the ECB and the European Court of Justice representing the community interest. Just like in the USA, the two houses, Senate and Congress, guarantee a balance between national interest and the community or general interests of the Union and in the case of the EP of the citizens too. Yet, within Economic and Monetary Union, this balance has not been ensured or not even constructed from the moment on that the possibility of an opting out had been granted and thus have led to the creation of the Eurogroup, leading to a situation that the more decisions had been taken on an intergovernmental basis, treaties have been signed and institutions have been founded on an intergovernmental basis, the more democracy has been eroded at national and at EMU level. However, within the EMU construction, the Commission could not assume the role it has been assigned within the EU Treaties: to defend the Community interest and to defend the European Treaties and laws. As Commissioner Moscovici notes "Yet the voice of the Commission does not carry as far as the Eurogroup – an informal and deeply intergovernmental forum without any pre-established rules and regulations – or it does not carry far enough, at any rate, to allow the general European interest to prevail" (Moscovici 2015).

The same lack of the priority or in some cases even vision of the "general European interest" together with the lack of capacity to negotiate a European compromise or grand deal is true for the national parliaments. The mandate of a member of a national parliament (NP) is to look after their national interest, which finds reflection in their divergent positions in the matter of economic governance. "There is no such a thing like a NPs' unitary position on how to cope with the democratic weaknesses of the system of coordination of national economic policies. Next to the divide between Eurozone vs. non-Eurozone NPs, there are divides between parliaments of rescued countries and parliaments of the states that most prominently offered financial assistance and between parliaments of 'Southern Europe', in favour of anti-cyclical policies, and parliaments of 'Northern Europe' supporting austerity measures" (Fasone 2019).

The European Parliament, in contrast to the national parliaments, is the locus, public space or agora, in which these deliberations and debates are being held and compromise positions are being negotiated, of which the numerous resolutions on the crisis and reform proposals are proof and may serve a precious advice for future reforms of EMU and its crisis management. In the European Parliament, directly elected members from all the Member States form ideological groups or parties and mostly vote along the ideological lines, which allows compromises that bridge the interest conflicts between creditor and debtor countries. However, given that EMU crisis management took place outside of the EU legal framework, the European Parliament was largely excluded from the real decision-taking process. P. Mocscovici resumed on the European Parliament's role and influence in the crisis management: "It was the great absentee in the Greek crisis. But then, to whom should it have turned? To the Commission in its capacity as negotiator? To the president of the Eurogroup, who is not answerable to it? To the IMF, which is even less answerable to it? Or to the European Stability Mechanism, which is a purely intergovernmental organisation? And the secondary question is this: how much weight did the European Parliament carry in the Greek crisis by comparison with the German Bundestag or the Finnish Eduskunta?" (Moscovici 2017).

Commissioner Moscovici's remarks reveal the further democratic regression provoked by the eurozone crisis having given rise to a quasi-oligarchic dominance among the MS, asymmetry and certainly an increasing disparity in democratic rights between creditor and debt countries. "Although there are exceptions, typically the parliaments of Eurozone countries receiving financial assistance or support (Cyprus, Greece, Ireland, Italy, Portugal, Spain) have been those most concerned by a significant loss of influence in budgetary matters. By contrast, the legislatures of some Eurozone countries regarded as fiscally virtuous, like Austria, Finland and Germany, have seen their budgetary powers, at least, safeguarded domestically in the constitutional framework emerging from the Euro-crisis" (Riekmann and Wydra 2013). Eurobarometer opinion polls on "My Voice counts in the EU" reflect the same picture since the outbreak of the crisis: citizens of the creditor countries consider with a large majority that their voice counts in the EU, while the citizens of the deficit countries have the opposite feeling that their voice does not count. As a consequence, we would have to conclude that the EMU architecture and eurozone crisis led not only to a regression in terms of economic and social convergence but also in terms of democratic decision-taking and accountability rights within the eurozone, reminding of the initial stage of democracies in Greece, where democratic rights were limited to a citizen of a certain level of wealth (and at that time also sex and nationality) and early stages of European democracies.

As a consequence of the euro crisis, the national parliaments of the deficit countries mostly only had the choice between the lesser of two evils: sovereign default and leaving the euro area or adjustment programmes, which in the end turned out to be economically either doubt or harmful, procyclical, socially and politically painful and destabilizing by leading to an internal devaluation of 25% by imposing austerity and social cuts. Democratically, these MoUs were largely imposed by the Eurogroup via the Troika, in many cases without considering the local economic, social and political situation or priorities, without a proper impact assessment and broader democratic consultation. It is rather doubtful that the "general European interest" has been in the focus of the crisis management of the eurozone, when considering the following three points: First, the burden of adjustment was entirely put on the deficit countries: both in the obligation to bail out the banks and in terms of the policy mix they had to follow. The IMF had already in 2011 given the same advice as the European Fiscal Board emphasizes in 2019 that the countries which find themselves with more fiscal space should run an expansionary policy while the countries with excessive deficits and debts need to undertake measures of budget consolidation. In reality, Germany and the other countries which should have played the role of the motors of the European recovery preferred to prove themselves as examples in budget consolidation, leading Europe's economy to the verge of recession.

Second, the Troika follows the instructions of whom and was/is accountable to whom? In other words, who decided these policies and on the basis of which rules, guidelines, principles and interests? Who carries the responsibility for their decisions and as was the case with the past adjustment programmes for their heavy economic, social and political costs? In any sound democratic system, there would be checks and balances; in the case of decisions taken by elected representatives, they would either be rewarded through re-elections or sanctioned by losing the elections and their political mandate in the case that the policies were not considered successful or appropriate. If the decisions were based on the expertise of some technocratic entity to which the decision-taking or at least shaping powers have been delegated, these experts or technocrats would lose their credibility and reputation and would sooner or later also lose their function or the entire institution to which the decision-taking or shaping power was delegated would be abolished or at least diminished in influence. In the case of the eurocrisis decision, the situation is not so clear. Some countries succeeded to push through decisions which were very much in their national interest, and from a national (short-term) perspective, these decisions were beneficial (to their nation) and thus will be rewarded. Other nations did not really have much choice and influence, in which case there would either occur a sanctioning through elections or on the contrary a sympathy and identification with the national leader against certain other European leaders or the EU as a whole. The prolonged crisis, fall of investment and growth and the fact that the adjustment programmes did not lead to a debt reduction in highly indebted countries but had rather increased them and prolonged and deepened the crisis are rather interpreted as consequences of not following the rules and insufficient reform efforts by the crisis countries than as wrong policy recommendations and procedures.

Transparency EU summarizes the malaise of the Eurogroup's accountability regime with two quotes: one by German finance minister Wolfgang Schäuble, "Elections change nothing. There are rules", and the other by the Finnish finance minister describing Germany's raw power: "Schäuble has been the treasurer of Europe and the de facto finance minister for the eurozone". It concludes "When votes and electoral outcomes can 'change nothing', while the finance minister of a 'creditor' country is described as the 'de facto finance minister' of several 'debtor' countries, citizens (rightly) see 'constrained government' and 'democracy without choice', with negative consequences for their participation in elections and their satisfaction with democracy". This is consistent with Seymour Martin Lipset's warning that without democratic participation and accountability, a society loses the capacity "to engender and maintain the belief that the existing political institutions are the most appropriate ones". In other words, what is at stake in the debate about economic governance in the euro area is nothing less than the legitimacy, and viability, of liberal democracy (Braun and Huebner 2019).

Third, the rise of the hegemon. Here, we touch a vulnerable point of the current decisions in the crisis management and in the shaping of the adjustment programmes. Clearly, the one institution with the strongest decision-taking power is the Eurogroup, on the basis of which decisions the Euro Summit takes the final decisions. The Troika itself is consisting of three very different institutions with different mandates: The Commission, the ECB and the IMF. Both the first two institutions are bound to the treaties and objectives of the EU, yet it seems that they have rather been "instrumentalized" by the informal Eurogroup without the adequate role assigned to them by the European Treaties, thus losing their "independence" vis-a-vis the Member States (in particularly the most powerful), by the fact that the Eurogroup is not an institution anchored in the EU treaties. The IMF has been added to form the Troika, for its "know-how", already having the appropriate reputation about its Washington consensus style adjustment programmes, which would lead to more neoliberal reforms in the adjustment countries. While Germany had initially been fiercely opposed that Greece as a euro area country would go to the IMF to ask for assistance of balance of payment problems, in a later phase it was particularly Germany who was most in favour of adding the IMF to the Troika, when the decisions on the first bailout programmes to Greece had already been taken. Indeed, the reason behind the change of attitude could be that the IMF usually assesses the debt sustainability of any candidate for an adjustment programme. In a case like Greece, the usual advice of the IMF would have been a haircut of the creditors, meaning a bailing-in of the banks which had provided the easy credits. In the case of Greece, this would have been mainly French and German banks (ESMT's Jörg Rochol).

The Commission had lost power within the euro area crisis management, in particular when we think of its "right to initiative". It had rather the role of a technocrat organization which had to prepare economic justifications for political guidelines or orders which came from the Eurogroup or single members of the Eurogroup and later execute them and monitor the implementation, for which the European Commission is being blamed as being the disadvantage of a more "politicized Commission" and for not having guarded its respective role as a guardian of the European Treaties and the acquis communautaire, including the Charter of Fundamental Rights and the Social Rights. One cannot but wonder if the Commission did take these decisions by Collegium and about the role of the Commissioner in charge of social policy. On the one hand, the Commission is blamed for not having been sufficiently strict in terms of monitoring the fiscal policies and situation of the Member States before the crisis. The later aspect has led to two reforms: on the one hand, a strengthened role for the Commission in the surveillance of the fiscal policies and, on the other hand, also to the establishment of the European Fiscal Board and analogous independent fiscal boards at national level.

The European Court of Justice warned in its Pringle Judgement of a certain conflict of interest of its role as the guardian of the Treaties and the one in the Troika. Additionally, the "instrumentalization" of the Commission by the Eurogroup within the Troika has also led to an increasing asymmetry of accountability of the European Commission between the EP and the Council.

The ECB's role was already addressed above; interestingly, the supranational pillar turned out to be the most effective regarding crisis management. However, on the downside was the "overreach" of an independent central bank on national governments policy priorities, with the double problematic that it cannot be its role and mandate and in particular without the "appropriate" democratic accountability neither at national nor at EU level. Should the ECB entitled to determine which kind of fiscal priorities, social policies and wage policies and collective bargaining a Member State should execute? Where in this scenario is the sovereign's will be playing a role and what meaning has the word democracy in within it? Additionally, a further criticism has been raised by Wehlan concerning the ECB's decision and cutting liquidity to Greece at the moment of the referendum on the austerity programme. It sheds a dubious light of political activism and interventionism on the ECB and exposes its conflict of interest as the central bank of all Member States, including of Greece, and its role as a creditor and supervisor of systemically relevant banks and within the Troika.

Schmidt (2015) argues that eurozone governance combined excessive intergovernmentalism with an increased supranationalism of the ECB pressing "Member States for more austerity measures and structural reforms in a quid pro quo for more vigorous monetary interventions" and the European Commission receiving more competences in budgetary oversight while the European Parliament remained largely sidelined. "The resulting rules-based and numbers-focused government framework has not only generated problems for the European economy; it has also cast doubts on the European Union's democratic legitimacy and its social solidarity". The eurocrisis has led to a regression of democracy in the EU, both at the national level of the periphery countries and at the regional level. Indeed, in parallel some core Member States parliaments have acquired increased power being able to impose to another MS policies and priorities, which have a strong impact on the lives of the citizens of other Member States. EMU has not only reduced the periphery and (later) indebted countries to the status of emerging countries by depriving them of the instrument of exchange rate devaluations, reducing their possibilities to let the automatic stabilizers work for a more rapid and social recovery but politically and democratically has degraded them to the status of colonies of the larger hegemons, by eroding the democratic rights of the peoples to decide on their economic and social policies and in the case of a crisis, at least on the priorities of which measures to take, thus undermining their sovereignty.

The intergovernmental framework with the exclusion or submission of the institutions standing for the general interest of the EU instrumentalized supranational institutions for the national interests of the hegemonic Member States by protecting their own national banks from major haircuts in a crisis caused by a global economic system and design of the EMU, which had largely been influenced by the same hegemons (and their banks), and even benefitting from the crisis through the interest. The involvement of the national parliaments of creditor countries in the decision-making process, including on the adjustment programmes, can in no way compensate the lack of decision power of the national parliament and social partners in determining the measures to combat the debt crisis in an equitable way and adjusted to local realities, needs and democratic priorities and to assist their economies in their recovery but rather illustrate the increasing asymmetry and disparity in democratic rights within the European Economic and Monetary Union. The EMU architecture has thus even led to an erosion of democracy both at EU level and at national level.

Conclusions

Ten years after the eurocrisis and more than 12 years after the global financial crisis broke out, EMU reforms have attempted to realize a banking union but have not completed it since it shies away from any risk-sharing instruments, schemes or tools such as a common backstop or a European Deposit Insurance Scheme. In the field of fiscal and budgetary policies, EMU actually strengthened the "risk avoidance" or ordo-liberal orientation and the straight jacket of the national finance ministers, giving greater surveillance powers to the European Commission, anchoring debt and deficit ceilings in national constitutions and facilitating sanctions at Council level. The "risk-sharing" or solidarity side of the economic governance framework with the creation of a possible euro area budget, a stabilization function, an unemployment insurance or reinsurance scheme or an EMF has not been realized to this date.

The paradigm change from Keynesianism to ordo- and neoliberalism has largely influenced the architects and design of monetary union, in particular leading to changes and omissions in regard to the more federalist predecessor, called the "Werner Plan", which had strong traits of Keynesianism. It is important to note that the paradigm change led to omission of central building stones of EMU which could have either helped to avert a crisis and increase crisis resilience or allowed a more efficient, equitable and democratic crisis management, such as the reflectance of the risks of deregulated financial markets, of internal imbalances, a euro area budget and other stabilization elements like the EMF, convergence policies, an evolution towards an economic union with the step-by-step transferral of decisions to the EU level and democratic accountability. While the EMU crisis management has avoided a sovereign default and the implosion of EMU, the new governance framework has prolonged and deepened the crisis and its economic and social consequences. In terms of equity, it has largely increased unemployment, poverty and income inequality; additionally it has led to a reversion of the achieved economic convergence. The measures implemented have not been able to reduce the debts of highly indebted countries and have worked largely procyclical, reducing growth and investment, also in the stronger economies, putting future competitiveness and the global role of the EU in question.

While economically the worst crisis is over, the political landscape has changed for good with an increase of political protest and historical mobilization of social movements, the mushrooming of new parties, the increasing polarization and radicalization of political parties. These developments can be interpreted as direct consequences of the negative input, output and throughput democracy (Schmidt 2015) and increasing disparity of democratic rights within the EU and at EU level.

Disclaimer The opinions expressed in this introduction/volume are the sole responsibility of the authors and do not necessarily represent the official position of the European Parliament or of any other EU institution.

Bibliography

Allen K., & Chazan G. (2018). Germany reaps a euro 2.9bn gain from Greek bond holdings. *Financial Times*, 22 June 2018.

Braun B., & Huebner M. (2019). *Vanishing Act: The Eurogroup's accountability*. https://transparency.eu/wp-content/uploads/2019/02/TI-EU-Eurogroup-report.pdf. Accessed 01 Mar 2020.

Danescu, E. (2018). The Werner report: A blueprint for EMU? In *Pierre Werner and Europe* (pp. 331–344). Cham: Palgrave Macmillan.

De Grauwe P. (2010). Fighting the wrong enemy, VOX CEPR Policy Portal, 19 May 2010.

De Grauwe P. (2011). A Fragile Eurozone in search of a better governance. CESifo Working Paper No. 3456, Apr 2011.

De Grauwe, P. (2015). Design failures of the Eurozone. In *The Eurozone crisis: A consensus view of the causes and a few possible remedies* (pp. 99–108). London: CEPR/VOX.

Draghi M. (2012). President of the European Central Bank, speech at the global investment conference in London, 26 July 2012. https://www.ecb.europa.eu/press/key/date/2012/html/sp120726.en.html. Accessed 01 Mar 2020.
Dijsselbloem J. (2017). Interview in the Frankfurter Allgemeine Zeitung, 20.3.2017.
ECB (2019). Occasional Paper Series No 232 / September 2019: Understanding low wage growth in the euro area and European countries. https://www.ecb.europa.eu/pub/pdf/scpops/ecb.op232~4b89088255.en.pdf
Eichengreen, B. (2012), European Monetary Integration with Benefit of Hindsight, *Journal Common Market Studies, 50*(S1), 123–36.
European Commission. (2008). Commission Communication COM (2008) 387 final on "The role of quality of public finances in the EU governance framework".
European Commission. (2015). Commission Communication COM (2015) 12 final on "Making the best use of the flexibility within the existing rules of the stability and growth pact", 13.1.2015.
European Council. (2014). Conclusions of 26/27 June 2014. https://www.consilium.europa.eu/media/39245/143477.pdf. Accessed 01 Mar 2020.
European Fiscal Board. (2019). Assessment of EU fiscal rules with a focus on the six and two-pack legislation. https://ec.europa.eu/info/publications/assessment-eu-fiscal-rules-focus-six-and-two-pack-legislation_en. Accessed 01 Mar 2020.
European Parliament. (2014a). Resolution of 13 March 2014 on the enquiry on the role and operations of the Troika (ECB, Commission and IMF) with regard to the euro area programme countries. https://www.europarl.europa.eu/sides/getDoc.do?pubRef=-//EP//TEXT+TA+P7-TA-2014-0239+0+DOC+XML+V0//EN. Accessed 01 March 2020.
European Parliament. (2014b). Working document on the on the review of the economic governance framework: stocktaking and challenges, ECON, Rapporteur Pervenche Beres, 17.10.2014.
European Parliament. (2016). Working document on the on the on a budgetary capacity for the Eurozone, ECON, Rapporteur Pervenche Beres, Reimer Boege, 19.2.2016.
European Fiscal Board. (2019), Assessment of EU fiscal rules with a focus on the six and two-pack legislation. https://ec.europa.eu/info/publications/assessment-eufiscal-rules-focus-six-and-two-pack-legislation_en. Accessed 01 Mar 2020.
Fasone, C. (2019). The emergence of 'Conflictual Cooperation' amongst parliaments in the economic and monetary union. *Reconnect Working Pape No. 3.* Feb 2019.
Folan O. E. (2015). Book review: The Lure of Technocracy by Jürgen Habermas. https://blogs.lse.ac.uk/europpblog/2015/08/09/book-review-the-lure-of-technocracy/. Accessed 01 Mar 2020.
Griffith-Jones, S. (2014). From austerity to growth in Europe: Some lessons from Latin America. In J. Stiglitz & D. Heymann (Eds.), *Life after debt: The origins and resolutions of debt crisis.* New York: Springer.
Hoffmann-Althelm, L. (2017). Two sides of the same coin? Independence and accountability of the European Central Bank. https://transparency.eu/wp-content/uploads/2017/03/TI-EU_ECB_Report_DIGITAL.pdf. Accessed 01 March 2020.
IMF (2009). Global Stability Financial Stability Report, April, (Washington DC: IMF). 48–49 pp, April 2009.
Kang, D. W., Ligthart, N., & Mody, A. (2016). The ECB and the Fed: A comparative narrative. VOX CEPR's Policy Portal, 19. January 2019.
Khan, M., & McClean P. (2017). Dijsselbloem under fire after saying Eurozone countries wasted money on alcohol and women. *Financial Times*, 21 Mar 2017.
Mersch, Governor of the Central Bank of Luxembourg, at a lecture in memory of Mr Pierre Werner, organised by the Official Monetary and Financial Institutions Forum (OMFIF), London, 14 Oct 2010.
Mody A. (2015). Living Dangerously (without) A Fiscal Union, Bruegel Working papers, 2015/03.https://bruegel.org/wp-content/uploads/imported/publications/WP_2015_03.pdf. Accessed 01 Mar 2020.
Moscovici P. (2015). After the Greek psychodrama, what improvements for the EMU? Notre Europe. https://institutdelors.eu/wp-content/uploads/2018/01/discoursmoscovicimacifen-jdisep2015.pdf. Accessed 01 Mar 2020.

Moscovici, P (2017). Interview in Corriere della Sera, 2 Sept 2017. https://www.corriere.it/economia/17_settembre_03/moscovici-l-italia-contenga-debito-si-ministro-finanze-ue-8ca48f7a-901e-11e7-90ab-5e72a21f32c7.shtml?refresh_ce-cp. Accessed 01 Mar 2020.

Oltermann P. (2015). Merkel 'gambling away' Germany's reputation over Greece, says Habermas. *The Guardian*, 16 Jul 2015. https://www.theguardian.com/business/2015/jul/16/merkel-gambling-away-germanys-reputation-over-greece-says-habermas. Accessed 01 Mar 2020.

Riekmann, S. P., & Wydra, D. (2013). Representation in the European state of emergency: Parliaments against governments? *Journal of European Integration, 35*(5), 565–582.

Rocholl, J., & Stahmer, A. (2016). Where did the Greek bailout money go. *ESMT White Paper No. WP–16, 2.*

Sachs, J. (2015). Death by debt-my response to The German Finance Ministry. *SZ (Süddeutsche Zeitung) International.*

Schmidt Vivien A. (2015), The Eurozone's crisis of democratic legitimacy: Can the EU rebuild public trust and support for European economic integration? European Commission, ISSN 2443-8022 (online), discussion paper 015 I Sept 2015.

Schoeller, M. G. (2017). Providing political leadership? Three case studies on Germany's ambiguous role in the eurozone crisis. *Journal of European Public Policy, 24*(1), 1–20.

Schulmeister, S. (2018). *From prosperity into the crisis and back: On the role of economic theories in the long cycle* (No. 571). WIFO Working Papers.

Singleton, J. (2011), Central Banking im the Twentieth Century, Cambridge University Press.

Smith-Meyer, B., & R. Heath (2017). Eurogroup confronts own deficit: governance. https://www.politico.eu/article/eurogroup-urged-to-tackle-its-own-deficit-governance/?utm_source=RSS_Feed&utm_medium=RSS&utm_campaign=RSS_Syndication. Accessed 01 Mar 2020.

Thompson, H. (2015). Germany and the Euro-zone crisis: The European reformation of the German banking crisis and the future of the Euro. *New Political Economy, 20*(6), 851–870.

Varoufakis, Y. (2017). *Adults in the room: My battle with the European and American deep establishment*. New York: Farrar, Straus and Giroux.

Veld Jan intl. (2013). Fiscal consolidations and spillovers in the euro area periphery and core. Economic Papers 506, European Commission, Oct 2013. https://ec.europa.eu/economy_finance/publications/economic_paper/2013/pdf/ecp506_en.pdf. Accessed 01 Mar 2020.

von Goethe, J. W. (1797). Der Zauberlehrling.

Werner, P. (1970). Report to the Council and the Commission on the realisation by stages of Economic and Monetary Union in the Community- "Werner Report"-(definitive text) [8 October 1970]. Bulletin of the European Communities, Supplement 11/1970.

Wolf, M. (2014). *The shifts and the shocks: What we've learned–and have still to learn–from the financial crisis*. UK: Penguin.

5

Crisis Management in the Eurozone: Democratic Legitimacy and Socioeconomic Impacts

Dimitris Katsikas

Abstract This chapter focuses on two significant aspects of crisis management in the Eurozone: (a) its democratic legitimacy and (b) its socioeconomic consequences. The two issues are very important, since both the socioeconomic effects of an adjustment program and its democratic credentials determine to a large extent its "ownership" by local societies and consequently its chances of success. Effectively, these two aspects refer to the "input" and "output" side of democratic legitimacy, that is, to legitimation through democratic processes and representation, and policy outcomes respectively. The analysis evaluates the first aspect of the legitimacy equation using criteria derived from democratic theory and applying them to the governance structure of the bailout programs. On the second aspect of legitimacy, that of outcomes, the socioeconomic consequences of the crisis management are reviewed, and their distributive aspects discussed. The chapter demonstrates that the EU's legitimacy has suffered along both aspects as a result of the crisis and the way it was handled. This leaves the EU in a particularly vulnerable state in the event of a future crisis.

Introduction

The European Economic and Monetary Union (EMU) proved the biggest victim of the global financial crisis that broke out in 2008. This was due to two factors: (a) the incomplete nature of the EMU and (b) the lack of a supranational crisis mechanism. By now, it is commonly acknowledged that before the crisis, significant imbalances had emerged among the economies of EMU's member states. Countries in the monetary union's periphery exhibited sluggish productivity growth which, coupled with high credit inflows, led to unsustainable current account deficits (Baldwin and

D. Katsikas (✉)
National and Kapodistrian University of Athens and Hellenic Foundation for European and Foreign Policy (ELIAMEP), Athens, Greece
e-mail: dkatsikas@eliamep.gr

Giavazzi 2015). Investors from the capital-rich North directed their funds to profitable investments in the relatively capital-poor South. However, these capital flows did not fund productive investments; they were instead directed toward the non-tradable sectors of these countries' economies, raising wages and inflation, undermining further their already weak international competitiveness, and boosting asset and real estate prices, thereby creating financial bubbles; in some countries, they were also used to fund mounting fiscal deficits. When, in the aftermath of the global financial crisis, there was a "sudden stop" of the capital flows, these countries had to face a harsh adjustment process. The EMU could not deal with such imbalances because of its flawed governance; its monetary pillar, built around the European Central Bank (ECB), had a clear institutional framework, a strong policy mandate and statutory independence from political interference. On the other hand, the remaining governance pillars were weak. In fiscal policy, the Stability and Growth Pact lacked enforcement powers and proved unable to control fiscal laxity in many member states (Begg 2011). Moreover, there was no supranational coordinating mechanism for the EU-wide stance of fiscal policy and its synchronization with ECB's monetary policy. In terms of broader economic policy surveillance, the Council's voluntary Broad Economic Policy Guidelines proved completely ineffective (Pisani-Ferry 2006). As a result, the EU lacked effective institutions with a clear mandate to prevent excessive imbalances.

Still, these imbalances did not have to lead to a full-blown regional debt crisis, which threatened the survival of the EMU itself. A major reason for this development was the absence of a crisis handling mechanism in the EMU, which led to an ad hoc, intergovernmental, and increasingly political handling of the crisis. In this context, "moral hazard" preoccupations prevailed; creditor countries worried that facilitating the recovery of crisis-hit countries would ease the pressure for fiscal adjustment and reforms. Such a rationale was also dictated by the politics of the time: bailing out crisis-hit countries that were depicted in the press as spendthrift and/or corrupt was not a particularly popular proposition, especially following the public bailouts of banks during the financial crisis only a couple of years earlier. The result was crisis management along an "individual responsibility" approach: every country needed to get its house in order (Katsikas 2012). This approach had two main characteristics:

(a) Individual bailout programs for each country that could not fund itself in the markets. The bailout loans were accompanied by conditionality; countries signed Memoranda of Understanding (MoUs), which spelled out the policy measures and structural reforms that had to be implemented in exchange for the funds. The design of the conditionality[1] and the supervision of its implementation were the responsibility of the Troika, which comprised representatives of

[1] The design of the programs was decided together with the governments of the countries receiving the loans, which had the opportunity to propose measures of their own, particularly regarding the more detailed aspects of the policies put forward; having said that, the proposed measures had to be approved by the Troika.

the creditors, namely, the European Commission, the ECB, and the International Monetary Fund (IMF). The reforms promoted had a liberal direction, aiming to improve the international competitiveness of these countries; in some cases, the MoUs also included comprehensive public administration reforms, with the aim to increase the efficiency and the fiscal sustainability of the state mechanism. It is worth noting that similar policies were promoted by countries which did not sign a bailout agreement, but faced similar problems, as was the case with Spain, which signed a more limited bailout agreement for its financial sector, and to a lesser degree, Italy.

(b) The cost of the adjustment process was entirely borne by the crisis-hit countries. The MoUs were the only way to deal with the crisis; there was no scope for any supranational mechanism of compensation for the economic and social losses of the adjustment process or for encouraging growth in the economies facing a deep recession, in large part, due to the promoted austerity policies. Some EU-wide growth funding initiatives, such as the Compact for Growth and Jobs agreed at the European Council of June 2012, were put forward but were never really implemented. An investment mechanism, the so-called Juncker Plan, was effectively put in place much later, after 2015, during the recovery of the European economy; it is worth noting that even this mechanism did not involve new public funding, but relied on the redeployment of already available funds in the EU budget and mainly the leveraging of new private funds.

This approach produced negative results not only for the affected economies but also for the cohesion and public support of the EU itself. The conditionality imposed through the MoUs in crisis-hit countries was extensive, ambitious, and in certain respects harsh, as was the case with the austerity policies promoted. This in turn caused or at the very least deepened the economic recession affecting the countries receiving the bailout funds. As a result, in the countries of the South, people living in adverse material circumstances felt alienated, disappointed, and increasingly angry by what they perceived to be a lack of solidarity by the European Union and the countries of the North, whom they often accused as responsible for the crisis. On the other hand, in the countries of Northern Europe, there was also a growing feeling of hostility developing toward the European project, as citizens questioned the decisions of their governments to "bail out" the countries of the South, which were often portrayed as "reckless" and "irresponsible." This rift, and more broadly the way the crisis was handled, ultimately undermined the legitimacy of the EU itself.

The aim of this chapter is to examine how the democratic legitimacy of the EU was affected by the crisis and the way this was handled, with a focus on the crisis-hit countries and particularly those of the European South. After a brief introduction in the issue of democratic legitimacy in the EU, different aspects of the crisis management will be analyzed, and their impact on the democratic legitimacy of the EU will be evaluated.

EU's Legitimacy Before the Crisis

The political authority to issue rules and policy dictates necessitates legitimacy, that is, a sense of obligation on the part of the subjects of authority to conform to its pronouncements (Flathman 1980). Authority is not obeyed because people consider its individual decrees and rules to be always in their individual interest but due to a sense of obligation and an acknowledgement of the legitimate right of authority to issue commands and pronouncements. In this sense, legitimacy is a prerequisite not only for the effective operation but also for the very existence of political authority.[2] In democratic regimes, this sense of obligation stems from the assurance that governments represent the people and that they will exercise their authority in ways which serve the people's interests in accordance with their values. These two aspects are often analyzed separately as two different forms of legitimacy: input and output legitimacy (Scharpf 1999; Schmidt 2013).[3] Input legitimacy refers to processes which ensure the representation of the interests and values of the people in policy-making, primarily by establishing the accountability of policy-makers to the people, for example, through electoral processes. Output legitimacy refers to policy outcomes; legitimacy is ensured when the promoted policies do in fact serve the common good and improve the lives of the citizens. Political authority in democracies necessitates both types of legitimacy, but there is a trade-off; if a political entity is somewhat lacking in one dimension, it can "make it up" in the other dimension (Schmidt 2015).

Before the crisis, EU's record in terms of democratic legitimacy was mixed. Its input legitimacy was considered by many as lacking. Indeed, there was a lively academic debate about the so-called EU's democratic deficit (Weiler et al. 1995; Majone 1998; Moravcsik 2002, 2008; Follesdal and Hix 2006; Hix 2008). Follesdal and Hix (2006) summarized the arguments of the critics into five distinct claims, which referred to the strengthening of the executive power, at both the national and EU levels, at the expense of parliamentary control; the related weakness of the European Parliament and the absence of truly "European" elections; the distance of EU from the voters, who do not really understand and identify with it; and as a consequence of all the above, a "policy drift" away from voters' "ideal" policy preferences. Others objected to this critique; Andrew Moravcsik, one the leading scholars in EU studies, has rejected the democratic deficit theory as a myth, arguing that the EU is a limited-purpose organization which should not be held to an ideal standard of democracy more appropriate for nation states. Indeed, he believes that even

[2] This is true not only for democracy but for all kinds of government. What changes are the criteria based on which authority is judged; for example, in monarchies it could be blood lineage and the divine right, or in more primitive societies the sanctity of tradition. Having said that, the prolonged deterioration of people's living standards will ultimately erode authority, irrespective of its source.

[3] Vivien Schmidt has added another aspect of democratic legitimacy in her analysis, the so-called throughput legitimacy, which effectively refers to the quality of governance processes (e.g., transparency, inclusiveness, etc.). This aspect is not examined here.

within the confines of its limited mandate, the EU "is at least as democratic, and generally more so, than its member states" (Moravcsik 2008, p. 332).

While Moravcsik may be right that the EU has a more limited mandate compared to national governments and that on the whole its function is subject to a – not inconsequential – array of democratic checks and balances, it is hard to deny the claim that the EU citizens do not understand or identify with the EU. Indeed, the very progress of European integration has been associated with the lack of citizens' participation; European elites have been thought to enjoy a "permissive consensus" by the general public, which allowed them significant leeway in promoting the project of European integration (Lindberg and Scheingold 1970). Democratization always came afterward in an effort to catch up with the integration progress, which was mainly driven by economic considerations (Fossum 2016).

In this context, the European integration process before the crisis was mostly driven by output legitimacy. As long as integration yielded economic benefits for the member states, it did not become an issue of strong political contestation in European societies. The advanced economies of the North took advantage of the benefits offered by the European single market to boost further their competitiveness and leverage the international presence of their companies, while the poorer countries of the South received significant economic aid in the form of structural funds, intended to help their economies adjust and gradually converge to those of the North. Later, the new entrants from Central and Eastern Europe also became beneficiaries of such funding and through their participation in the single market were able to link their economies to global value chains and receive substantial investment inflows. In this sense, before the crisis, the less than perfect record of the EU in terms of input legitimacy did not pose a major obstacle in European integration because the EU was thought to deliver prosperity to its citizens.[4]

EU's Legitimacy After the Crisis

The crisis undermined the legitimacy of the EU in a number of ways. The handling of the crisis raised serious concerns regarding its conformity to democratic norms, weakening further the already challenged input legitimacy of the EU. At the same time, the intensity and extent of the crisis, related to the austerity policies promoted through the MoUs, severely undermined its output legitimacy.

[4] Still, already before the crisis, problems in terms of legitimacy were becoming increasingly visible. The deepening and widening of the integration process that followed the Maastricht Treaty weakened the permissive consensus. European integration became increasingly intertwined with issues pertaining to core aspects of national sovereignty and identity, making it more controversial and politicized, and thus increasingly part of domestic party politics; as a result, it gradually started becoming subject to an intensifying "constraining dissensus" (Hooghe and Marks 2009).

EU's Input Legitimacy and the Crisis

Turning first to the issue of input legitimacy, the MoUs and the Troika challenged democratic norms of policy-making at both the national and EU levels. More specifically, at the EU level, the institutional set-up and operation of the Troika and the policies promoted through the MoUs produced a number of challenges for democratic legitimacy. First, the Troika was an ad hoc institutional mechanism, created in haste to deal with the crisis. This created several problems: there were no established procedures, in relation to the other EU institutions and in particular the European Parliament, which could increase the democratic accountability of its operation. Moreover, the IMF, being an international economic organization, had no obligation to inform or report to European institutions about its actions and decisions in the context of the Troika. All in all, there was lack of transparency in Troika's decision-making which undermined its accountability. Moreover, the Troika had no legal mandate stemming from the EU Treaties and no clearly defined objective. As a result, procedures were followed which did not have any legal basis, putting in doubt not only the legitimacy but also the legality of its actions; for example, Eurogroup's mandate to the European Commission to negotiate on its behalf the details of the bailout programs with the countries receiving the loans was legally unfounded, as such a procedure is not specified in EU law and because the Eurogroup is not an official EU body (European Parliament Report 2014, p. 16).[5]

Secondly, Troika's composition was highly problematic: both the European Commission and the European Central Bank faced serious conflicts of interest. More specifically, as part of the Troika, the European Commission was acting as an agent of the member states, which had authorized it to negotiate and supervise the implementation of the bailout programs. At the same time, the European Commission is considered the "guardian of the Treaties," the supranational organ entrusted to supervise the application of EU laws and norms. In other words, the European Commission came to act as both the agent and the "supervisor" of national governments, and more often than not, this conflict worked at the expense of the latter role, which however is the one institutionally assigned to the European Commission. Moreover, in terms of the MoUs' policy content, the bailout programs' conditionality extended to policy areas such as healthcare, labor, and social policy, which for the most part are outside the remit of EU policy competence. In addition, many of the policies promoted violated either directly or indirectly, through their results, the principles enshrined in essential EU legal texts such as the Charter of Fundamental Rights of the EU or strategic policy agendas like "Europe 2020," exposing once again the untenable position of the Commission as both the guardian and violator of EU principles.

Similar problems were also raised with relation to ECB's role in the Troika, as its role extended well beyond its mandate regarding monetary policy. Indeed, the ECB

[5] Regulation (EU) No 472/2013 changed this, as it provided an institutional basis for the operation of the Troika.

was involved in decisions relating to fiscal, wage, and financial policies and structural reforms in a number of policy areas, all of which were well outside its authority. These decisions had often significant distributional consequences (e.g., its decision not to bail in the senior-bondholders of the Irish banks in 2010), were employed by the Troika as leverage during the negotiations of the bailout agreements (e.g., the threatened termination of emergency liquidity assistance in the cases of Ireland and Cyprus in 2010 and 2013, respectively, and its actual termination in the case of Greece in early 2015), and/or constituted direct interventions in the political system of the countries in crisis, as was the case with the letters sent by the ECB to the governments of Spain, Italy, and Ireland. These actions proved controversial and had clear political ramifications, which undermined the status of the ECB and its credibility as a central bank independent from politics. What is more, the ECB's accountability framework was not appropriate for this kind of political decision-making, which further undermined the legitimacy of these decisions (Transparency International EU 2017).

The problems with the Troika's institutional set-up were not unrelated to the new mode of EU's operation during the crisis. In the course of the crisis, decisions were increasingly taken in the context of a renewed intergovernmentalism, where the European Council took the decision-making initiative and the Eurogroup acted as its "legislative-executive arm," setting out more detailed guidelines for the European Commission. The latter, in its role as the initiator of EU policies and the European Parliament as a co-decision agent and an accountability mechanism, were largely sidestepped. It is telling that both of EU's funding mechanisms, the European Financial Stability Facility (EFSF) and the European Stability Mechanism (ESM), were created on the basis of intergovernmental agreements, outside the EU legal framework. The same is true for one of the most important reforms of the EU's economic governance following the crisis, the so-called Fiscal Compact. Intergovernmental bargaining meant that the creditor countries, enjoying a highly asymmetrical negotiating advantage, came to dictate the terms of the bailout agreements according to their national preferences (Schimmelfennig 2015). In this context, established EU rules, norms, and practices often took second place in the negotiating table.

Beyond undermining democratic legitimacy at the EU level, the dominance of creditor countries' preferences in the design and implementation of bailout agreements affected negatively the input legitimacy of the MoUs in crisis-hit countries as well. The perception that the policies contained in the MoUs, and more generally the terms of the agreements, were dictated by the countries of the North and imposed on the countries in the South receiving the loans undermined from the beginning the "ownership" of the programs.[6] According to the IMF itself, ownership is a key factor for the success of a bailout program (IMF 2006). If the prevailing perception in

[6]According to the IMF, "National ownership refers to a commitment to a program of policies, by country officials who have the responsibility to formulate and carry out those policies, based on their understanding that the program is achievable and is in the country's best interests" (IMF 2006, p. 1).

a country is that conditionality is externally imposed, or that the program serves the interests of particular interest groups, in or even out of the country (Gould 2003), then opposition to the program conditionality is likely to be high, particularly when the proposed measures inflict economic losses on large parts of the population, as was the case with the MoUs' austerity and internal devaluation policies.

Moreover, opposition can be high against structural reforms. Structural reforms have distributional consequences, which can produce resistance not only from those that know that they stand to lose but also from broader population groups, which face uncertainty over the distribution of costs and benefits and opt for the risk-averse solution of the status quo (Fernández and Rodrik 1991). The MoUs promoted reforms, which were unrealistically ambitious, anticipating major restructuring in a wide array of policy areas, ranging from the labor and product markets to public administration and the welfare state, in a short period of time. This created uncertainty, disrupting further the depressed economies, undermined the effectiveness of the reforms, and created losers who resisted the MoUs' conditionality. The combined effect of austerity and structural reforms, in combination with the widely shared, and largely accurate, impression that the MoUs were imposed by the creditor countries, completely undermined ownership of the promoted policies; in other words there was a lack of socio-political consensus for the promoted policies, which for large parts of the population rendered them effectively "unauthorized" (Bellamy and Weale 2015).

This impression was progressively strengthened by the fact that the same kinds of policies were promoted despite the alternation of parties with different ideological orientation in government. It was as if it did not matter which government was in power; elections produced different governments, but not different policies. This effectively "hollowed out" the domestic political process, resulting in what has been termed "politics without policy" (Schmidt 2015) or "politics of constrained choice" (Laffan 2014). This political impression took on a substantive institutional manifestation in the way national parliaments operated during the crisis. The functioning of national parliaments became hostage to a permanent "state of emergency," which allowed incumbent governments to pass bills with limited parliamentary oversight under emergency procedures, which effectively forbade a comprehensive discussion of the proposed measures; in effect parliaments became rubber-stamping institutions for policies decided in intergovernmental negotiations at the EU level, while in some cases they were completely by-passed, as was the case in Portugal where the MoU was not brought to parliament for ratification. The continuous erosion of MoUs' input legitimacy undermined public trust in domestic political systems, which in turn created space for the emergence of populist and Eurosceptic parties. In other words, the way the crisis was handled undermined not only the democratic legitimacy of the EU but also that of the domestic political institutions, raising concerns about the quality and operation of democracy in crisis-hit countries.

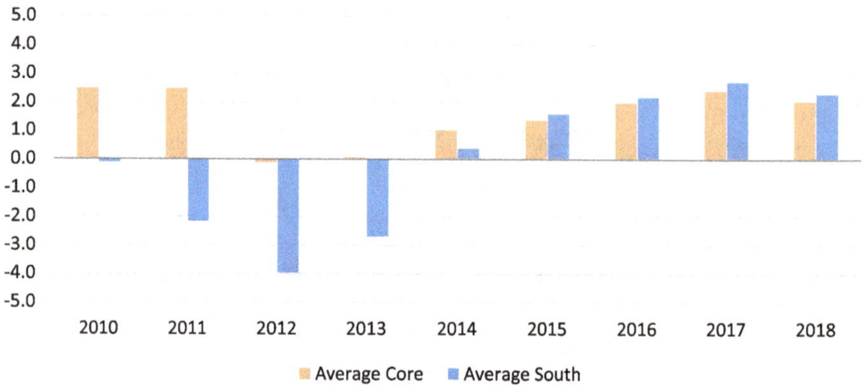

Fig. 5.1 Average growth rates in the EU Core and in the EU South (gross domestic product at market prices, chain linked volumes, percentage change on previous period, 2010–2018). Note: Core countries include Austria, Belgium, Finland, France, Germany, and the Netherlands; "South" countries include Cyprus, Greece, Italy, Portugal, and Spain. (Source: Author's elaboration of Eurostat data)

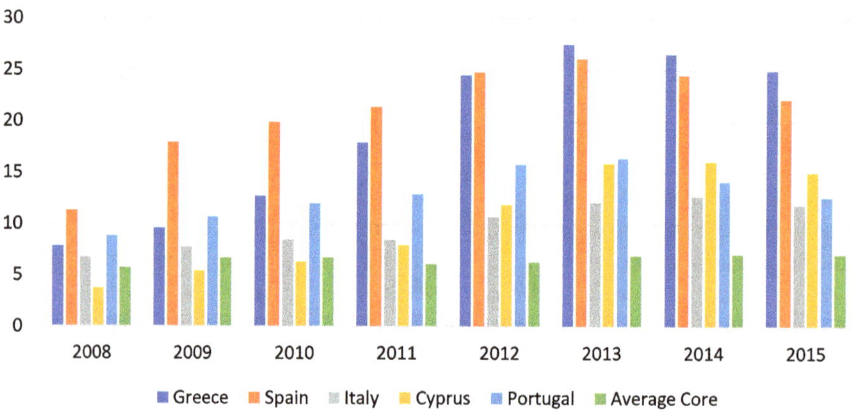

Fig. 5.2 Unemployment rate, countries of the EU South and average EU Core (% active population, 2008–2015). (Source: Author's elaboration of Eurostat data)

The Impact of the Crisis and EU's Output Legitimacy

The erosion of input legitimacy due to the policies promoted under the MoUs could have been perhaps tolerated by the publics in crisis-hit countries, if these measures improved their economic situation. On the contrary, the policies promoted produced severe negative short-term economic consequences, which undermined the hitherto strong pillar of EU's democratic legitimacy, that of output legitimacy.

The austerity and internal devaluation policies led to a sharp decline of disposable income and economic activity, which sent the crisis-hit economies into recession (Fig. 5.1).[7] The negative income shock was combined with problems in the banking sector, already ailing from the global financial crisis, and long-term structural weaknesses that kept productivity and international competitiveness low. These problems made recovery difficult, particularly as the Troika persisted in setting unrealistic fiscal targets, which did not take into account the effects of the recession, necessitating thereby new austerity measures, a process which drove economies into a downward economic spiral. As a result, unemployment rates rose fast, often reaching unprecedented levels, as was the case in Greece and Spain (Fig. 5.2). The situation in the labor market was in sharp contrast with that of the countries of the "core," which experienced mild increases in their unemployment rate if at all (e.g., Germany's unemployment rate kept falling from 2010 onward and throughout the crisis).

The large numbers of unemployed people in turn meant a deterioration of their material circumstances, made worse by the well-known weaknesses of the welfare systems in the countries of Southern Europe (Ferrera 1996). In addition to fragmentation and operational inefficiencies, the welfare system in these countries struggled to cope financially, under circumstances of declining income flows as a result of reduced insurance contributions (due to the rising unemployment) and state funding (due to austerity policies), while needs for expenditures rose (e.g., for

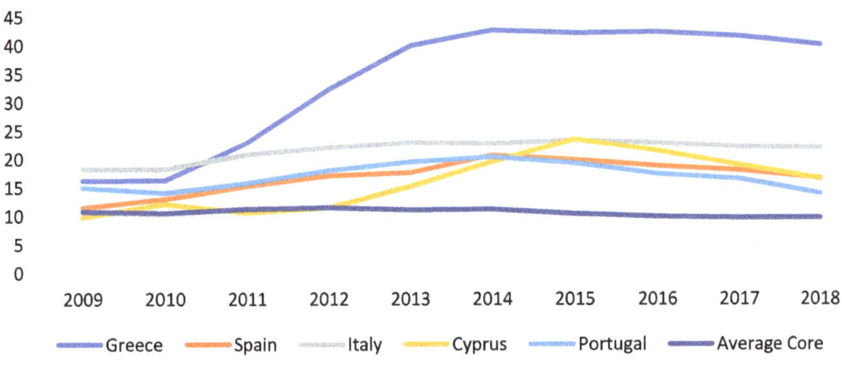

Fig. 5.3 At-risk-of-poverty rate anchored at a fixed moment in time (2005) by age and sex, countries of the EU South and average EU Core (% of the population 2009–2018). Note 1: A fixed poverty line measures poverty compared to a fixed level of income which does not change through time. A fixed poverty line can be a very useful analytical tool in cases of big and rapid positive or negative changes in economic output in a country. In such circumstances there is a tendency for the entire distribution to move upward (or downward), leaving thus relative poverty largely unchanged. Accordingly, in such circumstances it makes sense to compare peoples' level of living not with other people in the same society, but with the same peoples' living circumstances of only a few years ago, before the boom (crisis) took hold.) . Note 2: The "average core" excludes France due data unavailability. (Source: Author's elaboration of Eurostat data)

[7] The graph does not include Ireland due to some uncertainty regarding its GDP statistics, particularly during the recovery period after 2015. See, for example, Halpin (2016).

unemployment benefits). As a result, levels of poverty and/or social exclusion started to rise substantially, Greece being in a category of its own (Fig. 5.3). The result was a social crisis, which fed further people's anger, contributed to the delegitimation of domestic political systems and the quest for alternative solutions, often found in the rhetoric of populist parties.

Why did the creditors insist on policies that sent the crisis-hit economies in recession and stirred social and political turmoil? The answer lies in the way the crisis was handled; the intergovernmental and highly political handling of the crisis led to bailout programs whose overriding priority was the reduction of fiscal deficits and the sustainability of public debt. The reasons for this were twofold: firstly, the obvious desire of creditors to limit their funding to debtor countries, in order to safeguard their own fiscal integrity, but most importantly to address the concerns that dominated domestic political discourse about using taxpayers money to bail out the "irresponsible" partners in the South; secondly, to limit the "moral hazard" associated with bailing out the countries in crisis, that is, the danger that they would become dependent on such financing and relax their fiscal consolidation and reform efforts.

The desire to limit moral hazard was evident in the rhetoric adapted to justify the proposed policies; the crisis was typically presented as one of fiscal profligacy on the part of the debtor countries, which does not stand up to scrutiny given the solid fiscal record of countries like Ireland and Spain before the global financial crisis. Nonetheless this became the dominant narrative in the early stages of the crisis and affected the design of the programs, which emphasized front-loaded austerity and a "big-bang" of structural reforms. This unavoidably led to a "one-size-fits-all" approach, which proved problematic because there was disregard for the distinct features of these economies, as well as for the different causes of the crisis in different countries. As a result, Troika's projections proved highly erroneous (typically over-optimistic) and led to the oft-cited IMF's acknowledgement of its failure to calculate properly the fiscal multipliers (Blanchard and Leigh 2013), on which the design of austerity policies had been based. Similar mistakes were repeated in the area of structural reforms, where knowledge of local economic realities but also of political and institutional characteristics are more important. Rodrik (2016) has criticized the ambitious "big-bang" programs, which eventually resulted in micromanagement of the economy and/or the public service, costing precious political capital while producing moderate economic results.

The internal devaluation policies are a case in point; one of the factors that may account for the very different trajectories of Greece and Ireland during the crisis is the fact that Ireland's labor and product markets were considered flexible and dynamic before the crisis, which maximized the benefits of the internal devaluation policy that was adopted; in Greece on the other hand, the internal devaluation policy did not yield similar results, given the closed nature of the economy and the structural rigidities in the product and labor markets (see, e.g., Zografakis and Kastelli 2017). Indeed, it seems that in Greece, the focus on internal devaluation led to a sequencing of reforms in the labor and product markets which proved counter-productive in terms of economic results (Petralias et al. 2018), but highly disruptive in terms of its social and political repercussions.

All these problems were not new; they have all been documented before in the literature on the IMF, which has also been criticized for the "one-size-fits-all" approach (e.g., Stiglitz 2002; Ostry et al. 2016) and for biased, typically over-optimistic, projections (e.g., Atoyan and Conway 2011). Despite this knowledge and previous experience, the same mistakes were repeated causing social, political, and institutional backlash which not only undermined the effectiveness of the reforms but also strengthened Eurosceptic rhetoric, attitudes, and parties.

Conclusions

Before the crisis, EU's democratic legitimacy record was mixed. Its input legitimacy was challenged from many quarters, but European integration continued to progress given the material prosperity it was thought to deliver to Europeans. The crisis delivered a blow to the democratic legitimacy of the EU. Its already challenged input legitimacy suffered further, as the ad hoc, intergovernmental, and increasingly political handling of the crisis violated EU norms and institutions. The resulting policies were forced on crisis-hit member states, with limited parliamentary scrutiny and democratic debate, hollowing out the domestic political systems. Such practices created space for anti-systemic and Eurosceptic populist parties, which gained strength in a number of member states.

In recent years, economic recovery has improved the image of the EU once again, confirming to some degree the output legitimacy hypothesis. However, significant challenges remain. While the image of the EU has almost fully recovered, trust in the EU is still well below its pre-crisis levels for most countries (see Chap. 16, of Verney and Katsikas, this volume). Moreover, the damage to the credibility and legitimacy of domestic political institutions is harder to overcome; the refugee crisis of 2015–2016 added strength to the rise of populist, Eurosceptic, and nationalistic parties, not only in the crisis-hit countries but also in the countries of the North. Moreover, the economic and social consequences of the crisis are still not fully overcome in most of the crisis-hit countries. This increases their vulnerability to the effects of a new international or European crisis; indeed, such fears are on the rise again given the slowdown in the world and European economy in 2018 and 2019. In sum, while the EU was able to overcome the crisis, the way this was handled has left a negative legacy of political mistrust toward both the EU and the domestic political systems, which has undermined their democratic legitimacy. Given the additional pressures that have arisen due to the refugee crisis and the growing discontent about the effects of globalization, this legacy may be more lasting and consequential than it currently appears.

References

Atoyan, R., & Conway, P. (2011). Projecting macroeconomic outcomes: Evidence from the IMF. *Review of International Organizations, 6*(3), 415–441.

Baldwin, R., & Giavazzi, F. (Eds.) (2015). *The Eurozone Crisis: A consensus view of the causes and a few possible solutions*. A VoxEU.org eBook, CEPR Press.

Begg, I. (2011). Prevent or cure? Dilemmas facing economic governance. In I. Begg, A. Belke, S. Dullien, D. Schwarzer, & R. Vilpišauskas (Eds.), *European economic governance: Impulses for crisis prevention and new institutions*. Bertelsmann Stiftung. https://www.yumpu.com/en/document/view/49720762/european-economic-governance-bertelsmann-stiftung. Accessed 30 Oct 2019.

Bellamy, R., & Weale, A. (2015). Political legitimacy and European monetary union: Contracts, constitutionalism and the normative logic of two-level games. *Journal of European Public Policy, 22*(2), 257–274.

Blanchard, O., & Leigh, D. (2013). Growth forecast errors and fiscal multipliers. *American Economic Review, 103*(3), 117–120.

European Parliament. (2014). *Report on the enquiry on the role and operations of the Troika (ECB, Commission and IMF) with regard to the Euro area programme countries (2013/2277(INI))*, Committee on Economic and Monetary Affairs, A7-0149/2014, 28.2.2014. https://www.europarl.europa.eu/cmsdata/59739/att_20140305ATT80482-1284267003893663985.pdf Accessed 30 Oct 2019.

Fernández, R., & Rodrik, D. (1991). Resistance to reform: Status quo bias in the presence of individual-specific uncertainty. *American Economic Review, 81*(5), 1146–1156.

Ferrera, M. (1996). The "southern model" of welfare in social Europe. *Journal of European Social Policy, 6*(1), 17–37.

Flathman, R. E. (1980). *The practice of political authority: Authority and the authoritative*. Chicago and London: The University of Chicago Press.

Follesdal, A., & Hix, S. (2006). Why there is a democratic deficit in the EU: A response to Majone and Moravcsik. *Journal of Common Market Studies, 44*, 533–562.

Fossum, J. E. (2016). Democracy and Legitimacy in the EU: Challenges and Options. IAI Working Papers 16. http://www.iai.it/sites/default/files/iaiwp1601.pdf. Accessed 30 October 2019.

Gould, E. R. (2003). Money talks: Supplementary financiers and international monetary fund conditionality. *International Organization, 57*, 551–586.

Halpin, P. (2016, July 13). *Leprechaun economics' leaves Irish growth story in limbo*. Reuters. https://www.reuters.com/article/us-ireland-economy/leprechaun-economics-leaves-irish-growth-story-in-limbo-idUSKCN0ZT21K. Accessed 10 Nov 2019.

Hix, S. (2008). *What's wrong with the European Union and how to fix it*. Cambridge: Polity Press.

Hooghe, L., & Marks, G. (2009). A post-functionalist theory of European integration: From permissive consensus to constraining dissensus. *British Journal of Political Science, 39*(1), 1–23.

International Monetary Fund. (2006). *Statement of the IMF Staff principles underlying the guidelines on conditionality*, Revised January 9. https://www.imf.org/external/np/pp/eng/2006/010906.pdf. Accessed 20 Sept 2019.

Katsikas, D. (2012). Η ισχύς εν τη πιστώσει: Η Γερμανία και το έλλειμμα ηγεσίας της Ευρωζώνης. *Greek Review of Political Science*, 39, May–November.

Laffan, B. (2014). Testing times: The growing primacy of responsibility in the Euro area. *West European Politics, 37*(2), 270–287.

Lindberg, L. N., & Scheingold, S. A. (1970). *Europe's would-be polity: Patterns of change in the European community*. Englewood Cliffs, N.J: Prentice-Hall.

Majone, G. (1998). Europe's 'democratic deficit': The question of standards. *European Law Journal, 4*(1), 5–28.

Moravcsik, A. (2002). Reassessing legitimacy in the European Union. *Journal of Common Market Studies., 40*(4), 603–624.

Moravcsik, A. (2008). The myth of Europe's democratic deficit. *Intereconomics: Journal of European Public Policy*, (November–December), 331–340.

Ostry, J. D., Loungani, P., & Furceri, D. (2016). Neoliberalism: Oversold? *Finance and Development*, June, 38–41.

Petralias, A., Anastasatou, M., & Katsikas, D. (2018). Balancing adjustment policies and structural reforms in Greece: The case of product markets. In P. Manasse & D. Katsikas (Eds.), *Economic crisis and structural reforms in southern Europe: Policy lessons*. London and New York: Routledge.

Pisani-Ferry, J. (2006). Only one bed for two dreams: A critical retrospective on the debate over the economic governance of the Euro area. *Journal of Common Market Studies, 44*(4), 823–844.

Rodrik, D. (2016). The elusive promise of structural reform. *Milken Institute Review, 18*(2), 26–35.

Scharpf, F. W. (1999). *Governing in Europe*. Oxford: Oxford University Press.

Schimmelfennig, F. (2015). Liberal intergovernmentalism and the Euro area crisis. *Journal of European Public Policy, 22*(2), 177–195.

Schmidt, V. A. (2013). Democracy and legitimacy in the European Union revisited: Input, output *and* 'throughput'. *Political Studies, 61*, 2–22.

Schmidt, V. A. (2015). The Eurozone's crisis of democratic legitimacy: Can the EU rebuild public trust and support for European economic integration. Discussion Paper 015, September, European Economy, European Commission. https://ec.europa.eu/info/sites/info/files/dp015_en.pdf. Accessed 30 Aug 2019.

Stiglitz, J. E. (2002). *Globalization and its discontents*. New York: Norton.

Transparency International EU. (2017). *Two sides of the same coin? Independence and accountability of the European Central Bank*. https://transparency.eu/wp-content/uploads/2017/03/TI-EU_ECB_Report_DIGITAL.pdf. Accesses 20 Sept 2019.

Weiler, J. H. H., Haltern, U. R., & Mayer, F. (1995). European democracy and its critique. *West European Politics, 18*(3), 4–39.

Zografakis, S., & Kastelli, I. (2017). Is it true that reducing labour costs is sufficient to improve the competitiveness of the Greek economy? In D. Katsikas, K. Filinis, & M. Anastasatou (Eds.), *Κατανοώντας την Ελληνική Κρίση: Απαντήσεις σε Καίρια Ερωτήματα για το Κράτος, την Οικονομία και την Ευρώπη*. Athens: Papazisis Publications.

6

Financial Instability and FTT

Stephan Schulmeister

Abstract This chapter analyses the pros and cons of financial transaction taxes (FTT) as mechanisms to mitigate financial instability and the proposal of the European Commission to implement an FTT in the EU in September 2011 until its suspension, as well as the prospects for it to be adopted in the future.

Introduction

The proposal of the European Commission to implement a financial transaction tax (FTT) in the EU (September 2011) can be considered an attempt to mitigate the contradiction between rising financial instability in the "real world" and mainstream economists' unbroken belief in financial market efficiency. Such a tax would dampen asset price volatility, in particular caused by (ultra)fast trading techniques, yet it would represent a "softer" means of interference in market processes as compared to direct regulations. Based on empirical research on asset price dynamics, the Austrian Institute of Economic Research (WIFO) had presented already in February 2008 a comprehensive concept of a general FTT (Schulmeister et al. 2008). In contrast to a Tobin tax, the FTT should be levied on all transactions with any type of financial asset. The essential features of the WIFO proposal were as follows[1]:

- The FTT is levied on all transactions involving buying/selling of spot and derivative assets, traded either on organized exchanges or over the counter.
- The tax base is the value of the underlying asset, in the case of derivatives their notional/contract value.

[1] The WIFO concept was not the first one, which would propose a *general* FTT. Pollin et al. (2003) proposed a "securities transaction tax" for the US markets, Summers and Summers (1989) had made "a cautious case" for such taxes. However, the WIFO concept was the most detailed and most comprehensive concept.

S. Schulmeister (✉)
University of Vienna, Wien, Austria
e-mail: stephan.schulmeister@wifo-pens.at

- The tax rate should be low (between 0.01% and 0.05%).

This concept ensures the following: The "faster" an asset is traded and the higher is the leverage ratio, the more will the FTT increase transaction costs. Hence, an FTT with a low and uniform rate specifically dampens very short-term speculation in derivatives. High-frequency trading would become unprofitable even at a tax rate of 0.01% (or less). All other forms of short-term speculation would at least be dampened. As a consequence, asset price runs would occur less frequently and would become less persistent. Since long-term trends ("bulls" and "bears") are the result of the accumulation of short-term runs, an FTT would also dampen the long swings of exchange rates, commodity prices and stock prices. As the financial crisis 2008 was directly related to the "tilting" of the bull markets of stock prices, commodity prices and house prices into three bear markets, the concept of a general FTT got more attention than ever before in the subsequent years.

The struggle over the FTT developed in three phases. In the first phase (2009 to 2011), the supporters of the tax went on the offensive. This phase ended with their (preliminary) "victory" in the form of the FTT proposal of the European Commission (EC) in September 2011. The second phase was shaped by the search for ways how to implement the FTT within the EU. It ended with the publication of a modified FTT proposal by the EC in February 2013 as basis for the implementation in 11 Member States (EU11). In the last phase, a strong counter-offensive of big "financial players" like Goldman Sachs deepened the conflicts among the EU11 group. As a consequence, several member states called for more modifications of the FTT concept of the EC and finally gave it up.

After the Financial Crisis: Pros and Cons of an FTT and the Fight for Public Opinion

Almost all NGOs active in the field of development aid and fighting poverty had for many years called for the Tobin tax. In the aftermath of the financial crisis, these groups switched to demanding a general FTT. Their campaigning was so successful that already in November 2010 61% of the respondents of a "Eurobarometer" poll supported the introduction of an FTT (EC 2011a). At the same time, the leaders of the two most important EU Member States, Chancellor Merkel and President Sarkozy, began to endorse such a tax. The "counter-attacks" against the FTT were put forward by economists of the IMF and – at first – also of the EC (IMF 2010; EC 2010a, b). Their objections were derived from equilibrium theory in general and financial market efficiency in particular.

- Objection 1: An FTT reduces liquidity and therefore hampers the price discovery process. It is assumed that rational traders drive the asset price to its fundamental equilibrium known to everybody. In reality, however, information is (very) imperfect, uncertainty is particularly pronounced in financial markets, and trading is not only based on rational calculations but also on emotions and social interaction (contagion, herding, market sentiments).

- Objection 2: The FTT does not specifically increase the costs of destabilizing trading. In fact, an FTT with the notional value as tax base increases the tax burden the more the faster transactions are carried out and the higher their leverage is.
- Objection 3: The distortive effects of an FTT will be higher than those of other kinds of taxes, in particular of a VAT, because the FTT is a turnover tax. This analogy is misleading. Buying an asset does not represent an (intermediate) input, and selling an asset does not represent an (intermediate) output. A more precise analogy to an FTT would be taxes on gambling where usually any bet/transaction is taxed.
- Objection 4: An FTT would raise the cost of capital because it has the same effect as taxes on future dividends. The assertion is wrong since a tax on dividends would affect any stock, whereas the FTT would affect only those stocks which are (frequently) traded. Compared to the trading volume of stock (index) derivatives, the volume of stock spot transactions is low.
- Objection 5: Most financial transactions are not driven by (destabilizing) speculation but stem from distributing risk. Before something can be distributed, it has to be produced. The production of risk and uncertainty in financial markets has risen due to the dominance of (automated) trading systems which disregard market fundamentals and are therefore destabilizing.
- Objection 6: Derivatives should not be taxed because this would increase hedging costs. Hedging involves only two transactions, opening and closing a derivative (counter-)position. At an FTT rate of 0.01%, the hedging costs would be only 0.02% of the insured value.

The Proposal of the European Commission and the Attempts to Implement the Tax

The European Commission changed its position towards the tax fundamentally between August 2010 (when it still rejected such a tax – see EC 2010b) and September 2011 (when it proposed a common system of financial transaction tax – see EC 2011b, c). The reasons for this turn were predominantly political: NGOs continued to campaign intensively for the FTT, most people in the EU supported it (EP 2011), and the European Parliament as well as the German and French government called for the introduction of this tax. The main features of the FTT proposal of the EC (ECP) are as follows (EC 2013).[2]

The tax base is defined comprehensively. Almost all transactions in financial instruments carried out by financial institutions (FIs) are subject to the tax. Tax

[2] For a more detailed summary of the EU proposal as well as a theoretical discussion of financial transaction taxes in general, see Griffith-Jones and Persaud (2012).

revenues accrue to the FTT countries (FTTCs) according to the "residence principle" and the "issuance principle". The residence principle means that all transactions of FIs established in one of the 11 FTTCs are subject to the tax wherever the latter are carried out. The issuance principle means that also transactions in financial instruments, which are issued in an FTTC, are subject to the FTT even if none of the parties is established in an FTTC. For the minimum tax rates, the ECP proposes 0.1% as regards financial instruments other than derivatives (i.e. spot transactions) and 0.01% as regards derivative transactions. Each party has to pay the tax at the respective rates, i.e. 0.1% or 0.01%, respectively.

In February 2013, the EC published its modified proposal for an FTT implementation in the 11 EU Member States joining the ECP, among them all big euro countries. Finally, it seemed as if the FTT would soon be implemented in 11 countries. But it should come quite differently.

The Successful Counter-attack of the Financial Lobby Since 2013

Even though the modified proposal of the EC did not differ essentially from the original, the reaction of the financial lobby to its publication was completely different from the situation in fall 2011. This time, the respective institutions had enough time to prepare a most powerful campaign. Its targets were as follows:

- Bomb the public and politicians with as many assertions about the disastrous effects of an FTT as possible within a short period of time. What counts is quantity, not quality.
- Pretend that the interests of the national finance industry are national interests.
- Pretend that the interests of governments to finance their debts stay in conflict with the FTT proposal of the EC.
- Pretend that an FTT harms the interest of the (little) private investor in having his/her money "work", in particular for his/her retirement.
- Ignore all arguments of FTT proponents concerning trading practices, "manic-depressive" asset price fluctuations and their impact on the real economy.

The most important intermediate target of the campaign against the FTT was to play off groups of actors and their interests against each other: national interests against the interests of "Brussels bureaucrats", interests of EU Member States against each other, government's interest in easy debt financing against the interests of the civil society, the interests of the latter against the interests of the (little) private investor, etc. The campaign of the financial institutions materialized primarily in pamphlets and press conferences of practically all big banks (Goldman Sachs, Morgan Stanley, Deutsche Bank, JP Morgan, Citigroup, etc.) and lobby organizations (International Banking Federation, International Capital Market Association, European Repo Council, European Fund and Asset Management Association, etc.).

In all their messages, the financial lobby repeated over and over again: The tax would hamper liquidity, increase the cost of capital and of financing the government debt; the tax would reduce profits of banks and, hence, their tax payments; hedging costs would rise; and, as a consequence, overall financial stability would be reduced. These assertions were then used to drive a wedge between the 11 FTT countries, in particular between France and Germany: "Indeed, we think the FTT would de facto be a transfer of French taxes (on, e.g., derivative transactions of the French banks, which are the market leaders in Equity Derivatives) to other jurisdictions" (Morgan 2013, p. 2).

The intention to play off governments against each other was facilitated by the fact that France and Italy introduced their own FTT in 2012 and 2013, respectively. The French tax is essentially a "stamp duty" on the change of ownership of French stocks, the scope of the Italian tax is wider as it also covers some derivatives. Once there were national FTTs introduced, the respective governments did no longer stick to the FTT proposal of the EC but wanted the latter to be changed according to their national FTT concepts. For example, the French government wanted the residence principle to be removed and derivatives to be excluded from the tax as both measures would hurt their national banks (in France, all big banks have specialized in "finance alchemy", only Deutsche Bank). The financial lobby also mobilized the central banks. In May 2013, the then Governor of the Bank of England stated bluntly about the FTT: "Within Europe, I can't find anyone in the central banking community who thinks it's a good idea". At the same time, the Governor of the Banque de France and the President of the German Bundesbank criticized the FTT explicitly in the public (see Corporate Europe Observatory 2013).

In addition, the financial lobby opened a new "front": An FTT would almost destroy the repo market (with a repurchasing agreement, a bank raises cash by selling a security – usually a government bond – to the lender and commits itself to repurchase the security when the repo expires, in most cases just after 1 day). This assertion turned out to become the most effective weapon against the FTT proposal of the EC:

- As the EC had not dealt explicitly with the repo market, the lobby could pretend that the proposal had overlooked how this market would be affected.
- Politicians who had supported the FTT proposal became uncertain as they were in fact not familiar with repos.
- At first glance, it does indeed seem inconsistent that unsecured credits remain FTT-free whereas collateralized borrowing is taxed.
- The most important types of collateral in repos are government bonds. Hence, the financial lobby asserted that the FTT would raise the costs of financing the public debt.
- In a similar manner, it was argued that also pension funds would see lower returns as consequence of higher repo costs.

All this reasoning hides the core properties of repo transactions and of the repo market as the core component of the shadow banking system:

- Most repo transactions finance very short-term trading activities, in particular proprietary trading of banks.[3] Intraday trading is financed by so-called tri-party repos where purchasing and repurchasing take place within hours.
- Repos facilitate leveraged trading to the extreme in the sense that one can purchase an asset (almost) without cash by borrowing money to buy the asset and simultaneously posting the asset as collateral.
- Short-selling is fostered by the repo market. One lends money in the repo market, takes the security one intends to short as collateral and then sells the security.
- The extremely high leverage of repo transactions strengthens boom-bust cycles and increases systemic risks: Rising asset prices stimulate repo financing which feeds back onto the bull market and conversely in the case of a bear market.
- The possibility to reuse the collateral produces "repo chains" (e.g. bank A sells a security to bank B in return for cash, bank B sells the security to bank C, etc.), feeding back on the strength of bull or bear markets.[4]

It is no surprise that the increasingly short-term repo transactions developed in tandem with the increasingly short-term proprietary trading of banks. This type of trading is predominantly unrelated to market fundamentals (it is to a large extent driven by trading systems). The financial lobby rightly expects repo financing to become unprofitable due to the implementation of an FTT. This, however, would be an advantage to the economy as a whole as these transactions finance predominantly short-term and destabilizing asset speculation. The "production" of systemic risks by short-term repos is confirmed by their role in the recent financial crisis (e.g. Hördahl and King 2008; Gorton and Metrick 2010; Tuckman 2010; for a summary, see Gabor 2016): Banks and their "special purpose vehicles" created securities from loans which often were backed by subprime mortgages. These securities were then used as collateral for repos. In this way, "securitized banking" created liquidity which further fuelled the booms of asset prices.

When the confidence in the real value of mortgage-backed securities became weaker, the confidence crisis spilled over to the repo market as a whole. The subsequent "run on repo" caused interbank interest rates to shoot up, and the bankruptcy of Lehman Brothers in September then accelerated the simultaneous fall of stock prices, house prices and commodity prices dramatically, turning the liquidity crisis of the banking system into a solvency crisis. All these aspects were neglected in the "scientific" documentation of the harmfulness of an FTT provided by the financial lobby. The most influential study became a research report of Goldman Sachs, in the following termed "GS study" (Goldman 2013).

This study is a perfect example how economists develop methods guided by the interest in reaching certain results, in this case "blowing up" the costs of the FTT to the maximum extent. The GS study summarizes the main results right at the

[3]According to survey studies of the Bank of England, two thirds of repo turnover concern overnight deals (Hördahl and King 2008).

[4]For the different channels through which the repo market produces (avoidable) systemic risk, see the excellent paper by Gabor (2016) and the literature quoted there.

beginning: "On a 2012 pro-forma basis, the FTT would amount to €170 bn…for the 42 European banks we have analysed…. By affected balance sheet category, the bulk of the impact stems from the European banks' REPO books (€118 bn), followed by derivatives (€32 bn), equities (€11 bn) and government bond books (€4 bn). By bank, the impact extends across business models – investment, universal, global and domestic retail banks. Similarly, by geography, it has a reach well beyond the EU-11. Indeed, we show some of the most affected banks would be those in the UK and Switzerland. Individually, we show that the most affected banks are the French and German institutions. The six French and German banks show a 2012 pro-forma FTT as a percentage of 2015E PBT (i.e., profits before taxes) ranging from 168% (BNP), up to 362% (DBK) and finally 423% (Natixis). But even pure-play retail lenders – the Italian/Spanish domestic banks for example – stand to be significantly impacted (16–130% of 2015E PBT)" (Goldman 2013, p. 4).

In order to arrive at these "magic" figures, the GS researchers invented a new estimation procedure: "…we attempt to gauge what the 2012 FTT (theoretically) payable by individual banks would be, were they asked to apply FTT retroactively, to 2012 balances. This is a theoretical, 'all else equal', exercise…" (Goldman 2013, p. 16). In other words, when calculating the costs of the FTT, GS researchers assumed that transaction volumes remain unaffected by the tax – they call this the "pro-forma effect". The seriousness of this procedure can be illustrated using the following example. Trading volume in UK financial markets amounted to 563 times the British GDP in 2010 (even without repo transactions which are not covered by the BIS data base).[5] On a "pro-forma" base, an FTT rate of 0.1% would generate tax revenues of 56.3% of GDP; at a rate of 1%, the British government might even receive revenues amounting to 5.6 times the British GDP.

The GS researchers justify the "pro-forma" estimation arguing that "the results allow us to identify the business areas/product lines where the FTT impact would be most pronounced…". This is simply wrong: The structure of activities differs between European banks. Banks which are specialized on short-term trading and repo financing ("finance alchemy banking") will reduce these activities in reaction to the FTT implementation to a much greater extent than the more traditionally operating banks ("boring banking"). To serve its "research interest", GS researchers introduced the concept of an "effective annual tax rate". This means that the estimated *annual* FTT payments are related to the *average* repo value. In this way, one can document astronomically high "tax rates" as these rates become the higher the shorter the financing period of the REPO is. For tri-party REPOS which are turned over three to five times per day, GS Research arrives at an "effective annual tax rate" of the FTT of 360% (Goldman 2013, Exhibit 12 on p. 19). The absurdity of this procedure becomes evident if one considers the following example: A US household spends every day on average 100$ on consumption for which it has to pay 5$

[5] Based on data from the World Federation of Exchanges (WFE) and the BIS, overall transaction volume in 2010 on UK markets is estimated at 1270,4 tn. $.

in sales tax. What sense does it make to calculate an "annual effective sales tax" of 365 times 5% = 1825% instead of speaking of a general sales tax rate of 5%?

Another example for the predominance of the "research interest": When discussing the FTT impact on the profits of European exchanges, the researchers did not stick to their "pro-forma" estimation but assumed an FTT-induced reduction of trading volumes. In this way, the GS reports arrive at the following conclusion: "...we estimate that the average European Exchange & IDB (i.e., interdealer brokers) under our coverage would see pre-tax profits decline by 22% as a result of the tax..." (Goldman 2013, p. 44). An exquisite example of manipulation concerns the impact of the FTT on retail investors: "Our analysis suggests that much of the burden of the FTT would fall on retail investors rather than institutional investors... we estimate that a typical retail investor from the Euro-11 area could expect to incur an annual FTT charge of 33 bp, while a similar institutional fund manager would incur 11 bp in tax. On this basis, a 30-year-old retail investor in the Euro-11 area who invested €1,000 a year until retirement at 65 could expect to see 14% of the principal investment consumed by the FTT" (*GS Report*, p. 54).

These calculations are biased in three respects. First, it is assumed that investors would not reduce the turnover of their portfolio due to the FTT. Second, it is – unrealistically – assumed that the retail portfolio returns over 35 years 6% p. a. on average. Both assumptions result in a high sum of cumulative tax payments (4875 €). Third, this sum is then related to the cumulative cash invested (35,000 €) leaving out the interest-compound effect. If one takes the latter – correctly – into account, the cumulative tax burdens amount to only 4.1% of the closing portfolio (this ratio is documented in Exhibit 34 but not mentioned in the main text).

The "dirty" campaign of the financial lobby was successful: The tensions between members of the "coalition of the willing" rose, in particular between Germany and France. On May 6, 2014, finance ministers of the EU11 declared: "...Our commitment to the introduction of a financial transaction tax remains strong...We agree on the following key elements...The progressive implementation will first focus on the taxation of shares and some derivatives".

In plain language, this passage should read as follows: "The campaign of the financial lobby was too strong. This forced us to give up the 'all institutions, all markets, all instruments' approach proposed by the European Commission. Instead, as a first step we shall introduce a tax just on shares. We commit ourselves to call it 'financial transaction tax'".

It took the finance ministers of the ECP more than 4 years to finally arrive at this result. In December 2018, the German and French minister proposed the French model as the "new European Financial Transactions Tax": Only spot transactions of stocks issued in an EU country should be taxed. One year later, the German Finance Minister Olaf Scholz trimmed the concept further: Only transactions with stocks of companies with a market value of more than 1 bn € should be comprised by the new "FTT". This would mean that only less than 0.3% (!) of all financial transactions in the EU would be taxed[6] and it would also mean the "FTT" would tax exactly only those trades which are less used for short-term speculation and more for holding wealth (compared to derivatives). It won't be too difficult for pension and investment funds to carry out a campaign against such a one-sided "FTT". In addition, countries like Belgium and Austria which have been always supporting a comprehensive FTT (including derivatives) will leave the "coalition of the willing". This means that Scholz' "FTT" cannot not be implemented as the so-called enhanced cooperation needs the participation of at least nine member states (as yet, only ten have remained in the group). As a first indication of this development, the Austrian Ministry of Finance published a study immediately after the publication of the Scholz proposal which sharply criticized the "FTT" which would only tax stock transactions. However, in case of a new financial crisis, the idea of implementing a general FTT will pop up again.

References

Corporate Europe Observatory (2013). *Robbing the "Robin Hood" tax: The European Central Bank weighs in*. Corporate Europe Observatory. July 2013. https://corporateeurope.org/en/financial-lobby/2013/07/robbing-robin-hood-tax-european-central-bank-weighs. Accessed 2 March 2020.

European Commission (2010a). *Innovative financing at the global level, SEC (2010) 409 final*. April 2010. https://ec.europa.eu/economy_finance/articles/international/2010-04-06-global_innovative_financing_en.htm. Accessed 02 March 2020.

European Commission (2010b). *Financial sector taxation, SEC (2010) 1166*. August 2010. https://ec.europa.eu/taxation_customs/sites/taxation/files/resources/documents/taxation/gen_info/economic_analysis/tax_papers/taxation_paper_25_en.pdf. Accessed 02 March 2020.

European Commission (2011a). *Eurobarometer 74, Economic Governance in the European Union*. January 2011. https://ec.europa.eu/commfrontoffice/publicopinion/archives/eb/eb74/eb74_en.htm. Accessed 02 March 2020.

European Commission (2011b). *Proposal of a Council directive on a common system of financial transaction tax*. https://eur-lex.europa.eu/legal-content/EN/TXT/?uri=celex:52011PC0594. Accessed 02 March 2020.

European Commission (2011c). *Impact assessment accompanying the document Proposal of a Council directive on a common system of financial transaction tax*. https://ec.europa.eu/transparency/regdoc/?fuseaction=list&coteId=2&year=2011&number=1102&version=ALL&language=en. Accessed 02 March 2020.

European Commission (2013). *Proposal for a Council Directive implementing enhanced cooperation in the area of financial transaction tax*. https://eur-lex.europa.eu/legal-content/EN/TXT/?uri=celex:52013PC0071. Accessed 02 March 2020.

European Parliament (2011). *Eurobarometer 75.2, Europeans and the crisis*. June 2011. https://www.europarl.europa.eu/pdf/eurobarometre/2011/juin/22062011/eb752_financial_crisis_analytical_synthesis_en.pdf. Accessed 02 March 2020.

[6]Already in 2013, only 0.45% of all financial transactions in Europe concerned stock trading (spot). This share is nowadays most probably smaller as short-term speculation has increased above average and uses predominantly derivative instruments. In 2013, derivative trading in Europe comprised 83.5% of all transactions, foreign exchange spot trading accounted for 15.2%.

Gabor, D. (2016). A step too far? The European financial transactions tax on shadow banking. *Journal of European Public Policy, 23*(6), 925–945.

Goldman, S. (2013). *Financial transaction tax: How severe?* Goldman Sachs Research Report of May 1, 2013.

Gorton, G., & Metrick, A. (2010). *Securitized banking and the run on repo*. Yale ICF Working Paper No. 09 14, November 9. https://papers.ssrn.com/sol3/papers.cfm?abstract_id=1440752. Accessed 02 March 2020.

Griffith-Jones, S., & Persaud, A. (2012). Financial transaction taxes. Paper prepared for – and presented to – *the Committee on Economic and Monetary Affairs of the European Parliament*. 6 February 2012. https://www.europarl.europa.eu/document/activities/cont/201202/20120208ATT37596/20120208ATT37596EN.pdf. Accessed 02 March 2020.

Hördahl, P., & King, M. (2008). Developments in repo markets during the financial turmoil. *BIS Quarterly Review*. 8 December 2008. https://www.bis.org/publ/qtrpdf/r_qt0812e.pdf. Accessed 02 March 2020.

International Monetary Fund (2010). *A fair and substantial contribution by the financial sector*. Final Report for the G-20. June 2010. https://www.imf.org/external/np/g20/pdf/062710b.pdf. Accessed 02 March 2020.

Morgan, S. (2013). European rates/banks: FTT – Alternative scenarios. In *Paper by Morgan Stanley Research Europe*. June 5, 2013.

Pollin, R., Baker, D., & Schaberg, M. (2003). Securities transaction taxes for U.S. financial markets. *Eastern Economic Journal, 29*(4), 527–558.

Schulmeister, S., Schratzenstaller, M., & Picek, O. (2008). A general financial transaction tax – Motives, revenues, feasibility and effects. In *Study of the Austrian Institute of Economic Research (WIFO)*, Vienna. April 2008. https://papers.ssrn.com/sol3/papers.cfm?abstract_id=1714395. Accessed 02 March 2020.

Summers, L. H., & Summers, V. P. (1989). When financial markets work too well: A cautious case for a securities transactions tax. *Journal of Financial Services Research, 3*(2–3), 261–286.

Tuckman, B. (2010). Systemic Risk and the Tri-Party Repo Clearing Banks, CSF Working Paper, February 2, 2010.

7

Governance Institutions in Latin America and Economic Crisis Management

Maria Antonieta Del Tedesco Lins and Andrea Ribeiro Hoffmann

Abstract This chapter analyses the governance institutions in Latin America, i.e. norms, instruments and mechanisms designed to deal with macroeconomic and financial crisis management, and their use during the financial crisis which started in 2008 in the USA and reached the region mostly towards the mid-2010s. It argues that Latin American regional institutions never prioritized the harmonization or the development of common macroeconomic policies or mechanisms to deal with financial crises, and the few multilateral initiatives created were not successful.

Introduction

As the 2008 financial crisis evolved, the governments of most countries in the world assessed its potential impact on their domestic stability and adjusted their macroeconomic policies accordingly, complementing or substituting for with various levels of success. Some regions, such as Europe, have had or developed regional governance structures to deal with the crisis collectively, member-states measures given the existence of common regional arrangements, as discussed in several chapters of this volume. In Latin America, most regional organizations did not have or did not develop such structures, and the management of the crisis was handled mainly at the domestic level; the reactions by Argentina, Brazil and Mexico, for instance, are analysed by Lins in Chap. 11 of this volume.

The absence or weakness of common regional structures to deal with external financial crises in Latin America is quite puzzling given that, at the one hand, the region has been fertile for the establishment of regional institutions and structures

M. A. D. T. Lins
University of São Paulo (USP), São Paulo, SP, Brazil
e-mail: madtlins@usp.br

A. Ribeiro Hoffmann (✉)
Pontifical Catholic University of Rio de Janeiro (PUC-Rio), Rio de Janeiro, Brazil

Coordinator of the second phase of the Jean Monnet Network "Crisis-Equity-Democracy for Europe and Latin America", Rio de Janeiro, Brazil
e-mail: a_ribeiro_hoffmann@puc-rio.br

of governance over the years, as discussed by Briceño-Ruiz and Ribeiro Hoffmann in Chap. 18, and, on the other hand, it has been particularly vulnerable to global macroeconomic instability and financial crisis such as in the 1980s and 1990s. This chapter does not explore the reasons for the lack of more robust regional frameworks to respond to financial crisis; rather, it analyses if and how the (few) existing governance institutions played a role in the management of the 2008 crisis (Martins 2017; Kacef and Monti 2010). We argue that, despite the existence of a myriad of regional institutions, the level of cooperation among their member-states and their capacity to act in crisis situations has been extremely limited. It is worth mentioning that most Latin American organizations have norms, instruments and mechanisms in the social areas which were or could have been used to control the damages of macroeconomic instability by compensating for the lost in jobs, revenues and rights, either temporarily or permanently (Medeiros 2016). This chapter does not delve into these governance structures, but we acknowledge their relevance as policy instruments to deal with macroeconomic and financial crisis from a broader perspective.

The chapter is structured in three sections, covering, firstly, the governance structures set by the main regional organizations active during and since 2008 such as Mercosur, UNASUR, ALBA, the Pacific Alliance and CELAC, and secondly, other multilateral institutions such the Corporación Andina de Fomento (CAF) and the Fondo Latinoamericano de Reservas (FLAR), followed by the concluding remarks.

Regional Governance and Economic Crisis Management in Latin America by Regional Organizations

Despite the enormous variance in terms of issue areas covered and priorities, currently existing regional organizations have practically no norms, instruments and mechanisms to promote the harmonization, cooperation and integration in macroeconomic and financial matters. By the time the 2008 crisis burst, the main organizations active in the region were the key organizations created during the so-called first and second waves of regionalism, i.e. Mercosur, the Andean Community (CAN), the Central American Common Market (CACM) and the Caribbean Common Market (CARICOM), and ALBA, created in 2004 by Cuba and Venezuela to promote a counter-model of regional integration based on the twenty-first Century Socialism. In 2008, UNASUR was created, and soon after, the Pacific Alliance and CELAC (in 2011 and 2012, respectively). UNASUR and CELAC are exemplar of the regional trend in this period, which became to be known as "post-liberal" or "post-hegemonic", given the lack of consensus on free markets as the main motor of regional integration. The Pacific Alliance, instead, must be seen as a reaction to the twenty-first Century Socialism and a regrouping by free-trade countries in the Andean region and Chile. The return to a pro-market approach also led to the creation of Prosur in 2019, but it is too soon to include this organization in the analysis.

From among organizations, Mercosur and the Pacific Alliance have adopted a more liberal approach to development, even if Mercosur changed over time, as discussed in the already mentioned Chap. 18. UNASUR and CELAC were conceived as broad organizations, covering economic, social and cultural areas, but given their size of membership and diversity of policy preferences of their member-states, they have had a less coherent profile in their economic/development initiatives. One would expect that, independent their of more liberal or more developmentalist profiles, these organizations and their member-states would have an interest in creating buffers against global level instability and external shocks, but this has not been the case. Several reasons are pointed out in the literature, such as asymmetries of domestic macroeconomic indicators, lack of interdependence, political choices and ideologies, but the objective of this chapter is not to explore the causes but rather to map the existing mechanisms and to what extent they were used following the crisis.

Starting with Mercosur, despite many achievements in setting norms and standards, and establishing structures of governance in issue areas such as trade, migration and education, the regulation of services and capital has been a fiasco. The Protocol of Montevideo to foster the integration of financial services, concluded in 1997, entered into force in Brazil and Uruguay in 2019, but it did not play a role so far. Mercosur has actually a bad record in fostering cooperation in macroeconomic and financial matters; the unilateral decision in Brazil to devaluate its currency, the real, without discussing with Mercosur member-states, in 1999, following the contagion of the Asian crisis of 1997, has left a shadow in the region (Bouzas et al. 2002, p. 17–19). When the international liquidity crunch came in 2008, Mercosur countries responded to the crisis according to their domestic priorities, and as a consequence, no common policies were set nor were any specific common interests discussed. Countercyclical policies were effective in Mercosur countries, as all four member-states combined monetary and fiscal policies in order to avoid a heavier fall in consumption and investment than that which the decline in external demand would have originally imposed on their economies. Like in most countries around the world, quite traditional instruments were used: expansion of liquidity, tax exemptions and stimulus to specific sectors and expansion of credit by state-owned financial institutions. Mercosur countries were free from rigid exchange rate policies, even if to very different degrees. A great virtue of the floating exchange rate regime is precisely its ability to absorb external shocks and thus allow the domestic economy to accommodate to the new global situation. This was an important element of the varied reactions of Mercosur countries to the crisis. The four member-countries' exchange rates depreciated in the initial moments of the crisis, but this was followed by quick monetary accommodation. The exception in this case was Argentina who, as a matter of deliberate policy, allowed the peso to continue to depreciate even after the worst period of the crisis had passed. Monetary measures were all devoted to the expansion of liquidity and the reduction of interest rates. In Brazil, federal banks pursed an aggressive increase in the availability of credit through several different instruments according to their specific jobs. Foreign exchange and trade policies were also dictated by the need to protect companies from the shortage in international credit lines. Independently of their relative success, the point is that Mercosur member-states did not use the organization as a platform for discussion, coordination or the development of a common approach to handle the crisis.

UNASUR has provided space for a critical discussion about global financial architecture given its more developmentalist profile during the peak days of the "left turn." Meanwhile, Venezuela and Brazil supported the creation of a Bank of the South as an alternative source for the financing of infrastructure to the Bretton Woods institutions and the Inter-American Development Bank (IDB), such as the case of the New Development Bank (NDB) proposed by the BRICS countries in 2014. The Constitutive Act establishing the Bank of the South was signed by Brazil, Bolivia, Argentina, Ecuador, Uruguay, Paraguay and Venezuela in 2007, and the Constitutional Agreement was approved in 2009. The expectation was that it would have a capital of USD 7 bi from the founding members with contributions from Brazil, Argentina and Venezuela (USD 2 bi each), Ecuador and Uruguay (USD 400 mi each), Bolivia and Paraguay (USD 100 mi each), but, unlike the NDB, it was never capitalized, and the project was suspended with the paralysation of Unasur (Calixtre and Barros 2010; Palestini 2016).

ALBA openly promoted a non-capitalist model of regional integration, rejecting free trade and key principles of the capitalist system such as private property and intellectual property. In addition to the oil regime and the creation of Petrocaribe, one of the most ambitious economic initiatives was the creation of a common currency, the Sucre, but to be used mainly as a mechanism of compensation for trade. Cusack argued that although trade via Sucre "grew rapidly from 2010 to 2012, rather than being balanced, this boom consisted largely of Venezuelan imports from Ecuador (…) And beyond 2012, it also became clear that the system was facilitating forms of corruption" (Cusack 2018, p. 127). Benzi (2017, p. 110) also argued that Sucre was undermined by corruption. Venezuela was a partner in 98% of Sucre trade, and the Venezuelan-Ecuador relationship alone accounted for 89% of Sucre trade (Cusack 2018, p. 129). Exchange between Cuba and Ecuador, for example, represented just 5.5% of Sucre Trade in 2016 (Cusack 2018, p. 130). Apart from Sucre, ALBA did not develop any mechanism that could be used to design a common approach to handle with the financial crisis.

The Pacific Alliance was created in 2011 by Chile, Colombia, Mexico and Peru, and its priorities are to foster trade liberalization and establish investment partnerships with Asia, especially China. An innovative initiative in the area of macroeconomics was the creation of the Latin American Integrated Market (MILA), an agreement initially made between the Santiago Stock Exchange, the Colombia Stock Exchange and the Lima Stock Exchange, later joined by Mexico in 2014 to establish a regional market allowing for gains in scale by the trading of stock shares in each of the national markets.[1] Martins (2017, p.110) argues that by 2015 MILA had not achieved the expected results; the impact of its creation in terms of correlation, risk and profitability was marginal and in terms of volume negotiated

[1] https://mercadomila.com/en/who-we-are/our-history/

negative. Even if MILA's record improved since then, this mechanism was not relevant in terms of managing the impact of the 2008 crisis.

Finally, CELAC priorities have not included (macro)economic matters either. Moreover, as Sanahuja argues (Caetano and Sanahuja 2019, p. 31), CELAC can be well defined as another example of summit diplomacy in the region, where presidents have a key say but little interest in institutionalizing common approaches. That said, CELAC has received technical support by CEPAL and SELAC to foster harmonization and the consolidation of regional trade and investment markets (Vadell 2018, p.16), but this process has been hindered by the extreme divergence among its member-states. As highlighted by Bonilla and Jaramillo (2013), CELAC included countries which had very different approaches to trade and macroeconomic policies at the time of its creation, from the (neo)liberal Chile and Peru to (twenty-first century) socialists Venezuela and Cuba, and also countries from the Caribbean, which have also great variation of insertion in the global trade and financial markets. For that reason, it has also been deeply affected by the polarization around the Venezuelan crisis, and its last Presidential Summit took place in 2017, in Punta Cana, Dominican Republic, when only 11 from the 22 presidents were present.[2] CELAC has also promoted Ministerial Summits, but the last took place in 2015. The third ministerial summit foreseen to take place in 2017 was cancelled. Macroeconomic dialogue was not a priority even during the good times of CELAC,[3] but this channel was the most appropriate to foster cooperation with the EU (Ghymers discusses a proposal to strengthen this dialogue in Chap. 22 of this volume). In fact, in addition to its role within the region, CELAC has been a platform for the region to dialogue and cooperate multilaterally with partners such as the EU and China. The EU has given special attention to CELAC given its preference to structure its bi-regional relations in formal agreement frameworks. EU-LAC bi-regional relations include Special Partnerships with Brazil and Mexico, bilateral dialogue and/or agreements with individual countries and sub-regions such as the Andean Community, Central American Common Market and Mercosur.[4]

---

[2] http://observatorio.repri.org/artigos/celac-a-retorica-da-integracao/; http://observatorio.repri.org/artigos/celac-de-la-convergencia-a-la-paralisis/;http://revistafal.com/la-celac-en-el-nuevo-escenario-regional/

[3] The Plan of Action approved in 2013 established eight priorities: science, research, innovation and technology; sustainable development; climate change; regional integration and interconnectivity; social cohesion; migration; education; and labor, drugs, gender, investments and entrepreneurship; and the Action plan approved in 2015 added higher education and citizenship security. https://www.consilium.europa.eu/media/24235/read-the-assessment-of-programmes-and-actions.pdf. See as well http://alcuenet.eu/policy.php

[4] The EU and LAC countries have created a think tank to forward studies about the bi-regional relations, located in Hamburg. https://eulacfoundation.org/en. Veja também https://eeas.europa.eu/delegations/brazil/48562/rela%C3%A7%C3%B5es-ue-celac_pt

Other Multilateral Mechanisms to Manage Economic Crisis in Latin America

A matter of great importance in the debate between nations and as with multilateral institutions since the 1990s emerging economies' financial crises, the struggle to maintain global financial stability has given rise to a series of regional initiatives. The global financial crisis outbreak (2007–2009) reinforced the concern with market stability and brought to the floor the concept of global safety nets (Ocampo 2006; Fritz and Mühlich 2019). Since the establishment of the Chiang Mai Initiative in response to the impacts of the 1997 Asian crisis, a number of collaborative initiatives between regional partners have taken shape.

Although some regional integration initiatives were already present in Latin America, they did not play a decisive countercyclical role in the most recent crisis. Rather, national states have conducted their own stimulus policies taking into account their economic possibilities and political dynamics. Latin America has not been particularly fertile in establishing regional financial arrangements – RFA. When compared to the European and even Asian cases, the few initiatives carried out in Latin America reveal its limited character, both in terms of the extent of participation and in terms of financial collaboration among its members. To fairly look for all possible forms of regional coordination in the face of economic crises, long existing institutions are worth mentioned: the Corporación Andina de Fomento (CAF), the Fondo Latinoamericano de Reservas (FLAR), the Central American Bank for Economic Integration (created in 1961), the Caribbean Development Bank (1969) and the Financial Fund for the Rio de la Plata Basin, FONPLATA (1969) (Garcia 2015). From them, CAF and FLAR – though not bringing together a considerable number of countries in the region – could have played a more integrative role in the face of the crisis.

A veteran institution of financial integration, since it was first created in 1968 by the Andean Group, CAF is formally an Ibero-American development bank.[5] It has a contingent credit line, and its loan program has broadened to several sectors since the 2000s. However, the characteristics of CAF's financing lines and projects indicate that it operates mainly as a development bank and less as a regional relief fund, even considering its support to sovereign debt issuance and its increasing activities in global markets.

FLAR was created in 1978, by founding members Bolivia, Ecuador, Colombia, Peru and Venezuela. Its functions are typically those of a liquidity fund aimed at supporting countries in the face of problems in their balance of payments through loans and encouraging better management of international reserves, in addition to fostering financial cooperation between partners. Its institutional structure allows the fund to easily incorporate new members, and its very objectives could allow it

[5] CAF was created in 1970. It is owned by the 17 Latin American and the Caribbean countries and by Spain and Portugal. It has 13 private banks of the region as shareholders. https://www.caf.com/en/about-caf/who-we-are/

to turn into a powerful Latin American RFA (Lochagin 2015) should the largest economies of the region join. This could also enhance the FLAR's funding capacities.

Given the limited role of formal regional institutions in the region in combating the effects of the global recession, it is interesting to look for other actions carried out jointly by countries in the region to deal with the credit crunch that mastered the late 2000s in global economy. In the absence of regional institutions with macroeconomic cooperation programs, or multilateral financial arrangements or relief funds, some Latin American countries could have possibly established bilateral credit lines or other forms of bailout or mutual aid. The joint issuance of sovereign bonds by Argentina and Venezuela in 2006 – the Bonos del Sur – is an interesting case of credibility borrowing between countries. The markets saw this joint issue as a sign of Argentina's creditworthiness, which eased the country's access to debt financing. Phillips (2013) describes how the three different bonds (two Argentines and one Venezuelan) were initially issued as a package in the primary market but could be traded separately in the secondary market. Although there was no formal guarantee from the Venezuelan government to the Argentine issue, the market evaluated these bonds differently when compared to other Argentine sovereign bonds with similar maturity and yield. This was a very particular case that must be analysed in the perspective of Venezuela's struggle for greater regional leadership, against the backdrop of high availability of resources derived from oil and disputing this leadership with the Brazilian centre-left government.

Concluding Remarks

This chapter has shown that, despite the plurality and achievements of regional organizations and regional institutions created in Latin America in the past decades, they have never prioritized cooperation and integration on macroeconomic and financial matters. The few existing initiatives such as Mercosur's financial services protocol, UNASUR's Bank of the South, ALBA's common currency Sucre, Pacific Alliance's integration of stock exchanges (MILA) and the Fondo Latinoamericano de Reservas (FLAR) were not used or not effective to buffer the 2008 crisis. Latin American countries handled the impact of the 2008 crisis mainly at the domestic level as they lacked viable mechanisms to react collectively.

Literature

Benzi, D. (2017). ALBA-TCP. Anatomía de una integración que no fue. Quito: Ediciones Imago Mundi.

Bonilla, A. (2013). In G. Jaramillo (Ed.), *La CELAC en el escenario contemporâneo de América Latina y del Caribe*. San Jose: FLACSO-CAF.

Bouzas, R., da Motta Veiga, P., & Torrent, R. (2002). *In-depth analysis of Mercosur integration, its prospectives and the effects thereof on the market Access of EU goods, services and investments. Observatory of Globalization.* Barcelona: University of Barcelona.
Caetano, G., & Sanahuja, J. A. (2019). Integración regional y regionalismo en crisis. *Revista uruguaya de Ciencia Política, 28*(1), *7–14.*
Calixtre, A. B., & Barros, P. (2010). O Banco do Sul e o Brasil na Agenda da Nova Arquitetura Financeira Regional. *IPEA Boletim de Economia e Política Internacional, 3*, 22–23.
Cusack, A. K. (2018). *Venezuela, ALBA, and the limits of postneoliberal regionalism in Latin America and the Caribbean.* New York: Springer.
Fritz, B., & Mühlich, L. (2019). Regional Financial Arrangements in the Global Financial Safety Net: The Arab Monetary Fund and the Eurasian Fund for Stabilization and Development. *Development and Change, 50*(1), 96–121.
Garcia, L. E. (2015). Comparative advantages and challenges of Regional Development Banks: THE CAF experience. LSE Global South Unit Policy Brief Series No. 2/2015.
Kacef, O., & Monti, R. L. (2010). Latin America and the international crisis: Some considerations on macroeconomic policy. *The Perspective of the World Review, 2*, 1.
Lochagin, G. (2015). A ampliação do Fundo Latino-americano de Reservas como estratégia de integração financeira regional. In E. Iglesias, G. Daminani, A. Garcé, & F. W. Zibetti (Eds.), *Os Desafios da América Latina no Século XXI.* São Paulo: Editora da Universidade de São Paulo.
Martins, N. N. (2017). Integração Financeira na América Latina entre 2000 e 2014: avanços, limites e caminhos à frente. *Revista Tempo do Mundo, 3*, 2.
Ocampo, J. A. (2006). Regional financial cooperation: Experiences and challenges. In J. A. Ocampo (Ed.), *Regional financial cooperation* (pp. 1–39). Washington, D.C.: Brookings Institution Press.
Palestini, S. (2016). Development banks and regional powers: An analytical framework. KFG Working Paper n.77. Nov. 2016.
Phillips, L. M. (2013). The politics of joint sovereign borrowing: The Venezuelan/Argentine Bono del Sur. *Review of International Political Economy, 20*(3), 576–604.
Vadell, J. A. (2018). El Foro China-CELAC y el nuevo regionalismo para un mundo multipolar: desafíos para la Cooperación Sur-Sur. Carta Internacional, 13(1).

Part III
Nation-Level Impacts on Europe and Latin America

8

Explaining the Greek Crisis

Dimitris Katsikas and Pery Bazoti

Abstract The handling of the Greek crisis was not successful. Despite the sacrifices that the Greek people had to endure, the country's structural problems both in the public sector and the economy have not been resolutely resolved. This chapter offers an explanation for this failure. The main idea is to connect the externally imposed policy conditionality, with the particular characteristics of Greece's domestic political economy, seeking to integrate an analysis of impediments and opportunities for structural reform. While the literature on external institutional constraints emphasizes the possibility for achieving convergence, the institutionalist literature points towards divergence among national political economies, as institutional change and policy performance are conditioned by crucial intervening variables, namely, aspects of the domestic institutional infrastructure. In this context, Greece is a paradigmatic case of long-delayed or stalled reforms despite external pressures that promoted them. While most attention has been paid to the weaknesses of the EMU, this analysis' emphasis is on the role of crucial domestic factors. The analysis takes place in three steps: (a) the outline of Greece's institutional profile and growth trajectory based on an analysis of formal and informal domestic institutions; (b) the description and analysis of the design, implementation and impact of the adjustment programs; and (c) in view of (a) and (b) an assessment of whether the adjustment programs implemented in Greece took into consideration the characteristics of the country's political economy, and how and to what degree the failure to do so accounts for their results.

D. Katsikas (✉)
National and Kapodistrian University of Athens and Hellenic Foundation for European and Foreign Policy (ELIAMEP), Athens, Greece
e-mail: dkatsikas@eliamep.gr

P. Bazoti
Hellenic Foundation for European and Foreign Policy (ELIAMEP), Athens, Greece

Introduction

Greece has undergone a deep, long-lasting crisis with unprecedented consequences for its political and socio-economic system. Already before the onset of the crisis, Greece was facing a mounting public debt and a number of structural economic deficiencies. When in 2009, revelations about Greece's unexpectedly high fiscal deficit became known, the resulting loss of credibility, in combination with the country's fiscal and economic woes and international investors' low risk appetite in the aftermath of the global financial crisis, shut the country out of the markets forcing the Greek government to make an official request for aid. On 2 May 2010, Greece signed a bailout agreement for a 3-year, €110 billion loan, provided by the Eurozone member-states and the International Monetary Fund (IMF). The agreement came with strict conditionality in the form of a comprehensive policy program (Memorandum of Understanding (MoU)) that would be supervised by the so-called Troika (representatives of the IMF, the European Commission and the European Central Bank (ECB)).

The program called for an extremely harsh front-loaded austerity policy. The aim was to eliminate the deficit and achieve a sustainable primary surplus, in order to ensure the sustainability of public debt. At the same time, the memorandum required an extraordinary number of major structural reforms to streamline public administration and improve the economy's international competitiveness. However, things did not develop as predicted. The aggressiveness of fiscal adjustment led the Greek economy into deep recession, which in turn undermined the government's fiscal consolidation efforts, leading to new measures and plunging the country into a downward economic spiral (Katsikas 2012).

The second bailout agreement, signed in early 2012, did nothing to change the mood in a country that found itself in a desperate social, economic and political situation. Thousands of businesses had gone bust, while unemployment reached 22% in the first quarter of the year. Frustration and anger simmered among the population. These feelings were openly vented at the elections of May, which changed fundamentally the political map of Greece. The once mighty, socialist PASOK, which had come to power in the October 2009 elections and had handled the crisis until that point, was relegated to third place, losing more than 30 percentage points in the polls. New Democracy, PASOK's centre-right counterpart, did not fare much better; while taking first place, it recorded its worst electoral result ever. The winners of the election were radical parties on the left and the right, united by their opposition to the bailout agreement and the memorandum. Particularly impressive was the performance of Syriza, a radical left-wing party, which took second place. The transformation of the Greek political scene was completed in January 2015 when SYRIZA won an early election and formed a coalition government with AN.EL., a populist, nationalist and ultra-conservative right-wing party.

The new government embarked on a new and ambitious negotiation with the creditors to formulate an entirely new type of agreement, outside the framework of the bailout programs. The handling of the negotiation by the Greek government was extremely poor (Katsikas 2016) and resulted in the debacle of the summer of 2015, when the deadline for reaching an agreement expired, leaving the country without a program, and therefore without funding and the banks without access to ECB's liquidity.[1] Predictably, the country defaulted on an IMF payment, the banks were closed, and capital controls were imposed to prevent a bank run and capital flight. Despite the fact that the government won a hurriedly conducted referendum on a proposed draft agreement, with 61% of people rejecting the agreement (as was the government's proposal), the immediate danger of a Grexit ultimately led the government to sign a new bailout program. The new MoU continued where the previous left off, adding new austerity measures to make up for the lost time in 2015. Since 2017, the Greek economy has started growing again, and on August 2018, the third program was officially completed (the only one to be completed as planned). Although public finances have improved, the economic prospects of the country seem uncertain given the continued austerity of the post-bailout agreement with the creditors and the incomplete structural reforms program.

From this brief overview of the crisis, it is evident that its handling was not successful. The fiscal balance has been restored, but this came at a great economic and social cost; meanwhile many of the country's structural problems both in the public sector and the private economy remain unresolved. This chapter seeks to offer an explanation for this failure. The main idea is to connect the externally imposed policy conditionality, with the particular characteristics of Greece's domestic political economy, seeking to integrate an analysis of impediments and opportunities for structural reform. While the literature of external constraints emphasizes the potential for convergence, the institutionalist literature stresses the divergence among national political economies, as institutional change and policy performance are conditioned by crucial intervening variables, namely, aspects of the domestic institutional environment, including norms and practices.

The analysis will take place in three steps: (a) the establishment of Greece's political economy profile and growth trajectory before the crisis; (b) the description and analysis of the design, implementation and impact of the adjustment programs; and (c) in view of (a) and (b) an assessment of whether the adjustment program implemented in Greece took into consideration the country's institutional specificities and how to what degree the success/failure of doing so can account for the program's results.

[1] For a different view from the man who handled the negotiation, see Varoufakis (2018), and for a journalistic account that tells a very different story from that of Varoufakis, see Dendrinou and Varvitsioti (2019).

The Domestic Politico-Economic System

The present Greek political system was mainly consolidated in *Metapolitefsi*, a term referring to the period after the fall of the military junta in 1974 and the re-establishment of democracy. During this period, two parties dominated the political scene, the socialist-democratic PASOK and New Democracy on the centre-right. The two parties alternated in power, forming strong single-party governments, with smaller parties having a marginal role in governmental politics. During these years, the majority of the electorate was siding with one of the two dominant parties regardless of their policies. This kind of partisan identification reflected events of the Greek political history, mainly the Civil War of 1944–1949, when political divisions deteriorated to a prolonged armed conflict, a painful legacy whose shadow still lingers today.

Under such polarized circumstances, the formation of single-party governments has been relying mostly on the 'moving' voters between the two parties. Despite being a minority in numbers, this part of the electorate has proven to be a critical driver of elections' outcomes. Hence, political parties have traditionally sought to acquire control of this minority by creating and maintaining an extensive network of preferential relationships with potential voters, in exchange for their vote. Clientelism became the foundation of the Greek party system, in the form of privileges granted in specific social groups and/or areas, and permeated the functioning of the state and the private economy. State power has been used by political parties as a means to extend benefits and privileges in exchange for electoral support, resulting in the state's haphazard expansion into all areas of public life and the creation of what has been termed 'bureaucratic clientelism' (Lyrintzis 1984) or 'clientelistic state' (Sotiropoulos 2001).

This came mainly in the form of seeking employment in the public sector; a job in the public sector became exceptionally popular among citizens as it offered the advantages of job security and a relatively high wage. Consequently, it quickly became the subject of exchange in return for votes, at the expense of public finances. Although not disproportionally bigger than other OECD countries' public sectors, the Greek public sector has been more expensive, due to both higher remuneration costs and its inefficient operation (Ladi and Katsikas 2017). The fiscal impact of clientelism is well illustrated by the presence of politically induced cycles in Greece's public finance. A recent study by Chortareas et al. (2018) reveals that during election years in the era of Metapolitefsi, there was an annual increase in governments' expenses by 1.7% and a deterioration of the primary balance of almost 3%.

The favourable conditions for civil servants were not unrelated to the presence of their particularly strong trade union, ADEDY. Before the crisis, trade unions, in the form of formal organizations and institutions, were the sole actors of an underdeveloped civil society. Confederations of unions, and mainly ADEDY, or GSEE, representing employees of large private sector companies, had an active involvement in the political system and had established a quid pro quo bond with incumbent governments. This comes as no surprise if one considers that both political parties have infiltrated the labour and student movements (Sotiropoulos 2018).

Accordingly, a distorted collective bargaining process was forged. Unions pushed towards policies that were not aligned with the economic prospects and abilities of the state and the economy. General strikes and street protests were often used as a lever of pressure against incumbent governments. Such practices created an ineffective and fragmented labour market as the labour costs rose disproportionally to labour productivity and divisions between 'insiders' from influential labour unions and under-represented 'outsiders' (e.g. employees of small and medium-sized private businesses and the self-employed) were deepened. In these circumstances, undeclared work thrived. Clientelism ended up substituting social insurance and meritocracy and left no room for the development of a modern welfare system.

The private economy could not remain unaffected in these conditions. Growth was mainly based on domestic consumption of non-tradables fuelled by domestic and foreign credit as a result of the low interest rates that followed Greece's accession to the EMU and the liberalization of the Greek but also the European and international financial systems. This led to Greece's twin deficits. On the one hand, successive governments' 'largesse' led to a derailment of public finances, driving the fiscal deficit to an unprecedented 15.2% of GDP in 2009. On the other hand, Greece imported a large part of what it consumed, a tendency which led to an increasing current account deficit, which peaked at 14.9% in 2008.

The economy remained closed and introvert; exports of traded goods contributed less than 10% of GDP before the crisis, mostly in sectors of low technological content and value added (Zografakis and Kastelli 2017), while Greece ranked last in attracting Foreign Direct Investment (FDI) in the EU-27 (Papazoglou 2014). This situation was partly due to inflated labour costs, as explained above; the loss of competitiveness, however, was also due to other factors, such as the small size of Greek businesses and the low levels of competition in domestic product (goods and services) markets (Papazoglou 2014; Vettas and Kouranti 2014). Many of these problems were due to the adverse regulatory environment in Greek product and labour markets, which suffered from excessive and low-quality regulation, which, more often than not, served particular private interests. According to the Index of Economic Freedom (2018), for the period 1995–2008, the Greek economy moved between the moderately free and mostly unfree categories.

Indicative, and a direct result of the lack of openness and the close embrace between political power and economic interests, was the pervasive presence of corruption. The average score of the Corruption Perceptions Index of Transparency International (2018) for the years 2000–2009 was 4.4, with 0 standing for highly corrupt and 10 for 'clean' countries. At 2009, the year of the outbreak of the crisis, Greece had a score of 3.8 and ranked 94th among 180 countries.

Despite the absence of high-quality inclusive institutions, Greece managed to grow. After a slowdown of the growth rate in the 1970s and a drawn-out economic crisis during the 1980s, the economy recorded substantial growth from the mid-1990s up until the crisis; according to Eurostat data, between 1995 and 2007, Greece's GDP was growing by 3.74% annually, a growth rate well above the EU and Eurozone averages. However, this growth had a *plateau* given that it was driven by the effects on consumption and construction due to the partial liberalization of the economy, particularly in the financial system, during an era of global prosperity and de-regulation and the constant flow of EU structural funds. Favourable external conditions sustained the distortions and weaknesses of the Greek political and economic institutions, creating a socioeconomic framework which was at the same time ineffective and stable but also highly vulnerable to abrupt changes in the external environment.

External Conditionality: An Overview of the Policy and Institutional Aspects of the Adjustment Programs

The main objectives of the three Economic Adjustment Programs were to restore fiscal sustainability and international competitiveness and to secure the stability of the financial system. To achieve these objectives, the MoUs agreed between Greece and its creditors included a wide array of measures both in the expenditure and revenue side of the government's budget, a major structural reforms' program in both the public administration and the private economy and an ambitious plan of privatizations.

The focus of the first program was on restoring fiscal sustainability and therefore promoted tax increases and horizontal cuts in government expenses (e.g. through reductions in salaries, pensions and social benefits). These policies had an immediate effect, and by the end of 2010 the government was able to boast a spectacular reduction of the fiscal deficit by more than 5 percentage points. However, further progress in reducing the fiscal deficit, but also in the crucial task of restoring the country's competitiveness, required complex, difficult and time-consuming structural reforms in both the state apparatus and the private economy. In addition to their complexity, these reforms elicited strong and well-organized opposition from interest groups that stood to lose from their implementation. As a result, the structural reforms' program soon came to a standstill. At the same time, despite the improvement in public finances, the deep recession meant that public debt as a percentage of GDP rose to 172% in 2011, fuelling fears about an impeding Greek bankruptcy. Under these circumstances, markets' expectations regarding the country's economic course sank, and the sovereign debt crisis became a crisis of the banking sector as the Greek banks were heavily exposed to Greek public debt. The Troika gradually and reluctantly accepted the necessity of negotiating a second bailout agreement with additional funds, accompanied by an agreement to reduce Greek debt to more sustainable levels.

The second bailout program was signed in March 2012 by an interim three-party coalition government under Lucas Papademos, former ECB Vice President, which had formed following a governmental crisis in late 2011. The funds made available through the second bailout agreement were €174 billion; €117.8 billion were related to the bail-in of the private sector creditors (PSI), while the remainder were meant to cover the operational financing needs of the Greek government and the repayment of public debt falling due (European Commission 2012). The terms of the second loan agreement were more favourable than the first (whose maturity was also extended); the new loans had long maturities (15–30 years, with a grace period of 10 years for the European loan) and a reduced interest rate margin. At the same time, the PSI deal reduced the privately held Greek debt by €106 billion, while extending the remainder for up to 30 years, imposing on investors losses of up to 75% in terms of net present value.

Despite the aforementioned benefits, the agreement sparked a domestic political crisis, due to the new round of measures mandated by the memorandum that accompanied the loan agreement. More specifically, the memorandum dictated a new round of austerity measures including the abolition of most tax exemptions, a new round of reductions in salaries, pensions and benefits and more cuts in several areas of public spending. However, what caused the greatest consternation were the interventions in the labour market. The minimum wage was reduced by 22% and by an additional 10% for young people up to the age of 25. At the same time, the new memorandum abolished the status of existing collective agreements as a minimum framework of reference for labour rights and wages, until new agreements were negotiated between employers and employees, opening thus the way for the replacement of sectoral agreements by company-level and individual agreements. The memorandum also stipulated that personnel in the public sector would be reduced by at least 150,000 until 2015. Finally, the agreement included an extremely ambitious privatization plan which was originally thought to bring to the public coffers €50 billion, a projection that proved wildly optimistic.

The government coalition of the radical left SYRIZA and the nationalist right-wing AN.EL. signed the third Economic Adjustment Program after a period of dramatic and ultimately failed negotiations with the country's creditors, which led to the highly controversial and polarizing *referendum* of June 2015. The third loan agreement, signed in August 2015, was in line with the previous ones, adding new measures to make up for the off-track course of the Greek economy during the negotiations' period. The new reform agenda was based on four main pillars. First, the restoration of fiscal sustainability with a gradual increase of primary surplus targets to 3.5% of GDP from 2018 onwards through a set of upfront fiscal measures such as VAT increases, a comprehensive pension reform meant to reduce the fiscal burden of future pensions and measures to enhance tax compliance. To ensure compliance with the targets, the first program review in May 2016 added a mechanism which automatically triggered additional measures in case of fiscal imbalances. Second, the restoration of financial stability by addressing in a decisive way the issue of non-performing loans (NPLs) and by recapitalizing the banks by end-2015. Third, in order to strengthen growth and restore competitiveness, Greece undertook the responsibility to implement a new privatization plan, policies that would support further investments as well as a wide range of reforms in the labour and product markets. Finally, a key priority was the creation of a modern structure in public administration with measures aiming at enhancing its efficiency, fighting corruption and ensuring the independence of key institutions such as the revenue administration and the statistics institute (European Commission 2016).

Assessing the Compatibility of the External Constraint and Domestic Institutions

The policy conditionality promoted through the MoUs had all the characteristics of the 'traditional' IMF recipe: fiscal consolidation, liberalization of the economy and, due to the inability to engage in external devaluation, labour market reforms aimed at internal devaluation. This policy program failed to adequately take into account the particular characteristics of Greece's political economy.

First, while there is no doubt that a certain degree of austerity would have to be implemented in the case of Greece, given its huge fiscal deficit, the fiscal consolidation program was extremely ambitious. The first MoU called for an array of fiscal measures with a view to reducing the fiscal deficit by 11.2% of GDP by 2013, that is, a reduction of more than 3% of GDP per year, with primary surpluses projected thereafter. This kind of adjustment is not unprecedented but has been achieved in only a handful of cases, typically not in circumstances of deep recession, which Greece found itself in already from 2008, and in countries with very different characteristics from Greece, namely, open and extrovert economies (Anastasatou 2017). The fiscal consolidation program underestimated the dependence of the Greek economy on the state budget and domestic consumption and therefore the consequences that a drastic reduction in state spending and disposable income, as a result of austerity, would have on economic growth. Indeed, the program's projections were constantly and overwhelmingly optimistic regarding a number of macroeconomic variables, such as private consumption and investment and therefore GDP growth (Petralias et al. 2013).

The unprecedented decline of economic activity and the consequent dramatic increase in unemployment (Fig. 8.1) translated into reduced tax revenues and social security contributions, at a time that the government bill for unemployment and other social benefits was increasing. As a result, fiscal targets were missed, which led to the adoption of new austerity measures to make up for the deviations, which in turn deepened the recession.[2] This downward economic spiral derailed the creditors' plans and made obvious the need for a second MoU, which however continued on the same policy path, as did the third.

In addition to miscalculating the impact of austerity on the Greek economy, given its structural characteristics, it seems that the designers of the MoUs also ignored two other features of the Greek political economy. First, the dependence of

[2] Governments also tried to meet the fiscal targets by reneging on their own obligations, by delaying tax returns and payments towards domestic suppliers and by cutting down repeatedly the public investment account in the budget; these tactics deprived the economy from much-needed liquidity, deepening the downward economic spiral.

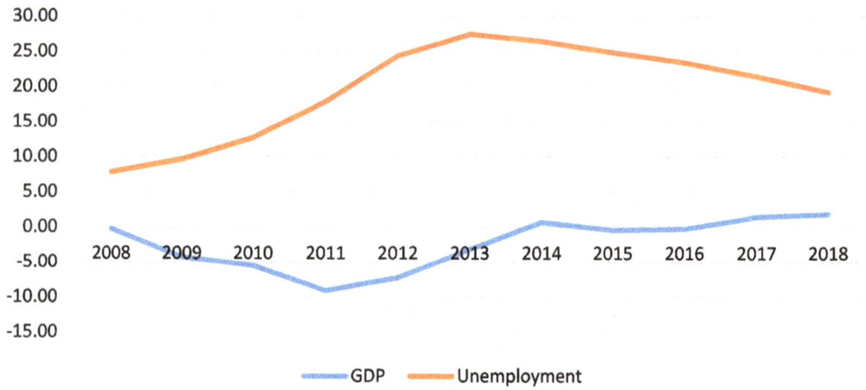

Fig. 8.1 GDP growth rate and unemployment rate (Source: ELSTAT)

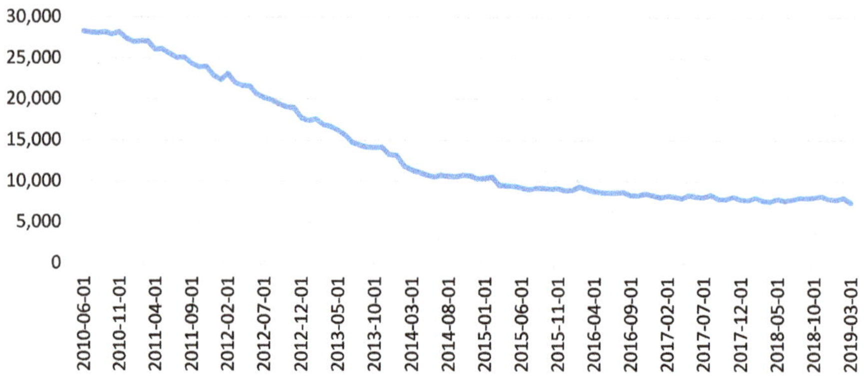

Fig. 8.2 Volume of new bank euro-denominated loans to non-financial corporations, Greece, June 2010–February 2019 (in millions of euros). (Source: Bank of Greece)

both the private economy and the state on the domestic banking system for funding. Given the banks' high exposure to Greek public debt, the impact of the sovereign debt crisis on Greek banks was tremendous as it cut them off from the interbank market and imposed on them substantial losses through the PSI. Moreover, as the economy deteriorated and uncertainty rose, there was a massive outflow of deposits and a dramatic increase in NPLs.[3] The resultant credit crunch left Greek businesses not only without access to capital for investment purposes but lacking even working capital to meet their daily operational needs (see Fig. 8.2). In the rare cases that

[3]According to the Bank of Greece (2015), banks' non-performing exposures (a measure similar to NPLs) in the first quarter of 2015 accounted for 40.8% of all loans and amounted to more than 100 bn euros.

funding was available, the high cost of capital discouraged most businesses from borrowing, despite their dire circumstances.[4]

Secondly, the MoUs did not take into account the limited support available through the weak and fragmented Greek welfare state, which traditionally catered mostly to the needs of pensioners. The insufficiency of social benefits (including unemployment benefits) meant that many people went for years with minimal or even no support at all.[5] As a result, the economic crisis led to social degradation (Matsaganis and Leventi 2014; Katsikas et al. 2015), as poverty rates soared to unprecedented levels (Fig. 8.3). The severe social crisis not only impeded economic recovery but fuelled even more the social and political reaction against the continued austerity policies and the MoUs in general, raising further the political cost of their implementation.

While austerity was driving the Greek economy into depression, an ambitious program of structural reforms was also under way. It had two main objectives: (a) to improve the effectiveness and efficiency (in fiscal terms) of the public administration and (b) to restore the economy's international competitiveness. Pursuing the first objective called for a broad array of structural reforms with a fiscal impact, such as the establishment of a single payments authority for all public servants, a complete overhaul of the financial administration of the Greek National Health System, an overhaul of the Greek tax and pension systems and even reforms in the country's judicial system.

The reforms promoted were appropriate and much needed in most of the cases; however, their design and implementation were far from optimal, partly because

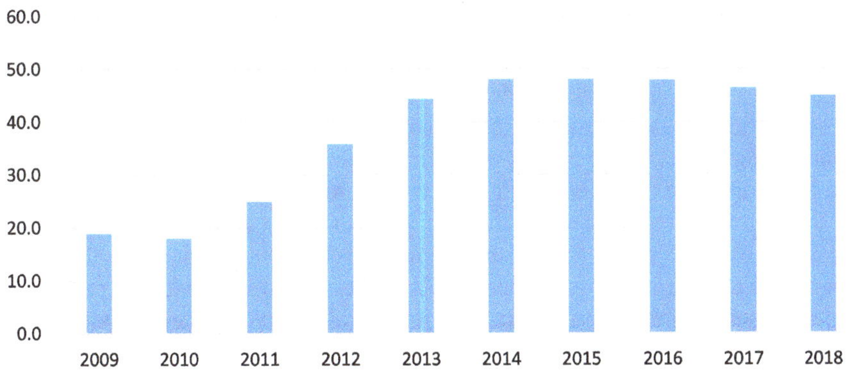

Fig. 8.3 At-risk-of-poverty rate anchored at a fixed moment in time (2008) by age and sex, Greece. (Source: Eurostat – EU-SILC Survey)

[4] Between the summer of 2010 and October 2015, the average interest rate for credit lines to non-financial corporations ranged between 6 and 8% (Bank of Greece). It is worth noting that for most of this period ECB's official rate was below 1%.

[5] It is telling that during the crisis, typically less than 15% of the unemployed received unemployment benefits.

they did not adequately take into account the institutional capacity and characteristics of the Greek public administration. A first problem was the sheer size and scope of the reform program, designed to be implemented in a relatively short period of time, which strained the limited resources of an already weak administration (Spanou 2018). This led to outright failures to promote certain reforms and partial and delayed progress in the implementation of others. The structural weaknesses of the public administration were compounded by the focus on fiscal consolidation, which affected adversely the priorities of many reforms (Spanou 2018).

Secondly, the design and handling of administrative reforms were often driven by a misunderstanding of the broader normative and political framework surrounding the operation of public administration. This became clear with one of the most controversial reforms, a commitment to reduce the number of public servants by 150.000 by 2015. Leaving the arbitrariness of that number aside, the reform was based more on calculations about its fiscal impact and the desire to send a 'message' about the creditors' determination to end the political protection enjoyed hitherto by civil servants. The announcement of the reform served only to create insecurity to civil servants amidst a deep economic crisis, which created a political backlash both by the public servants' unions and the opposition parties. Threatening massive lay-offs in the public sector ignored the dependence of the ruling political elites on the goodwill of civil servants to produce results in an administration which lacked clear, common and high-quality operating procedures but also violated a 'taboo' of Greek society, which views lay-offs as a means of restoring efficiency, as ethically reprehensible. While the government was quick to give public assurances that personnel reductions would happen without resorting to lay-offs, the political backlash sidetracked other necessary reforms, such as the introduction of a personnel evaluation system or a mobility scheme.

Similar problems emerged with reforms intended to restore the international competitiveness of the Greek economy as the internal devaluation approach ignored the structural and institutional characteristics of the Greek economy. The small export sector, specializing mostly in agricultural and low-technology products, could not capitalize on lower labour costs to a degree that would have a significant impact on the economy. Indeed, in the early years of the crisis, there was hardly any increase in exports despite the fact that labour costs had been reduced considerably (Zografakis and Kasteli 2017). Since 2015, exports have been gradually increasing but not at a pace sufficient to sustain economic recovery, and the Greek economy is still a long way from being considered an open and extrovert economy (Fig. 8.4).

Indeed, given the structural and institutional characteristics of the Greek economy, such as the small scale of production, specialization in low value-added activities, high dependence on imports for intermediate products and the bureaucratic burden which impedes competition and productive investment, the belief that the reduction of labour costs alone would be sufficient to substantially improve the competitiveness of the Greek economy should be considered naïve at best.

Given these problems, a more rational scheme would involve early and ambitious reforms in the business environment and the product markets, before moving to labour market reforms. Such a reform sequence is compatible with the findings of

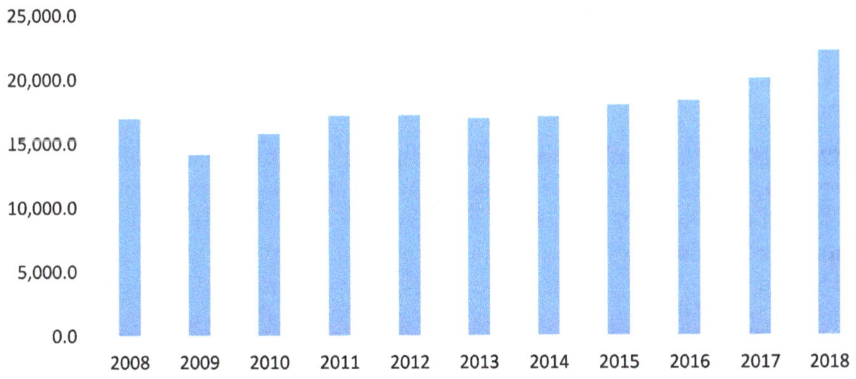

Fig. 8.4 Exports of traded goods (excluding ships and fuel), 2008–2018 (in millions of euros), Greece. (Source: Bank of Greece)

empirical bibliography internationally (Bouis et al. 2012) but also for the case of Greece (Petralias and Katsikas 2018). Unfortunately, significant reforms in the product markets, such as the so-called OECD's toolkit,[6] which has been shown to have affected positively employment and prices (Petralias et al. 2018), were only introduced in 2014, as was the crucial reform of the regulatory framework for the licensing of productive investments, a reform which has yet to be completed.

Conclusions

Greece's crisis was one of the deepest and longest-lasting crises in the post-war period internationally. During a period that lasted more than 8 years, the country implemented three consecutive adjustment programs which imposed strict austerity policies and a host of ambitious reforms. While the fiscal balance has been restored, the economic and social cost incurred were tremendous, as more than 25% of GDP was lost and unemployment and poverty rates soared to unprecedented levels. At the same time, the sustainability of Greece's debt has not been restored, because the huge drop in GDP has increased the ratio of debt to GDP well above its pre-crisis levels (181% in 2018). Moreover, despite progress in many areas of public administration and the regulation of the private economy, some of Greece's most important structural problems remain unresolved. These problems continue to undermine both the efficient and effective operation of the public administration and Greece's

[6]The 'OECD Competition Assessment toolkits' are packages of measures that aim to reduce the regulatory burden in product and service markets, based on comprehensive studies of several key sectors. In the Greek programs, there were three waves of such studies, in 2013, 2014 and 2016. In total, the toolkits identified 1276 regulations which inhibited competition and proposed 773 measures relating to 14 major sectors of the Greek economy (SEV 2016).

potential to become an extrovert, competitive economy. The country has gone through a period of tremendous social and political unrest, which led to a radical change of its political landscape and at times threatened Greece's place in the Eurozone.

On balance therefore, one would be hard-pressed to argue that Greece's bailout has been a success story. One of the most important reasons for this failure has been the lack of ownership of the policies promoted. This in turn is due not only to the character of the policies themselves (e.g. extreme austerity) but also to the shallow and incomplete understanding of Greece's political economy. The policies promoted magnified the economic and social crisis as they failed to take into consideration the public administration's and the economy's structural and institutional features. Beyond its adverse economic impact, this failure also had significant political repercussions, as it allowed populist parties to take advantage of people's anger and frustration and dominate the political scene, increasing political uncertainty, undermining progress in much-needed reforms and ultimately delaying the country's exit from the crisis.

The creditors' attitude of zero tolerance for deviations from the program, which at times seemed to stem not only from ignorance but also ideological fixations, particularly on the crucial issue of austerity, did not facilitate incumbent governments' efforts.[7] On the contrary, it fed social discontent both against the incumbent governments and the European Union. It is telling that, in 2018, following Greece's completion of the third adjustment program, three quarters of Greeks still did not trust the EU, the highest number among all member-states (Eurobarometer 90.3). All in all, it seems that too much economic, social and political capital was spent to achieve too little, too late.

References

Anastasatou, M. (2017). Είναι αλήθεια ότι η διατήρηση υψηλών πρωτογενών πλεονασμάτων για σειρά ετών είναι εφικτή. In D. Katsikas, K. Filinis, & M. Anastasatou (Eds.), *Κατανοώντας την Ελληνική Κρίση: Απαντήσεις σε Καίρια Ερωτήματα για το Κράτος, την Οικονομία και την Ευρώπη*. Athens: Papazisis Publications.

Bank of Greece (2015). *Monetary Policy*. Annual Report. Athens

Bouis, R., Causa, O., Demmou, L., Duval, R., & Zdzienicka, A. (2012). The short-term effects of structural reforms: An empirical analysis. *OECD Economics Department Working Paper, No* 949.

Chortareas, C., Logothetis, V. E., & Papandreou, A. A. (2018). Elections and opportunistic budgetary policies in Greece. *Managerial and Decision Economics, 39*(8), 854–862.

Dendrinou, V., & Varvitsioti, E. (2019). *The last bluff: How Greece came face-to-face with financial catastrophe & the secret plan for its euro exit*. Athens: Papadopoulos Publishing.

[7] That is not to say that incumbent governments always put in the required effort; governments seeking to reform the Greek state and economy would have to clash with a wide array of interest groups, turning in effect against their own political clients. In many cases, therefore, they chose to safeguard partisan interests, hoping to preserve some of their political capital.

European Commission (2012). The Second Economic Adjustment Programme for Greece. Occasional Papers 94. Brussels.

European Commission (2016). *Compliance Report: The Third Economic Adjustment Programme for Greece. First Review.* June. Brussels.

Index of Economic Freedom (2018). Figure the data. https://www.heritage.org/index/visualize. Accessed 25 Apr 2018.

Katsikas, D. (2012). The never-ending greek crisis: A tragedy without a catharsis. *Revista de Estudios Europeos*, *60*(Jul-Dec), 33–52.

Katsikas, D. (2016). An old crisis, a new government and the creditors: 'Plus ca change plus c'est la même chose'? In P. Morrilas & T. Dokos (Eds.), *Greece and the EU: Lessons from a long-lasting crisis*. Barcelona: CIDOB MonoFigures, Barcelona Centre for International Affairs.

Katsikas, D., Karakitsios, A., Filinis, K., & Petralias, A. (2015). *Social profile report on poverty, social exclusion and inequality before and after the crisis in Greece*. Crisis Observatory and Hellenic Open University. http://crisisobs.gr/en/2015/01/ekthesi-gia-to-kinoniko-profil-tis-elladas-se-schesi-me-ti-ftochia-ton-kinoniko-apoklismo-ke-tin-anisotita-prin-ke-meta-apo-tin-ekdilosi-tis-krisis/. Accessed 20 Sept 2019.

Ladi, S., & Katsikas, D. (2017). Είναι αλήθεια ότι ο δημόσιος τομέας στην Ελλάδα είναι υπερβολικά μεγάλος. In D. Katsikas, K. Filinis, & M. Anastasatou (Eds.), *Κατανοώντας την Ελληνική Κρίση: Απαντήσεις σε Καίρια Ερωτήματα για το Κράτος, την Οικονομία και την Ευρώπη*. Athens: Papazisis Publications.

Lyrintzis, C. (1984). Political parties in the post-junta Greece: A case of "bureaucratic clientelism"? *West European Politics, 7*(2), 99–118.

Matsaganis, M. & Leventi, C. (2014). Poverty and Inequality during the Great Recession in Greece. *Political Studies Review*, 12, 209–223.

Papazoglou, C. (2014). Ελληνική Εξαγωγική Επίδοση: Ανταγωνιστικότητα και Άμεσες Ξένες Επενδύσεις. In: M. Masourakis, & C. V. Gortsos (Eds.), *Ανταγωνιστικότητα για Ανάπτυξη: Προτάσεις πολιτικής*. Hellenic Bank Association.

Petralias, A., Petros, S., & Prodromidis, P. (2013). Greece in recession: Economic predictions, mispredictions, forecast suggestions and policy recommendations. *Cyprus Economic Policy Review* 7(2), 53–80.

Petralias, A., & Katsikas, D. (2018). Μεταρρυθμίσεις στην αγορά προϊόντων και στο επιχειρηματικό περιβάλλον. In D. Katsikas, M. Anastasatou, E. Nitsi, A. Petralias, & K. Filinis (Eds.), *Διαρθρωτικές Μεταρρυθμίσεις στην Ελλάδα κατά τη Διάρκεια της Κρίσης (2010–2014): Επισκόπηση, Αποτίμηση και Προτάσεις Πολιτικής*. Athens: Bank of Greece and ELIAMEP.

Petralias, A., Anastasatou M., & Katsikas, D. (2018). Balancing adjustment policies and structural reforms in Greece: the case of product markets. In P. Manasse & D. Katsikas (Eds.), *Economic Crisis and Structural Reforms in Southern Europe*. London and New York: Routledge.

SEV. (2016). *Η εφαρμογή της εργαλειοθήκης του ΟΟΣΑ για την αξιολόγηση των συνθηκών του ανταγωνισμού στην Ελλάδα…σε αριθμούς. Πορεία υλοποίησης και νέες συστάσεις*. Athens: Business Environment Observatory, SEV.

Spanou, C. (Ed.) (2018). *Reforms in Public Administration under the crisis: Overview, Description, Evaluation*. Athens: ELIAMEP.

Sotiropoulos, A. D. (2001). *Η κορυφή του πελατειακού κράτους*. Athens: Potamos.

Sotiropoulos, D. A. (2018). A fragmented but strengthened civil society? In D. Katsikas, D. A. Sotiropoulos, & M. Zafiropoulou (Eds.), *Socioeconomic fragmentation and exclusion in Greece under the crisis*. New York: Palgrave Macmillan.

Transparency International (2018). *Corruption perceptions index 2000*. https://www.transparency.org/research/cpi/cpi_2000/0. Accessed 15 Mar 2018.

Varoufakis, Y. (2018). *Adults in the room: My battle with the European and American deep establishment*. New York: Farrar, Straus and Giroux.

Vettas, N., & Kouranti, F. (2014). Ανταγωνισμός, ανταγωνιστικότητα και εξωστρέφεια: Η φύση και ο ρόλος των εμποδίων εισόδου. In M. Masourakis, & C. V. Gortsos (Eds.), *Ανταγωνιστικότητα για ανάπτυξη: Προτάσεις πολιτικής*. Hellenic Bank Association.

Zografakis, S., & Kastelli, I. (2017). Is it true that reducing labour costs is sufficient to improve the competitiveness of the Greek economy? In D. Katsikas, K. Filinis, & M. Anastasatou (Eds.), *Κατανοώντας την Ελληνική Κρίση: Απαντήσεις σε Καίρια Ερωτήματα για το Κράτος, την Οικονομία και την Ευρώπη*. Athens: Papazisis Publications.

9

Euro Crisis and Portugal's Reaction

Kai Enno Lehmann

Abstract This chapter analyses the reaction of Portugal to the Euro crisis, in particular, the absence of popular revolt, and explores the possibilities to replicate the 'Portuguese experience' elsewhere.

Introduction

To say the global economic crisis from 2008 onwards hit Portugal hard would be both a statement of the obvious, as well as an understatement. The country went through a deep recession, painful 'structural reforms' and suffered high unemployment and a 'brain drain' of mostly young people. In this sense, Portugal has been no different to the experiences of Spain, Greece or Italy from within the European Union (EU). Yet, unlike those three other countries, Portugal has *not* suffered a 'populist revolt' from the political Right or Left. Instead, Portugal today is often seen as an example of a successful economic recovery without suffering social or political rupture.

The present chapter asks not only whether such a statement is accurate but what explains this apparent absence of a popular revolt. Looking at social, political and economic indicators, it will trace the evolution of Portugal over the last 10 years since the onset of the financial crisis. The central argument put forward here will be that, whilst it is useful to look at the Portugal case in the context of the global economic crisis to see what 'lessons can be learned', we should be careful in drawing too many conclusions for other cases and replicating the 'Portugal experience' elsewhere since much of what has happened in the country needs to be put into the context of its particularities. Therefore, any attempt to replicate its approach elsewhere will most likely fail. Any lessons need to be 're-adapted' to the particular circumstances of other countries.

K. E. Lehmann (✉)
University of São Paulo, São Paulo, Brazil
e-mail: klehmann@usp.br

The Context: Portugal Before the Crash—Not All Well, Even Then

There is a lot of literature today looking at the origins of the economic crisis of 2008 or the origins of the Eurozone crisis (Giddens 2015; Krugman 2012; Lane 2012; amongst many). Whilst this literature is hugely informative, it frequently overlooks national particularities. In the case of Portugal, one of the key factors in this respect is the fact that, by 2008, the country had essentially been in economic crisis mode for many years.

As Reis (2013) argued, the country had been in economic difficulties since at least the year 2000, suffering a serious economic contraction between 1999 and 2000.[1] This was accompanied by rising unemployment and years of anaemic productivity (ibid: 144). The then Chief Economist of the International Monetary Fund, Olivier Blanchard, warned in 2007 that 'Portugal is in serious trouble [...] Growth is very low. The budget deficit is large. The current account deficit is very large ... In the absence of policy changes, the most likely scenario is one of competitive disinflation, a period of sustained high unemployment until competitiveness has been reestablished' (Portugal 2015: 6).

Subsequent history confirmed these warnings. Apart from a crisis of growth, the country was also dealing with a chronic budget deficit which, in 2005, already stood at 6.2% of GDP,[2] way above the 3% stipulated by the rules of the Eurozone. In fact, according to Pereira and Wemans (2012), from the year of its re-democratization to the onset of the economic crisis, there had never been a surplus in the state budget. As such, it should come as no surprise that the Portuguese state accumulated high levels of debt over the decades. In fact, Portugal's fiscal position since democratization had been so perilous that, since 1976, the International Monetary Fund instigated 'fiscal consolidation programs' for the country on three different occasions (Lourtie 2011). When, therefore, in 2009, the debt-to-GDP ratio was at 83.6% (a ratio which worsened steadily in subsequent years), it was, whilst alarming, not actually anything new.[3] Rather, it followed a historical pattern which the country had gone through several times. Just as importantly, household debt in the country had also risen steadily prior to 2008. Whereas in 1995, it was 35.1% of GDP, by 2008, it had already reached more than 90%.[4] These figures hint at deep structural problems within the Portuguese economy which both pre-date, at least partially caused, and overlay the crisis from 2008. In order, therefore, to understand the *extent* and *impact* of the 2008 crisis, it is worth having a look at these issues.

---

[1] See https://data.worldbank.org/country/Portugal. Accessed 15 May 2019.

[2] See https://countryeconomy.com/deficit/portugal. Accessed 15 May 2019.

[3] Data from https://tradingeconomics.com/portugal/government-debt-to-gdp. Accessed 15 May 2019.

[4] https://www.ceicdata.com/en/indicator/portugal/household-debt%2D%2Dof-nominal-gdp Accessed15 May 2019.

One such structural issue is the size of informal economy. According to some estimates, the informal sector in Portugal accounted for approx. 23% of GDP, significantly above the share of most—though by no means all—EU member states prior to 2004 (Barbosa et al. 2013). To give just one example, in Austria, a comparable country in terms of size, just under 10% of the economy was classed as informal in 2007 (ibid). This informality, in turn, has an impact on the tax base from which the Portuguese state can finance its activities. In 2008, on the eve of the crisis, the tax-to-GDP ratio was a touch over 21%.[5]

A second structural issue has been a long-standing problem with the *quality* of jobs created. According to the European Union itself, '[t]he prevalence of low qualified workers in the Portuguese labour market has been considered as one of the most important constrains to national competitiveness and development'.[6] Such jobs tend to be less secure and low-paid, making those holding them far more susceptible to economic shocks. An economy based on such type of employment simply lacks the *resilience* to be able to cope with economic shocks over which the country in question itself may have very little influence. This lack of resilience is underpinned by an education system which does not adequately prepare Portugal's young population for the changing working environment (OECD 2015; Pereira and Wemans 2012). Uneven educational attainment contributed to an entrenchment of a lack of social mobility and high levels of social inequality.

The critical point is to realize that, when the economic crisis hit the Eurozone in 2008, Portugal was both already in economic difficulties as a result of a myriad of factors as well as ill-prepared to withstand any further shocks. In simple terms, the economy was not resilient enough to be able to cope with, or adapt to, the crisis which unfolded from 2008 onwards. As a consequence, Portugal was one of the countries hardest hit. This was most obviously shown in the country's unemployment rate, which rose from a little under 8% in 2008 to just under 18% by 2013, underpinning in the process two of the structural problems touched upon above: the persistence of a large, informal economy as well as a brain drain from the country of primarily young people (Khalip 2015).[7]

This being the case, there was general gloom around Portugal's prospects of escaping this vicious economic cycle it seemed to be trapped in. This gloom was added to by problems within the political system which, once again, were long-standing. At national level, Portuguese politics since re-democratization has been marked by extended periods of—more or less stable—coalition and/or minority governments (Lloyd-Jones 2001; Lobo 2001). Particularly on the left of the political spectrum, the country has been marked by political fragmentation and instability (Bale 2008). This situation did not lend itself to long-term planning and strategic thinking to make the country more resilient and address the structural factors touched upon above.

---

[5] https://data.worldbank.org/indicator/GC.TAX.TOTL.GD.ZS?locations=PT. Accessed 15 May 2019.

[6] https://www.eurofound.europa.eu/publications/report/2009/portugal-quality-of-work-and-employment-of-low-qualified-workers. Accessed 15 May 2019.

[7] See https://tradingeconomics.com/portugal/unemployment-rate. Accessed 15 May 2019.

The impact of the economic crisis, then, has to be seen within this context: a country with a relatively young, and fragile, democracy which had proved itself to be incapable of developing and implementing policies capable of tackling the deep structural economic problems the county faced. It is here that we need to look at the role of the European Union within this scenario.

The Response and Role of the European Union

The above argument has some critical implications for the role of the European Union in the crisis and prior to it. Historically, Portugal's membership of the EU has been seen as enormously beneficial to the country in general and its economy in particular. For instance, from the year before its accession in 1986 to the eve of the economic crisis in 2008, GDP per head in the country rose from $2705 to 24,816.[8] Equally, for most of its life as an EU member, Portugal saw an inflow of foreign direct investment.[9] As a result, public opinion surveys have consistently shown large support in Portugal for EU membership over the years, as well as for membership of the single currency, of which Portugal is a founding member.[10]

This public support, as well as the severity and long-standing nature of the crisis as described above, gave the EU some political cover and freedom to act, particularly bearing in mind that Portugal has had experience of receiving outside 'assistance' or 'interference' (depending on one's point of view) in macroeconomic management in response to economic crises or challenges, as was the case in preparation of entry to the single currency during the 1990s (Bale 2008; Lloyd-Jones 2001). The response of the EU to the crisis was what one 'traditional'. In agreeing a so-called 'bailout' programme to stop the country falling into bankruptcy, the EU—together with the European Central Bank and the International Monetary Fund, the 'Troika'—required Portugal to undertake some significant macroeconomic adjustments. In return for a three-year loan worth approximately 78bn euros, the country undertook to implement:

- A public sector wage freeze and limiting promotion opportunities
- An increase in sales tax (VAT) on some items, such as cars
- The privatization of parts of the national energy company as well as the whole of the national airline TAP
- The reduction of some pensions and the freezing of others and
- A further limiting of the amount of time unemployment benefit can be paid.

[8] See https://www.macrotrends.net/countries/PRT/portugal/gdp-per-capita. Accessed 15 May 2019.

[9] See https://data.worldbank.org/indicator/BM.KLT.DINV.WD.GD.ZS?locations=PT.Accessed 15 May 2019.

[10] For the historical series, see https://ec.europa.eu/commfrontoffice/publicopinion/index.cfm/Chart/index. Accessed 15 May 2019.

In putting forward these measures, the key objectives were to 'maintain the stability of the Portuguese financial sector and to buffer the domestic impact of the crisis' (Portugal 2015: 10). Unsurprisingly, as elsewhere in Europe, the measures put forward by the Troika were heavily contested. From an economic point of view, many have argued that the austerity measures contained in the bailout plan would have a detrimental impact both on the economy as a whole and people's living standards individually (Pedroso 2014). Politically, there was strong criticism from many quarters about the fact that the European Union, at least initially, did nothing to address the flaws in the design of the single currency and associated fiscal processes despite the fact that, after Ireland and Greece, Portugal was the third Eurozone country needed to be bailed out in order to avoid sliding into bankruptcy (Costa et al. 2016). This suggests that there are evident, and profound, structural problems in the design of the EU's monetary union, and these are *those* which need to be addressed in order to avoid future crises.

This ties into broader arguments made about the policy focus of the European Union. As outlined above, Portugal has suffered from *long-standing* structural problems in its economy which were somewhat masked by the macroeconomic performance of the country since it joined the EU in 1986. As a result, the failure to address these structural problems was often overlooked, including by the EU. As Bittner (2010) has argued, the unwillingness and/or inability of the EU to address structural problems has been one of the most striking defects of its work over a long period of time, and the crisis which came about in Portugal (as well as elsewhere) was only one of the many manifestations of this failure (see also Lehmann 2018).

In the specific case of Portugal linked to this was also the worry of the country following in the footsteps of Greece, Spain and Italy—amongst others—which have had to content with the rise of populist parties from both the right and left in response to the economic crises the respective countries passed through after 2008 (Giddens 2015). Yet, in Portugal, the surge of populist parties has not occurred. There has been an intense debate in the academic literature as to what, in contrast to several other European countries, explains this absence of populism in Portuguese politics and society at large. In this literature, one can detect several explanations, roughly grouped under demography, history, culture and specific local contemporary factors. It is worth looking at these briefly in turn.

The Absence of Populism in Portugal?

The first factor explaining the absence of a strong, anti-establishment party in Portugal is the make-up of its political, and party, system. Critically in this respect, Portugal actually has a long history of having relatively strong 'outlier' parties. Ever since democratization from the mid-1970s onwards, the Portuguese Communist Party, for instance, has consistently polled in the region of 10% of the vote, be it in local or national elections (Llana 2015). That means that there is little room, on the Left at least, for a 'protest party'. It already exists but is part of the political mainstream.

Linked to this is Portuguese history. Unlike Greece or Spain, the country does not have a contentious recent history. It has not had the experience of a civil war, like Greece, or strong regional separatist movements which, in some cases, have included a long-lasting terrorist campaign, as in the case of Spain. Portugal's history is, in this sense, more consensual, lacking both the precedents and incentives to pursue radical policies and radical politics aimed at overthrowing 'the system'. The experience of relatively consensual coalition governments since 1974 plays into this context. Portugal is not a country to which 'revolution' comes easily (Morlino and Raniolo 2017; Lloyd-Jones 2001).

The second key factor when discussing the absence of explicitly populist parties is the way politics is *done* in Portugal (Magalhães 2011). Critically, Portugal's mainstream political parties are primarily associations for the attainment of power. Yet, this also means that they have a strong sense of when to *leave* power in order to preserve themselves long term. In the specific case of the Portuguese bailout programme, this meant, for instance, that the then Socialist government asked for a bailout from the Troika of European Union, European Central Bank and the International Monetary Fund, yet then resigned to call for a snap general election. This meant that, in some ways at least, the established parties remained untarnished by what was to unfold: The Socialists could credibly claim not to be directly responsible for the *consequences* of the bailout and associated austerity programmes, whilst the Conservatives could credibly claim not to be responsible for the situation which *led to* the need for a bailout in the first place.

A third factor which explains the absence of an explicit populist movement in the country is demographic. In simple terms, those who might lead such a movement—the young—voted with their feet (and not at the ballot box) and left the country. Youth migration has surged since 2010 (Heinke 2016), leading some to claim that Portugal's younger generation has chosen 'emigration, not revolution' (Llana 2015). A potential revolutionary movement was therefore killed off, at least for the time being, by the very economic circumstances that might facilitate it. As a consequence, what protests there have been in Portugal have come largely from the older generation, hit hard by pension reforms and cuts to public services such as healthcare (ibid). These protests might be vociferous, but they do not threaten the system as a whole.

Finally, in Portugal, it has been possible to claim that the intervention by the Troika has been a success and one achieved in a relatively short time. The country exited its bailout programme in 2014 with governments claiming that the country can, once again, 'stand on its own two feet' (Amaro 2017). Recent data suggests that GDP per head in 2018 was just under 19,000 euros in 2018, compared with just over 16,000 euros in 2013.[11] Whilst the country was, at the time of the bailout, in a deep economic recession, GDP has now been growing at more than 2% per year since 2016. At the same time, unemployment has fallen from more than 16% in

[11] Data for this section from https://www.focus-economics.com/countries/portugal. Accessed 15 May 2019.

2013 to less than 10% in 2018. Linked to this, personal consumption has grown consistently since 2014, reflected in retail sales growth.[12] The medicine might have been bitter, so the argument goes, but it has had the desired effect, a line which the EU has certainly been pushing hard (Centeno 2018).

Yet, the above only tells part of the story. Populism may not be explicit in the way it is in Greece or Spain or Italy. However, this does not mean that there are no populist tendencies. First of all, it is worth noting that, following the inconclusive legislative election of 2015, a relatively radical-looking left-wing government did take power, replacing the centre-right government which had implemented the austerity measures described above (De Georgi and Santa-Pereira 2016). This does suggest that there was 'punishment' for these measures at the ballot box. Equally, it is worth noting that the government which took power, a minority administration led by Prime Minister Antonio Costa, has since relied on the support of the Portuguese Communist Party which, as argued above, has traditionally been the party of protest in times of crisis (ibid.). There *was*, therefore, protest, albeit within the context of the relatively benign conditions of Portugal.

It is also noticeable that the government has, since taking power in 2015, veered leftwards politically. Developing a strong anti-austerity narrative, some measures with a populist appeal—such as partially reversing public sector salary cuts—have sustained the government's popularity whilst changing the tone of the domestic debate of one from crisis management to optimism (Jones 2017). In other words, the government has managed to adopt some populist measures and tactics (the importance of narrative, for instance) and applied it to the country's specific circumstances whilst following a clear political line which was different from previous years and previous governments. In doing so, it attended to at least some of the demands that were made by civil society during the worst years of the crisis and the austerity which followed. It also provided a 'human touch' to its policies, focusing on such issues—the partial reversal of salary cuts, for instance—which make a clear, and almost immediate, difference to people's lives. In other words, it has *adapted* populism to the particular circumstances of the system within which it worked (Lorenz 2018).

The critical point, then, is that Portugal was *not* that different from other countries in having within its society and political system populist tendencies (see also Freire and Santana-Pereira 2019), but how the system managed to absorb and utilize these tendencies without causing it to rupture. It had adaptive capacity. This adaptive capacity, however, will be tested in the coming years as Portugal faces up to some of the structural challenges discussed above which resulted in, and sustained, the crisis in the first place and which have the potential to alter the dynamics of society and the current political system.

[12] Data from https://tradingeconomics.com/portugal. Accessed 15 May 2019. It is worth noting that the causal link between the policies of the troika and the more positive economic outlook has been questioned. See, for instance, Pedroso (2014); Jones (2017).

Future Challenges

In spite of the good news on the economic front, there have been some suggestions from analysts that the current recovery may not be all that it seems. The first reason for this is simply the impact the depth of the recession has had in terms of confidence, both in the country as a whole and on the part of the population. Yet, trust in the sustainability of the economic recovery—and the government policies to ensure such sustainability—is absolutely vital. Portugal still has the third-highest debt ratio of the European Union, standing currently at 120% of GDP.[13] In other words, the country is in no way 'out of the woods'.

More critically still, however, than this snapshot are long-term trends. Most crucial, perhaps, is the demographic development already touched upon above. The great exodus of the country's young population during the crisis years represents Portugal with a significant demographic challenge: It has one of the oldest populations in Europe, with all that this implies for the Labour market but also for the health and pension system. Therefore, it has to either try and 'repatriate' and retain its youngsters or encourage immigration. Yet, this in itself may shift the very conditions which have insulated the country from an explicit populist challenge (Khalip 2015). Furthermore, the government will have to tackle, structurally, the country's social security system to be sustainable in the long term.

Equally, the country's economic base remains fragile. A significant part of the current recovery has been based on a booming tourism sector. Yet, this sector is notoriously fickle and subject to outside influences and factors over which the government itself may have little to no control. International competitiveness of Portuguese businesses remains a significant concern, linked to age-old problems of the education system, already referred to at the start of this text, which, in simple terms, does not produce enough people with the kind of skills which would allow for a profound reform of the economic system of the country. These challenges, in turn, are linked to the structure of the Portuguese state, which is still often seen as too slow and unresponsive, both to the demands of business and the population at large (IMF 2018; OECD 2015). In other words, having overcome the immediate crisis, the government is now facing up challenges very similar to those which previous governments faced and whose inability to confront these challenges significantly contributed to the crisis in the first place.

Yet, it is unclear whether the current government has the capacity to deliver such reforms. In many ways, in fact, the current government was given sustainability and purpose by the gravity of the situation it found itself in upon assuming power. With the immediate emergency passed, the political dynamics inevitably change which may expose more of the differences between the partners in the left-wing alliance than had previously been the case. In recent months, there has been a noticeable emergence of tensions between those advocating a wholesale abandonment of aus-

[13] Data from https://tradingeconomics.com/portugal/government-debt-to-gdp. Accessed 15 May 2019.

terity policies and those, around the current Prime Minister, advocating for a more moderate and incremental change of course away from the policies of the 'bailout era'. It remains to be seen how these changes impact on the current left-wing coalition elected in October 2019 (Ames 2019).

In this respect, Portugal faces very similar types of challenges to the ones that it has faced ever since re-democratization: Structural reforms which would allow the country to become far more pro-active in *avoiding* crises rather than *react* once a crisis has hit. The key challenge, then, for a system which has shown itself remarkably resilient is to become one whose conditions allow for crisis avoidance. This is critical since, as has been shown, the absence of explicitly populist parties does *not* mean the absence of conditions which can foster and incubate populism. In fact, as has been argued, the make-up of the current government and some of the policies it pursues are signals that populist tendencies exist within society which governments are happy to respond to. History over the last 45 years suggests that the country is very capable to controlling and channelling these populist tendencies in a constructive and productive manner. Yet, with the challenges it still faces, vigilance is needed to ensure that this continues and can be used in such a way as to allow the country to address the strategic problems it clearly still has, even, or because of, years of crisis and austerity.

Conclusions

Portugal has often been held up, not least by the European Union, as a posterchild of its policies in response to the crisis of 2008 and beyond. As shown, the data clearly illustrates the improvement the Portuguese economy has undergone during the last few years after emerging from a deep recession. The fact that it has done so without throwing the political system into turmoil through the emergence of explicitly populist parties from either the Left or the Right is a testament to the system's robustness and adaptability. It is obviously, based on the historical evidence since re-democratization in 1974, a remarkably adaptive and resilient system. Yet, as I hope to have illustrated, it would be too simplistic to make a linear connection between the policies and Portugal's economic upturn. In fact, many have questioned both this link and the depth and sustainability of this upturn.

The reasons for these doubts are founded in the historical realities of the country. As illustrated, Portugal has had a history of booms and busts over the last few decades, grounded in an inability to address the structural weaknesses of the economy, ranging from education to productivity to the over-reliance on foreign capital and economic sectors more vulnerable to outside shocks. As yet, the country has shown relatively little, even in this crisis cycle, to suggest that it can overcome these cycles of boom and bust.

It is this lack of evidence in terms of profound structural reforms which means that the spectre of a populist surge cannot be discounted for definitive. So far, populist tendencies and demands have been absorbed into the mainstream of this system.

Yet, the lack of change in the fundamentals of the Portuguese economy and society suggests that another crisis could well occur. Whether the resilience of the systems would hold again in such a scenario is open to question. Portugal, in short, needs to remain vigilant.

References

Amaro, S. (2017). How Portugal came back from the brink — And why austerity could have played a key role. https://www.cnbc.com/2017/08/02/how-portugal-came-back-from-the-brink.html. Accessed 15 May 2019.

Ames, P. (2019). Portugal splashes the cash ahead of elections', *Politico*, 10th January 2019. https://www.politico.eu/article/as-elections-loom-portugal-backs-major-infrastructure-investments-antonio-costa-socialists/. Accessed 15 May 2019.

Bale, T. (2008). *European politics-A comparative introduction*. Basingstoke: Palgrave.

Barbosa, E., Pereira, S., & Brandão, E. (2013). The shadow economy in Portugal: An analysis using the MIMIC model. In *FEP Working Papers 514, December 2013*. Porto: Universidade do Porto.

Bittner, J. (2010). So nicht, Europa: Die drei grossen Fehler der EU, (Munich: DTV Premium).

Centeno, M. (2018). From sick man to poster boy: Portugal's successful recovery from the euro crisis. *Speech by Eurogroup President and Portugal's minister of finance, Mário Centeno*, Harvard University, 18th March 2018. https://www.consilium.europa.eu/media/33780/speech-peg-harvard-april-2018.pdf. Accessed 15 May 2019.

Costa, L., Martins, N. O., & Guedes de Oliveira, F. (2016). Portugal's bailout and the crisis of the European Union from a capability perspective. *Cambridge Journal of Economics, 40*, 1479–1496.

De Georgi, E., & Santana-Pereira, J. (2016). The 2015 Portuguese legislative election: Widening the coalitional space and bringing the extreme left in. *South European Politics and Society, 21*(4), 451–468.

Freire, A. & Santana-Pereira, J. (2019). From austerity politics and democratic crisis to austerity relief and democratic renewal? The Portuguese case, 2008–2019. Paper presented at the conference '*Crisis management and democracy in EU and Latin America: Lessons learned*', Athens, Greece, June 2019.

Giddens, A. (2015). *Turbulent and mighty continent – What future for Europe?* Cambridge: Polity.

Heinke, R. (2016). Portugal's unwanted youth. Heinrich Böll Stiftung, 14th January 2016. https://eu.boell.org/en/2016/01/14/portugals-unwanted-youth. Accessed 15 May 2019.

IMF (2018). Portugal-recovery and risks. *IMF Country Focus*. https://www.imf.org/en/News/Articles/2018/09/11/na091318-portugal-recovery-and-risks. Accessed 15 May 2019.

Jones, O. (2017). No alternative to austerity? That lie has now been nailed. *The Guardian*, 24th August 2017. https://www.theguardian.com/commentisfree/2017/aug/24/austerity-lie-deep-cuts-economy-portugal-socialist. Accessed 15 May 2019.

Khalip, A. (2015). Portugal's brain drain spells lasting headache for election winner. https://uk.reuters.com/article/uk-portugal-election-braindrain-idUKKCN0RU1HZ20150930. Accessed 15 May 2019.

Krugman, P. (2012). *End this depression now*. London: W. W. Norton & Company.

Lane, P. R. (2012). The European sovereign debt crisis. *Journal of Economic Perspectives, 26*(3), 49–68.

Lehmann, K. (2018). The crisis of the European Union as a complex adaptive system. *Journal of Common Market Studies, 56*(4), 971–988.

Llana, S. M. (2015). Austerity bites Portugal as much as Greece. Why no populist movement?, *Christian Science Monitor*, 10th August 2015. https://www.csmonitor.com/World/Europe/2015/0810/Austerity-bites-Portugal-as-much-as-Greece.-Why-no-populist-movement. Accessed 15 May 2019.

Lloyd-Jones, S. (2001). Portugal's history since 1974. *CPHRC Working Papers, 2*(1).

Lobo, M. C. (2001). The role of political parties in Portuguese democratic consolidation. *Party Politics, 7*(5), 643–653.

Lorenz, T. (2018). As Europe moves right, Portugal veers left-and thrives. *World Politics Review*, 2nd January 2018. https://www.worldpoliticsreview.com/articles/23899/as-europe-moves-right-portugal-veers-left-and-thrives. Accessed 15 May 2019.

Lourtie, P. (2011). Understanding Portugal in the context of the euro crisis. *Paper prepared for resolving the European debt crisis, a conference hosted by the Peterson Institute for International Economics and Bruegel, Chantilly, France, September 13–14, 2011*. https://piie.com/publications/papers/lourtie20110913.pdf. Accessed 15 May 2019.

Magalhães, P. (2011). Elections, parties and policy-making institutions in democratic Portugal. In A. C. Pinto (Ed.), *Contemporary Portugal: Politics, society, and culture*. New York: Columbia University Press.

Morlino, L., & Raniolo, F. (2017). *The impact of the economic crisis on South European democracies*. Basingstoke: Palgrave.

OECD. (2015). *OECD skills strategy diagnostic report: Executive summary Portugal*. Paris: OECD.

Pedroso, P. (2014). Portugal and the global crisis: The impact of austerity on the economy, the social model and the performance of the state. In *Study*. Berlin: Friedrich Ebert Stiftung.

Pereira, P. T., & Wemans, L. (2012). Portugal and the global financial crisis – Short-sighted politics, deteriorating public finances and the bailout imperative. In *WP 26/2012/DE/UECE*. Lisbon: Technical University.

Portugal, P. (2015). The Portuguese economic crisis: Policies and outcomes. In *Policy brief*. Gütersloh: Bertelsmann Stiftung.

Reis, R. (2013). The Portuguese slump and crash and the euro crisis. *Brookings papers on economic activity*, NBER Working Paper No. 19288. Washington, DC: Brookings Institution. https://www.brookings.edu/bpea-articles/the-portuguese-slump-and-crash-and-the-euro-crisis/. Accessed 15 May 2019.

10

Economic and Political Issues in Italy

Simone Romano

Abstract Italy went through an economic and political crisis in 2011. The trigger was the Sovereign debt crisis that shook the Eurozone due to its incomplete structure. The ingrained causes were the long-term structural problems that have plagued the Italian economy for a long time, leaving it vulnerable to external shocks. The reaction to the crisis took the form of austerity measures and reforms implemented by a technocratic Government. These policies, carried out with no external financial assistance, were meant to send a signal to markets and stop the spiral of distrust and negative self-fulfilling expectations, but they did not address the sources of the problems. Since then much has been done at both national and European levels, but it is still not enough to guarantee resilience. Italy needs to finally solve its structural problems, and the European Monetary Union (EMU) needs to complete its architecture, starting with the completion of the Banking Union. Considering the increasing social discontent and political intolerance, failing to act now might imply severe consequences when the next crisis hits.

When Did the Crisis Start? International Triggers and National Ingrained Causes

On the 16th of November 2011, the Government headed by Mario Monti took office, replacing the Cabinet presided over by Silvio Berlusconi. This change in the political leadership, due to the state of emergency and not to standard political dynamics, is the clearest symbol of the economic and political crisis which Italy went through in 2011 (Bosco and McDonnell 2012). It is certainly not the starting point though. That crisis was due to both cyclical and structural conditions and to national and international factors, making it a deep-rooted and complex phenomenon, whose causes and origins are not easy to pinpoint.

S. Romano (✉)
G7/G20 Sherpa Unit, Office of the Prime Minister of Italy, Rome, Italy
e-mail: simone.romano@uniroma3.it

At the beginning of November 2011, the spread that measures the difference between the 10-year treasury bond yields of Italy and Germany was at 574 basis points, while at the beginning of that same year, it was 400 basis points lower. This worrisome dynamic was self-sustaining, fostering a vicious cycle of negative self-fulfilling expectations about the soundness of Italian public finances. These negative expectations contributed to plunge the country into a second and longer recession, after the one that followed the 2008 financial crisis, which, in turn, replenished the pessimistic predictions (Henningsen 2012). Albeit Italy had run larger budget deficits and had borrowed with substantial higher interest rates in its recent years,[1] the unfolding of the events in 2011 urged an unprecedented move, such as the change of government. Was the heavy public debt burden the driving cause of this negative spiral? Was the contagion of the crisis that had started in Greece the precedent year? Was it the lack of confidence towards the Italian government? Was it the structural weakness of the Italian economy? As a matter of fact, the 2011 crisis in Italy was the result of a complex combination of different causes, with short-run external triggers building on national long-run problems.

The international context played a key role in exacerbating the negative perception over a national economic situation that, albeit not sound and prosperous, in other circumstances would have been judged far away from the possibility of a sovereign default. The so-called Sovereign Debt Crisis of 2011 started in Greece the precedent year and was triggered by the Greek reckless handling of public finances, hiding a prolonged period of overspending through "books-cooking" practices. This crisis though, as described by Baldwin and Giavazzi (2015), was not only explainable in terms of sovereign debt (un)sustainability, but it was rather originated by growing and undisputed imbalances that developed over time in the European Monetary Union (EMU) since its inception. The unfolding of the crisis enlightened the flawed nature of the EMU due to its incomplete construction: without adequate tools at the European level to curb the contagion, when the Greek problem exploded, the financial markets promptly started fearing about the resilience of other national economies that for many reasons seemed less equipped to counteract the negative shock spread by the collapse of the Greek economy throughout the Eurozone.

As Fig. 10.1 illustrates, while for Portugal, Ireland and Spain the main problem was the soaring level of deficit due to the bailout of key actors of their banking and financial sector, for Italy, the Achilles heel was the high level of public debt (Fig. 10.2).[2]

---

[1] While the peak for the interest rates on the Italian Government Bond registered in December 2011 was around 7%, the interest rate on the same security was around 21% at the end of 1981 (IMF Database). In that year, Italy had a public deficit of around 10% of GDP, so higher than the ones registered in the period 2009–2011, when the peak was around 5% (EU Commission dataset).

[2] The higher level of primary deficit (and so of public debt) registered in Italy in the aftermath of the global financial crisis was not due to discretionary fiscal stimulus or bailouts, but mainly it was the result of the slowdown of the economy and its consequent pressure on public budget through automatic stabilizers.

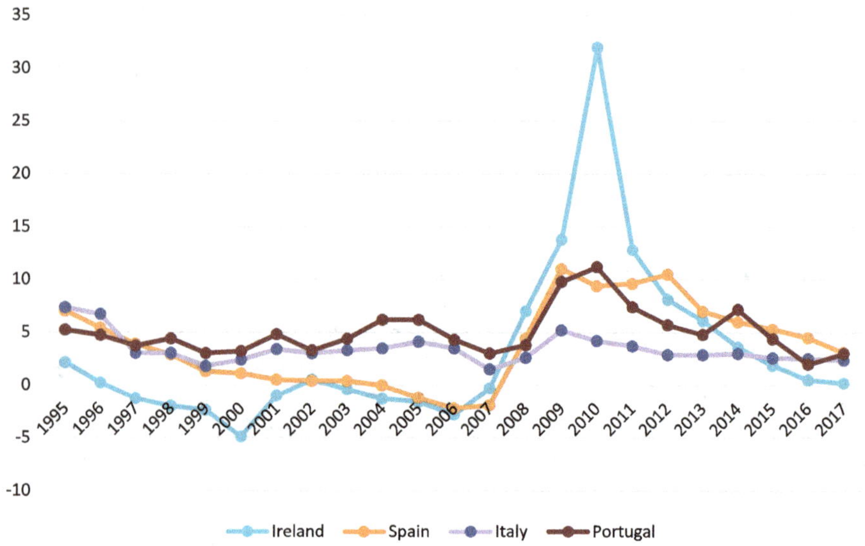

Fig. 10.1 Deficit levels (as % of GDP). (Source: Eurostat)

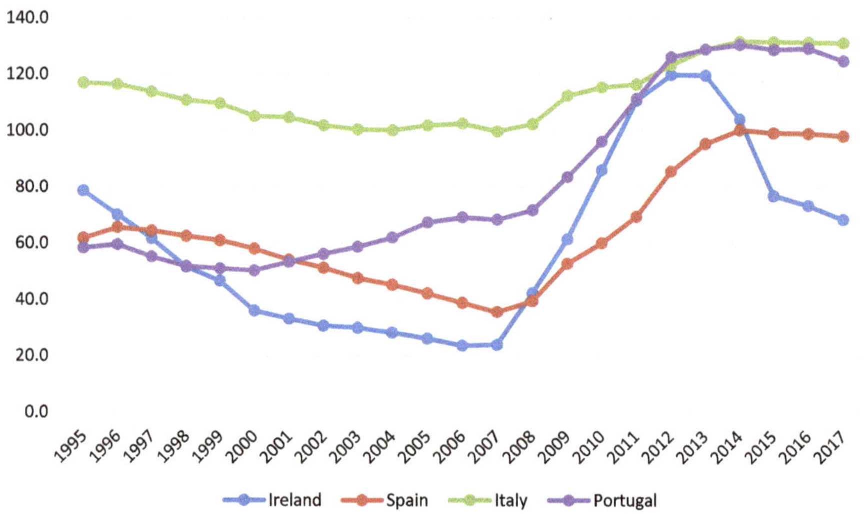

Fig. 10.2 Public Debt (as % of GDP). (Source: Eurostat)

The mounting lack of confidence towards the resilience of the Italian public finances was fuelled by national characteristics as well: the widespread mistrust towards the Government and its capability of guiding the country in such a difficult moment and the long-term structural weaknesses of the Italian economy, such as the low productivity growth and the high level of unemployment, tax avoidance and corruption. All of this quickly fostered the view that Italy could be one of the next

EMU member countries to face a situation similar to the one that was happening in Greece, spreading fears about its ability to honour its sizeable sovereign debt.

Against this background, with the spread sailing straight to the 400 basis point, on the 5th of August 2011 the European Central Bank (ECB) sent a letter, meant to be secret, to the Italian government. The missive, signed by both Trichet and Draghi, urged the Italian government to act baldly and swiftly. Among the urgent measures advised by the ECB were the increase in competition to foster efficiency and strengthen economic growth, large-scale liberalization and the decentralization of wage bargaining. Albeit the government headed by Silvio Berlusconi promptly reacted, starting immediately to implement some of these measures, many European political leaders—above all the German Chancellor Angela Merkel and the French President Nicolas Sarkozy—thought it was not enough. This judgement was shared by investors, which were increasingly reluctant to buy Italian Treasury Bonds, driving up interest rates and spread. The publication of the Trichet–Draghi letter in the late September by an important Italian newspaper did not help to cool the situation off, eroding the thin confidence on which the cabinet was hinging. At this point, a strong signal was needed: the change in government was the inevitable last resort.

The described unfolding of events demonstrates the key role played by both the flaws in the architecture of the EMU that paved the way for the 2011 crisis, and the long-standing fragility of the Italian economy. The next two paragraphs briefly extend the analysis on both factors.

Deep-Rooted National Weaknesses

The Italian economy has been dragged down for long time by structural problems that all Governments, regardless of their political colour, have struggled to solve or even just to address.

Italy is one of the countries with the highest level of value-added tax (VAT) avoidance in Europe, and it has faced the problem of generalized tax evasion for a long time. This phenomenon coupled with the wide dimension of its black economy subtracts important resources from the public budget, exacerbating its fiscal sustainability issues.

The narrow fiscal space that these factors shape is detrimental for economic growth. Italy has difficulties in attracting private capitals: the scarce efficiency in its bureaucracy and judiciary system together with the high level of corruption scares away international investors, while the uncertainty stemming from its chronic political instability discourages national investment. Since the lack of investment depresses the productivity growth, Italy needs public investment, but the government cannot afford to step in because of its tight budgetary constraints (Henningsen 2012).

All of this is coupled with an inefficient labour market where, moreover, the portion of graduates in the work force is very small if compared with other advanced economies. The sluggish or flat economic growth resulting from these factors increases the debt burden, requesting a very tight budgetary policy to maintain its dynamics under control. This policy does not sustain aggregate demand and growth, further fuelling the vicious circle.

International Context

The EMU is a unique case of a currency union without a centralized fiscal policy design. This implies that the common monetary policy can deal only with union-wide shocks, while the reaction to idiosyncratic shocks is left in the hands of national policies. Even though these national policies may be not enough, the Eurozone lacks union-wide stabilizers: the labour and capital mobility among member countries has been scarce, the level of coordination on the union-wide fiscal stance has not been sufficient and the EMU still lacks common fiscal capacity. In such environment, a sizeable national shock can easily become systemic as the Greek case of 2010–2011 clearly demonstrated.

This background is particularly worrisome in the light of the enhanced economic interdependence among member states due to the currency union and the common market: inside the EMU, many banks, funds and firms hold sovereign bonds of other member countries, and many firms do business with their counterparts in other member states. Hence, if a member state is to default on its debt or to face a deeply troublesome economic situation, its economy would not be the only one to be severely hit, but the shock would spread to other member countries through both financial and trade channels.

As a consequence, national Governments could be called to intervene to help distressed financial institutions or to avoid an ulterior slowdown of their economies. Many of these Governments, though, have budgetary positions which are already worrisome, as it was the case in 2010–2011, when many of them were already in dire straits. At this point, financial markets, which are forward looking for their own nature, started pricing in the higher risk. In 2011, these jitters were further fuelled by the famous and improvident Deauville beach walk, when President Sarkozy and Chancellor Merkel decided that the private sector had to bear part of the burden in case of sovereign defaults. Albeit the decision could be right in principle, the timing was highly inappropriate and ended up igniting the financial contagion that transformed the Greek sovereign crisis into a union-wide crisis, hitting Italy as well (Haas and Gnath 2016).

The Policy Responses: Austerity and Reforms

When the Monti cabinet took office, the situation was highly distressed. Markets had lost confidence in the Italian capacity to honour its debt: the prices of the Italian Treasury bonds were collapsing, increasing the interest rate on the debt and, in turn, narrowing further the fiscal space. Time was ticking and a strong signal was needed to calm the markets and show that the new Italian leadership was able to steer away from disaster.

The strong response took the form of the so-called "*Salva Italia*" (Saving Italy) decree, launched by the Cabinet just roughly 2 weeks after its appointment. The timing of the decree, the fact that the budgetary law there contained was the fifth of the year and the sizeable net balance (with a net surplus of 20 billion euros) well describe the scope and the urgency of this manoeuvre.

The decree comprised three chapters: public budget, social security and growth. The spending cuts were crafted to reach the amount of 12–13 billion euros in 3 years, while the increase in taxes was designed to bring new revenues in the amount of 17–18 billion in the same time span. Of this grand total of 30 billion euros, 20 of them were thought to be used to reduce the deficit (and so preventing the debt from soaring), while 10 were destined to growth-enhancing measures (Baldini 2014).

On the spending reduction side, the *Salva Italia* decree provided for a radical change in the role of the provinces as territorial administrations, diminishing their competences as a first and quicker step towards their complete abolition.[3] On the same line, the decree reduced the number of employees of all the authorities, while many of the existent authorities were abolished.

Remaining in the first chapter, on the revenue side, the real estate taxation, already introduced, was anticipated (so as to start in 2012 and no longer in 2014), and it was extended to first homes as well. Furthermore, a luxury tax was introduced on cars, boats and private aircrafts. The VAT was designed to increase from 21% to 23% in 2012 but, in the end, only increased to 22% during the Government headed by Enrico Letta, in 2013.

The most important measure for its long-term impact was contained in the second chapter: social security. The retirement reform known as Fornero law (from the name of the Ministry who crafted it) changed the former defined benefit pension scheme into a defined contribution pension scheme. It also raised the retirement age and provided incentives for people who postpone their retirement. This translated into a substantial long-term structural improvement of the Italian budgetary position, quickly making it one of the most honourable member countries for the EU Sustainability Index produced by the Marktwirtschaft Stiftung (2014), which takes into account not only the outstanding level of debt, but also its projection into the future.

Regarding the third chapter, the measures to spur economic growth were inspired by the need to improve the budgetary position as well, resulting in the usage of widespread liberalizations as the main tool. Just as a matter of example, the limits regarding the opening times for any kind of shop or commercial activity were abolished, and the territorial criteria determining the number of pharmacies were modified as to increase competition. Beyond liberalizations, the decree established as deductible the regional income tax paid by firms and employers on workers, and

[3] As of today, the provinces, albeit further modified, still exist and function.

aimed at refinancing many public infrastructure projects considered key for future development (Culpepper 2014). Albeit for timing and scope the strongest response, the *Salva Italia* decree was not the only clear signal that the emergency cabinet sent to markets, investors and other political leaders. In fact, while already started by the former government, the parliament speeded up the approval of the balanced budget constitutional amendment, and the government proposed a spending review, meant to save up on unproductive expenditures, with a cut in the civil servants and military forces (among others).

To better understand the Italian response to the crisis, it is important to stress that, differently from Greece, Ireland, Portugal and Spain, Italy did not receive any financial assistance from the EU Commission or the International Monetary Fund (IMF). This implies that it did not have any external authority directly involved in the policy design. In the immediate aftermath of the *Salva Italia* decree, the spread, thermometer of the market sentiment towards Italy, decreased and reached 374 points. At the end of the year though, it increased again, reaching 500 points. In 2012, the spread followed a fluctuating trend, with a new peak over 500 in the summer of 2012. This shows that while the austerity measures pushed by the Monti cabinet managed to avoid the worst from happening, breaking the negative spiral that threatened to plunge Italy into a sovereign debt crisis, they did not succeeded in solving the problem at its source but, truth be told, they were not meant to do so.

The problem with the Italian economy has been the passiveness used to address the underlying structural problems. This made a "shock therapy" in necessary the worst moment: in the context of 2011, with a huge slack in the economy and an accommodative monetary policy, the fiscal multiplier was bigger than usual (Chinn 2013). In these conditions, a stark package of austerity measures, albeit necessary in that moment of emergency, had a very negative and long-lasting effect on the already troubled Italian economy, prolonging the time needed to recover from recession and shaping what has been happening in the years up to now, both on the economics and politics. Even though a strong tightening of the public budget was inevitable in that difficult moment, a technocratic Government could have been braver in designing the measures, looking only at their long-time effect, with no need to consider the inevitable political discontent that they were to originate.

Despite the efforts, the 2011 crisis in Italy and the Eurozone was not over until the summer of 2012. In fact, the spread in the Eurozone as a whole (and so in Italy as well) decreased in a lasting and sizeable way only after the famous "Whatever it takes" speech pronounced by the ECB President Mario Draghi in July 2012. These words made history as the perfect example of the forward guidance tool aimed at shaping expectations, declaring that no matter the challenges, the ECB was ready to do whatever was needed to save the Euro and, quoting President Draghi, that would have been enough. As a matter of fact, it was.

The fact that only the intervention of a European power was able to solve the problem demonstrates how the 2011 Sovereign debt crisis was not only an issue of national public finances, but rather an EMU-wide problem. There is no doubt that Italy had a structurally flawed economic situation with a too high debt burden. This entailed that, sooner or later, in order to avoid a crisis, it would have been necessary to "put the house in order". The "house in order" approach indeed was—and still is—necessary to prevent the spreading of new crises in a currency union shaped as the EMU, calling each member state to be responsible and conscious of the spillover effects of its national economic policies. This said, what happened in the period 2010–2012 clearly demonstrated that the "house in order" approach, albeit necessary, is not sufficient, and a completion of the EMU architecture is desperately needed.

The Economic and Political Legacy

Seven years have passed from the peak of the crisis. Since then, much has been done to avoid repeating past mistakes, both at national and European levels. Nevertheless, it is not enough: many of the problems that led to the 2011 crisis, at both levels, are still unresolved. On the Italian side, it suffices to think that in the weeks that preceded the drafting of this paper, Italy lived a sort of strange deja-vu, with a growing attention (or rather mistrust) from financial markets and other member states towards the conduct of economic policy carried out by the Government. Once again, the capability of the Cabinet to face the economic challenges, linked with the very high level of public debt and the stagnating economic growth, was questioned. This led investors to ask for a higher premium when buying Italian bonds, ending up increasing the interest rates and pushing the spread beyond 300 points. The similarity with what happened in 2011 clearly indicates that the underlying structural problems have not been resolved.

The Governments that followed the Cabinet headed by Mario Monti were successful in maintaining the debt dynamic under control and bringing Italy outside recession, but the country has not succeeded in recovering the pre-crisis level.[4] While many other Western and European countries have experienced a period of substantial growth in the last 2–3 years, with the pace of crisis-hit countries like Spain or Ireland outperforming Italy substantially, Italian economy did not manage to fuel a convincing growth.[5]

This further confirms that the structural problems that paved the way for the 2011 crisis are still unresolved. The productivity growth is still very low, and the level of investment, both public and private, is not sufficient. The unemployment, above all among young people, is still very high,[6] creating a concrete risk of hysteresis that, together with ageing, can lower further the productivity and any prospect of growth.

[4] The level of real GDP in 2016 was still much lower than in 2006, roughly at the level of 2001. Please refer to the table in the appendix for all the detailed figures.

[5] Both Ireland and Spain experienced an annual growth rate of their real GDP that was higher than 3% in the period 2015–2017, while the Italian rate in the same period was hardly higher than 1% (OECD StatExtra Database).

[6] The unemployment rate had been higher than 10% until the end of 2017, while the youth unemployment rate has been higher than 30% (Eurostat and OECD).

Corruption, inefficient bureaucracy and public administration are still there as well, together with the high public debt burden.

To worsen further the situation, the two crises and the long recession that followed left a heavy legacy that adds on to old structural problems. The long-lasting decline of economic activity implied a very high share of firm destruction. This exacerbated the unemployment problem and contributed to the mounting problem of non-performing loans (NPL), which jeopardized the resilience of the whole Italian financial system. The Italian banks were not heavily engaged in derivatives, and this left them in a better shape in 2008 if compared with other international counterparts. The deep and long recession that followed the 2008 financial crisis brought many borrowers to default on their debts or to be delinquent with their payments. This situation put a strain on the balance sheets of many Italian banks, creating a concrete threat for the resilience of the Italian banking sector. In turn, this problem affected the capability of financial institutions to lend to the real economy, curbing further economic growth.

While the worst phase of the NPL issue seems behind our backs as the peak of the 2011 crisis, the Italian economy is still in a bad shape. This long-standing difficult economic situation has important consequences that go beyond the economy, affecting the political and social spheres as well. The lack of a proper economic recovery together with the unpopular austerity measures approved as a solution to stop the contagion of 2011 created a fertile ground for the spread of populism. The absence of tangible positive results in face of the sacrifices that the austerity measures imposed to a big part of population has led people to become increasingly angry and disappointed at elites and the establishment. In an enduring period of uncertainty such as the present one, people have started seeking prompt protection and fast solutions. While standard political parties failed to understand and address these needs, the populist forces responded directly to the people requests, offering simple solutions and wide protection regardless of their real feasibility. This paved the way for the first openly populist Government in Italy, one of the founder and main member states of the EU. As demonstrated by the first 6 months of the populist Cabinet, this is not only an Italian problem but it spills over to the EU and the Eurozone. For the future of the EU construction, it is of paramount importance not to label this as a bump in the road or something strictly related to Italian dynamics. On the contrary, this has to be considered a wake-up call: the way the double crisis was handled had flaws and, in order to thrive, it is important to rethink social and economic policies at all levels.

Widening the focus to the European level, it is clear that the 2011 crisis has spurred an effort to provide the EMU with new and more adept instruments to face critical situations. To this end, the creation of the Banking Union and the European Stability Mechanism (ESM) are the two most important pillars. While in the aftermath of the crisis the pace for their creation was impressively quick and efficient, the impetus has lost momentum afterwards. The Banking Union provides the perfect example. What happened during the crisis highlighted the inadequacy of the national character of banking supervision in a common financial market where the main actors had a systemic importance. To this end, the Single Supervisory

Mechanism (SSM) was created, shifting the competence for supervision of the systemic actors directly to the ECB. On top of this, the Single Resolution Mechanism was created, to handle in a homogenous way the solution of troubled systemic financial institutions. Although this effort has gone in the right direction, the construction has been left incomplete and, as it stands, it cannot function properly (exactly as it happened with the creation of the EMU). The third block of the Banking Union, the European Deposit Insurance Scheme (EDIS), needs to be created to diminish the probability of bank runs and self-fulfilling crises. Political divide between prioritizing risk reduction over risk sharing, or the way around, still hinders the creation of this third pillar, leaving the EMU exposed to shocks. The situation seems better on the ESM side, where a concrete reform of the international treaties shaping the ESM is currently under discussion, adding important features to the mechanism, such as its role of backstop for the Single Resolution Funds (SRF).

What Have We Learned or What We Should Have Learned?

The dynamics that led to the crisis of 2011, the unfolding of the events and the years that followed teach us important lessons for both Italy and Europe. At the Italian level, these years have stressed the importance to address the structural problems that have been ignored or badly addressed for too long, both in the economic and the political system. Policy uncertainty, lack of social capital, low productivity, increasing inequality, corruption and tax avoidance have been hampering the growth potential and policy stability for many years now. Addressing them only in a state of emergency, as it was the case in 2011, brings negative consequences that, considering the current economic and social situation in Italy, could be even worse. Moreover, these factors undermine Italy's economic and social resilience, making it very vulnerable to external shocks.

At the European level, the events of the last 7 years have showed the need to wisely complete the structure of the EMU, providing it with all the mechanisms that a currency union requires in order to function well. On a practical level, the first moves need to be the completion of the Banking Union, the revision and enhancement of the ESM and the provision of a fiscal capacity or any kind of fiscal stabilization tool at the European level (Shambaugh 2012).

None of these tasks is easy, none of them is free of high political costs, but if we do not act now, the cost in the future could be very high. A wise proverb states that the roof has to be repaired when the sun is shining. Now, with the positive economic moment of the last couple of years that is starting to fade, there is no longer room to postpone difficult decisions. Italy and the EMU have survived previous severe crises as the one in 2011, but, if they do not act baldly and swiftly to make their systems more resilient, they might be in deep trouble when the next crisis hits. The political and social capital has clearly eroded since 2011, and the economic situation, above all in Italy, offers less room for manoeuvre than in 2008. Errare humanum est, *perseverare autem diabolicum.*

Appendix: Table with Economic Indicators

Date	Real GDP - Levels	Real GDP - %	10Y Interest Rates	Deficit (Surprulus)	Deficit (Surprulus)	Government gross DEBT	Unemployment Rate	Gini Index	Gini Index	Government
	Millions of Chained 2010 Euros, Annual, Seasonally Adjusted Eurostat (Fred)	Percent Change from Year Ago, Annual, Seasonally Adjusted Eurostat (Fred)	Percent, Annual, Not Seasonally Adjusted OECD (Fred)	Percent of GDP, Annual, Not Seasonally Adjusted IMF	Percentage of gross domestic product (GDP) Eurostat	Percentage of gross domestic product (GDP) Eurostat	Total: All Persons, Percent, Annual, Not Seas. Adjusted OECD	Index, Annual, Not Seasonally Adjusted World Bank	Perc. Chan. from Year Ago, Annual, Not Seas. Adj. World Bank	
1995-01-01	1412032,0		**12,20583333333330**	**-7,253**	-7,3	116,9	11,18333333333330			**Dini**
1996-01-01	1426978,2	1,1	9,40066666666666	-6,651	-6,7	116,3	11,16666666666670			
1997-01-01	1454851,7	2,0	6,86025000000000	-3,012	-3,0	113,8	11,21666666666670			**Prodi**
1998-01-01	1475958,1	1,5	4,88250000000000	-3,021	-3,0	110,8	11,30000000000000			
1999-01-01	1498201,2	1,5	4,72750000000000	-1,805	-1,8	109,7	10,86666666666670			**D'Alema**
2000-01-01	1558066,5	4,0	5,57608333333333	-1,324	-2,4	105,1	10,05000000000000			
2001-01-01	1582391,1	1,6	5,18708333333333	-3,393	-3,4	104,7	9,00833333333333			**Amato**
2002-01-01	1586300,8	0,2	5,03416666666667	-3,073	-3,0	101,9	8,47500000000000			
2003-01-01	1590126,7	0,2	4,29583333333333	-3,414	-3,3	100,5	8,43333333333333	34,9		
2004-01-01	1612046,4	1,4	4,25867500000000	-3,567	-3,5	100,1	8,00000000000000	34,3	-1,7	**Berlusconi**
2005-01-01	1630398,0	1,1	3,55542166666667	-4,173	-4,1	101,9	7,70833333333333	33,8	-1,5	
2006-01-01	**1664709,2**	2,1	4,04614166666667	-3,587	-3,5	102,6	6,79166666666667	33,7	-0,3	
2007-01-01	**1686846,3**	1,3	4,48725833333333	**-1,527**	-1,5	**99,8**	**6,07500000000000**	32,9	-2,4	**Prodi**
2008-01-01	**1669161,4**	**-1,0**	4,68106666666667	**-2,692**	-2,6	**102,4**	6,70833333333333	33,8	**2,7**	
2009-01-01	**1576786,5**	**-5,5**	4,31118333333333	**-5,269**	**-5,2**	**112,5**	7,75000000000000	33,8	0,0	
2010-01-01	1602776,4	1,6	4,03570833333333	**-4,246**	-4,2	**115,4**	8,35000000000000	34,7	**2,7**	**Berlusconi**
2011-01-01	**1614317,0**	0,7	**5,42275833333333**	-3,712	-3,7	**116,5**	**8,35000000000000**	35,1	1,2	
2012-01-01	**1568281,1**	**-2,9**	**5,49267500000000**	**-2,927**	**-2,9**	**123,4**	**10,64166666666670**	35,2	0,3	**Monti**
2013-01-01	**1540846,8**	**-1,7**	4,31642500000000	**-2,950**	**-2,9**	**129,0**	**12,13333333333330**	34,9	-0,9	
2014-01-01	**1543656,4**	0,2	2,89320000000000	-2,986	-3,0	131,8	**12,65000000000000**	34,7	-0,6	**Letta**
2015-01-01	1556448,7	0,8	1,71395000000000	-2,576	-2,6	131,5	11,89166666666670			**Renzi**
2016-01-01	1571579,6	1,0	1,48643333333333	-2,477	-2,5	**132,0**	**11,67500000000000**			

References

Baldini, M. (2014). *Fiscal austerity and income distribution in Italy*. Center for the Analysis of Public Policies (CAPP) 0112.

Baldwin, R., & Giavazzi, F. (2015). *The Eurozone crisis. A consensus view of the causes and a few possible solutions*. VoxEu.org book.

Bosco, A., & McDonnell, D. (2012). The Monti government and the downgrade of Italian parties. *Italian Politics, 27*(1), 37–56.

Chinn, M. (2013). Fiscal multipliers. *The New Palgrave Dictionary of Economics, 7*, 1–10.

Culpepper, P. D. (2014). The political economy of unmediated democracy: Italian austerity under Mario Monti, *West European Politics, 37*(6), 1264–81.

Haas, J., & Gnath, K. (2016). *The Euro area crisis: A short history*. Bertelsmann Stiftung Policy Papers.

Henningsen, D. M. (2012). *The origins of the Italian sovereign debt crisis*. CMC Senior Theses Paper 379.

Marktwirtschaft Stiftung (2014). *Honorable states?* EU Sustainability Ranking, 2014.

Shambaugh, J. C. (2012). *The Euro's three crises*. Brookings Papers.

11

Handling of Economic Crisis in Mexico, Brazil and Argentina

Maria Antonieta Del Tedesco Lins

Abstract Through a comparative case study analysis, the chapter seeks to retrace the recent history of Argentina, Brazil and Mexico in dealing with economic crises. Despite their different institutional arrangements and macroeconomic trajectories, the comparison shows that domestic concerns were the main drivers of economic policies. Particularly regarding each country's approaches to exchange markets and capital controls—here called financial policy—the chapter evaluates the extent to which they contradict international perceptions and even the International Monetary Fund's (IMF's) stance on financial regulation and the management of capital flows. A close relationship between domestic political demands and the design of economic policy indicated that even in the face of some similarity between the challenges posed to the three countries and more than responses to changes in the world economy and the quest to keep these economies integrated, economic policy aimed to accommodate internal political pressures.

Introduction

Crises are a common feature to barely all analyses of Latin American economic history. The 1980s' debt crisis besides blocking the region's access to international financial markets led to economic stagnation, hiking inflation and poverty increase. Since the late 1980s, debt renegotiation, programs of macroeconomic adjustment and liberalization policies opened a new phase for the region. Hand in hand with the economic transition was the political one. Democracy building on the onset of military regimes and the reign of long-lasting ruling parties was a remarkable challenge to be conciliated with macroeconomic and institutional reforms. Argentina, Brazil and Mexico, the three largest economies in the region, shared this experience but, although having adopted several similar policies in their economic reform programs

M. A. D. T. Lins (✉)
Universidade de São Paulo – Institute of International Relations, São Paulo, SP, Brazil
e-mail: madtlins@usp.br

since the 1990s, they cannot be considered resembling fragments of a common model. Their respective political idiosyncrasies have led to quite diverse economic policy arrangements ever since. The chapter recovers the economic and political trajectories of these three countries since the early 1990s, against the backdrop of the 1980s' debt crisis, its impacts and the ensuing liberalization reforms. Financial and exchange rate policies are in the spotlight to analyze the countries' performances throughout the different crises and their financial insertion in the world economy. In all three cases, monetary, exchange rate and financial openness policies were instrumental in determining both the intensity of each country's financial integration and the degree of vulnerability to which they were subject when the global financial crisis hit. It is argued that despite their very diverse political trajectories, flirts with populism inspired economic policy in critical moments in the three cases.

The 1980s' Latin American foreign debt crisis and the ensuing lost decade reflect the previous period during which the presence of military dictatorships in several countries of the region is key to understanding economic policy focused on maintaining high rates of output growth, despite rising inflation, especially in Argentina and Brazil. High liquidity in international financial markets in the run-up to the oil crisis granted these countries the access to credit from abroad at floating and initially low interest rates, allowing them to postpone necessary reforms and preserve growth. The fight for economic normalization in Latin American countries following debt renegotiation in the late 1980s was uneven and consisted of two big challenges: macroeconomic stabilization and long delayed structural reforms as necessary conditions to resume growth. Most of the reforms were inspired by what was labeled the Washington Consensus, a set of liberalizing measures which, in the three cases here, were coupled with the adoption of pegged currency exchange regimes. These profound macroeconomic transformations both led the three countries to a new phase of increasing integration into the world economy and gradually triggered the financial crises that followed. However, the intensity of their crises in 1994 (Mexico), 1998–1999 (Brazil) and 2001–2002 (Argentina) was quite diverse and proportional to the commitment to the hard-pegged exchange rate regime of each one (Wiesner 2008; Kaminsky et al. 2009).

The literature on Latin American financial systems and central bank reform tends to emphasize international actors and pressures as key determinants of policy change. In contrast, and furthering the argument that economic policy had pinches of populist inspirations in a number of episodes of recent history, this chapter argues that domestic concerns were the main drivers of financial policy making after the 2008 crisis even in countries with different institutional arrangements and macroeconomic trajectories such as Brazil, Mexico and Argentina. Through a comparative case study analysis, the chapter seeks to retrace the three countries' approaches to exchange markets and capital controls and evaluate to which extent they contradict international perceptions and even the International Monetary Fund's (IMF's) stance on financial regulation and the management of capital flows. Populist economic policies can be traced despite a number of government shifts after democratization—broadly situated in the late 1980s.[1] As the following discussion intends to put, populist temptations prevailed mostly in Argentina and Brazil.[2]

The text is divided into three main sections besides this introduction and the concluding remarks. Next section recovers in broad lines the Latin American debt crisis, distinguishing each country's political situation before 1982, thereafter and leading to the liberalizing reforms of the 1990s. The third section focuses on the three nations' respective financial crises during the 1990s and 2000s and their political and economic consequences. The fourth section scrutinizes the reactions of Argentina, Brazil and Mexico to the 2008 global financial crisis, a period during which three very distinct political orientations were in place in each of the three countries.

From Over-Indebtedness to Economic Collapse: Latin American Saga

The literature on the legendary Latin American debt crisis usually points to the national state as the main source of instability (e.g. Skidmore and Smith 2005). Bresser-Pereira (1992) summarizes the different positions on the Latin American crisis and groups them into two explanatory theories from which arise reform proposals: the neoliberal and the fiscal crisis approaches. The neoliberal view, giving birth to the so-called Washington Consensus, was the international financial bodies' common view and enjoyed strong influence over Latin American leaders. The heterodox approach stressed the state's inability to follow previous development policy. The neoliberal approach identifies two major causes for the crisis in Latin America: the extreme growth of the state manifested by too much intervention in the economy with emphasis on protectionism; and the economic populism that would prevent the state from controlling social demands in accordance with the sanitation needs of public finances. Following this logic, the crisis must be initially countered by a rebalancing of public accounts and stabilization before a market-oriented growth policy is launched, where the state would have its space reduced. The return of the development process would be a logical consequence of adjustment.

---

[1] Latin America experienced new forms of populism at the turn of the twenty-first century, with the rise to power of governments that made up the so-called 'Pink Tide'—a period characterized by the presence of several center-left governments in the 1990s and 2000. But right-wing populism would still come back in more recent versions, as the world has been experiencing a surge of these "not so new populisms." They arise as a reaction to the deepening globalization and its effects on national production, population flows and capital movements, among other social and economic transformations, but their emergence do not replace the so-called "old populisms." This chapter is aligned with the definitions of populism presented by Rodrik (2018) and Grigera (2017).

[2] A thorough analysis of the economic policy shifts in Mexico and Brazil after their elections in 2018 and 2019 goes beyond the chapter's time frame.

The approach to the fiscal crisis suggests that the loss of the state's ability to save and invest, which stems from stabilization programs, precludes it from resuming its control of long-term development policies. The shift from public to private investment is not automatic, and the economy stagnates until the private sector sees no greater interest in investing. Government deficit as a structural problem leads to a broader crisis of the state coupled with the loss of credibility of governments in power as the crisis deepens. Despite the direction of causality between the state crisis and adjustment policies being reversed among them, arguments from both approaches can be used to understand the crises that followed.

Mexico was not under military rule in the 1970s and 1980s but faced a crisis of a similar kind to the other two countries. With the exception of Colombia, all Latin American countries that took massive credit during the 1970s went bankrupt in the 1980s (Damill et al. 2005, p. 189). In the early 1980s, falling international oil prices, rising US interest rates and the high level of accumulated foreign debt from the previous period led the Mexican economy to extreme external vulnerability. It was the dawn of insolvency crisis. During Miguel de la Madrid's government (1982–1988), an intense debate about the orientation of economic policy took place confronting structuralist positions with groups clearly in favor of liberal reforms (Maxfield 1992). According to Santín Quirós (2001), the government's political support coalition was mostly "financial." The nationalization of the banking sector carried out by the Mexican government in 1982 was conceived against a crisis backdrop and was defined within an unambiguously liberal inspiration, from the appointment of the president de la Madrid's economic team, through a design of reform that was frankly favorable to the financial sector, both regarding the amounts paid by the state for the nationalized financial institutions and the main framework to redress the national financial system (Santín Quirós 2001).

In Brazil, the 1974 presidential transition had a broader political significance, as a group with a project of political distension who would lead to the gradual opening of the regime came to power. Economic policy was executed considering this political circumstance for the new government could not achieve a worse economic performance than those obtained by its predecessors. The world economy's cyclical reversal forced Brazilian policy makers to face different problems: conforming to a new international reality; adjusting domestic macroeconomic situation, given that inflation was accelerating; and maintaining high growth rates. With the outbreak of the Mexican crisis in 1982, it was no longer possible for the military to postpone a request for IMF financial aid. This point in time can officially be considered the beginning of Brazilian debt crisis (Garriga and Lins 2014, p. 60). What followed was a struggle for macroeconomic stability amid a complete imbalance in external accounts and a long series of failed economic plans under the IMF's agenda. This process generated a decade and a few years lost.

The 1980s began with Argentina facing serious deadlocks. The retreat of military regime was marked by a hard defeat in the Malvinas war against Britain. Election in 1982 brought a civilian back to power, Raúl Alfonsin (1983–1989), with an expectation that his mandate could confront major problems: inflation rates of over 200% a year as early as 1982, rising to 400% the following year, and the undisputable inaptitude to manage and repay private foreign debt. The next inescapable step would be to turn to the IMF and face structural adjustment policies as a conditionality of obtaining a loan (Skidmore and Smith 2005). Referring not only to the 1980s' chronic Argentine indebtment but also to the succeeding crisis of 2002, Damill et al. (2005) state: "for around three decades external debt was almost constantly one of the main issues of economic policy."[3]

Hence, those who agree with the diagnosis of the fiscal crisis see the Latin American debt crisis as the major consequence of the financing model adopted as economic stimulus in the previous period, which resulted in excessive indebtedness and also prolonged maintenance of the import substitution policy (Griffith-Jones and Sunkel 1986, inter alia). Structural problems persisted throughout the 1980s, despite all attempts to adjust. The crises' fiscal feature translated into public accounts deficits but also brought financial and political components to all those crises.

Adjustment programs have not been effective in rebalancing external accounts and controlling inflation nor have they ensured output growth that would lift countries out of crisis with even the IMF policies not being strictly followed by governments. Argentina and Brazil have reached hyperinflation, which has profoundly deteriorated personal income, particularly in the lower classes. Although not attaining Argentine and Brazilian levels, inflation in Mexico also remained very high, particularly after 1982. Thereafter, overcoming the 1980s' crises should be achieved by combining macroeconomic stability and the pursuit of greater international integration of countries, which was accomplished in the following decade.

Liberalization Policies Cum Financial Crises in the 1980s and 1990s

From debt renegotiation and restructuring, Latin American countries have been implementing reforms in their economic policy framework. The rhythm and intensity of the reforms were defined by each country's political trajectory and the readjustment needs. Regarding financial liberalization, quite different patterns were taken. Net inflows of foreign capital in emerging markets resumed and increased substantially in a short period of time since 1990.

Several similarities that marked the three largest Latin American economies during the 1980s and through part of the 1990s seem to vanish as Argentina, Brazil and Mexico delineated distinct economic policy paths since the late 2000s. The unfolding of the late 1990s–early 2000s and 2008–2009 crises was quite particular in each one of the three countries due to both their general economic conditions and the political choices that have been made during and after the crises. Generally

[3] In the original: "Por cerca de tres décadas la deuda externa fue casi ininterrumpidamente una de las preocupaciones centrales de la politica econômica." (Damill et al. 2005: 187).

speaking, since 2007 Argentina has adopted a model of state-led economic strategy quite diverse than both Brazil and Mexico economic models. While Argentina was taken away from the international financial markets and was implementing an increasingly protectionist and interventionist economic policy, both Brazil and, to a greater extent, Mexico maintained a stable macroeconomic pattern, at least until late 2010s, in the Brazilian case.

Mexico

Mexico began to open to global financial markets as early as the late 1980s, under the IMF structural adjustment programs. The Mexican authorities have since launched financial reforms that spanned the domestic financial system and opened the capital account. In addition, interest rates were liberalized, selective credit policies were eliminated and a system of multiple banks was established until the privatization of banks in the early 1990s. The opening of the capital account allowed the presence of foreign investors in public securities markets and capital markets and gave Mexican companies the opportunity to issue bonds in foreign markets. The inflow of foreign direct investment was stimulated by an institutional reform in 1993. The Mexican case presents some peculiar features. The banking system was nationalized during the 1980s amidst the debt crisis. Financial institutions' re-privatization and the financial reforms led by the Salinas government (1988–1994) were clearly motivated by neoliberal ideas and can be seen as a coordinated attempt to build legitimacy and political support for the government (Santín Quirós 2001; Sandoval 2011).

Similarly to Argentina and Brazil, stabilization centered around monetary and exchange rate policies since the 1980s. The external financing constraint and fiscal problems imposed limits to growth, and inflation control became the top priority. A crucial reform in conducting monetary policy was introduced in 1993 via constitutional amendments. This change effectively institutionalized the operational autonomy of the Mexican Central Bank as constitutional independence. Priority was given to the stabilization of the Mexican currency's purchasing power. However, the heightened confidence in the monetary authority was not strong enough to prevent the currency crisis of 1994.

Since 1992, the Mexican currency was clearly over-valued. Along with a deteriorating balance of payments, political instability set off a speculative attack against the peso. The rigidity of the adjustment mechanism that had been adopted made adjustment in the face of market pressures a difficult proposition. When new Zedillo government (1994–2000) tried to change the mechanism of bands, performing a more or less controlled devaluation, the decision set off a wave of panic. Confidence in the Mexican economy deteriorated even further with an intense capital flight (Garriga and Lins 2014). The Mexican crisis was an important but not yet the final chapter in the epic of fixed exchange rate regimes in Latin America. This concurred with the implementation of the Real Plan in Brazil and with an extremely prosperous—albeit unsustainable—time in Argentina's convertibility regime.

Argentina

In Argentina, financial openness was a key element of the Convertibility Plan adopted in 1991. To protect against inflation, the economy had been steadily "dollarized" since mid-1980. The adoption of the currency board and, therefore, the establishment of legal tender status for the dollar led to total freedom for capital flows in the country. Besides the previous rules facilitating transactions in dollars, the Convertibility Law allowed the establishment of contracts in any foreign currency. Deregulation of the capital account in 1991 complemented this move to convertibility (Klagsbrunn 2010; Damill et al. 2011).

The literature describes two major growth episodes since the 1990s. The first period, from 1992 to 1998, may be considered as the apex of the convertibility model. The economy was organized around market institutions, and modernizing reforms were introduced. However, contrarily to the success obtained by the 1991 monetary reform, the process of fiscal reordering process was much less evident. The long persistence of the exchange regime, high interest rates and insufficient financial development would be the explosive ingredients that, in addition to the international financial turmoils, would detonate the crisis (Crisitini 2008, Labaqui 2014; Damill and Frenkel 2012, 2013; Damill et al. 2011; Fanelli 2013). In January 2002, the country lost 50% of its foreign reserves—that occurred even with the establishment of the *corralito*, limiting banking withdrawals—and the currency lost 40% of its value in the month the crisis began and 265% in the following 6 months (Kaminsky et al. 2009).

After the 2001–2002 crisis, Argentina witnessed episodes of intense growth. Policy patterns in Argentina, however, changed over time as state interventionism became more prominent under President Cristina Kirchner's consecutive mandates (Labaqui 2012). Government control spread to all spheres of economic life, including increasingly less reliable official statistics.

Argentina benefited from the world economy's prosperity period until 2007, particularly due to the rising price of commodities, which gave the country some comfort in the external accounts to set up the guidelines of economic policy in accordance with domestic policy priorities. However, and as expected, Argentina has been almost completely excluded from the international financial markets since 2001. Despite broad acceptance among Argentina's creditors of the 2005 and 2010 restructuring offers, a group of holdout creditors successfully litigating against Argentina in US courts has effectively posed an obstacle to the country's ability to issue debt abroad. The risk is that these disgruntled creditors will cease any assets distributed overseas as part of their standing legal claims for repayment. As a result, since the mid-2000s, Argentina has engaged in "creative" and interventionist funding schemes such as the nationalization of pension funds (Labaqui 2014).

Brazil

The Brazilian liberalization process was discreet compared to those of Mexico and particularly Argentina. Brazilian authorities began in the late 1980s–1990s opening different segments of financial markets (currency, fixed income and equity) to the entry of foreign capital. The banking system was not completely opened and transactions in other currencies were never permitted (Gottschalk and Sodré 2008; Freitas and Prates 2001). With monetary stabilization, a profound restructuring of markets took place, leading to the disappearance of several institutions and the promotion of higher market concentration.[4] The whole process led to a decrease in the number of public banks given the privatization of state banks and the strengthening of federal banks that remained in operation. The entry of large foreign banks and a greater concentration among domestic private ones drove to more competition amid larger financial institutions. These moves to reorganize the financial system, coupled with fairly rigid financial supervision and a relatively low degree of openness, ensured that the amount of international transactions of the financial system did not set up high vulnerability and dependence on external funds.

Either to attract portfolio investments in periods of current account deficit or to keep the process of reserve accumulation at times of international liquidity, high interest rates were a constant element of Brazilian economic policy, both during the pegged exchange regime and when flotation was embraced. Between 2003 and 2007, Brazil witnessed increasing portfolio capital inflows (see Fig. 11.1).

Brazil never granted *de jure* autonomy or independence for its central bank. After modifying the exchange regime and adopting the inflation targeting system in 1999, the Brazilian central bank worked "autonomously" for about 10 years. This can be explained by the priority given to inflation control due to its huge political and economic importance in a context of benign global economic conditions.

Policy Responses to the 2008 Crisis

On the eve of the 2008 global crisis, Argentina was experiencing twin surpluses (fiscal and current account) since its post-2002 resurrection. The economy was boosted by both the commodities boom and the new type of macroeconomic populism[5]

[4] Price stabilization after 1994 led to a deep reduction in banks' earnings from inflation and indexation praxis. Large private banks such as Econômico (August 1995) and Nacional (November 1995) went bankrupt. State government banks were privatized, and federal banks were recapitalized and reformed (Mettenheim 2010).

[5] The idea and paradigm of "macroeconomic populism" were defined by Dornbusch and Edwards (1992), and has been widely applied to economic policy experiences in Latin America. As they define: "Macroeconomic populism is a policy perspective on economic management that emphasizes economic growth and income redistribution and deemphasizes the risks of inflation and deficit finance, external constraints and the reaction of economic agents to aggressive non-market policies." (op.cit, 247).

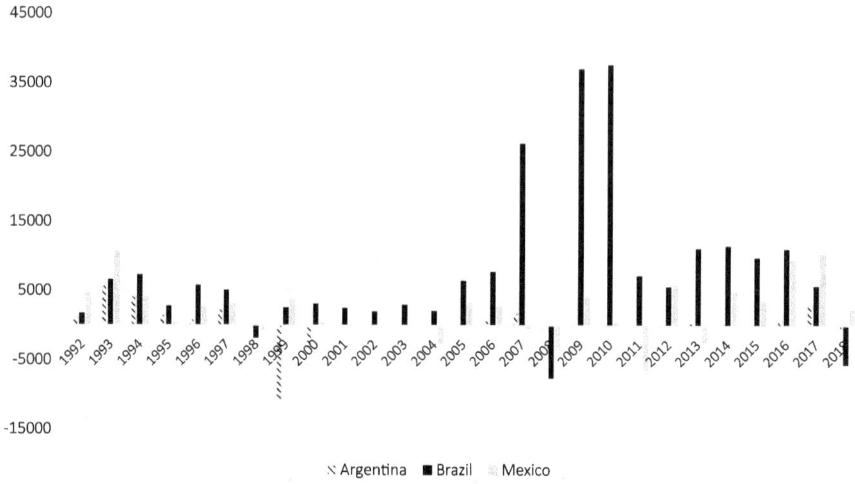

Fig. 11.1 Portfolio equity net flows, current US$ millions. (Source: World Bank)

established since 2007 (Labaqui 2014; Damill and Frenkel 2013; Fanelli 2013). The Brazilian economy too was undergoing a prosperous phase when the crisis deepened in 2008. After a few years of fiscal discipline that restored international credibility and helped the country regain a certain level of stability, Brazil was in the midst of an expansionary turn in economic policy, characterized by measures to stimulate domestic consumption and investment in specific sectors. Therefore, countercyclical policies marked the expansion and specialization of some policies already in place, such as credit expansion by state-owned financial institutions and tax exemptions to particular industrial sectors related to domestic consumption or potential exporters (Wise and Lins 2015).

In contrast, Mexico was severely hit by the crisis, a temporary reversal of an upward growth trend from 2002 to 2007. This was a result of higher oil prices, exports to the USA, larger remittance inflows and consequent currency appreciation. All contributed to over expenditure before the 2008 global crisis. The proximity to the US economy, that had fueled Mexican exports, meant that the effects of the crisis were deeper, notably through currency depreciation. However, Mexico rebounded relatively quickly from the initial shock. According to the IMF's Assessment on the Mexican financial system, the commitment to the inflation targeting and floating exchange rate scheme, combined with the effort to maintain fiscal discipline, were key factors explaining Mexican rebound since 2010 (IMF 2012). Financial sector restructuring after 1995, its lower external exposure and a quite moderate central bank reaction to the crisis were peculiar characteristics of the Mexican case (Esquivel 2015).

Despite their different reactions to the crisis, the three countries were capable of holding high amounts of foreign reserves in absolute terms. Yet, when considering the rate international reserves to GDP, Argentina's figures declined significantly since 2007 to recover after 2015 (Fig. 11.2). Capital flight from Argentina started in

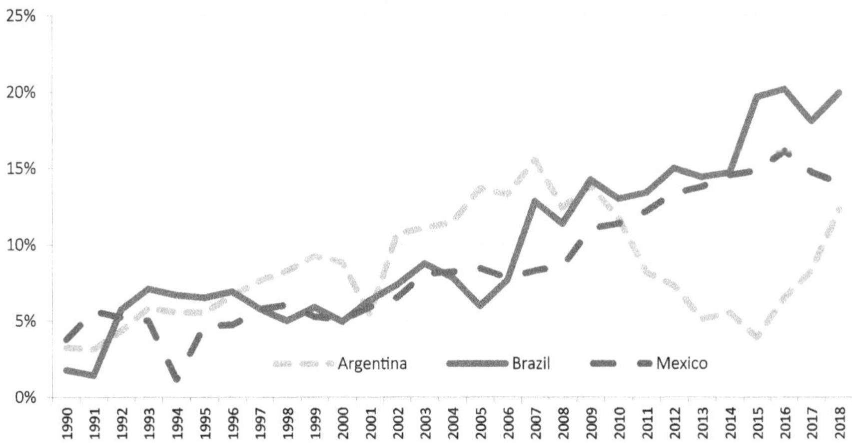

Fig. 11.2 Foreign Reserves/GDP Ratio, %. (Source: World Bank, author's calculation)

early 2007 precisely when underestimation of inflation rates became a public and ongoing practice, and from then on, the credibility of the economic policy went steadily declining. The falling prices of the country's government bonds in international currency and the higher spreads measured by markets relatively to non-risk assets illustrate the process (Damill and Frenkel 2012).

Argentina, Brazil and Mexico experienced very unstable portfolio investment inflows after the crisis. Besides the fluctuations in international markets, the ability to attract foreign capital was extremely uneven among the three countries, as Fig. 11.1 depicts. Since late 2011, large emerging economies showed a trend to growth at a slower path. Shifts in industrialized countries' monetary policies, and consequently higher interest rates in safe markets, brought less capital to large emerging economies than before. At the same time, these economies started managing capital account more closely, in order to protect themselves and/or with other policy goals (Gallagher and Tian 2017). Brazil has been a pioneer in using taxes to control capital outflows. Mexico, on the contrary, has been rewarded by risk agencies for its conservative approach to economic policy. Shortly, in different extents, emerging economies implemented new policies or reformed old ones, bringing new facts to the markets and new configurations to their own policy frameworks.

Policy Changes

Argentina, Brazil and Mexico took advantage of long and pronounced increases in commodity prices during the 2000s. Regarding financial flows, Brazil and Mexico were able to attract capital and issue bonds in external markets, when considering the various differences among these assets. Argentina was gradually isolated from the international financial markets both by the lost credibility of government bonds and by the constraints imposed on the private sector access to external credit markets.

Since 2007 Argentina had been experiencing stronger state intervention which also included government intervention at the federal statistics institute, the nationalization of private pension funds and other previously privatized corporations,[6] a conflict between the administration and the central bank, and a confrontation with the agriculture sector (Labaqui 2012; Damill and Frenkel 2013).[7] These facts substantially deteriorated the risk perception of international markets and contributed, along with the crisis, to the severe capital outflows the country experienced since late 2007, whose adverse impacts on the balance of payments were offset by the benign effects of international commodity prices. Labaqui (2012) describes how President Cristina Fernández de Kirchner tried to regain the confidence of international financial markets', and thus reduce Argentine bonds' spread, by normalizing external debt payments (albeit not engaging with holdout creditors). She then proceeded to try to convince skeptical observers and investors about the economic stability of the intra public sector financing scheme by using resources that originated from the nationalized pension funds to pump up national reserves. From there on, Argentina experienced a sequence of discretionary policy changes and institutional uncertainty.

In Brazil, the political scenario was mainly favorable to the government in 2008–2009. President Lula was in the middle of his second term and, despite major corruption scandals involving his party and important political leaders connected to him, popular approval of the government remained high. Gains that had been achieved by the lowest income groups provided an important source of political support to the government, as well as the image of Brazil as an emerging power. The worsening economic situation after the crisis was hence not a politically acceptable alternative for the country.

In fact, since the beginning of Lula's first term, a particular group dissatisfied with the direction of economic policy within the president's Workers' Party had been criticizing its "neoliberal" features. Once macroeconomic stability was achieved, for this group, it was time to change policy goals and directions. Pro-growth measures should be combined with stability in normal times. When the crisis came, pro-growth measures were already in place and, while they were being implemented, a broader set of new measures was created, as a program intended to

---

[6] Examples are the airline Aerolineas Argentinas and the oil company YPF.

[7] "Enfoquemos ahora en mayor detalle el canal financiero. Los cambios en el contexto financiero global se reflejaron principalmente en una variable: las salidas de capitales privados. La denominada "huida hacia la calidad" afectó a muchas economías en desarrollo, particularmente en el último trimestre de 2008. En el caso argentino, varias fuentes internas de incertidumbre se adicionaron al impacto de los shocks externos negativos. Cuatro factores se destacan como los más importantes. Ya hemos comentado la manipulación de las estadísticas oficiales de inflación desde comienzos de 2007 y el conflicto entre el gobierno nacional y los productores agropecuarios. Se agregarían luego la nacionalización del sistema privado de pensiones a fines de 2008 y, finalmente, el conflicto relacionado con la utilización de reservas de divisas del Banco Central para hacer frente al servicio de la deuda pública, en 2009." Damilll and Frenkel (2013), p. 18.

be a new industrial policy, which increased tax benefits to selected sectors and incentives to producers with export potential.[8] With the transition from Lula's to President Dilma Rousseff's administration, there was an important shift in the economic team. In light of the poor economic performance since 2011, state interventionism gained more ground to the detriment of the commitment to macroeconomic stability. The relationship between the executive and the central bank took on a more "intimate tone," largely at the expense of the monetary authority's credibility. Rousseff's first mandate favored a long waited—by the developmentalist group in PT—shift in the relationship between the central bank and the Finance ministry. Under Lula, the arm wrestling between the two institutions has mostly been won by the central bank. Its governor Henrique Meirelles and his team enjoyed a de facto operational autonomy and kept the commitment to the inflation target.

Mexico, despite the various previous internal reforms and the pro-market approach of its policy framework, as mentioned above, was far from shielded from the adverse impacts of the crisis. Mexican political scene is much more complicated than the relatively short list of presidents in recent years might lead one to believe. Democracy is relatively new and younger than that of Argentina and Brazil, considering the transition of power from the previously hegemonic PRI to the PAN with the election of Vicente Fox in 1999. This event broke the cycle of over 70 years of PRI administrations.[9] However, 12 years of PAN administrations did not bring about fundamental change despite the party's more conservative (right-wing) platform compared to that embraced by the PRI.

Indeed, during most of the twentieth century, Mexico experienced a very particular political regime, which some political scientists have called "exceptional." While many Latin American countries were plagued by political instability, coups and military crises of governance, the Mexican political system was largely stable, while dominated by the PRI. These 70 years of authoritarianism and clientelism had effects on the practice of politics that the 12 years of the PAN administrations failed to overcome. When the global crisis erupted, Mexico was highly dependent on the US economy and torn by violence from confrontations related to drug trafficking. In December 2012, Enrique Peña Nieto returned the PRI back to power, bringing with him a "well trained" team of technocrats to the Finance Ministry and central bank, most of whom had been educated in the USA.[10] This was a totally different approach to Mexico's economic policy design than those found in Argentina and Brazil at that time.

To sum up, Brazil, Argentina and Mexico presented very different political scenarios when dealing with the impact of the 2008 crisis. These differences are relevant in regard to both the general political orientation of the parties in power and the

[8] *Plano Brasil Maior* (Greater Brazil Plan), launched in August 2011. (http://www.brasilmaior.mdic.gov.br/inicio).

[9] Partido Acción Nacional – PAN (in Spanish), National Action Party and Partido Revolucionario Institucional – PRI, Institutional Revolutionary Party (in Spanish).

[10] See *The man from MIT*. The Economist, March 22, 2014.

more immediate motivations of economic policy in the post-critical phase of the global crisis.

Conclusion

Through a comparative case analysis study, this chapter sought to understand how the three largest Latin American economies dealt with their economic crises in the past four decades. The argument was that, despite the close relations maintained by these countries with multilateral organizations such as the IMF, and the intense financial integration process that marked the period and brought profound changes to the region, domestic political choices prevailed over possible international pressures on crisis management and policy making.

Since 2000, among the three countries, Argentina suffered the most instability and output volatility as a result of the crises. Its own crisis in 2001–2002, when the macroeconomic framework broke and strong uncertainty, recession and inflation increased, and during the attempt to stabilize and reform made by Mauricio Macri government (2015–2019). In Brazil, the severe crisis that deepened from 2014—precipitated by the Rousseff's government "growth at any cost" policy—was used as a pretext for conservative forces in Congress to engender a parliamentary coup that led to the impeachment of the president, and even more instability. Mexico maintained a more disciplined economic policy, anchored in its institutions, such as the independent central bank. But that was not enough to prevent a growing social discontent that led to the election of a left-wing populist proposal presented by Antonio Manuel López Obrador in 2017.

In the three cases, a close relationship was observed between domestic political demands and the design of economic policy. Although there were similarities between the challenges faced by the three countries, such as the need to respond to changes/shifts in the world economy, each country's economic policy sought, above all, to accommodate internal political pressures.

References

Bresser-Pereira, L. C. (1992). *A crise do Estado. Ensaios sobre a economia brasileira.* São Paulo: Nobel.

Crisitini, M. (2008). Argentina. In P. Fischer-Bollin & E. Saavedra (Eds.), *Crecimiento y progreso social en América Latina* (pp. 17–46). Rio de Janeiro: Konrad Adenauer Stiftung.

Damill, M. & Frenkel, R. (2012). Macroeconomic policies, growth, employment, and inequality in Latin America. UNU-WIDER Working Paper No. 2012/23.

Damill, M., & Frenkel, R. (2013). La economía argentina bajo los Kirchner: Una historia de dos lustros. Instituto de Transparencia Financiera-ITF. *Documentos técnicos*, 1–41.

Damill, M., Frenkel, R., & Rapetti, M. (2005). La deuda argentina: Historia, default y reestructuración. *Desarrollo Económico, 45*(178), julio-setiembre, 187–233.

Damill, M., Frenkel, R., & Simpson, L. (2011). Regulaciones financieras y macroeconomía: La experiencia paradigmática de la Argentina en los años noventa. *Desarrollo Económico, 50*(200), 547–578. www.jstor.org/stable/41408181.

Dornbusch, R., & Edwards, S. (1992). The macroeconomics of populism. In R. Dornbusch, & S. Edwards (Eds.), *The macroeconomics of populism in Latin America* (pp. 7–13). National Bureau of Economic Research conference. Chicago: The University of Chicago Press.

Esquivel, G. (2015). Mexico's recovery from the global financial crisis. In C. Wise, L. E. Armijo, & S. N. Katada (Eds.), *Unexpected outcomes: How emerging markets survived the global financial crisis*. Washington, DC: Brookings Institution Press.

Fanelli, J. M. (2013). Mirando el 2014 en Argentina: ¿dónde está el piloto? Observatorio Económico de la Red Mercosur, Diciembre. Available at: http://www.oered.org/index.php?option=com_content&view=article&id=252%3Amirando-el-2014-en-argentina-idonde-esta-el-piloto-&lang=es

Freitas, M. C. & Prates, D. M. (2001). A abertura financeira no governo FHC: impactos e consequências. *Economia e Sociedade, Campinas, 17*, Dezembro, 81–111.

Gallagher, K. P., & Tian, Y. (2017). Regulating capital flows in emerging markets: The IMF and the global financial crisis. *Review of Development Finance, 7*, 95–106.

Garriga, A. C., & Lins, M. A. D. T. (2014). El camino hacia la estabilidad: Treinta años de la moneda en Brasil y en México. In M. M. Sousa & C. Maldonado (Eds.), *En Busca del Desarrollo: Una Comparación de las Estrategias de Desarrollo de Brasil y México* (pp. 55–103). México: CIDE.

Gottschalk, R., & Sodré, C. A. (2008). The liberalization of capital outflows in Brazil, India and South Africa since the early 1990s. In P. Arestis & L. F. Paula (Eds.), *Financial liberalization and economic performance in emerging countries*. New York: Palgrave Macmillan.

Griffith-Jones, S. & Sunkel, O. (1986). *Debt and development crises in Latin America: The end of an illusion*. New York: Oxford University Press.

Grigera, J. (2017). Populism in Latin America: Old and new populisms in Argentina and Brazil. *International Political Science Review, 38*(4), 441–455.

IMF (2012). Mexico Financial System Stability Assessment. IMF Country Report No. 12/65. Available at: https://www.imf.org/en/Publications/CR/Issues/2016/12/31/Mexico-Financial-System-Stability-Assessment-25810.

Kaminsky, G., Mati, A., & Choueiri, N. (2009). Thirty years of currency crises in Argentina: External shocks or domestic fragility? *Economía Journal*, The Latin American and Caribbean Economic Association – LACEA, *0*(Fall 2009), 81–123, August.

Klagsbrunn, V. (2010). Brazil and Argentina in the global financial system: Contrasting approaches to development and foreign debt. In G. R. D. Underhill, J. Blom, & D. Mügge (Eds.), *Global financial integration thirty years on: From reform to crisis*. Cambridge: Cambridge University Press.

Labaqui, I. (2012). Living with our own means: The role of financial policy in the Nestor and Cristina Fernandez de Kirchner Administrations. Paper prepared for the XXX International Congress of the Latin American Studies Association (LASA), San Francisco, May.

Labaqui, I. (2014). Who's afraid of reversing neoliberal reforms? Financial statecraft in Argentina and Venezuela. In L. E. Armijo & S. N. Katada (Eds.), *The financial statecraft of emerging powers. Shield and sword in Asia and Latin America* (pp. 21–46). New York: Palgrave Macmillan.

Maxfield, S. (1992). The international political economy of bank nationalization: Mexico in comparative perspective. *Latin American Research Review, 27*(1), 75–103. Retrieved 20 Feb 2019, from www.jstor.org/stable/2503718.

Mettenheim, K. (2010). *Federal banking in Brazil: Policies and competitive advantages*. London: Pickering and Chatto.

Rodrik, D. (2018). Populism and the economics of globalization. *Journal of International Business Policy, 1*(1), 12–33. https://doi.org/10.1057/s42214-018-0001-4.

Sandoval, I. E. (2011). Crisis, rentismo y intervencionismo neoliberal en La banca: México (1982–1999). México: Centro de Estudios Espinosa Yglesias, A.C.

Santín Quirós, O. (2001). *The political economy of Mexico's financial reform*. Basingstoke: Ashgate.

Skidmore, T., & Smith, P. H. (2005). *Modern Latin America* (6th ed.). New York: Oxford University Press.

Wiesner, E. (2008). *The political economy of macroeconomic policy reform in Latin America: The distributive and institutional context.* Northampton: Edward Elgar Publishing.

Wise, C., & Lins, M. A. D. T. (2015). Macro-prudence versus macro-profligacy-Brazil, Argentina and the global financial crisis. In C. Wise, L. E. Armijo, & S. N. Katada (Eds.), *Unexpected outcomes: How emerging markets survived the global financial crisis* (pp. 148–180). Washington, DC: Brookings Institution Press.

12

Impact of the Financial Crisis on Brazilian Democracy

Andrea Ribeiro Hoffmann and Bettina De Souza Guilherme

Abstract This Chapter explores the impact of the financial crisis on Brazilian democracy. We argue that while Brazil is one among many countries facing systemic effects of the 2008 crisis, domestic factors are also important to understand the level of the crisis, and the fragility of democracy at the present. Domestic factors explain, therefore the differences between Brazil and other countries in Latin America and in Europe.

Introduction

Brazil has gone through major changes since the beginning of the twenty-first century, including economic growth and political activism at the global level, symbolized by its participation in the BRICS group of countries, and the role of the latter in the changes of the post–Cold War global order. These positive trends were abruptly interrupted, if not reverted, in the period following the global financial and economic crisis of 2008. In the first years following the crisis, the country was not affected, but by the end of 2012, reduction of growth and rise of inequalities marked the end of the boom. With the impeachment of President Dilma Rousseff in 2016, a U-turn in economic policy towards a neoliberal approach took place, pushed by the opposition as an alternative about how to deal with the economic crisis, but the

A. Ribeiro Hoffmann
Pontifical Catholic University of Rio de Janeiro (PUC-Rio), Rio de Janeiro, Brazil

Coordinator of the second phase of the Jean Monnet Network "Crisis-Equity-Democracy for Europe and Latin America", Rio de Janeiro, Brazil
e-mail: a_ribeiro_hoffmann@puc-rio.br

B. De Souza Guilherme (✉)
Founder and Co-coordinator of the Jean Monnet Network "Crisis-Equity-Democracy for Europe and Latin America", IRELAC, Rio de Janeiro, Brazil

European Parliament, Brussels, Belgium
e-mail: bettina.desouza@europarl.europa.eu

economic results have been meagre and the political effects have been dramatic, leading the more profound and serious threat to democracy since the end of the military regime in the 1980s.

In this chapter, we focus on the political crisis. We argue that the global financial crisis was a trigger of the crisis, but that domestic factors are key to understand the depth of the crisis, and the fragility of democracy at the present, and therefore the differences between Brazil and other countries in Latin America or other regions such as Europe.

With that aim, we firstly situate the current political crisis in the recent history of Brazilian democratization, relying on the seminal work of Brazilian political scientist Leonardo Avritzer, specially his last book, published in 2019. We analyse the key political changes and popular reaction from 2013, when popular demonstrations erupted, to the election of extreme-right President Bolsonaro in 2018. We highlight key facts such as the imprisonment of former President Lula and the assassination of Rio de Janeiro Deputy Marielle Franco to illustrate the degradation of the rule of law and the fragility of democracy. We conclude by pointing to some major challenges ahead.

Pendular Democracy: The Democracy Paradox from 2013 Demonstrations to the Election of Bolsonaro

The crisis of the Brazilian democracy is not a minor 'detour', rather a demonstration of some of the structural instabilities of Brazilian institutions and inequalities of Brazilian society. Avritzer (2018) analyses the developments from the 2013 demonstrations to the election of President Bolsonaro, and argues that the process of construction of Brazilian democracy can be characterized as 'pendular' both in empirical and normative terms. In this sense, the current period is seen as a setback and reversion from the previous phase of consolidation of democracy and is characterized by another cycle of democratic instability as those that peaked in 1954 and 1964, when two models of development were in contest, a more developmentalist and a more liberal. A key difference, however, is that while during those crises the divergence between Brazilian domestic society reflected Cold War opposing economic models, the current global context is of neoliberal hegemony, and the alignments seem to reflect the contest between the USA and China for leadership (Acharya 2018; Ikenberry et al. 2018).

Despite this difference, as Avritzer identifies a 'democracy paradox' in the fact that the current cycle of discontent ('mal-estar') with democracy began with demonstrations for better public service, social justice, anti-corruption and more democracy in June 2013, and triggered a set of actions and events, which had the reverse effect. This is not a unique phenomenon, but can be observed as well in other countries (i.e. Arab Spring, USA), where major social movements had appeared and were expected to lead to a major leap forward of democratizations and answering the call for a better global governance and more equity, but indeed brought about instability, unrest and setbacks for democracy and social justice. It is not rare that the momentum created by indignation, anger and social protest end up being hijacked by one of the movements for the realization of its particular objectives as was the case of the Muslim Brotherhood, or diverted by a counter-movement to the new social movements (case of Trump's populism as a reaction to Occupy Wall Street).

2013 Demonstrations

In the case of Brazil, the original protests of June 2013 were organized by the Movimento Passe Livre (MPL) in protest of a minor increase of the metro and bus tickets in several Brazilian cities and promoting free transport in Brazil. After an initially repressive reaction by the police and security forces and the unjust stigmatization as vandals by the traditional press, the mobilization through social media more than outperformed the expectations of the organizers. While the MPL as well as the participants refused any participation of political parties, they did not engage in 'framing activities' to discuss and find an agreement on the main demands as in Spain (indignados) and the USA (Occupy Wall Street). However, the aims of the June 2013 protests were not to bring the government down but to request more and better public services (transport, education, health service) and to fight corruption: thus to improve governance.

The 2013 demonstrations led to a twofold weakening of the Dilma Rousseff government. First by revealing criticism and a diminishing support within the classical electorate of the PT shown by the rise of a considerable protest movement demanding more and better public service during the PT government. Second, it led to the appropriation of (traditional left wing) social movement repertoire such as demonstrations and social media by (centre-)right wing movements officially with the 'noble' motivation to combat corruption and ended up bringing down the left-wing government of the Labour Party (Partido dos Trabalhadores—PT) which was in power since 2003. The social movements protests of the years 2015 and 2016 were clearly directed 'against' the government and PT, and as later revealed financially supported by some industrialists and finance representatives, and stimulated and supported by the special anti-corruption taskforce Lava Jato, Judge Sergio Moro and the traditional media, in particularly the media conglomerate Globo, which gave broad coverage to the demonstrations against the PT and in particularly against Dilma Rousseff and Lula.

While these 2015 and 2016 social movements were 'officially' protesting against corruption, their main purpose and motivation was to bring down the PT government. This became clear when there were neither 'paneladas' nor demonstrations when acting president Michel Temer was wiretapped in a conversation with newspaper JB revealing his implication in a network of corruption, indicating persons of confidence to receive the corruption money who were filmed receiving the bribe the following day. Just as well astonishing was the silence on the revealed implication of family members of the later president Bolsonaro in corruption and relationships with militias who were involved in the murder of Marielle Franco. The political crisis led to the non-acceptance of the election results of 2014, when President Dilma Rousseff was re-elected.

During 2013, a major media campaign against President Rousseff and PT evolved, blaming them for corruption and incompetence to improve economy. The surprise and narrow (51,64%) victory came as a major shock. The opposition refused to accept the results of the elections for the first time since 1989, and started to boycott all proposals from the government to improve the economy following the strategy of 'the worse the better' (quanto pior melhor) and of searching reasons to impeach the president. In this context, the 'national pact to stop the bleeding' and the Operation Car Wash were created.

Dilma's Impeachment

The impeachment process followed clean procedures at the formal level.[1] The deterioration of the economy resulted not necessarily by 'bad administration' but from global level structural factors such as financial crisis, the fall of global demand for primary resources and the fall of petrol price. Dilma's government lacked willingness and capacity to build coalitions with other parties and lost political support in Congress and Senate. Dilma herself lacked charisma and lost support of her own electorate after hiring orthodox finance minister Levy and engaging into budget consolidation measures after the re-election.

Economic downturn, Car Wash Operation and street movements during 2015 and 2016 culminated with the impeachment of Dilma in August 2016. Vice President Temer became interim President and changed completely the government programme; he announced a neoliberal strategy 'Bridge to the Future (*Ponte para o Futuro*)' in line with the decade-old Washington consensus and a conservative approach in politics, the picture of a white-(old)-men-only government being quite symbolic. According to Carta Capital of 23 September 2016, Michel Temer explained on 21 September 2016 to a group of entrepreneurs and investors in New York that the reason for the impeachment was that Dilma Rousseff refused the proposals of the neoliberal programme. In a television interview in SBT at the end of 2018, Michel Temer admitted that he considered Dilma Rousseff as correct and honest person and did not have the impression that she was somebody to take over the government to enrich herself with public property. His statements and the

[1] The main milestones of the impeachment process were: Dec 2015—acceptance of case by the Congress (Pres. Eduardo Cunha after the PT had voted for lifting his immunity in a major corruption case for which he was later condemned; April 2016—Approval at the Congress by the Commission (11/4 38x27) and the Plenary (17/4 367x137); May 2016—Approval at the Senate by the Commission (12/5 55x22) and the Plenary (10/8 59x21); August 2016—Judgement at the Senate presided by the President of the Supreme Court (31/8 61x20 but 42). Note that the Supreme Court supervised the procedure but never examined the merit (cause) of the impeachment.

wiretapped conversation of the Senate PMDP party leader Juca lead to the conclusion that the main purposes of her impeachment were not to fight corruption, but to stop or limit the investigations of Lava Jato and to bring about a complete policy change, thus the dismantlement of the young welfare state introduced by Lula and Dilma into a neoliberal system, what they would not have succeeded by democratic elections.

Temer's Government and the Neoliberal U-Turn

Temer was elected as a vice president, however, for a political programme in line with the former government, explicitly opposing the austerity programmes contained in the 'bridge for the future'. Temer's government quickly went about to adopt policies to reduce workers' rights and protection with the pretext of modernizing and increasing Brazil's attractiveness for investors, weakening the trade unions, and with an extensive possibility of 'outsourcing', deregulated the labour market. While Temer's finance minister had promised the creation of six million new jobs in Brazil, the policy change resulted in an increase of informal work and of unemployment from 11.2% (in May 2016) to 13.1% (in April of 2018). A further measure of the dismantlement of the welfare state were cuts of the social programmes such as the Bolsa Familia, Minha Casa Minha Vida and the programme Universidade para Todos (ProUni). In November 2016, Temer's government succeeded to reduce the minimum quota of 30% of participation of the company in petrol exploitation and lift the exclusive exploitation right for the deep sea (pré-sal). Last but not least, the Temer government succeeded in their attempt as both the Congress and the Senate adopted the so-called 'Teto de gasto' by a constitutional amendment which limits the budget for 20 years to only increase along the inflation rate. All these reforms and sacrifices (of the poorer part of the society) should lead to the economic recovery, which so far turned out rather modest GDP growth of 1.06% for 2017 and 1.12% for 2018. In the same period, inequalities increased; according to the Instituto Brasileiro de Economia da Fundação Getulio Vargas (FGV IBRE), Brazil reached in March 2019 its record rate of inequality of 0.6257%, the highest level of inequality of any democracy in the world.

Foreign policy orientation was also completely reformulated under Temer, from a south–south approach to an alignment with the USA. During the governments of President Lula, from 2003 and 2010, growth was accompanied by an active foreign policy (Vigevani and Cepaluni 2016); since the re-election of Dilma, foreign policy had become practically paralysed (Saraiva 2014; De Oliveira et al. 2018), as well captured in Mello's article title, which states that Brazil changed 'From Euphoria to Inertia' (Mello 2018). The same trend is analysed by Milani et al. (2017), who introduce the concept of 'graduation dilemma' to address structural constraints to changes of the international position of second-tier non-nuclear states, such as Brazil:

> At the outset of the 21st century, Brazil was praised for being a responsible rising power. It was held aloft as a development model for other nations of the Geopolitical South, as well as an example of incremental political transition from a civil—military dictatorship to a rights-based society. Brazil's fight against hunger, its inclusive public policies, the increase in the number of public universities, the recognition of a diversified multiracial society, multilateral leadership, a political vision of regional integration processes, and its outreach to African countries, *inter alia*, contributed to Brazil's world-wide acclaim. Developing countries sent envoys to Brasília to analyse the gradual results of social policies being implemented.... In 2017, however, the situation is totally different from that at the beginning of the twenty-first century. Although Fernando Henrique Cardoso, Lula da Silva and Dilma Rousseff had their respective differences and relevant distinctive traits, the three presidents did not deviate from the 1988 Constitution and subsequent political pact that supported Brazil's re-democratization and macroeconomic stabilization. Nevertheless, in 2015–2016 the sense of progressive advancement was disrupted. Something has happened in Brazil in the last two years, and the country now faces one of the greatest institutional, political and economic crises of its Republican period. (Mello 2018, p. 4)

Temer's policies did not manage, however, to revert the economic downturn, and his approval rate was only 5% by the end of his term. According to an opinion poll of the CNI-Ibop at the end of 2018, 74% of the interviewed persons considered Temer's government negative. Moreover, and ironically, he was accused of corruption. In the context of the revelation of Temer's involvement with corruption, there is a twofold puzzle: first why did the chamber of deputies and senate the federal, both institutions that had violently and explicitly been demonstrating zero tolerance for Rousseff, not immediately start an impeachment? Second, where were the social movements against corruption which had been protesting in millions against Dilma Rousseff under the allegiance of creative accountancy (pedaladas), when everybody could 'hear' president Temer being implicated in corruption and 'see' the video where his person of trust was collecting and transporting a suitcase with corruption money.

Concerning the first puzzle we have to be aware that most of the deputies which had voted for the impeachment of Dilma would be against the impeachment of Temer, because they would have to admit that they had made a mistake and might face the consequences by not being re-elected. Additionally, a considerable number of deputies were implicated in corruption charges and did not want to risk losing their political mandate, which would lift their immunity, in the case of new elections. Third, according to the journal Estadao de SP of 7 January 2018, the government of Temer liberated a record of R$ 10.7 billion for parliamentary amendments to buy the support of the deputies against an impeachment and in favour of the unpopular bills adopted during the Temer's era. These budgetary amendments dedicate investments in the electorates of the deputies for infrastructure or other needs.

The second puzzle is the relative 'non-reaction' of civil society and the voice of the street, in particularly of the ones, which were protesting with pans and the big anti-corruption movements 'vem pra rua' (come to the street). However, reading the leaked information of the Lava Jato Telegram conversations reveals that some of these movements had been 'instrumentalized' for a regime change rather than for the fight against corruption. Additionally, some of these movements appear to be financed by major oligarchs who are sympathetic with the economic agenda of Temer. Some interpreted it with the demoralization of the population and the giving up of hope in positive change, considering all politicians as corrupt. But the comeback of the military also signalled that protest was not totally absent, but rather that control has increased.

Federal Intervention in Rio de Janeiro and the Comeback of the Military

Carnival 2018, which is of major importance in Brazilian culture, surprisingly turned out to be the main manifestation and expression of indignation, outrage and protest. In particularly in Rio de Janeiro, two of the major Samba Schools Beija Flor and Tuiuti thematized the corruption and deception and exploitation of the workers in their performances, showing Temer as a vampire, surrounded by dancers with suitcases full of corruption money, workforce as exploited slaves and so on. The audience joined the dancers, and the songs are being played in Samba bar as a sign of resistance. Shortly after the Carnival had ended and around the date of Lula's arrest, Temer's government announced the military intervention in Rio de Janeiro, officially to contain violence, in reality to intimidate the population and to oppress any resistance to the arrest of Lula and against the government measures. This military intervention did not decrease violence, but on the contrary, according to Pablo Nunes, coordinator from the Observatório da Intervenção (2018 report), resulted in the increase of 17% of homicides and 174% of shootings, and achieved a historic record of 1532 deaths caused by public security agents which implies an increase of 34% in relation to 2017.

The Election of Bolsonaro

The economic crisis and change of approach that began in Temer's government evolved into a crisis of democracy that led to the election of extreme-right President Jair Bolsonaro in the end of 2018. Bolsonaro's government was elected with the support of three main groups, which can be referred to as the 'neoliberals', the 'military' and the 'ideological' (Pinto 2019). The 'neoliberals' are represented by Minister of Economics Paulo Guedes, who has a de-regulation, privatization and free-trade agenda. This agenda is not new in Brazilian politics, as it was advanced in the beginning of the 1990s by President Fernando Collor, and parts of the agenda by most governments since then. The 'military' is a less homogeneous group, including lower-patent pro-Bolsonaro groups and high-ranking groups with a sometimes divergent approaches to international security matters such as Venezuela, UN peacekeeping and domestic security matters such as the Amazon. The ´ideological' is an even less homogenous group, labelled here mainly for the dogmatic approach to normative issues including environment, human rights, religion and gender, often inspired by Olavo de Carvalho, a Brazilian living in the USA referred in the media as Bolsonaro's 'guru', and the US-based 'alt-right' movement. Carvalho has kept contact with other right-wing politicians and instigators in the world such as Steve Bannon, Victor Orban and Matteo Salvini, in addition to Donald Trump. This group has also influence in the Minister of Foreign Affairs, Araújo. These groups and their political agendas do not share a coherent political project, rather they advance mostly in clientelist fashion, specific interests which are often contradictory. Despite this weakness and mounting discontentment, Bolsonaro's government has been successful to be proactive and keep the opposition in a defensive position.

Lula's Imprisonment and the Assassination of Marielle: Rule of Law Under Threat

Two developments during the political crisis evolving in the last years are key to understand the depth of the democratic crisis in Brazil and the threat to the rule of law, namely, the imprisonment of former President Lula and the assassination of Rio de Janeiro-elected Deputy Marielle Franco.

As already discussed, the campaign against corruption during PT governments was empowered by the creation of the so-called operation Car War (Operação Lava-Jato), instituted by the Federal Public Ministry (Ministério Público Federal). Despite the successes in many investigations, the operation has been criticized in terms of the use of plea bargaining (delação premiada) and its bias against PT and former President Lula, which included a strategic cover by the media such as Rede Globo, a powerful conglomerate by Marinho family (Bottino 2016; Cioccari 2015). Lula was sentenced in two cases and accused in five other penal cases, and is in prison since April 2018.[2] Lula's imprisonment has launched a campaign to set him free (Lula Livre), led by PT and Brazilian artists such as Chico Buarque, who was a symbol of the resistance against the military regime and includes the support from a broad range of intellectuals and institutions worldwide such as the UNHR High Commissioner in 2018 and the UNHR Council in 2019; Lula was also nominated a candidate to Nobel Peace Prize for his Fight Against Hunger and Poverty, following a petition led by Perez Esquivel.

The second development which is key to understand the crisis of Brazilian democracy is the assassination in March 2018 of then elected member of the Rio de Janeiro city Council, Marielle Franco, and the interconnected relations between Bolsonaro's family and the militia. As David Miranda, also member of Rio's City Council and husband of American journalist Glenn Greenwald, stated: 'Finding who ordered her death is key to the most important political cause of our time:

[2] The cases were (1) July 2017—sentenced for money laundering and passive corruption by then Federal Judge Sergio Moro TRF-4 (beach apartment Guaruja worth USD 1mi bribe); January 2018—appeals court upheld decision; April 2018—started sentence in Curitiba; and (2) February 2019—sentenced by Federal Judge Gabriela Hardt (renovation Works in ranch in Atibaia Worth USD 460,000 bribe).

stopping authoritarianism in Brazil'.[3] Miranda claims that Marielle 'was executed by a group known as "The Crime Bureau" – a shadowy and elusive organisation which commits murder at the bidding of politicians, criminals, right-wing paramilitary "militias" – and whoever else has a few hundred thousand reais to pay for the murder of someone they don't like'. Even if the formal investigation remains inconclusive, Miranda's accusation is supported by academic and investigative journalism research.[4] A direct link between Bolsonaro's family and Marielle's assassination was not proved, but the President's son, Flávio, supported politicians who celebrated her death and is also linked to the militia in other affairs.[5] Lima (2019) argues that it is important 'to understand the historical continuance of lethal violence as one of the most striking social characteristics of Brazil…[and that].. preventing and tackling of homicides - understood in a broad sense that includes all intentional murders - are political and institutional operations ensuing from a symbolic simulacrum that causes incremental initiatives to fail to reach the architecture of institutions of criminal justice and public security'. This simulacrum leads the police and other institutions of the criminal justice system to continue operating from a core of criminal policies that do not comply with the democratic public security project, that is, with the protection of life and civil and human rights envisioned by the 1988 Constitution (Lima 2019, p.1).

Conclusions: Challenges Ahead

We have argued in this chapter, in line with Avritzer (2018), that from a long-term perspective, Brazilian democracy has followed a pendular trend, but we have highlighted the relevance of the impact of the global financial/economic crisis and the (mis)managements of Brazilian government as key triggers for the current rupture. The U-turn to a neoliberal approach since the impeachment of President Rousseff has had a crucial impact not only on the growth and economic inequalities, but also on the Brazilian democracy. We have also argued there that three main challenges can be highlighted, which require different short- and long-term reaction and measures, namely, a politico-institutional, an economic and a socio-cultural challenge.

The politico-institutional challenge is not new; some of the weaknesses of Brazilian political institutions have been discussed in the academia and in the political parties during the last decades, and proposals for political reforms have been advanced. Some of these weaknesses are the weak presidentialism and the large amount of political parties. The judicialization of politics or politicization of the

[3] https://www.theguardian.com/commentisfree/2019/mar/14/marielle-franco-murder-brazil

[4] https://brasil.elpais.com/brasil/2019/01/29/politica/1548794774_637466.html; https://theintercept.com/2019/01/17/marielle-franco-brazil-assassination-suspect/

[5] https://politica.estadao.com.br/noticias/eleicoes,flavio-bolsonaro-defende-destruicao-de-placa-pro-marielle-por-correligionarios,70002532531; https://brasil.elpais.com/brasil/2019/01/22/politica/1548165508_401944.html

judiciary became a caricature in Bolsonaro's government, but is also not new. Newer phenomena are the participation of Armed Forces in the government (active and retired military), the reversion of evolving relations between civilian and military, and the direct involvement of the militia in the government, as exemplified in the case of Marielle.

The economic challenge is the reversion of the neoliberal approach to development embraced by Bolsonaro's government, which added a denial of the climate change and the impact of the increase of a strategy of growth based on extractivism and agribusiness to the cost of a sustainable development approach. Finally, socio-cultural challenges and the appeal of an extreme-right populist regime to the population are explored by Salgado in this volume, but we would like to emphasize here the challenges posed by the expansion of a new (conservative) social base grounded in the Pentecostal churches, and the 'contamination' of cultural policy and therefore the support to a conservative approach to culture.

Disclaimer The opinions expressed in this introduction/volume are the sole responsibility of the authors and do not necessarily represent the official position of the European Parliament or of any other EU institution.

References

Acharya, A. (2018). *The end of American world order*. 2nd Edition. Cambridge, UK; Medford, MA, USA: Polity.

Avritzer, L. (2018). The pendulum of democracy in Brazil: An approach of the 2013–2018 crisis. *Novos estudos CEBRAP, 37*(2), 273–289.

Bottino, T. (2016). Colaboração premiada e incentivos à cooperação no processo penal: Uma análise crítica dos acordos firmados na "Operação Lava Jato". *Revista Brasileira de Ciências Criminais, 122*(2016), 359–390.

Cioccari, D. (2015). Operação Lava Jato: Escândalo, agendamento e enquadramento. *Revista Alterjor, 12*(2), 58–78.

de Oliveira, F., Pennaforte, C. P., & Martins, M. A. F. (2018). Da crise de governabilidade à crise de legitimidade: Os impactos da crise política sobre a política externa brasileira. *Revista de Estudios Brasileños, 5*(9), 148–160.

Ikenberry, G. J., Parmar, I., & Stokes, D. (2018). Introduction: Ordering the world? Liberal internationalism in theory and practice. *International Affairs, 94*(1), 1–5.

Lima, R. S. D. (2019). Segurança pública como simulacro de democracia no Brasil. *Estudos Avançados, 33*(96), 53–68.

Mello e Silva, A. (2018). From Euphoria to Inertia: Brazil's international rise and decline, *E-International Relations*. Apr 29.

Milani, C. R., Pinheiro, L., & De Lima, M. R. S. (2017). Brazil's foreign policy and the 'graduation dilemma'. *International Affairs, 93*(3), 585–605.

Pinto, E. C. (2019). Bolsonaro e os Quartéis: A loucura como método. UFRJ Instituto de Economia. Texto para Discussão 006/2019.

Saraiva, M. G. (2014). Balanço da política externa de Dilma Rousseff: perspectivas futuras? *Relações Internacionais* (R: I), (44), 25–35.

Vigevani, T., & Cepaluni, G. (2016). *A política externa brasileira: a busca da autonomia, de Sarney a Lula*. Editora Unesp.

13

Economic, Political and Social Crisis in Venezuela

José Briceño-Ruiz and Kai Lehmann

Abstract This chapter aims to answer the following questions: What is the nature of the crisis confronted by the country and what are the conditions which led to, and sustain, it? What do these conditions mean for any attempts to address this crisis? Finally, what can be done in practical terms to address this crisis especially considering the country's increasing isolation not only in the region but in the world?

Introduction

That Venezuela is in crisis is beyond dispute. This crisis has economic, political and social dimensions and is accompanied by an internal political polarization that makes a peaceful agreement or transition difficult to achieve. The involvement of external actors (Cuba, the United States, the Rio Group China and Russia) has made the Venezuelan situation a regional and global issue. This chapter aims to answer the following questions: What is the nature of the crisis confronted by the country and what are the conditions which led to, and sustain, it? What do these conditions mean for any attempts to address this crisis? Finally, what can be done in practical terms to address this crisis especially considering the country's increasing isolation not only in the region but in the world?

We argue that the room of maneuver of regional institutions, and the international community as a whole, is very limited. The defense of democratic institutions, the avoiding of a military solution and the assistance to the Venezuelan people to deal with the economic crisis are certainly worthy goals. Nevertheless, the mechanisms to promote them have been not easy to implement.

It is vital that the countries of the region cooperate—be it through existing regional and sub-regional structures or through ad-hoc arrangements. However, the

J. Briceño-Ruiz
National Autonomous University of México (UNAM), México City, Mexico
e-mail: bricenoruiz@unam.mx

K. Lehmann (✉)
University of São Paulo, São Paulo, Brazil
e-mail: klehmann@usp.br

region is not homogeneous, and schemes such as the Union of South Americas Nations (UNASUR) have been accused to favor the Venezuelan regime (Burges 2018). A new regional bloc, the Forum for the Progress and Development of South America (PROSUR), was created in March 2019 (Calvacanti 2019), but excluded Venezuela. The Organization of American States (OAS) has also failed to find a solution to the crisis. This has led to the creation of the Lima Group with the participation of various Latin American and Caribbean countries and Canada.[1] More recently, after the proclamation of Juan Guaidó as interim President, in January 2019, a Contact Group was created by Mexico, Uruguay, the Caribbean Community (Caricom) and the European (EU) (European External Action Service 2019). However, the capacity of all these institutions to deal with the Venezuelan crisis is limited.

The Context: What Type of Crisis in Venezuela?

It is not difficult to attest to the existence of a crisis in Venezuela. This is acknowledged by both supporters and critics of the Venezuelan regime. The crisis is multidimensional in the sense that it encompasses economic, social, political and institutional aspects.

The Economic Crisis

In March 2013, a few days after the death of Hugo Chávez, Moises Naím described what were already the evident distortions of the Venezuelan economy: "Venezuela has one of the largest fiscal deficits in the world, the highest rate of inflation, the worst adjustment of the exchange rate, the fastest increase in debt and one of the biggest drops in productive capacity, even in the critical oil sector. In addition, during the Chávez era, the country fell to the bottom of the lists that measure international competitiveness, ease to do business and attractiveness for foreign investors, and rose to the top among the most corrupt countries in the world" (Naím 2016).

Despite these warnings, the Venezuelan government did not implement a serious economic plan to resolve the crisis. Rather, the Maduro administration continued exchange controls, control of prices and interest rates, and increased public expenditure. International organizations such as the World Bank or the International Monetary Fund, as well as various ratings agencies, estimate that the country has the highest inflation rate in the world: 3,300,000% in 2018. The International

[1] See https://www.cancilleria.gob.ar/en/announcements/news/declaration-lima-group for its opening statement on Venezuela.

Table 13.1 Venezuelan crude oil production

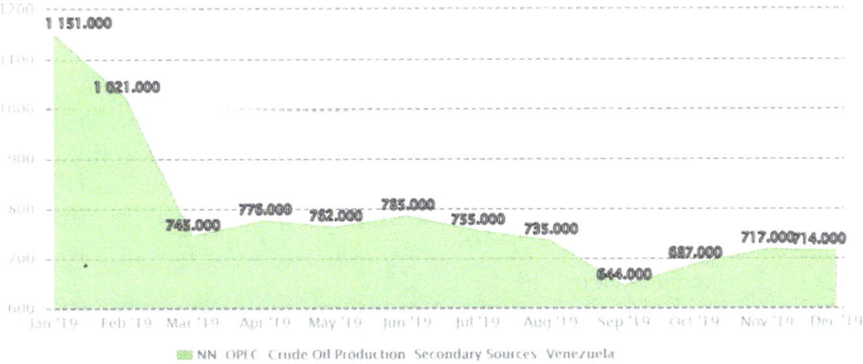

Source: www.CEICDATA.COM | Organization of the Petroleum Exporting Countries

Monetary Fund foresees a rate of 10,000,000% for 2019.[2] The indicator to compare recessions is GDP (gross domestic product). According the International Monetary Fund, Venezuela's GDP will fall 25% in 2019.[3] "That is a significantly sharper contraction than during the 1929–1933 Great Depression in the US, when US GDP is estimated to have fallen 28%. It is slightly bigger than the decline in Russia (1990–1994), Cuba (1989–1993), and Albania (1989–1993)" (Hausmann 2017).

To this fall in economic activity must be added the fall in oil production. A recent report from Andrew Stanley and Frank Verrastro of Center for Strategic and International Studies in Washington asserts that: "In the last 3 years (…) Venezuelan oil production plummeted by over 50% from 2.3 million barrels per day (b/d) in January 2016 to 1.1 million b/d in January of this year. Production continues to collapse and is now well below the 1 million b/d mark following the implementation of U.S. sanctions on PDVSA, and more recently in the aftermath of widespread electrical blackouts" (Verrastro and Stanley 2019). Table 13.1 shows the decline of Venezuelan oil production and evidences that in November 2019 the country produced around 717.000 barrels per day.

Consequently, the fall in government revenues is not only due to the collapse of prices in the international oil market, but also to a collapse in production. The absence of any policy to prepare for a price fall is a factor that also indicates deep structural problems in the Venezuelan economy, such as an absence of a policy of economic diversification, investment in the productive sector and, in general, a total

[2] "El FMI prevé hiperinflación del 10.000.000% en Venezuela y una caída del 25% del PIB". https://www.lavanguardia.com/economia/20190409/461567333424/fmi-venezuela-inflacion-pib-nicolas-maduro-juan-guaido.html

[3] "El FMI prevé hiperinflación del 10.000.000% en Venezuela y una caída del 25% del PIB". https://www.lavanguardia.com/economia/20190409/461567333424/fmi-venezuela-inflacion-pib-nicolas-maduro-juan-guaido.html

absence of long-term planning, problems identified, but not addressed, long ago (Karl 1997). This failure also explains why countries like Ecuador, Trinidad and Tobago or Saudi Arabia have not entered into a crisis similar to the Venezuelan one despite the collapse in oil prices.

Another manifestation of the crisis is indebtedness of the country. Hausmann affirms that "Venezuela is currently the most indebted country in the world. There is no other nation with an external public debt as high as a proportion of its GDP or its exports, or that faces a higher debt service as a proportion of its exports" (Hausmann 2017). According to CEIC's data, Venezuela's External Debt reached USD 110.2 billion in March 2019 (CEIC 2020).

The Venezuelan government's political strategy has been to pay its debt commitments at almost any cost, even if that implies new loans or issuing new bonds. Two examples serve to illustrate this point: the first was the purchase by Goldman Sachs in May 2017 of bonds for an amount of 2800 million dollars that expire in 2022 with a discount of 69%, which implies that the U.S. Company disbursed only 865 million dollars. The second was a loan of 2 billion dollars made by the Russian company Rosneft with the commitment of a collateral of 49.9% of the stock of the company in Citgo as loan guarantee in benefit of the Russian. Citgo is a Venezuelan firm based in the United States.[4] Despite these efforts, the default arrived in 2018. According to the Venezuelan consulting firm Aristimuño Herrera & Asociados, the Venezuelan debt in default in 2019 amounted USD 17.048 million (elimpulso.com 2019).

The Social Crisis

A study by three of the most prestigious Venezuelan universities (Universidad Central de Venezuela, Universidad de Carabobo and Universidad Simón Bolívar) reports that in 2017, around 25.8% of the Venezuelan households lived in poverty, while 61.2% were in extreme poverty. The report also showed that 8.130 millions of Venezuelans had two or less meals per day in 2017. The result of this is that people have lost weight, around 11 kilos in the first two decades of the twenty-first century (UCAB et al. 2017).

The shortage in foodstuff and medicaments is explained by the Venezuelan dependence on imports and the attack to the private sector during the Chávez era. Between 1999 and 2012, imports went from 16.7 billion dollars to 59.3 billion dollars (Hernández 2015). However, as a result of the fall in income of the Venezuelan government and its strategy of paying the debt at any cost, there has been a severe reduction in imports. According to Hausmann (2017), "imports of goods and services per capita fell by 75% in real terms (adjusted for inflation) between 2012 and

[4] https://www.reuters.com/article/venezuela-pdvsa-idUSL1N1EI1FO

2016, with an even greater decline in 2017". To this is added the reduction of agri-food national production due to the existence of an adverse economic and institutional context.

These crises have led to massive migration of Venezuelans to other Latin American countries, the United States and Spain. It is estimated that around four million Venezuelans have decided to leave their country. Colombia has received around 2.5 million Venezuelan in the last 2 years. Peru, Ecuador, Brazil, Argentina and Chile have also been affected by the massive arrival of Venezuelan to their territories, as have Spain and the United States, particularly the state of Florida.

The implication of such a chaotic wave of migration in the recipient countries is significant, in particular in terms of incorporation of such population in the labor market as well as in the provision of social services like education and health. The risk of xenophobic behavior in the recipient countries is high. Thus, this wave of migration is the first regional effect of the Venezuelan economic and political crisis (Goldberg 2019). All these scenarios have led to describe the situation as a humanitarian crisis.

The Political Crisis

Hand in hand with an economic crisis goes a political crisis. Venezuela has been marked in recent years by violent oppression of opposition protests, the imprisonment of political opponents of President Maduro and the gradual, but now almost complete, destruction of the democratic political system and any semblance of checks and balances within the state, with the judiciary dominated by appointees loyal to Maduro and the National Assembly dominated by the opposition, sidelined through the creation of a so-called "constituent assembly" entirely in the hands of Maduro's Venezuelan Socialist Party (McCoy 2017). Independent media have essentially been destroyed, often through somewhat innovative methods of, for instance, giving preferential access to paper to government-friendly outlets, while forcing critical newspapers to cease production, paper being essentially unavailable on the open market (Nagel 2014).

The most recent chapter of this political crisis began in a public appearance in front of thousands of Venezuelans in Caracas Juan Guaidó, proclaimed himself as Venezuela's interim president, based on articles 233 and 333 of the Venezuelan Constitution, because on January 5, the National Assembly declared that Nicolás Maduro had usurped the presidency (see Briceño-Ruiz, 2019).

After winning the May 2018 Presidential elections—considered illegal by both national and international observers (Rendon 2018)—Maduro was sworn in in front of the Supreme Court (TSJ) on 10 January. For Guaidó, by being sworn in by the Venezuelan Supreme Court of Justice to validate an election that had been considered null and void, Maduro had usurped the office of the presidency, in violation of article 333 of the Venezuelan Constitution.[5] In this case, according to article 232 of the Venezuelan Constitution, elections must be called before the lapse of 30 consecutive days, and in the meantime, the presidency of the republic is held by the president of the National Assembly (Herrero and Casey 2019).

Since then, the crisis in Venezuela has not stopped. A failed attempt to send humanitarian aid to the country took place on 23 February 2019. At the end of April, some military, among them the Director of Bolivarian Service of Intelligence (SEBIN in Spanish), decided to recognize Guaidó as President, and the main opposition leader, Leopoldo Lopez, was released after 4 years in jail. After hours of silence, Maduro appeared on TV denouncing a coup d'État organized by the United States. However, it was known later that the action was a plot in which participated the Minister of Defense Vladimir Padrino López, the Chief of the Supreme Court Maikel Moreno and the Director of Counter-Intelligence José Hernández Dala. For reasons unknown to the public, the key actors decided to abandon the plot and declared the support to Maduro (Bronner and Rosati 2019). Despite the failure of this action, Guaidó remained as interim President for more than 50 countries, but in January 2020, a political maneuver of some dissidents from the opposition appointed Luis Parra as new President of the national Assembly. Other governments did not recognize this election due to the lack of transparency.

The crisis remains, and the external variables play an even more crucial role. The Trump administration has upped its rhetoric, declaring that "all options are on table", potentially increasing the risk of a military intervention (Parvaz 2019). However, the United States is not the only external actor in play. Cuba is accused of controlling the intelligence services and to monitor any attempt to act against Maduro in the Army. It is argued that around 20,000 Cubans are in Venezuela, including troops and intelligence services. Russia has given military assistance by sending a limited number of troops. There are also allegations that the Colombian guerrillas FARC and ELN and the Hezbollah are present in Venezuela. This has caused reactions in most of Latin American countries, particular the Venezuelan neighbors that foreseen as a menace the presence in Venezuela of all those actors (Specia 2019).

The Response of the International Community

There has been considerable concern on the part of the broadly defined international community with the deteriorating situation in the country. At a humanitarian level, several agencies, including from the United Nations, have expressed alarm at the deteriorating social indicators and public health crisis (UNHCR 2018). Regional

---

[5] This articles state that: "it should not lose its validity if it were to be put aside due to an act of force or were to be repealed by any other means than what it provides for. In such a case, any citizen granted or not with authority, shall have the duty to help to reestablish its effective validity" (Constitución de la República Bolivariana de Venezuela 2000, article 333).

organizations, such as UNASUR or OAS, have raised the alarm and, in the case of UNASUR, offered to act as mediators to resolve the political crisis in the country (Sabatini 2017). During the 2015 parliamentary elections, there was a significant presence of international electoral observers, as the one of authors witnessed first-hand.[6] There have been bilateral tensions, especially between Colombia and Venezuela, in relation to refugees and alleged criminal activities on and across the border between the two countries, tensions which go back many years (Haddad and Lehmann 2017). New regional initiatives such as the Lima Group, created in 2017, and the Contact Group, established in 2019, have unsuccessfully tried to resolve the crisis. The issue has been even discussed in the UN Security Council. Most recently, Norway has been a mediator to facilitate talks between government and opposition (Dobson 2019).

Therefore, it is not the case that the crisis in Venezuela has gone unnoticed. It has received considerable political attention internationally. Equally, it has been analyzed exhaustively from a large number of different angels. For instance, there have been detailed analyses of the causes of the economic crisis from both a political economy angle as well as a historical perspective (Carroll 2013, as one example). As we shall see later, these different frameworks make a significant difference to the analysis. Current period in Venezuelan history, starting with the election of Hugo Chavez as President in 1998, has been analyzed in detail by both academic and journalists, investigating, among other things, Chavez' politics, his personality, the background to "Chavismo's" rise to power and ability to maintain it, its policies and their consequences, etc. (*ibid.*, InSight Crime 2018a, b).

Similarly, it is true that, within these analyses, one can find no shortage of suggestions on how to overcome the current problems, or at least shift the current situation to a state which may, in time, allow the country to come out of its current predicament. Most prominent in these analyses have been those in the economic field which have looked at the question of how the country can overcome its current economic crisis as well as its structural economic problems. These range from hyperinflation to an extreme over-reliance on oil as the country's export item to a lack of productive capacity to make the country self-sustainable to the collapse of its social infrastructure. Within the political sphere, there have been several attempts to break the deadlock between government and opposition, ranging from mediation attempts led by UNSUR and, at some points, the Catholic church to the imposition of sanctions on members of the Venezuelan political and economic elites to the suspension of Venezuela from MERCOSUR to the threat, uttered by U.S. President Trump, of military intervention (Sabatini 2017; New York Times 2016; Jacobs 2017).

Yet, what is striking is the utter failure of any and all of these initiatives to even minimally move the situation forward. In fact, Maduro's position, and those of the "Chavista" regime he leads, seems to be stronger today than they have been for several years, at least in the short term, *despite* the multiple crises he is confronting

---

[6] One of authors (Kai Lehmann) personally spoke with several observers during a visit to Caracas during the 2015 elections.

(Latouche 2018a, b). This suggests that one of the key problems faced by the international community at large is the fact that it has not managed, in any way, to change the conditions which both led to, and sustain, the economic, political and social crises which are ravaging Venezuela. The question, then, becomes what needs to be done to be able to have any influence on Venezuela and how this can be done. It is this which we will turn to now.

The Reasons for Failure—And (Limited) Options for Action

The key problem the international community has in responding to the crisis in Venezuela is one of extreme incoherence. Both the international community but, crucially, domestic actors in Venezuela almost comically, hopelessly, disagree on just about every aspect of the crises described above: What is the crisis? Who is responsible for it? What are the objectives when addressing the crisis? What are the actual options for action on the part of the international community and what are the chances of success for any given mediation?

One point where one might find some agreement on the need for immediate, and relatively uncontroversial, action is the humanitarian aspect linked to the incredible flow of refugees out of Venezuela, the country being estimated to have lost approximately four million people in the last few years.[7] While this helps Maduro to keep control domestically, the refugee movement is actually a potential source of action and change in the longer term. Firstly, Venezuela is running out of people. This is only sustainable for so long, though we do not know when a tipping point of the sort described above will come. At some point, however, Maduro will have to address the flight of human capital (Bahar 2018).

Secondly, the problems the refugee movement are creating region-wide are at least *beginning* to bring about a regional response, albeit tentatively, hampered, as explored elsewhere in this volume by Lins & Hoffmann and Hoffmann & Briceño-Ruiz, by the effective collapse of the formal structures of existing South American regional organizations (Goldberg 2019). Nevertheless, regional action may create more pressure on Maduro to change course or, at least, cause friction within and between his allies between the more pragmatic and the more hardline members of his inner circle. This new dynamic could then be exploited to pressure for change.

Thirdly, the refugee movement includes some of those economic and political leaders from Venezuela that may, one day, have the capacity to rebuild the country (see Winter 2018). The presence of literally millions of Venezuelans spread through the region, while creating severe tensions, may also create a groundswell of opinion that "something must be done" to address this situation (Marques 2018; Valencia and Taj 2018). This may not happen, but it could, and will, depend to a significant

[7] See https://www.aljazeera.com/news/2019/06/venezuela-exodus-surpasses-4-million-190607140601790.html

extent on the capacity of the Venezuelan diaspora to organize itself and create, in effect, a plan for "the day after Maduro". Finally, in relation to this point, the urgent humanitarian need evident in the refugee movement opens space for broad political agreement on the need to respond vigorously to this need (if only to relieve pressure in the receiving countries).

This, in turn, could transform the political atmosphere in the region toward a reanimation of regional cooperation in this as well as other matters. In other words, the dynamics of the political situation in Latin America will be influenced one way or another which, in and of itself, will influence the calculations by political actors inside Venezuela. In relation to this, such focus on humanitarian needs—a need which is overwhelming—also allows for the opening up of space for the involvement of civil society. There is no doubt that dealing with the humanitarian consequences of the current crisis requires the involvement of organizations that work "on the ground" and can more easily reach those in most need. This, also, will give these organizations a stake in the future development of the country and might open up space for the involvement of such groups in any discussions about the future of Venezuela.

A second issue which can and should be taken up by the international community is planning for a worsening of the situation. A solid political institutional structure at regional level is vital since the consequences of a total collapse of Venezuela will be felt in the whole region. Therefore, one very useful service the international community could provide right now is to gently probe and assist South American countries to re-activate regional cooperation efforts. In this sense, however, the attempt to replace UNASUR with PROSUR without the existence of regional consensus will be a counterproductive policy. Seeing that there are profound disagreements between member states about whether and how to move forward with the organization, it is vital that the international community give support—logistical, political, etc.—to the informal cooperation efforts being made now. This means engaging, for instance, with Ecuador, Colombia and Brazil, who have taken a leading role in addressing the refugee crisis engulfing their countries. What help would they need to start and maintain political and humanitarian process which can contribute to at least addressing some of the most immediate causes and consequences of the crisis?

However, the involvement of the international community must not be limited to the humanitarian issue. The international community should continue to find a political solution to crisis. On the one hand, it is crucial to put aside radical views demanding military intervention. On the other hand, it is need to promote the re-establishment of the democratic institutions severely weakened in the last few years. In particular, the demands for free elections and balance among the public powers are goals that international community must propose. It is true that ideological divisions in Latin America and the growing interventionism of foreign power make this goal not easy to achieve, but giving up is not an option.

In many ways, none of these suggestions are particularly satisfactory nor are there any guarantees that they will lead to the desired outcome. The most likely scenario appears to be the continuation of the current status quo, always with the fear that there will arrive a tipping point at which the system will change quickly and radically, if not necessarily, desirably.

Conclusions

In this chapter, we have argued that the crisis in Venezuela is multifaceted and the *consequence* of the interplay of a host of interdependent factors and conditions: economic, social and economic. Considering this complex interdependence, the crisis defies simple solutions. With this in mind, the options of the international community to influence developments in Venezuela are very limited. The best one can hope for is to try and change some of the conditions over which said community can have some influence. In practice, this means focusing not on the government of Maduro or the internal situation in the country but on the external consequences that have manifested themselves all across South America.

Assisting the region in dealing with the enormous flow of refugees, preparing for the possible consequences of the total collapse of Venezuela and the sketching out of some possible future scenarios for the rebuilding of this ravaged country are, at the current time, the options from a very limited menu of choices with the aim of re-establishing some kind of coherence to the country in the future. Obviously, this does not mean stopping the pressure for the re-democratization and re-institutionalization in Venezuela. However unsatisfactory this might seem bearing in mind the scale of the catastrophe unfolding in the country, it is the best that can be done now.

References

Bahar, D. (2018). Latin America is facing a refugee crisis: Why it matters that we call fleeing Venezuelans refugees, not migrants. *Foreign Affairs Snapshot*, 23rd October 2018. https://www.foreignaffairs.com/articles/venezuela/2018-10-23/latin-america-facing-refugee-crisis. Accessed 14 Jan 2019.

Briceño-Ruiz, J. (2019). The crisis in Venezuela: A new chapter, or the final chapter? *Latin American Policy, 10*(1), 180–189.

Bronner, E. & Rosati, A. (2019). Venezuela's failed uprising: How a deal to oust maduro unraveled. *Bloomberg News*, 3rd May 2019, accessible via https://www.msn.com/en-us/news/world/venezuelas-failed-uprising-how-a-deal-to-oust-maduro-unraveled/ar-AAAOS9C. Accessed 10 May 2019.

Burges, S. (2018). UNASUR's dangerous decline: The risks of a growing left-right split in South America. *Americas Quarterly*, 3rd May 2018. https://www.americasquarterly.org/content/unasurs-dangerous-decline-risks-growing-left-right-split-south-america. Accessed 22 June 2019.

Calvacanti, L. (2019). Com o fim da Unasul, países latino-americanos preparam o Prosur', *Correio Braziliense*, 22 March 2019. https://www.correiobraziliense.com.br/app/noticia/politica/2019/03/22/interna_politica,744711/com-o-fim-da-unasul-paises-latino-americanos-preparam-o-prosur.shtml. Accessed 22 June 2019.

Carroll, R. (2013). *Comandante-Hugo Chavez's Venezuela*. London: Penguin Books.

CEIC. (2020). Venezuela external debt. https://www.ceicdata.com/en/indicator/venezuela/external-debt. Accessed 27 Jan 2020.

Constitución de la República Bolivariana de Venezuela. (2000). available at https://www.oas.org/dil/esp/constitucion_venezuela.pdf, accessed: 28 October 2020.

Dobson, P. (2019). Venezuela. New round of 'face to face' talks to be held in Norway. *Venezuela Analysis*, 27th May 2019. https://venezuelanalysis.com/news/14510. Accessed 23 Jan 2020.

Elimpulso.com (2019, October 17). Deuda en default de Venezuela cerrará en US$ 17.048 millones el 2019 #17Oct. https://www.elimpulso.com/2019/10/17/deuda-en-default-de-venezuela-cerrara-en-us-17-048-millones-el-2019-17oct/. Accessed 27 Jan 2020.

European External Action Service. (2019).Venezuela: International Contact Group's political mission to Caracas, *Press Release*, 18th May 2019. Brussels: EEAS. https://eeas.europa.eu/headquarters/headquarters-homepage/62744/venezuela-international-contact-group%C2%B4s-political-mission-caracas_en. Accessed 1 June 2019.

Goldberg, M. L. (2019). Venezuela is a refugee crisis. *U.N. Dispatch*, 12 February 2019. https://www.undispatch.com/venezuela-is-a-refugee-crisis/. Accessed 2 June 2019.

Haddad, C. P., & Lehmann, K. (2017). The EU, Regional Conflicts and the Promotion of Regional Cooperation: A Successful Strategy for a Global Challenge?: Colombia's Case. In *The EU, Promoting Regional Integration, and Conflict Resolution* (pp. 155–173). Palgrave Macmillan, Cham.

Hausmann, R. (2017). Venezuela's economic decline is 'sharper than the US Great Depression'. https://www.weforum.org/agenda/2017/07/venezuela-s-economic-decline-is-sharper-than-the-us-great-depression. Accessed 17 Sept 2019.

Herrero, A. V. & Casey, N. (2019). How Juan Guaidó Rose from being virtually unknown to lead Venezuela's opposition. *The New York Times*, 22 January 2019. https://www.nytimes.com/2019/01/22/world/americas/juan-guaido-facts-history-bio.html. Accessed 3 June 2019.

Hernández, J. (2015) *Importaciones y escasez en Venezuela*. Revista Sic, 27 de marzo de 2015, accesible via: http://revistasic.gumilla.org/2015/importaciones-y-escasez-en-venezuela/, accessed 1 de September de 2020.

InSight Crime. (2018a). Venezuela: A Mafia State? https://www.insightcrime.org/wp-content/uploads/2018/05/Venezuela-a-Mafia-State-InSight-Crime-2018.pdf. Accessed 18 Oct 2018.

InSight Crime. (2018b). Venezuela's Maduro administration strengthens criminal ties. Gamechangers. https://www.insightcrime.org/news/analysis/gamechangers-2017-venezuela-maduro-administration-strengthens-criminal-ties/. Accessed 26 Nov 2018.

Jacobs, B. (2017). Trump threatens 'military option' in Venezuela as crisis escalates. *The Guardian*, 12 August 2017. https://www.theguardian.com/world/2017/aug/11/donald-trump-venezuela-crisis-military-intervention. Accessed 23 Nov 2017.

Karl, T. L. (1997). *The paradox of plenty – Oil booms and petrol states*. Berkeley: University of California Press.

Latouche, M. A. (2018a). Why an election won't topple Venezuela's Maduro. *The Conversation*, 24 January 2018. http://theconversation.com/why-an-election-wont-topple-venezuelas-maduro-89332. Accessed 23 Nov 2018.

Latouche, M. A. (2018b). Venezuela is now a dictatorship. *The Conversation*, 24th May 2018. http://theconversation.com/venezuela-is-now-a-dictatorship-96960. Accessed on 25 Nov 2018.

Marques, R. (2018). Venezuelanos são atacados em Roraima após assalto a comerciante. *O Globo*, 19 August 2018. https://oglobo.globo.com/brasil/venezuelanos-sao-atacados-em-roraima-apos-assalto-comerciante-22991479. Accessed 2 Sept 2018.

McCoy, J. L. (2017). Venezuela's controversial new constituent assembly, explained. *The Washington Post*, 1st August 2017. https://www.washingtonpost.com/news/monkey-cage/wp/2017/08/01/venezuelas-dubious-new-constituent-assembly-explained/?utm_term=.66d14407ee61. Accessed 23 Sept 2018.

Naím, M. (2016). "Chávez: lo bueno, lo malo y lo feo", en: Naím, Moisés, Repensando el mundo. 111 sorpresas del siglo 21, Caracas, La Hoja del Norte, pp. 228–232.

Nagel, J. C. (2014). Why Venezuela's newspapers can't afford the paper they're printed on. *Foreign Policy*, 6th February 2014. https://foreignpolicy.com/2014/02/06/why-venezuelas-newspapers-cant-afford-the-paper-theyre-printed-on/. Accessed 21 Sept 2018.

Parvaz, D. (2019). Trump considers military options in Venezuela that experts say will 'freak out' the hemisphere. *Think Progress*, 2nd May 2019. https://thinkprogress.org/trump-military-option-venezuela-destablize-region-6e51c49b1c87/. Accessed 22 Jan 2020.

Rendon, M. (2018). Venezuela's Presidency in Jeopardy. *Commentary*. London: Centre for International & Strategic Studies. https://www.csis.org/analysis/venezuelas-presidency-jeopardy. Accessed 23 Jan 2020.

Sabatini, C. (2017). Mediation in Venezuela is doomed to fail. *Foreign Affairs Snapshot*. https://www.foreignaffairs.com/articles/venezuela/2017-07-07/mediation-venezuela-doomed-fail. Accessed 14 Jan 2019.

Specia, M. (2019). What is happening in Venezuela and why it matters. *New York Times*, 30 April 2019. https://www.nytimes.com/2019/04/30/world/americas/venezuela-crisis.html. Accessed 15 May 2019.

The New York Times. (2016). Venezuela's downward spiral. 17 May 2016.

UNHCR. (2018, November 8). *Number of refugees and migrants from Venezuela reaches 3 million*. Geneva: UNHCR. https://www.unhcr.org/news/press/2018/11/5be4192b4/number-refugees-migrants-venezuela-reaches-3-million.html. Accessed 14 Jan 2019.

Universidad Católica Andrés Bello (UCAB), la Universidad Central de Venezuela (UCV) y la Universidad Simón Bolívar (USB) (2017). Encuesta Nacional de Condiciones de Vida de la Población Venezolana (ENCOVI). https://encovi.ucab.edu.ve/que-es-la-encovi/. Accessed Jan 29 2020.

Verrastro, F. A., & Stanley, A. J. (2019). *The Oil Industry Won't Save Venezuela, Commentary*. Center of Center for Strategic and International Studies, Washington, March 28, available at: https://www.csis.org/analysis/oil-industry-wont-save-venezuela, accessed 1rst Novembre 2020.

Valencia, A. & Taj, M. (2018). Ecuador, Peru tighten entry requirements for Venezuelans as influx swells. *Reuters*. https://www.reuters.com/article/us-ecuador-venezuela/ecuador-peru-tighten-entry-requirements-for-venezuelans-as-influx-swells-idUSKBN1L12IM. Accessed 14 Jan 2019.

Winter, B. (2018). After Maduro-Meet the 10 people who will (one day) rebuild Venezuela. *Americas Quarterly*, *12*(2). https://www.americasquarterly.org/fulltextarticle/meet-10-people-who-will-one-day-rebuild-venezuela/

Part IV
Regional Impacts of the Crisis

14

European Right-Wing Populism: A Psychoanalytical Study

Paula Sandrin

Abstract This chapter aims to provide a psychoanalytically informed interpretation of the rise of right-wing populism in Europe. It argues that explanations for the growing support for right-wing populist political parties and groups in European countries which stress the role of economic, migratory, and political factors can be deepened by a reading which takes into account the role of affects in politics.

Introduction

The tide of right-wing populism in Europe has been steadily rising in the twenty-first century. In the last 2 years alone, we have witnessed election victories or significant increases in the share of votes by right-wing populist parties in several European countries. In the French presidential elections of May 2017, far-right presidential candidate Marine Le Pen, of the National Rally, got 34% of votes, the party's best electoral result ever. In September 2017, the far-right Alternative for Germany (AfD) won 12.6% of the vote and entered the Bundestag for the first time, with an anti-euro and anti-immigration platform. This election happened in a context already marked by anti-migrant demonstrations by far-right political movements, such as Pegida (Patriotic Europeans Against the Islamisation of the Occident). In October 2017, the Freedom Party of Austria (FPÖ), founded by a former SS officer in the 1950s, won 26% of the vote and joined the then governing coalition. Also in 2017, the far-right Volya Movement entered the Bulgarian parliament for the first time and, in the Netherlands, the anti-Islam Party for Freedom became the second-largest party in the House of Representatives. In March 2018, the anti-establishment Five Star Movement became Italy's largest party and formed a coalition government with the far-right League party. In April 2018, Prime Minister Victor Orbán, leader of the Hungarian right-wing populist Fidesz party, who has been in office since 2010, won his third consecutive term. In Poland, the right-wing

P. Sandrin (✉)
Pontifical Catholic University of Rio de Janeiro (PUC-Rio), Rio de Janeiro, Brazil

populist party Law and Justice (PiS) has been in power since 2015. In Sweden, the far-right Sweden Democrats have steadily increased their share of the vote since 2010, gaining 17.6% in the 2018 elections, and becoming the third largest party in the country's parliament.

Several explanations have been put forward to account for this trend. First, the economic impacts of globalization and neoliberal policies, advanced by national governments and the European Union (EU), have generated a mass of discontented "left-behind", which becomes easy target of right-wing populists. This economic malaise is compounded by the rise in immigration, which creates anxieties about the potential (further) loss of jobs and pressures on the welfare state; about threats to national security (when migrants are perceived as likely terrorists and criminals); and about the loss of national identity. This situation is made even worse by the state's inability to manage the economy and control national borders, due to the loss of sovereignty entailed in EU integration process and as a result of neoliberal globalization. Traditional political parties are perceived as unable or unwilling to change this state of affairs, leading to frustration and opening the way for populist parties.

This chapter aims to provide a psychoanalytically informed interpretation of the rise of right-wing populism in Europe. It argues that explanations for the growing support for right-wing populist political parties and groups in European countries which stress the role of economic, migratory, and political factors can be deepened by a reading which takes into account the role of affects in politics. This chapter will, first, review the three main accounts—economic, migratory, and political—of the surge in support for right-wing populist political parties and groups in Europe, discussing their shortcomings. It will, then, put forward the argument that it is necessary to take into account the role of affects in identification processes, including identification with right-wing populist ideologies, in particular a sense of loss (of national sovereignty, security, identity, and economic prosperity) which leads to resentment.

It's the Economy,[1] Stupid: The Role of Economic Factors in the Rise of Support for Right-Wing Populism

This type of explanation has been advanced to account for several unexpected phenomena, such as the election of Donald Trump in the US, the decision of the UK to exit the EU, and the rise in support for right-wing populist parties and groups across Europe. The current global trade and financial order, marked by neoliberal globalization, has led to the Global Financial Crisis of 2008 and the Eurozone crisis and has significantly impacted on the economic well-being of many societies.

---

[1]The famous phrase "It's the economy, stupid" was created by Bill Clinton's 1992 presidential campaign strategist James Carville.

Globalization has contributed to unemployment due to the reallocation of industries from developed countries to places with cheaper labor costs. Neoliberal ideology of consumerism and competition and neoliberal economic policies of austerity, privatization, corporate trade, and financial deregulation, coupled with the weakening of labor unions, have led to the concentration of capital, rise in housing costs, cuts to welfare provisions, stagnation of wages, precarious jobs, and unemployment, all contributing to a growth in inequality, disempowerment, disenfranchisement, and dissatisfaction (Monbiot 2016). Such dissatisfaction is, then, mobilized by right-wing populist parties.

For example, in Germany, economic disparities between East and West have been invoked as a likely explanation for Euroscepticism, right-wing extremism, and anti-migrant sentiments, which are manifested more strongly in the country's poorer former East. In the UK, the BREXIT vote has been attributed to the poor economic conditions of some of country's regions. Left-wing commentators argued that many of those who voted Leave were "the 'left-behind' – often citizens of post-industrial towns across the Midlands and the North" (Russell 2016). They were "ordinary working class folks [...] simply fed up with the erosion of their living standards, the disintegration of their communities, and the lack of responsiveness of their political representatives and the unaccountable technocracy that has 'taken control' over their lives" (Roos 2016). The vote to leave the EU, thus, cannot be attributed to "stupidity, racism or lack of information" but to "a combination of hopelessness and isolation coupled with a collapse in material living conditions" (Russell 2016). Hence, Brexit was "first and foremost a political statement by the dispossessed and disempowered" (Roos 2016). Even though "feelings of powerlessness, discontent and alienation [..] had very little to do with Brussels", the EU referendum allowed those dissatisfactions to be voiced (Russell 2016).

Although Russell (2016) thinks that discontent in the context of BREXIT had little to do with the EU, neoliberalism as an economic theory and a set of policies have also influenced European Union economic thinking, even though Union representatives have presented the EU's social market economy as a resistance force against Anglo-American neoliberalism. German ordo-liberalism of Walter Eucken and Wilhelm Röpke has increasingly influenced EU's economic and monetary policies, gaining ground against alternative economic traditions from the 1980s onward, when neoliberal ideology began to spread across the globe (Dardot and Laval 2013). As recognized by Frits Bolkestein, former European Commissioner for Internal Market and Services, "the Economic and Monetary union [...] is one of the most important policy instruments for stabilising the vast free-market economy that Europe constitutes and, as such, is a typical product of ordo-liberal thinking" (in Dardot and Laval 2013: 217).

Naomi Klein explained Trump's election, Brexit, and rise of right-wing populism in Europe as reactions to the effects of "neoliberal policies of deregulation, privatisation, austerity and corporate trade", which have led to a decline in living standards, lost jobs, lost pensions, lost safety nets, and a "precarious present". "For the people who saw security and status as their birthright – and that means white men most of all – these losses are unbearable. Donald Trump speaks directly to that pain. The Brexit campaign spoke to that pain. So do all of the rising far-right parties in Europe" (Klein 2016). Thus, neoliberal globalization, marked by "constant threats of relocation, redundancies, and, ultimately, loss of employment", heightens "the fear of losing the conditions necessary for the reproduction of material life" (Lordon 2014: 35 and 36). This fear is then invoked and captured by right-wing populist parties which promise to placate it by transforming it into hatred, and directing it toward several targets: the EU, migrants and refugees, and against traditional national political parties. These targets of hatred and resentment are not mutually exclusive.

Thus, economic bureaucracies, "whether Washington, the North American free trade agreement, the World Trade Organisation or the EU", have been in the line of fire of right-wing populist politicians. The EU has been lambasted for being a bureaucratic elitist institution, distant from the concerns of "the people", robbing sovereignty, contributing to economic malaise, and being a catalyst for migration—either because of the freedom of movement or because of refugee quotas. Marine Le Pen's 2017 party program blamed globalization, neoliberalism, the EU, and immigration for undermining the country's national sovereignty, security, identity, and economy. Matteo Salvini, former Italian interior minister and leader of the far-right League party, claimed that the 2019 European parliamentary elections would be "a referendum between the Europe of the elites, banks, finance, mass migration and precariousness versus the Europe of peoples, work, tranquility, family and future" (Salvini in Heath et al. 2018).

This explanation, which stresses the economic impacts of neoliberal globalization, however, fails to explain why the "left-behind" are not the only ones supporting right-wing populist parties. In the UK, 39% of the top quarter of UK earners voted Leave (Curtice 2016). The Brexit campaign was led by wealthy politicians, and several rich counties also voted Leave (Milburn 2016), possibly moved by "imperial and colonial nostalgia" and fantasies about making Britain great again by setting up trade relationships with the Commonwealth, "our extended family in the world", "our Kith & Kin", according to Nigel Farage, former UKIP leader (Ashe 2016). In the US, 48% of the top third of US earners voted for Trump, whereas the majority of those in the bottom fifth of US earners (53%) voted for the Democratic candidate Hillary Clinton (Curtice 2016). In fact, we can identify a coalition between "winners" and "losers" of neoliberal globalization, united on an anti-immigration platform and sharing a sense of loss of national identity, security, and sovereignty. Therefore, the economics-based explanation must be complemented by other approaches.

They Steal Our Jobs, Rape Our Women, and Refuse to Integrate: The Role of Migration in the Rise of Support for Right-Wing Populism

When discussing the effects of globalization on individual and collective identities, Stuart Hall (2014) diagnosed three outcomes. First, cultural flows among nations and global consumerism can lead to cultural homogenization, creating global forms of identification and erasing national identities. Second, migratory flows can lead to the production of new hybrid identities, espoused by diasporic communities, who share and belong to different cultures and histories at the same time, widening the possibilities of identity. Third, migratory flows can also lead to the strengthening of identities. Dominant ethnic groups, feeling threatened by the presence of "others" in "their" territory, react defensively. Minority groups, in response to experiences of racism and exclusion, also strengthen their identities. In this last case, instead of creating homogenous or hybrid identities, globalization can lead to a polarization among groups who appeal to the "essence" of identities under threat by the presence of a different other.

The strengthening of national identities has clearly been the response given by right-wing populist parties in Europe to increasing migration flows resulting from globalization, the Syrian Civil War, and/or economic deprivation, political instability, and violence in the wider neighborhood. These parties tend to frame foreigners as threats to national security (for being violent sexual abusers, dangerous criminals, terrorists); to national welfare (for stealing jobs, putting pressure on the welfare state, being benefit scoundrels); and to national identity (for not integrating). The impacts of migration on the economy and national security are sources of controversy. The links between immigration and decline in economic well-being and between immigration and national (in)security are far from certain (see OECD 2014; Ousey and Kubrin 2018). These shaky grounds on which articulations about the threat posed by foreigners rest do not prevent right-wing political parties from inciting, invoking, and mobilizing such fears in their political discourses.

This leaves us with the relationship between immigration and (loss of) national identity. Why is the presence of difference considered so threatening to the nation? These are key issues which will be developed further in the following sections. At this moment, it is sufficient to say that the presence of difference can feel so threatening because modern nations are all cultural hybrids (Hall 2014). As imagined political communities (Anderson 2006) and products of specific historical contexts, nations must be politically and socially reproduced and performed through foreign and domestic policies "in which resistant elements to a secure identity on the 'inside' are linked through a discourse of 'danger' with threats identified and located on the 'outside'" (Campbell 1998: 75). In addition, narratives about national unity and national homogeneity are only made possible by the forgetting of violent pasts and violent presents which suppress(ed) and exclude(d) (ethnic, racial, religious, linguistic) differences (Hall 2014).

The increasing visible presence of "others" due to globalization, the free movement of people, and the migration and refugee crisis expose the cracks, fractures, and inconsistencies of an already precarious project. This presence destabilizes certainties which were constructed and maintained through discursive practices always opened to contestations. As will be discussed below, destabilization of the nation as an object of identification elicits such strong emotional responses, which are successfully mobilized by right-wing populist parties, because the nation has had a central role in structuring subjectivities and socio-political realities. The nation provides meaning to our existence, connecting our lives to a national destiny which has preceded us and which will outlast us (Hall 2014) *and* functions as object of affective investment (Solomon 2015; Stavrakakis 2007).

They Do Not Represent Us: The Role of Traditional Political Parties in the Rise of Support for Right-Wing Populism

This situation of economic precarity and fears of foreigners' threats to national security, welfare, and identity is compounded by the feeling that traditional political parties are unable or unwilling to address such anxieties and fears. Mainstream parties of both right and left of the political spectrum would be unable to provide meaningful solutions because state sovereignty has been eroded by neoliberal form of globalization and EU integration process. The state can no longer control the flow of capital, goods, services, and people; it can no longer control its borders. In addition, established parties would be unwilling to change this anxiety-inducing state of affairs because they have embraced neoliberalism not only as set of economic policies, but as a rationality, which concludes that globalization is irreversible and that there is no alternative. The differences between right and left have become minimal. These "post-democratic" political parties identify "democratic form with the 'necessities' of globalized capital" (Stavrakakis 2007: 264): "The absolute identification of politics with the management of capital is no longer the shameful secret hidden behind the 'forms' of democracy; it is the openly declared truth by which our governments acquire legitimacy" (Rancière in Stavrakakis 2007: 264).

According to Mouffe (2005), political mobilization requires the clear establishment of opposing poles with which people can identify. In order to act politically, we need to identify with a collective identity which provides meaning to our existence and functions and an anchor of affective investments. Therefore, politics needs to have a partisan character, clearly discerning between two poles of identification which offer real alternatives. It is in this context marked by a lack of political alternatives, by a "centrist consensus" (Mouffe 2017), that right-wing populist parties are able to capture the political imaginations and mobilize the affects of the population by offering a clear alternative; discernible poles of collective identity; an "us v. them" no longer based on the opposition between right and left, but based on "the people" and detached and distant elites who no longer represent us, and between "the people" and immigrants (Mouffe 2005: 70). A political context marked by the hegemony of neoliberal globalization, immigration, and the sameness of traditional right and left-wing political parties constitutes fertile ground for fringe political parties who present themselves as the only real alternative to mobilize those fears of loss of economic prosperity, (national) sovereignty, identity, and security.

But why is the message of right-wing populists so appealing to some? What are they appealing to and why do their narratives of national loss resonate among certain segments of the population? In order to answer these questions, we need to discuss the affective dimension of identification processes, including identification with certain conceptions of the nation advanced by right-wing populist groups.

The Nation as a Privileged Object of Identification: The Role of Affects in the Rise of Support for Right-Wing Populism

The nation, as a specific object of identification, emerged at the end of the eighteenth century as a result of several historical processes, such as the emergence of print capitalism and the Enlightenment (Anderson 2006), the French and Industrial Revolution, the Revolutions of 1848, and the emergence of mass electorate and workers' movements (Hobsbawm 1983), which destabilized the previous political and social orders and their traditional sources of legitimacy. This vacuum was occupied by the nation, which became a new source of legitimacy to states.

Most historical, sociological, and post-structuralist accounts of the nation (Anderson 2006; Hobsbawm 1983; Campbell 1998) stress its lack of essence and foundations; its contingent character; its historical, political, and social constructedness; and reproduction through linguistic and non-linguistic practices (including narratives about national histories, heroes and memories; public ceremonies, holidays and monuments; national anthems and flags; domestic and foreign policies) which allow the nation to come into being as an entity with supposedly ancient roots which survive into the present and (hopefully) will survive into the future. These symbolic and material practices which attempt to produce historical continuity between the past, the present, and the future contribute to the framing of the nation as possessing essential or natural attributes which survive through time. Through boundary-making practices (including foreign and migration policies), which delimit who is in and who is out, who belongs and who does not belong, the nation is produced and reproduced.

In spite of this constructed and performed character, the nation as an object of identification persists and commands deep affective attachments. As will become clear, "the durability and salience, the depth and longevity, of national identifications" (Stavrakakis 2007: 192) cannot be attributed solely to the historical, political, and social conditions which allowed nations to emerge, nor to the array of linguistic and material practices which produce and reproduce it, but also to their affective appeal.

According to psychoanalyst Jacques Lacan, both the subject and the Symbolic order (the order of language and representation) are characterized by a lack (of essence) (Stavrakakis 1999). Meanings we attribute to ourselves and to our objects of identification (including the nation) are established by the relationship between signifiers. These signifiers form chains of signifier which also relate to other chains (Stavrakakis 1999: 57). This means that, in principle, an infinite number of meanings can be produced and that meaning (attributed to ourselves and to our objects of identification) is always unstable. However, meanings can be partially and temporarily fixated in nodal points (Laclau and Mouffe 2001: 112), which are privileged discursive terms which arrest the endless flow of signification by binding "together groups of words and concepts into meaningful statements and narratives" (Solomon 2015: 64).

The individual only becomes a subject when s/he enters the Symbolic order, which provides several resources with which the subject can identify. The subject hopes that those resources will fully represent him and provide him with a stable identity, but this is impossible, because these resources do not hold stable meanings. This frustration compels the subject to keep on identifying, in the hopes that full representation will finally be achieved. What the subject desires through these identification processes, however, is not only discursive coherence and closure, but to recapture what Lacan calls enjoyment, or "pre-symbolic *jouissance*", a "state of bliss, unity and fullness", which is posited as lost and sacrificed when the subject accedes to the Symbolic (Stavrakakis 1999: 48). Thus, objects of identification which circulate in the Symbolic order, including the nation, are invested with affects because they promise to recapture this lost enjoyment.

There are types of enjoyment, according to Lacan, two of which are relevant here: enjoyment as fantasy and enjoyment of the body (Stavrakakis 2007: 196). In fantasy, it is offered the possibility of recapturing lost enjoyment through identification with social-symbolic signifiers, such as the nation. All nationalist projects make reference to a mythical past in which things were better and which can be retrieved if we get rid of others who are framed as obstacles to this achievement. These others can vary according to historical, social, and political contexts, but they are crucial to maintain the appeal of the nation. They are crucial because the instability, inconsistency, and incoherence of discourses and the impossibility of attaining wholeness and completeness through identification with discourses are attributed to others, the thieves of our enjoyment, instead of being attributed to the lack in the subject and the lack in the Symbolic or, in other words, to the absence of essence, foundations, stability, consistence, and coherence of our individual and collective identities and of our social and political realities. Thus, fantasmatic frames or narratives mask the lack in the subject and the lack in the Symbolic by attributing the impossibility of enjoying a full identity to external (or internal) others who prevent us from doing so (be they the EU, Muslims, Jews, traditional political parties, migrants, or refugees).

In enjoyment as fantasy, Eros, the libidinal drive of love, and Death, the drive of destructiveness and aggressiveness, are two sides of the same coin (Stavrakakis 2007: 198). As Sigmund Freud explained in *Civilization and its Discontents*, in order to inhibit, weaken, and disarm the aggressive and destructive drives, which threaten to disintegrate society, civilization employs several mechanisms, including directing the derivatives of the death drive outward, toward other objects (as in sadism) or the external world in general, as a kind of non-erotic aggressivity and destructiveness (as in enmity among nations, hatred and hostility towards foreigners, or other groups of people) (Freud 1962: 61, 65–67 and 70). Thus, "it is always possible to bind together a considerable number of people in love, so long as there are other people left over to receive the manifestation of their aggressiveness" (Freud 1962: 61).

As we have seen, signifiers never fully deliver on their promise of discursive coherence and of an encounter with enjoyment. What they deliver is a partial enjoyment of the body, momentary experiences in which the subject seems to achieve the desired full identification and enjoyment, such as in wars and national football teams' victories (Stavrakakis 2007: 197). All national projects organize rituals—ceremonies, festivals—in which this momentary encounter with enjoyment is made possible. These rituals vary according to nations and historical moments, but they organize enjoyment as a knot between Eros and Death, or libido and aggression, in unique ways. There is, thus, a "very visceral dimension of identity. Nationalism works through people's hearts, nerves and gut. It is an expression of culture through the body" (Jusdanis in Stavrakakis 2007: 200).

Therefore, the appeal of the nation comes from the promise to provide stable signification and representation; enjoyment as a sense of wholeness and completeness; and the momentary delivery of full identity and enjoyment in certain circumstances. What is at stake in identification processes, thus, is discursive coherence and stability *and* affects. In times of crisis, when the stability and fixity of our social constructions unravel, when certainties shatter and the lack in the Symbolic becomes visible, new identities can be articulated, such as the hybrid types discussed by Hall above. However, these moments of rupture can also lead to the strengthening of the identity under threat and resentment of the others deemed responsible for the unwelcomed instability. "Even relatively stable identity formations when encountering a dislocatory event, when entering a state of crisis or a 'critical juncture', often lose the appearance of stability and fullness. Under such conditions they can only attempt to retain their hegemonic status by blaming someone else" (Stavrakakis 2007: 195).

We can read the Eurozone crisis and the migration and refugee crisis as dislocatory events which rendered visible the contingent character of socio-political realities taken for granted (such as that EU integration inexorably brings about economic prosperity, peace, and stability, for example). These are moments in which new political possibilities and new identities can be articulated, but also moments in which the old ones dig in their heels and offer fantasmatic narratives which promise to restore a previous state of affairs which was lost, or could be lost, as a result of these dislocatory events, by taking back control (from the EU, from traditional political parties) and protecting our economy and our borders (from migrants and refugees).

Considering that the nation as an object of identification has had a central role in structuring subjectivities and socio-political realities and has been invested with visceral affects, these right-wing populist discourses resonate with certain segments of society because they (1) place the nation under threat in privileged position, inciting and invoking, in a time of crises, fears of instability and uncertainty of subjectivities and socio-political realities; and (2) tap into, and promise to satisfy, deep-seated desires for stability and wholeness which have historically been articulated around the nation as a nodal point.

These discourses resonate more strongly with those segments of the population which are abler to identify with articulations of the nation as a homogenous and nativist entity: white men, or the "Endangered White Male", in the words of Michael Moore (2016). After all, one can only fear and feel for the loss of the nation if one identifies with it and invests its affects in it. Thus, the rise of right-wing populist parties, Brexit, and the election of Trump cannot be simply explained by the (economic) discontent of "ordinary working class folks", since support for right-wing populist parties, Brexit, and Trump is not restricted to these segments of society and since fears and resentments are articulated around (the possible loss of) the nation, located at the intersection between economic, political, and identity factors. "Working-class folks" who fear for the loss of the nation and support right-wing political parties and groups are mostly white and part of those resented for the demise of the nation are non-whites, who must be kept out for they do not belong to "the people", to the territory, and to "us" and, therefore, are not entitled to the same protection. These non-whites can also be losers of globalization, can also be left-behind, but their predicament do not elicit much sympathy from the segment of white left-behinds who identify with homogenous versions of the nation mobilized by right-wing political parties.

It is important to clarify what is understood by racism in this context. "Racism is a global hierarchy of superiority and inferiority along the line of the human that have been politically, culturally and economically produced and reproduced for centuries by the institutions of the capitalist/patriarchal Western-centric/Christian-centric modern/colonial world-system" (Grosfoguel 2016: 10). Those placed "above the line of the human" are considered entitled to rights (including citizenship, jobs, and access to the welfare state) while those placed below the line of the human are not. In this definition, the marker of racism does not need to be only skin color, but also ethnicity, language, culture, and/or religion (Grosfoguel 2016). Thus, although "the others" present in right-wing populist discourses are varied (including people placed above the line of the human, such as EU and traditional political parties' members) and are also dependent on historical, social, and political contexts, they include segments of the world population which historically have had their humanity questioned and, as such, barred from rights. That is why, contrary to what some left-wing commentators reviewed here argued, racism cannot be ruled out as a layer of explanation for support for right-wing populist parties. This is not to say that those whose desires are oriented toward the discourses of right-wing populists are intrinsically racist, because there are no intrinsic essences to the subject or Symbolic objects of identifications, as has been argued. However, through several historical processes, some bodies become saturated with affects. Fear, hatred, and resentment circulate and are distributed across several figures which come to embody the threat of loss (of conditions of material and symbolic reproduction) and which are aligned together through a "metonymic slide" (Ahmed 2014: 44) between signifiers: the migrant, the refugee, the terrorist, the rapist, the invader, the violator. This circulation of affects produces the boundaries between "us" and "them", and moves us away from those bodies which are bound together.

Thus, the explanation advanced here for the rise in support for right-wing populist parties and groups in Europe stresses the economic distress and precarity brought about by neoliberal globalization, which was worsened by neoliberal solutions to the Eurozone crisis; the historical appeal of the nation as an object of identification which has been promising stability and enjoyment and is now being framed as under threat by multiple crises by right-wing populist parties' discourses; *and* the increasingly visible presence of others who have been historically racialized and are, thus, ideal for scapegoating. This scapegoating helps sustain the appeal of right-wing populist parties' discourses because the lack in the subject and the lack in the Symbolic are masked by attributing inconsistencies and lack of enjoyment to historically racialized others.

Concluding Remarks

This chapter aimed to interpret the growing support for right-wing populist parties and groups in Europe taking into account not only "material" and "discursive" factors—economic precarity, the surge in the number of migrants and refugees, the sameness of traditional political parties, the structures of populist discourses—but also "affective" factors. It has argued that we cannot account for this growing support by only emphasizing the deleterious economic and political effects of neoliberal globalization and migration patterns, although these are certainly part of the interpretation, since these effects have generated affects (anxiety, fear, hatred, resentment) which are successfully mobilized by right-wing political parties. We must also take the strong attachments to the nation as an object of identification and the historical dehumanization of certain groups of people seriously if we are to understand why populist discourses resonate among some segments of the population and if we are to devise an effective and ethical counter strategy.

This effective and ethical counter strategy would have to involve political discourses which are appealing to large segments of the population *and* which are inclusionary and pluralist. In order to achieve that, we need to find ways to "expand the chain of significations associated with the people" (Stavrakakis 2017, p. 8), to "integrate heterogeneous identities and demands in a broader chain of equivalences" (Stavrakakis et al. 2017, p. 8), and to articulate "an expanding plurality of social demands" (Stavrakakis et al. 2017, p. 8). In concrete terms, the concept of "the people" would need to be widened to include traditional working classes, and precarious middle classes also affected by austerity, feminist, and anti-racist movements. Naturally, these do not constitute detailed roadmaps or strict guidelines on how to establish hegemony, since the "chain of equivalence through which the 'people' is going to be constituted will depend on the historical circumstances. Its dynamics cannot be determined in isolation from all contextual reference" (Mouffe 2018: 43).

There is one thing we can be sure, though: this effective and ethical counter strategy should not present the political arena as a battle between "the Reasonable, the Moderate and the Good" versus "the Unreasonable, the Radical, and the Evil", for it has been precisely this type of political discourse that has alienated many voters and opened the way for right-wing populist parties that claim to actually listen to the woes of the population. Instead, this progressive political discourse should attempt to articulate a response to these very real fears and anxieties which is attuned to different historical, geographical, and cultural contexts, inclusive, pluralist, and agonistic.

References

Ahmed, S. (2014). *The Cultural Politics of Emotion* (2nd ed.). Edinburgh: Edinburgh University Press.

Anderson, B. (2006). *Imagined communities: Reflections on the origin and spread of nationalism*. London: Verso.

Ashe, S. (2016). UK, Brexit and postcolonial melancholia. *Discover Society*, 01/06/2016. https://discoversociety.org/2016/06/01/ukip-brexit-and-postcolonial-melancholy/. Accessed 12 Sept 2018.

Campbell, D. (1998). *Writing security: United States foreign policy and the politics of identity* (Rev. ed.). Minneapolis: University of Minnesota Press.

Curtice, J. (2016). US election 2016: The Trump-Brexit voter revolt. *BBC News*, 11/11/2016. https://www.bbc.com/news/election-us-2016-37943072. Accessed 12 Sept 2018.

Dardot, P., & Laval, C. (2013). The ordo-liberal origins of the construction of Europe. In *The new way of the world: On neoliberal society*. London: Verso.

Freud, S. (1962). *Civilization and its discontents*. New York and London: W. W. Norton & Company.

Grosfoguel, R. (2016). What is racism? *Journal of World-Systems Research, 22*(1), 9–15.

Hall, S. (2014). *A identidade cultural na pós-modernidade* (12ª ed.). Rio de Janeiro: DP&A.

Heath, R., Baume, M., & Barigazzi, J. (2018). Macron and Salvini face off over Continent's future. *Politico*, 19 July 2018. https://www.politico.eu/article/emmanuel-macron-matteo-salvini-showdown-over-europe-future/. Accessed 10 Sept 2018.

Hobsbawm, E. (1983). Introduction: Inventing traditions. In E. Hobsbawn & T. Ranger (Eds.), *The invention of traditions*. Cambridge: Cambridge University Press.

Klein, N. (2016). It was the Democrats' embrace of neoliberalism that won it for Trump. The Guardian, 09 November 2016. https://www.theguardian.com/commentisfree/2016/nov/09/rise-of-the-davos-class-sealed-americas-fate. Accessed 12 Sept 2018.

Laclau, E., & Mouffe, C. (2001). *Hegemony and socialist strategy* (2nd ed.). London: Verso.

Lordon, F. (2014). *Willing slaves of capital - Spinoza and Marx on desire*. London: Verso.

Milburn, K. (2016). Divide and conquer? The politics of the generation gap. *Open Democracy* UK, 20 July 2016. https://www.opendemocracy.net/uk/keir-milburn/divide-and-conquer-politics-of-generation-gap. Accessed 12 Sept 2018.

Monbiot, G. (2016). Neoliberalism – The ideology at the root of all our problems. *The Guardian*, 15 April 2016. https://www.theguardian.com/books/2016/apr/15/neoliberalism-ideology-problem-george-monbiot. Accessed 12 Sept 2018.

Moore, M. (2016). 5 reasons why Trump will win. https://michaelmoore.com/trumpwillwin/. Accessed 12 Sept 2018.

Mouffe, C. (2005). *On the political.* Abingdon: Routledge.
Mouffe, C. (2017). We urgently need to promote a left-populism. *Verso Books*, 04 August 2017. https://www.versobooks.com/blogs/3341-chantal-mouffe-we-urgently-need-to-promote-a-left-populism. Accessed 17 Sept 2018.
Mouffe, C. (2018). *For a left populism.* London: Verso.
OECD. (2014). Is migration good for the economy?. *Migration Policy Debates*, May 2014. https://www.oecd.org/migration/OECD%20Migration%20Policy%20Debates%20Numero%202.pdf. Accessed 12 Sept 2018.
Ousey, G. C., & Kubrin, C. E. (2018). Immigration and crime: Assessing a contentious issue. *Annual Review of Criminology, 1*, 63–84.
Roos, J. (2016). Brexit confirms: The neoliberal center cannot hold. *Roar*, 29 June 2016. https://roarmag.org/essays/brexit-crisis-europe-britain-referendum/. Accessed 12 Sept 2018.
Russell, B. (2016). Brexit, self-harm, and a method for taking control. *Plan C*, 18 July 2016. http://www.weareplanc.org/blog/brexit-self-harm-and-a-method-for-taking-control/. Accessed 12 Sept 2018.
Solomon, T. (2015). *The politics of subjectivity in American foreign policy discourses.* Ann Arbor: University of Michigan Press.
Stavrakakis, Y. (1999). *Lacan and the political.* London and New York: Routledge.
Stavrakakis, Y. (2007). *The Lacanian left: Psychoanalysis, theory, politics.* Edinburgh: Edinburgh University Press.
Stavrakakis, Y. (2017). Discourse theory in populism research - Three challenges and a dilemma. *Journal of Language and Politics, 16*(4), 1–12.
Stavrakakis, Y., et al. (2017). Extreme right-wing populism in Europe: Revisiting a reified association. *Critical Discourse Studies*. https://doi.org/10.1080/17405904.2017.1309325.

15

Economic Crises and the Development of Right-Wing Populist Parties

Eleonora Poli

Abstract Europeans have experienced a variety of challenges in recent years. The rise of sovereignism is one of them. Against this backdrop, this chapter analyses the link between the economic crises and the development of right-wing populist parties. It assesses that while the European economic governance, through a set of mechanisms and institutions, acquired a renovated economic and financial equilibrium, it failed to deal with other salient imbalances concerning wage and fiscal policies across European Union (EU) member countries allowing sovereign parties to gain more legitimacy.

Introduction

Europeans have experienced a variety of economic challenges in recent years. The multifaceted economic crisis that started in the aftermath of the 2008 Credit Crunch had important economic but also political consequences all over the Eurozone and in the European Union (EU) in general. Not only a crisis of competitiveness and productivity was followed by a banking crisis and, in member countries with high public debt, a sovereign debt crisis, but such downturns highlighted a problem of institutional imbalances at the very heart of the EU, caused by the incompleteness of the economic and monetary union (Christakis 2017, 1–43). To face such an unprecedented economic downfall and overcome the limitation of the institutional setting, the EU achieved more integration by reshaping and reinforcing its system of economic governance. The aim was that of building a better economic and monetary architecture than the one emerged during the 1990s. Yet, as this paper argues, more integration was probably not enough to appease social dissent, feeding the ranks of right-wing populist parties, here defined as the "sovereignists".

The development of the European Stability Mechanism (ESM) to financially assist Eurozone Member States in trouble or the Banking Union, the Fiscal Compact and the European Semester were all measures meant to increase control over

E. Poli (✉)
Istituto Affari Internazionali (IAI), Rome, Italy
e-mail: E.POLI@iai.it

national budgetary, financial and economic policies in order to overcome structural imbalances. Yet, while the European economic governance, through such mechanisms and institutions, acquired a renovated economic and financial equilibrium, it failed to deal with other salient imbalances concerning wage and fiscal policies across EU member countries. In other words, as the paper will highlight, while the EU was busy in guaranteeing the future of the euro and the European economic system, it failed in securing citizens about their economic welfare, economic perspectives and future wellbeing. Moreover, since the economic crises did not hit all countries equally or uniformly, with some European countries experiencing good economic performances over the years and other that did not, austerity policies together with the absence of harmonised economic rules created even more disparities across member states. At the same time, "more integration" lacked democratic accountability as it resulted in more power exerted top-down by the Commission and the European Council, often bypassing national and European Parliaments.

This chapter argues that economic shortage and lack of democratic accountability are keys in explaining the relative success of right-wing populist parties. Many of which are now part of the Identity and Democracy Group (ID) within the European Parliament, as it will be discussed in more details below. Indeed, while populism is not a novelty in the EU, the increasing support towards the sovereignist parties experienced in the years after the crises has been unprecedented, and it has recently resulted in the creation of the above-mentioned new Eurosceptic group within the European Parliament (75 seats). Certainly, the ID group does not have a majority in the EU Parliament and, so far, its impact on the EU policymaking has been marginalised by the majority, formed by traditional political forces. Yet, the re-emergence of populist extreme right-wing sentiments in Europe cannot be undervalued.

Several experts have linked the upsurge of such forces to various factors such as globalisation, a mix of anger against political elites, fake news, migration and rapid social changes as well as a diffused perception that Brussels is an inefficient bubble, intrusive and out of touch with ordinary citizens. Yet, leaving aside cultural and security reasons, with three European citizens out of five worried about their economic future and two out of four believing their voice does not count in the EU, this paper argues that the European governance and the way economic resources have been distributed among citizens and countries might well play a role when it comes to voters' support to those parties (European Commission 2018).

The chapter is structured as follows. The first part will analyse the characteristics of the sovereignist parties in the EU and what differentiate them from traditional nationalist or right-wing movements. The section will introduce an analysis of whether, why and how the European Economic governance might have fuelled their electoral support. Against this backdrop, the second part will instead provide an overview of the economic governance reforms applied by the EU in the aftermath of the crisis. Specifically, it will try to highlight how greater integration has also resulted in more discontent across those citizens who felt the EU was already not answering to their needs. Finally, the paper will explain the link between the success of ID parties and the reforms of European economic governance, arguing that despite differences in economic performances, such reforms acted as a catalyst for the support those parties still enjoy.

Populism: The Mother of All European Sovereignist Parties

Populism is not a novelty in the European political panorama. It is an unpleasant reflection of history. All the European "isms" one can think of—from German Nazism, to Italian Fascism, up to Spanish Franchism or Soviet Communism of Eastern European countries—detained elements of populism, even though they were based on different ideological backgrounds. Although in Europe, populism has been recently associated more with radical right-wing than left-wing ideas, in other parts of world, such as in Latin America, populism is often a product of the political left. When it comes to populism, political philosophy is not fundamental. Populist parties build their identity upon a thin host ideology, which can either be on the left or on the right of the political spectrum. There are no sets of economic, health or security policies, which can be defined as populist per se, while it is easy to identify a communist economic plan or a fascist security programme.

As underlined by philosopher Isaiah Berlin, populism is indeed characterised by a Cinderella complex (Krastev 2008, 43). Like the famous Cinderella's shoe, a definition of populism will fit perfectly just one party or movement, but not all of them. For this reason, one should think of European populism as a box and focuses on its perimeters instead of attempting to find out what is inside of it. The common standing that characterises all populist movements and parties across EU member countries is that the people are the central point of reference of any political discourse or action. Secondly, building on a diffused resentment felt by groups of the society who feel excluded from the advantages of globalisation, populism comes with a Manichean vision of society (Van Kessel 2015). Against this backdrop, the good people are to be protected by the corrupted elites, in the shape of Brussels bureaucrats, traditional politicians, the European establishment, etc.

Populist parties push forward a simplification of reality, which is particularly useful in political campaigns as it allows communicating directly to the voters and providing them with what appears as an easy solution to existential problems (Müller 2017; Mudde and Kaltwasser 2017). This simplification can also be defined as a moralisation. Indeed, by simplifying the political landscape, populist parties surge themselves as the representative of purity, against the evil and corrupt establishment. To date, considering the outcome of the 2019 EP elections, it is evident that anti-establishment and radical right-wing movements have shaped the recent upsurge of populist sentiments in the EU. Going beyond the national and regional differences that still characterise the EU, in the aftermath of the 2019 EP elections, around 16 out of 28 member countries have at least one party, whose characteristics correspond to the above-mentioned ones and the ID group is represented by parties coming from 9 different countries.

Country	Party	N. seats in national parliament	N. seats in the EP	Political group
Austria	Freedom Party (FPO)	31	3 of 18	ID
Belgium	Flemish Interests (Vl. Belang)	18	3 of 21	ID
Bulgaria	Bulgarian National Movement (IMRO)		2 of 17	ECR
Czechia	Freedom and Direct Democracy (SDP)	22	2 of 21	ID
Denmark	Danish People Party (DS)	16	1 of 13	ECR
Estonia	Conservative People's Party of Estonia (EKRE)	19	1 of 6	ID
Finland	Finns Party (PS)	39	2 of 13	ID
France	National Rally	7	23 of 74	ID
Germany	Alternative for Germany	94	11 of 96	ID
Greece	Golden Dawn (XA)	0	2 of 21	
Hungary	Fidesz	133	13 of 21	EPP
Italy	Lega Nord	182	28 of 73	ID
Poland	Law and Justice (PIS)	235	26 of 51	ECR
UK	Brexit Party	0	29 of 73	
Spain	Vox	52	3 of 54	ECR
Sweden	Sweden Democrats (SD)	62	3 of 20	ECR

Source: Author's elaboration of European Parliament's data

While academics do not agree whether this form of right-wing populism is only a communication strategy or a specific political style, what is certain is that right-wing populist parties in Europe, defined here as sovereignist, are all characterised by five fundamental elements (Pajnik and Sauer 2017; Wodak 2019). First, sovereignist parties are different from nationalist or fascist parties. Although they put the nation as the main actor able to solve citizens' problems and support "fortress" security policies and welfare chauvinism, their political campaigns lack a deep ideological backing (Halikiopoulou 2019, 1–15; Kriesi and Takis 2015). Moreover, differently from nationalist parties, they do not always oppose the nation against the rest of the world, but they often build on the vertical collusive relationship between "the people" and "the elite" (Rooduijn 2019, 362–372). Against this backdrop, sovereignist parties do not develop coherent policies, being able to change their own nationalistic perspectives, when forms of cooperation are preferable. They are anti-pluralist groups with an anti-elitist and anti-intellectual attitude (Wodak 2015). Finally, they are normally led by a charismatic leader, who is portrayed as a national hero or a strict but fair father, whose success is fuelled by a collective sense of insecurity.

Against this backdrop, the next section will argue that there is a link between the EU economic governance and sovereignism. It will highlight that, despite the different GDPs and economic performances of EU member countries, the European economic policies adopted in the aftermath of the crises as well as the lack of democratic accountability of the European decision-making process became catalysts for social discontent and rising insecurity, allowing ID sovereignist parties to achieve an unexpected electoral support.

European Economic Governance and Citizens' Welfare

According to the European Commission, the European economic governance has been developed as a tool to "monitor, prevent, and correct problematic economic trends that could weaken national economies or negatively affect other EU countries". Yet, its institutional framework, which emerged in the following of the Maastricht Treaty, has been often defined as incomplete and imbalanced (Chang 2019). Before the reforms introduced in the aftermath of the crises, the European economic institutions did not provide Eurozone Member States with a lender of last resort, and there were no clear European mechanisms for preserving financial stability or dealing with potential adverse shocks. This resulted in the multiple crises experienced so far.

Rising from the 2008 Credit Crunch, the economic crisis developed in Europe followed three different paths. There has been a crisis of competitiveness and productivity, a banking crisis and, in countries with high public debt, a sovereign debt crisis. At the same time, while the European monetary policy provided Eurozone deficit Member States' economies with a huge expansionary push, the absence of a banking union resulted in Member States respectively protecting and promoting their banks, fuelling various bubble, especially in the property market. Moreover, the lack of common fiscal and wage policies allowed some countries, such as Germany, to boost their own competitiveness by pursuing a policy of disinflation. The latter contributed to increment macroeconomic imbalances within the Eurozone. This happened in a context where countries had already divergent economic performances (Börzel and Risse 2018). In 2007, according the European Commission published data, the volume of German real GDP growth was 3.3, while in the EU 28 it was 3.1, in Italy 1.5, in Finland 5.2, in Slovakia 10.8 and in France 2.4.

Despite the above-mentioned divergences, the need to overcome the economic crises and save the euro resulted in the EU system of economic governance being radically reshaped and reinforced, achieving an unprecedented integration. The European Stability Mechanism (ESM) was established in 2012 as a permanent intergovernmental organisation to provide financial assistance and fiscal liability to Eurozone Member States under attack on the bond markets. Although the ESM has allowed to overcome one of the imbalances of the European economic system and save the euro, national parliaments have no control on its board of Governors, as the latter was established through an intergovernmental Treaty. Similarly, the Fiscal Compact, signed by all EU Governments with the exception of the UK, imposed strict budgetary rules on Member States, binding them to the activation of specific mechanisms to correct any significant deviations (Christakis 2017, 1–43). Again, the Fiscal Compact lacks democratic accountability as it provides the Commission with the power to unilaterally propose sanctions for Member States not respecting these commitments.

The creation of the Banking Union increased the instruments of the ECB to keep the "euro" alive, breaking the vicious cycle of speculation about both Member States and banking sectors' solvency so as not to endanger the financial stability of the Eurozone as a whole. On the other hand, the European Semester attempted to boost compliance of national budgetary and economic reforms with European requirements reinforcing the monitoring of member state policies by the Commission.

The above mechanisms had certainly the merit to save the euro and stabilise EU and Eurozone economies. To be fair, the urgency caused by the unprecedented economic crises of the last years made it impossible to have the above reforms properly discussed and checked by democratically elected national institutions and digested by citizens. While the restructurings were aimed to allow EU member countries, and in particular, the Eurozone, to achieve more integration, overcome the economic deadlock and provide more financial stability, the lack of direct communication channels between the EU decision-making process and the wide electorate made the former appearing as a distant actor with an unprecedented authority over national policies (Börzel 2016, 8–3; Schimmelfennig 2014, 321–337).

Moreover, such reforms did not solve the crises of competitiveness and productivity affecting the EU. These were seen as issues to be solved at national level, preferably by applying austerity policies and "internal devaluation" (Van Gyes and Schulten 2015. Schulten and Müller 2015, 331–363).

Although the EU has no formal competences on wage policies and collective bargaining, the necessity for member countries to respect rigid parameters imposed by the Fiscal Compact and the European Semester resulted in a so perceived top-down approach, whereby the EU recommended the reforms needed, especially in countries with lower economic performances. In a nutshell, the effectiveness of the reformed European economic governance in saving the "euro" and the European integration project has been at the expenses of democratic trends in some EU countries, creating a fertile common ground for sovereignist parties to emerge. More economic integration allowed for substantial powers to be transferred from the national to the European level, making the decision-making process mostly based on an "executive federalism". While the European governance fixed the debt and the banking crisis, the crisis of competitiveness did not receive an adequate answer. On the contrary, it stimulated new forms of competition among Member States, whereby surplus Member States could pressure the ones in deficit. To reduce national debts and remain in the rigid EU parameters, the majority of European governments enforced strict fiscal consolidation programmes with significant cut on education, health care, worker's rights and family policies. According to Eurostat data, since 2010, the percentage of people at risk of poverty raised by 2% in EU countries in general. In Germany, it passed from 8.9% in 2010 to 10.6% in 2017. In France, from 7.8% it reached 8.4%, and in Italy, from 11.8% it touched 12.4%. One exception to this trend is Finland, where it went from 8.4% to 7%. Yet inequality growth in all

EU countries, specifically in Finland and in Germany, where by 2010 to 2016, the middle class was squeezed respectively by 6.9% and 5.7% (Eurostat 2020).

The absence of a European wage policy resulted in all EU countries reducing the extent of their national collective bargaining, contracting wages and workers' rights. Indeed, the growing competition at the EU level among Member States made irrelevant any centralised bargaining as companies could move in other countries or hire remotely workers from other member states. These trends were catalyst of popular support to populist and more specifically sovereignist parties. They amplified two key factors that according to Frieden (2018) were at the basis of their success. On the one hand, they undermined an effective democratic accountability of the EU economic policies. On the other, they amplified the perception that the EU was not tackling citizens' rising insecurity and inequality.

Sovereignism and the Economy

Sovereignist parties did not gain political power in all the EU countries, and the ID group is represented only in nine states. Yet, even in those, such as Germany and Finland, with relative good GDP performances, sovereignist parties were able to win. They did so by highlighting the need to take back control from undemocratic Brussels institutions as well as to fight against rising inequality within and across countries. Those are the two fundamental factors that the European economic governance has, even if indirectly, contributed to fuel.

As populist movements normally do, ID sovereignist parties do not have any answer to solve the above issues, but they mount on citizens' economic insecurity, pushing forward a "fear propaganda".

To date, 51% of the European citizens are indeed afraid of the state of the society, and 67% believe that the world used to be a better place. Citizens fear about their future economic conditions and the loss of their cultural identity, or they have simply nostalgia of a mystified past. In not all countries citizens are concerned by the same issue or in the same way. Still the economic factors, the need for protection and anxiety about the state of society are deeply connected to a dissatisfaction with the quality of EU and Member States' democracies and the idea that European institutions are too complicated and fail to provide what is needed (De Vries and Hoffmann 2019). Indeed, 48% of the European citizens tend not to trust the EU, 38% believe the EU is not positively influencing their lives and 30% think we need less integration (European Commission 2018; European Parliament 2019; De Vries and Hoffmann 2019).

Sovereignist parties appeal to all social groups with specific economic concerns (Kriesi and Takis 2015). First, they receive support from the working class by building on a well-diffused negative condition of labour-market competition, mounting their exposure to immigrants' workforce who are allegedly keen to work longer hours and with lower salaries (Dancygier and Walter 2015, 133–56). This, together with the need to stop "welfare tourists", is the battle horse of the Austrian Freedom

Party (FPO) (Reuters 2017). Secondly, they received support by a declining middle class who is worried to lose its current social and economic status (Antonucci 2019; Hillje 2018; Michel 2017). For instance, supporters of the National Rally or Alternative for Germany (AfD) or even the Italian League fear unemployment, the worsening of working conditions and the weakening of social safety nets. AfD and FN voters believe that the future generation will be financially worse off than that of their parents (Hillje 2018).

Anxiety about other countries' economic performances is also an issue. Indeed, the absence of European common policies to overcome the crisis of competitiveness and productivity was detrimental, especially for Southern European countries, which experienced low growth. This allowed northern European sovereignist parties to create a new argument to discredit the EU and its economic governance around the capacity of Southern Europeans to repay their debt. Parties such as Alternative for Germany or the Finns Party constructed part of their European agenda on that, maintaining that their countries should protect their own citizens and fight against any form of bail out policy for rescuing the euro and underperforming EU member countries (The Finns Party 2019; Kim 2018). As far as rising inequality is concerned, those parties did not replace traditional left-wing agenda. They offer broader forms of protection in terms of tighter security with tax reduction, to compensate the loss of social status. They do not confront the EU and its economic governance to ask for more social guarantees or effective welfare policies. They indeed replace the idea of social equity with protectionism and the promise of lower taxes, combined with an ideological appeal to nationalism and a nostalgic desire to "make the country great again".

In conclusion, the economic crisis and the consequent EU institutional response, through the reforms of the European economic governance, did not directly cause the rise of sovereignist parties, but they acted as a catalyst of their success. They basically favoured the development of two key conditions: lack of democratic accountability and rising inequality, which fuelled citizens' insecurity at the basis of populist parties' fear propaganda.

Conclusion

Beyond the cultural backlash, which posits the origin of the radical right vote mainly to the diffusion of liberal values or the migration crisis, European economic governance is relevant when it comes to understand the success of the above-mentioned parties (Rydgren 2008, 737–765). Indeed, the inability or impossibility of national governments to face rising national inequality issues resulted in the politicisation of the European economic governance and its lack of democratic accountability, which became central to sovereignist parties' agenda (Börzel and Risse 2018, 23; Norris and Ingehart 2018). While economic and social inequalities grew larger, the migration crisis increased social pressure and concerns about additional strains on existing welfare systems (Meuleman et al. 2018). Unhappiness about the status quo was coupled by anxiety about the future and efforts made by EU institutions to reach more economic integration, as a way out of the crisis appeared useless by many. Europe ceased to be perceived as a "win-win" project for all. While austerity policy became the new scapegoat for all, the high social costs and increased economic and financial disparities among Member States boosted myopic national egoism. In this respect, the EU economic governance did save the Euro and provided financial stability to Eurozone and non-Eurozone countries, yet it lacked adequate measures to tackle rising citizens' economic insecurity, which were left in the hand of national governments. Yet, the need to respect strict budgetary rules resulted in traditional parties failing to deliver what was needed and provided sovereignist parties with the perfect political and economic background to emerge as alternative political forces.

References

Antonucci, L. (2019). *Fixing the European social malaise: Understanding and addressing the grievances of European workers*. IAI Commentary.

Börzel, T. A. (2016). From EU governance of crisis to crisis of EU governance: Regulatory failure, redistributive conflict and Eurosceptic publics. *JCMS: Journal of Common Market Studies, 54*, 8–3.

Börzel, T. A., & Risse, T. (2018). *A litmus test for European integration theories: Explaining crises and comparing regionalisms*. KFG working paper.

Chang, M. (2019). The (ever) incomplete story of economic and monetary union. *Journal of Contemporary European Research., 12*(1).

Christakis, G. (2017). Economic governance in the EU after the Eurozone crisis: A state of affairs. *Trasform Europe*, 1–43.

Dancygier, R. M., & Walter, S. (2015). Globalization, labor market risks, and class cleavages. In P. Beramendi et al. (Eds.), *The politics of advanced capitalism* (pp. 133–156). Cambridge: Cambridge University Press.

De Vries, C. E., & Hoffmann, I. (2019). The hopeful, the fearful and the furious. *EuOpinions*.

European Commission. (2018). *Standard Eurobarometer*.

European Parliament. (2019). *Flesh Eurobarometer, emotions and political engagement towards the EU.*

Eurostat. (2020). *People at risk of poverty or social exclusion*. Dataset Details. General and regional statistics.

Finns Party. (2019). The Finns Party's European Union Policy. https://www.perussuomalaiset.fi/kielisivu/in-english/

Frieden, J. (2018). *The politics of the globalization backlash: Sources and implications*. Annual meeting of the American Economics Association, Philadelphia.

Halikiopoulou, D. (2019). Right-wing populism as a nationalist vision of legitimating collective choice: A supply-side perspective. *The International Spectator, 2019*, 1–15.

Hillje, J. (2018). *Return to the politically abandoned. Conversations in right-wing populist strongholds in Germany and France*. Das Progressive Centrum.

Kim, J. (2018). The radical market-oriented policies of the Alternative for Germany (AfD) and support from non-beneficiary groups–discrepancies between the party's policies and its supporters. *Asian Journal of German and European Studies 3.1*, 1–24.

Krastev, I. (2008). The populist moment, new presence. *The Prague Journal of Central European Affairs, 11*(4), 43.

Kriesi, H., & Takis, S. P. (2015). *European populism in the shadow of the great recession* Colchester: Ecpr Press.

Meuleman, B., et al. (2018). The past, present and future of European welfare attitudes: Topline results from round 8 of the European Social Survey ESS Topline Series.

Michel, E. (2017). Welfare politics and the radical right: The relevance of welfare politics for the radical right's success in Western Europe (Doctoral dissertation).
Mudde, C., & Kaltwasser, C. R. (2017). *Populism: A very short introduction*. Oxford: Oxford University Press.
Müller, J. (2017). *What is populism?* Penguin UK.
Norris, P., & Ingehart, R. (2018). *Cultural backlash and the rise of populism: Trump, Brexit, and the rise of authoritarianism populism*. Cambridge: Cambridge University Press.
Pajnik, M., & Sauer, B. (2017). *Populism and the web: Communicative practices of parties and movements in Europe*. Abingdon, Oxon: Routledge.
Reuters. (2017). https://www.reuters.com/article/us-austria-politics-alliance-idUSKBN1781P9
Rooduijn, M. (2019). State of the field: How to study populism and adjacent topics? A plea for both more and less focus. *European Journal of Political Research, 58*(1), 362–372.
Rydgren, J. (2008). Immigration sceptics, xenophobes or racists? Radical right-wing voting in six West European countries. *European Journal of Political Research, 47*(6), 737–765.
Schimmelfennig, F. (2014). European integration in the euro crisis: The limits of postfunctionalism. *Journal of European Integration, 36*(3), 321–337.
Schulten, T., & Müller, T. (2015). European economic governance and its intervention in national wage development and collective bargaining. In *Divisive integration: The Triumph of failed ideas in Europe–Revisited* (pp. 331–363). ETUI, Brussels.
Van Gyes, G., & Schulten, T. (2015). *Wage bargaining under the new European Economic Governance: Alternative strategies for inclusive growth*. ETUI.
Van Kessel, S. (2015). Populist parties in Europe: Agents of discontent?. Palgrave Macmillan, London.
Wodak, R. (2015). *The politics of fear: What right-wing populist discourses mean*. Sage, London.
Wodak, R. (2019). Entering the 'post-shame era': The rise of illiberal democracy, populism and neo-authoritarianism in EUrope. *Global Discourse: An Interdisciplinary Journal of Current Affairs, 9*(1), 195–213.

16

Crisis, Euroscepticism and the Future of European Integration

Susannah Verney and Dimitris Katsikas

Abstract The crisis that started in Greece in 2010 gradually spread to other Eurozone member states. Things were worse for the crisis-hit countries of the Eurozone periphery, some of which implemented harsh adjustment programmes in the context of financial assistance agreements, while others adopted similar policies even though they had not officially entered a bailout agreement (e.g. Spain and to a lesser degree Italy). In this environment of deteriorating material conditions, Euroscepticism reached new heights. This chapter examines the impact of the crisis, and the way it was handled, on regionalism in Europe, through its effects on Euroscepticism. The authors compare Eurobarometer data from European Union (EU) member states, in order to develop a comparative outlook on attitudes towards European integration during the crisis. The analysis employs data at discreet time intervals, in order to capture the evolution of attitudes from the pre-crisis environment in 2008, to the peak of the crisis in 2012, its gradual resolution in 2016 and its official ending (with the exit of Greece from its third bailout programme) in 2018. This analysis is complemented by an overview of the political developments in crisis-hit countries with the objective of documenting and analysing the emergence and, in some cases, dominance of Eurosceptic parties. The objective is to present a comprehensive overview of political developments and the public attitudes that shaped them, vis a vis the EU, during the crisis and offer a tentative conclusion on their impact on the European integration process.

S. Verney
National and Kapodistrian University of Athens, Athens, Greece

D. Katsikas (✉)
National and Kapodistrian University of Athens and Hellenic Foundation for European and Foreign Policy (ELIAMEP), Athens, Greece
e-mail: dkatsikas@eliamep.gr

Introduction

The Eurozone sovereign debt crisis was the most important economic challenge the European Union (EU) has ever faced. The economic decline was mainly driven by the deep recessions experienced in the crisis-hit countries of the Eurozone periphery, particularly in the European South. Some of these countries (Greece, Portugal, Cyprus and Ireland) implemented harsh adjustment programmes in the context of sovereign bailouts. Spain adopted similar policies in parallel with a bailout of its banks by the European Stability Mechanism (ESM), and so did Italy, although to a lesser extent, as a result of pressure both from the markets and the EU. Thus, in all six countries, austerity policies were delivered as EU-mandated. In this environment of deteriorating material conditions, intra-European political divisions arose, as EU member states divided into creditor and debtor camps. The latter blamed the former for the imposition of harsh austerity policies and the consequent economic deterioration. Meanwhile, the creditors resented providing bailout funds to countries, which in their view were guilty of irresponsible fiscal behaviour and/or poor economic performance. In these circumstances, EU cohesion looked very fragile; popular support for the European integration project weakened and political parties critical of the EU gained in electoral influence.

The aim of this chapter is to examine the impact of the crisis and its management on Euroscepticism. Although the word was first used in the 1980s, the phenomenon of Euroscepticism—which can be defined simply as opposition to European integration—is as old as the process itself. Defined by what it is against rather than what it stands for, Euroscepticism is a rather all-encompassing term which embraces opposition to integration originating from multiple ideological viewpoints and expressing different intensities of disagreement, from simple criticism to outright rejection of the project. Study of the subject has tended to focus either on Euroscepticism's popular or public dimension, i.e. mass attitudes, or else on its expression within political party systems. This article will adopt both lenses. More specifically, it will first examine the impact of the crisis on levels of public support for European integration, comparing two regions of the Eurozone: its periphery and its West European core. It will then move on to investigate the changing strength of party Euroscepticism in the crisis-stricken Southern periphery. The objective is to present an overview of some important developments and the shifting public attitudes that shaped them in relation to the EU during the crisis and offer a tentative conclusion on their impact on the European integration process.

The Crisis and Public Support for the EU and the Euro

During the years of the Eurozone debt crisis, public support for European integration declined (Serricchio et al. 2013, Nancy 2016). However, the impact was not uniform across countries or through time. This section aims to provide a temporal and comparative overview of trends in public support for the EU during the period 2008–2018. The analysis compares countries grouped in 'core' and 'periphery' categories in order to capture the different dynamics of popular Euroscepticism in the crisis-hit and creditor regions. Our 'periphery' group consists of Greece, Italy, Portugal, Spain, Cyprus and Ireland, and the 'core' group consists of Austria, Belgium, France, Finland, Germany and the Netherlands. The analysis proceeds by comparing aggregate averages for each of these two groups and then looking at individual country results. It employs data at four discrete time intervals, from the pre-crisis period (2008), through periods of crisis intensity (2012) and gradual recovery (2016),[1] to the crisis' 'official conclusion' with the completion of Greece's third bailout programme in 2018. The data comes from the European Commission's biannual Eurobarometer surveys and specifically from reports 70.1 (10/2008), 78.1 (11/2012), 86.2 (11/2016) and 90.3 (11/2018).

In assessing support for the EU during the Eurozone crisis, we employ the well-known distinction made by David Easton. He defined 'diffuse support' for any political system as 'support that underlies the regime as a whole'. In his view, such 'generalized attachment' to a political system is more enduring and 'will not be easily dislodged because of current dissatisfaction with what the government does'. In contrast, 'specific support' refers to popular satisfaction with the outputs and performance of a political system and can be expected to be more easily affected by passing developments (Easton 1975, pp. 445–6, 437). Here, we opt to test the impact of the crisis on diffuse support for European integration. This decision is premised on our expectation that specific support is far more likely and indeed expected to suffer, given the adverse consequences of the crisis and the way this was handled; what is more interesting, however, is whether people's reactions reflect a broader disaffection with the EU and not simply the rejection of specific policies or institutions.

To test for the effects on diffuse support, we employ three questions: first, a question concerning the EU's image which clearly complies with Easton's definition of ways to measure diffuse support as 'evaluations of what an object represents – the general meaning it has for a person – not what it does' (Easton 1975, p.445). Secondly, 'Trust in the EU', which is often employed in related research and is generally considered a valid way to measure diffuse support for the EU (Ioannou et al. 2015). Thirdly, a question about the single currency was chosen as this was the aspect of European integration which was most questioned during the crisis. The crisis was centred on the Eurozone, and much of the criticism targeted its imbalanced architecture and incomplete governance, which made its handling more difficult and prolonged its duration. It is for this reason that in the countries that suffered from the crisis, the question of 'exit' from the Eurozone was often raised. Accordingly, a question on support for the euro, which is the central pillar and basic constituent element of the Eurozone, was an obvious choice. These questions are

[1] In 2014, both Ireland and Portugal successfully completed their bailout programmes, while the Eurozone economy as a whole turned once again into positive growth rates.

available for all four surveys and can thus be used to trace the evolution of attitudes during the crisis.[2]

The EU's Image

Before the crisis, the EU's image was overall positive, with few negative views,[3] but a substantial degree of ambivalence, as more than one in three EU citizens adopted a neutral stance (Fig. 16.1). The breakdown of views between the two country groups shows that the majority of citizens in the Eurozone periphery were positively disposed towards the EU (51%), and their 'approval rate' was higher than that of their counterparts in the core (43%). The percentage of negative opinions about the EU in the periphery was both very low (13%) and below that of respondents in the Eurozone core. In terms of individual countries,[4] Ireland recorded the highest support levels with 63% of respondents having a positive image of the EU, while other

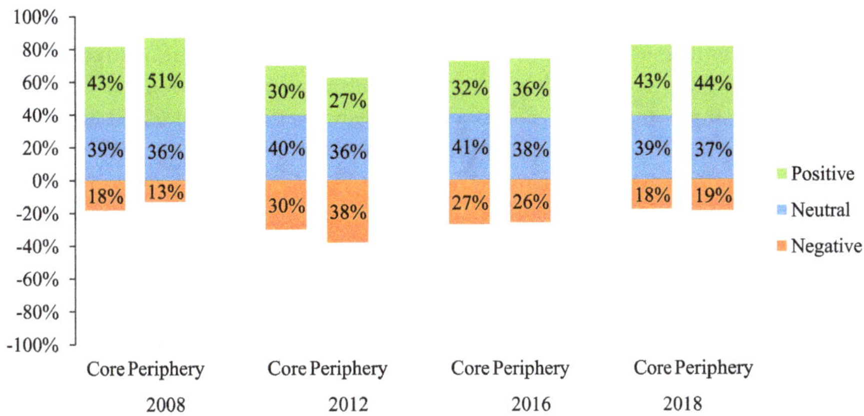

Fig. 16.1 EU image: Core vs periphery. Source: Authors' elaboration of Eurobarometer data (surveys 70.1, 78.1, 86.2 and 90.3)

[2]More specifically, the questions were: (a) EU Image: *In general, does the EU conjure up for you a very positive, fairly positive, neutral, fairly negative, or very negative image?*

(b) Trust in EU: *I would like to ask you a question about how much trust you have in certain media and institutions. For each of the following media and institutions, please tell me if you tend to trust it or tend not to trust it: The European Union.*

(c) Single currency: *What is your opinion on each of the following statements? Please tell me for each statement, whether you are for it or against it: A European economic and monetary union with one single currency, the euro.*

[3]For this question, positive/fairly positive and negative/fairly negative answers are grouped into two groups respectively (positive/negative).

[4]Although reference to data for individual countries is made throughout the text, the full presentation of such data is not possible due to space limitations.

periphery countries also recorded approval rates close to or above 50% (but with a lower score of 41% for Greece). Among the core countries, Austria and Finland had the lowest levels of support, with less than one in three respondents holding a positive image of the EU. In other core countries, support levels were similar to the periphery (close to or above 50%).

After the outbreak of the crisis, the picture changed completely. In 2012, positive views had declined across the board. In the periphery, the percentage of positive image responses had almost halved, whereas in the core, the drop was close to 30%. As a result, in the periphery group as a whole, negative responses exceeded positive ones, while they were evenly balanced in the core group. A closer look at individual countries demonstrates the intensity of the change. The lowest levels of support were recorded in Greece, where positive responses dropped to a mere 18% while 50% of respondents gave negative answers.

Spain, Portugal and Cyprus also recorded a negative balance of answers, with negative views in the latter two being well over 40%. On the other hand, Ireland held onto a small positive balance of 6% and Italy to a larger one of approximately 13%. Even in these countries however, the turnaround in public opinion was dramatic; for example, in Ireland, positive image responses fell from 63% before the crisis to 37%. Although less striking, the drop in positive views of the EU was also considerable in the core; Austrian and Finnish respondents, already more reserved in their support before the crisis, now gave more negative than positive answers. The remaining four countries retained a positive balance, but by a narrow margin.

The gradual resolution of the crisis, from 2014–2015 onward, changed the picture again. By autumn 2016, 2 years into economic recovery, European citizens' image of the EU started improving, particularly in the crisis-hit countries. Thus, in the periphery group, positive views increased from 27% to 36% with a corresponding drop in negative responses. In the core countries on the other hand, the improvement was minimal, with positive views increasing from 30% to 32%. However, the group averages hide significant differentiations. In the periphery, Portugal and to a lesser extent Ireland, almost recovered their pre-crisis positive image levels, whereas Cyprus and particularly Greece remained more sceptical. Italy, while recording a marginally positive balance of answers, was the only country in this group where the popular image of the EU continued to deteriorate in 2016. Interestingly, this was also the case for France in the core group. Austrians displayed stability in their opinions, whereas citizens of the remaining core countries had a modestly improved image of the EU. By 2018, the EU's image had improved substantially in all countries of both groups, including Italy and France. In some countries, like Ireland and Portugal, positive image responses now surpassed pre-crisis levels.

Trust in the EU

Turning to the question of trust, as with the image of the EU, pre-crisis replies indicate overall support for the EU among European citizens. In both groups, a majority of respondents tended to trust the EU (Fig. 16.2). Again, slightly more respondents in the periphery tended to trust the EU compared to those in the core countries (58% vs 54%). At the individual country level, the picture is more differentiated. Respondents in the periphery showed substantial levels of trust towards the EU (ranging roughly between 60% and 65%), except the Italians, where a majority (53%) tended not to trust the EU even before the crisis. In the core countries, mistrust prevailed in Austria (54%) and Germany (52%), while the French were equally split on the question. On the other hand, Belgium and the Netherlands showed high levels of trust (over 60%), while Finland recorded a positive, albeit marginal, balance.

Once again, the outbreak of the crisis changed the picture completely. In the crisis-hit periphery, the deterioration in trust was dramatic; the balance moved deeply into negative territory, with over 70% of respondents replying that they did not trust the EU in 2012. In the core countries, the direction of change was similar, but its intensity was less dramatic; trust levels receded to 42%. Looking at individual countries, in Greece, the country which suffered the deepest crisis, the loss of trust was truly overwhelming; 82% replied that they did not trust the EU, while Spain, also undergoing a deep crisis, recorded similar levels of mistrust (78%). In the remaining crisis-hit countries, approximately two thirds of respondents gave negative answers. In five of the core countries, a majority of respondents mistrusted the EU. The exception was Finland, where answers were evenly split.

The economic recovery had a positive impact on levels of trust in the EU, but not of the same magnitude as with the EU's image. Initially, the recovery of trust was

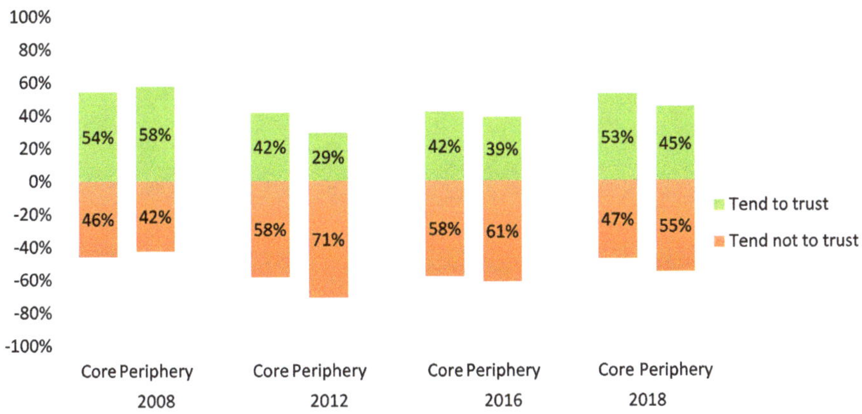

Fig. 16.2 Trust in EU. Source: Authors' elaboration of Eurobarometer data (surveys 70.1, 78.1, 86.2 and 90.3)

most evident in the crisis-hit group, which by 2016 recorded an overall improvement of 10 percentage points, while trust levels in the core remained unchanged. Looking at individual countries reveals significant differentiations once again. As was the case with the EU's image, Ireland and Portugal were the countries that came closest to their pre-crisis levels of trust; on the other hand, in Italy and Cyprus, trust continued to decline in 2016. Greeks remained overwhelmingly sceptical, with 80% of respondents stating they did not trust the EU. The picture in the core was also complicated in 2016. Some countries (Germany, Finland and Belgium) saw a modest recovery in trust levels, but in the Netherlands, the situation remained unchanged, while in Austria and especially France, trust levels declined further (72% of respondents mistrusted the EU in France). By 2018, the picture had improved substantially in all countries; but while trust levels had fully recovered to 2008 levels in core countries, in the periphery they remained more than 10 percentage points below the pre-crisis period.

Support for the Single Currency

Before the crisis, support for the Euro was high across the board, with respondents in the core group being more enthusiastic than those of the periphery group (Fig. 16.3). Apart from Ireland, where 92% of respondents supported the euro, in the other periphery countries, support ranged roughly between 60% and 70%. On the other hand, in all the core countries, support for the euro was above 70% and in some cases (Belgium, Netherlands and Finland) above 80%.

As with the previous two questions, the crisis brought a decline in popular support for the euro. However, contrary to the other aspects reviewed previously, the

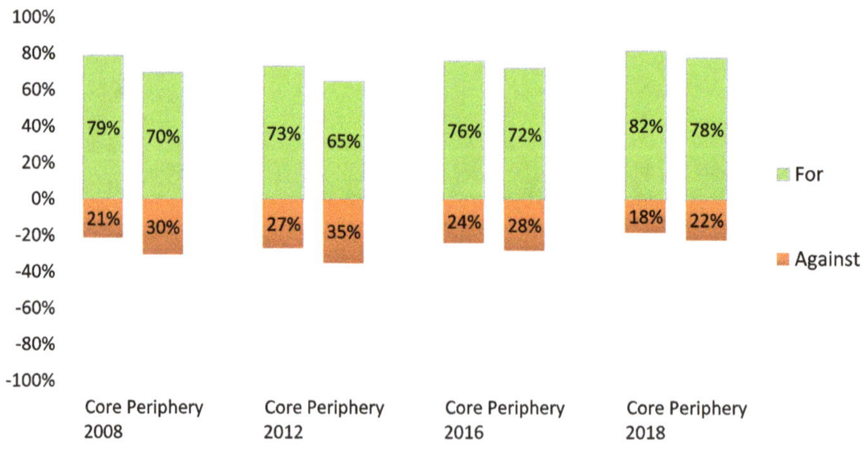

Fig. 16.3 Support for the Euro. Source: Authors' elaboration of Eurobarometer data (surveys 70.1, 78.1, 86.2 and 90.3)

impact here was limited. In the periphery group, average support for the euro fell by just 5 percentage points to 65% and in the core group by 6 percentage points to 73%. Individually, all the core and four of the periphery countries displayed a modest decline. In crisis-hit Ireland, the decline was more substantial (18 percentage points—but compared to the very high pre-crisis level noted above). Intriguingly, in Greece, which was then teetering on the verge of Eurozone exit, support for the euro actually rose to 67% from 58% before the crisis.

The economic recovery saw the popularity of the euro returning to pre-crisis levels, or even surpassing them, particularly in the crisis-hit countries. In the latter group, support for the single currency was stronger in 2016 compared to 2008. Support in Greece continued to rise, while Ireland and to a lesser degree Cyprus moved close to their pre-crisis levels. Only in Italy did support for the euro continue to decline, falling to 59% in 2016 from 65% in 2012. The only other two countries where support for the euro continued to fall were Austria (where nonetheless approximately two thirds of respondents continued to be pro-euro) and marginally, France. In the rest of the core countries, there was a modest increase in support, bringing them closer to their pre-crisis levels. By 2018, most countries recorded a substantial increase in support compared to 2016; as a result, at this point, all countries in both groups exhibited similar or higher levels of support for the euro compared to the pre-crisis period.

The Crisis and Public Support for the EU and the Euro: Implications for European Integration

The data presented above shows that the three different measures employed to gauge support for the EU were affected differently during and/or after the crisis. What explains these trends and what are the implications for European integration? First, support for the euro proved surprisingly resilient. A somewhat unexpected result, given the widespread critique of the functioning and institutional set-up of the Eurozone, is that the single currency has come stronger out of the crisis, at least in terms of popular support. Even more unexpected is that this support seems to be stronger in the crisis-hit countries, where criticism of the monetary union has been fierce. Studies have attributed this resilience of support to the stability benefits of the euro (Roth et al. 2016) and the prevalence of utilitarian criteria in citizens' judgments, given the increased salience of economic and redistributive issues during this time (Hobolt and Wratil 2015). It seems that European citizens thought the crisis could be best addressed in the EU/Eurozone framework compared to any other alternatives (Ibid). In the case of Greece for example, as Clements et al. (2014) note, despite citizens' dissatisfaction with the EU, they recognized that staying in the euro was the most realistic option.

On the other hand, contrary to expectations, our other measures of diffuse support proved more vulnerable to the crisis, and both declined substantially after 2008.

In both cases, the shock of the crisis was greater in the periphery than the core. However, both indicators closely followed the evolution of economic trends, showing a strong recovery after the crisis peaked. Again, however, there was a difference. Our aggregate figures show that by 2018, in our core countries group, diffuse support had returned to pre-crisis levels. In the periphery group, although the trend was moving in that direction, this was not yet the case. In particular, there remained a distinct 'trust gap' in the periphery, where in Autumn 2018, a majority of 55% of citizens still mistrusted the EU.

Perhaps this is to be expected, given that trust is a concept which denotes a deeper bond, acquired through time and experience. Once lost, recovering it is usually a difficult and long-term process. Research has shown that material considerations are an important factor in public support for the EU (e.g. Gabel 1998; Boomgaarden et al. 2010). For South European societies in particular, European integration traditionally represented a promise of material benefits and convergence with the living standards of the more affluent North. The austerity policies promoted during the crisis kick-started a negative economic spiral which plunged the economies of the South into deep recessions. For many people, the deterioration of their personal circumstances was so dramatic that it completely derailed their previous life expectations. In this context, the policies promoted by the EU were viewed as a 'betrayal' of hopes and promises.

Such an interpretation is consistent with the fact that trust declined most dramatically during the crisis in Greece and Spain, two countries which shared two important features: (a) the biggest surge in unemployment (reaching a staggering 27% in both countries) and (b) the most active and massive political mobilizations (the so-called 'indignados' movements) against the politics of austerity promoted by the EU. Both of these features are related with lower levels of trust in the EU; empirical analysis of Eurobarometer data for the periphery countries during 2008–2016 has shown that at the peak of the crisis, the unemployed were more likely not to trust the EU, while after the outbreak of the crisis, including the recovery period, individuals' financial situation and life satisfaction became more important criteria for trust in the EU (Katsikas 2017). Moreover, people who actively engaged in political discussions were more likely to mistrust the EU (Ibid), a finding consistent with the emergence of new Eurosceptic parties in these countries—the topic to which we will now turn.

The Rise of Eurosceptic Parties in the Southern Periphery

How were these shifting patterns of public Euroscepticism reflected in national politics? Prior to the crisis, attitudes towards European integration had been described as a 'sleeping giant' (van der Eijk and Franklin 2004): a question of low political salience which generally did not affect political behaviour. Other issues were deemed more important to voters when deciding which political party to support. Meanwhile, as noted in a seminal article by Paul Taggart (1998), Euroscepticism tended to be marginalised within national party systems: a politics of protest usually limited to minor opposition parties. In this section, we will investigate to what extent this picture changed during the crisis decade (2008-18), under the pressure of the decline in diffuse support for European integration which we saw above.

The Eurozone crisis turned European integration into a salient issue with a direct and visible impact on citizens' pockets. The management of the crisis proved controversial in both core and periphery countries, offering opportunities for Eurosceptic parties to gain a new prominence. Thus, in some of our core countries, electoral campaigns based on opposing bailouts of indebted peripheral states with 'our money' proved effective vote mobilizing tools. For example, in Finland in 2011, hostility towards the second Greek bailout helped the True Finns[5] to more than quadruple their electoral support, emerging as third party nationwide with a vote share just 1.3 percentage points behind the frontrunner. In Germany two years later, the anti-bailout AfD (Alternative for Germany), just 5 months after its foundation, won over two million votes in a federal election, bringing it only marginally below the 5% parliamentary threshold. Meanwhile in the periphery, the Eurozone crisis and the popular backlash it generated created major opportunities for parties campaigning against EU-led austerity. For reasons of space, our focus in this section will be on the four main countries of the Southern Eurozone (Italy, Spain, Greece and Portugal). As we have seen, it was in the crisis-hit Southern periphery, deeply affected by EU-mandated economic austerity, that the impact on diffuse support for the EU was greatest and more lasting.

The Marginality of Party Euroscepticism in the Pre-Crisis Southern Periphery

In three of our four South European countries, before the crisis the national party system was dominated by two pro-integrationist parties belonging to the two main political groups at European level, the European People's Party and the Party of European Socialists, respectively. In all three national systems, the two major parties usually alternated in power. In the last national elections before the outbreak of the Eurozone crisis, their combined vote shares accounted for 83.8% in Spain (2008), 77.4% in Greece (2009) and 65.7% in Portugal (2009). This meant that any Eurosceptic parties could only be minor forces, consigned to permanent opposition.

In these three countries, the Eurosceptic space was traditionally a left-wing monopoly. The Eurosceptic forces represented in the three countries' national parliaments included two hard-line communist parties in Greece and Portugal, which would have preferred their countries not to participate in the EU. Another three radical left parties (the Left Bloc in Portugal, SYRIZA in Greece and the United Left in Spain) did not oppose their countries' membership but wanted radical reform of the

[5] Now known just as 'The Finns'.

EU and particularly its neoliberal economic policy. Then in 2007, just before the crisis, LAOS, a radical right party advocating a Europe of the Nations, also entered the Greek Parliament. Meanwhile in Italy, since the party system crash of the early 1990s, a bipolar system had developed with power alternating between two party camps of the centre-left and centre-right, whose combined vote share in 2008 was 84.3%. Each of these Italian coalitions was dominated by a party belonging to the two main pro-integrationist European party groups. While recent Italian centre-right governments had included a Eurosceptic party, the Northern League's stance on European issues did not seem to impact on national European policy.

Eurosceptic Breakthroughs

The Eurozone crisis transformed this picture in a way which is only comprehensible in the light of the decline of diffuse support for the EU recorded in the previous section. The way the crisis opened up electoral space for Eurosceptic forces in Southern Europe can be seen first, in a series of parliamentary breakthroughs. These included three new parties: the Independent Greeks in 2012, the Five Star Movement in Italy in 2013 and the Spanish Podemos in 2015. Of varying ideological orientations, these parties also expressed different degrees and types of Euroscepticism. In Greece, an existing fringe group, the Neo-Nazi Golden Dawn, also entered parliament on the back of the reaction to the country's second EU/IMF bailout in 2012. Secondly, some parties which already existed in national parliaments were able to extend their appeal to new constituencies. In 2011, the United Left in Spain increased its vote by 80%. Most notably, however, SYRIZA in 2012 more than tripled its share of the vote in Greece. Thirdly, as a result of this expanded electoral appeal, Eurosceptic parties moved 'from the margins to the mainstream' (Brack and Startin 2015). In 2012, SYRIZA emerged as second party, becoming the official opposition in Greece. The following year, the Five Star Movement became the most voted party in Italy, a feat then achieved twice by SYRIZA in the two Greek parliamentary elections of 2015.

The exception was Portugal, where none of these phenomena occurred. As we have seen, in this country, levels of diffuse support for the EU recovered rapidly, already approximating pre-crisis levels by 2016. During the crisis period, there were no breakthroughs by Eurosceptic parties in Portugal. In the 2011 election, held shortly after the signature of the country's EU/IMF bailout, the joint vote share of the two Portuguese Eurosceptic parties actually decreased. Subsequently, the combined electoral support for these two parties has not reached the level of the last pre-crisis election in 2009. Despite this, however, Portugal also participated in the second major Eurosceptic development in Southern Europe during the crisis decade: the opening up of government to Eurosceptic party participation.

Eurosceptic Impact

The first indication that the crisis was opening new governing opportunities for Eurosceptic parties in the Eurozone's Southern periphery came in Greece. In 2011, LAOS was included as a junior partner in a government coalition. Four years later, Portugal experienced a major rupture in its post-dictatorship politics, when its radical left-wing Eurosceptic parties, previously regarded as non-coalitionable, were invited to support a minority socialist government with a programme of rolling back economic austerity. Even more striking, in Greece in 2015, SYRIZA not only became the senior coalition partner but also preferred as its governing ally the Eurosceptic Independent Greeks from the far right rather than a pro-EU party closer to it on the left–right spectrum. In 2018 in Italy, the Five Star Movement, with a vote share 13 percentage points ahead of the second party, also became the senior government party and also chose a Eurosceptic coalition partner, the now re-named League. Thus, overturning the patterns of the pre-crisis period, in three out of our four Southern periphery countries, Eurosceptic parties became government participants in the period 2011–2018.

This impressive growth in Eurosceptic party strength in Southern Europe marked a significant rise in opposition to the EU. But to what extent did this pose a significant threat to the integration project? As indicated above, the Eurosceptic forces were a variegated group with different viewpoints and aims in relation to integration. The common target of the South European Eurosceptic parties was the austerity policies which had so undermined public support for the EU in this region. But for most of the 'breakthrough' parties, their scepticism about EU policy did not extend to rejection of the Union itself. The exception was the Greek Golden Dawn, whose economic and political programme was incompatible with EU membership. However, Golden Dawn talked very little about the EU, so its hard-line opposition was not very visible. In any case, because of its general anti-system nature, this party remained in opposition and on the political margins. What though was the impact of the Eurosceptic parties in power?

In Portugal, the Eurosceptic forces were junior partners who supported the government but did not participate in it. Moreover, the socialist party had made it a pre-condition of government formation that the programme to reverse austerity would comply with the requirements of the EU's Stability and Growth Pact. As a result, while the Eurosceptic parties came in from the cold in the sense of being accepted as legitimate government partners, their government participation did not generate Eurosceptic policy outcomes. In contrast, in the other two countries, the Eurosceptic parties dominated government and, in both cases, engaged in confrontational politics with the EU. In Greece in 2015, this concerned whether the country should repay its debt as well as the terms of continued financial assistance. What proved crucial in this case was the strength of Greek popular support for the euro noted above. After a 6-month standoff, the government changed course and accepted a new bailout rather than risk a disorderly Eurozone exit which would have been highly unpopular with the electorate. With the Italian government formed in 2018, the confrontation concerned compliance with the EU's Stability and Growth Pact. After several months, when faced with the prospect of an EU Excessive Deficit Procedure, the Italian government agreed to reduce its budget deficit. As a result, it is a striking point that during the period of the Eurozone crisis and despite all the political discontent it generated in the region, there was no South European rupture with the EU or the single currency.

Conclusions: Crisis, Euroscepticism and the Future of European Integration

Usually, political dissatisfaction with government policies and performance is not expected to undermine support for a political system as a whole. But in 1975, David Easton wrote that 'there may be instances ... in which the sudden frustration of expectations can so jolt the deeper loyalties of the members of a system that their diffuse support falls into a precipitous decline' (p.445). It appears this happened during the Eurozone crisis. European integration, previously of low salience to voters, began to impact on citizens' lives in highly visible and unpopular ways. The management of the crisis generated resentment in both the core and the periphery of the single currency area. It did not simply leave citizens dissatisfied with the policies implemented, but also resulted in a sharp and steep drop in affective support for the European Union itself. In a climate of widespread criticism of the EU, the way was opened for the rise of the political opposition in the form of Eurosceptic parties. As we have seen, in Southern Europe, this led to the formation of Eurosceptic governments but did not, during the duration of the crisis, produce major Eurosceptic policy outcomes.

In the case of the Eurozone crisis, once the immediate cause of discontent—the economic pressures—began to ameliorate, Eurosceptic sentiment among the public also began to dissipate. Thus, on this occasion, the loss of legitimacy proved potentially reversible when the problem which had caused it ceased to be so acute. No doubt it was important that this reversal happened fairly fast before Eurosceptic sentiment became more deeply entrenched. The scale and rapidity of the decline in popular support for the EU after 2008 should serve, however, as an important warning. The experience of the Eurozone crisis suggests that future EU policy failures could have the potential to undermine the viability of the system as a whole.

References

Boomgaarden, H. G., Schuck, A. R. T., Elenbaas, M., & de Vreese, C. H. (2010). Mapping EU attitudes: Conceptual and empirical dimensions of Euroscepticism and EU support. *European Union Politics, 12*(2), 241–266.

Brack, N., & Startin, N. (2015). Introduction: Euroscepticism, from the margins to the mainstream. *International Political Science Review, 36*(3), 239–249.

Clements, B., Nanou, K., & Verney, S. (2014). We no longer love you, but we don't want to leave you: The Eurozone crisis and popular euroscepticism in Greece. *Journal of European Integration, 36*(3), 247–265.

Easton, D. (1975). A reassessment of the concept of political support. *British Journal of Political Science, 5*, 435–457.

Gabel, M. J. (1998). Public support for European integration: An empirical test of five theories. *Journal of Politics, 60*(2), 333–354.

Hobolt, S. B., & Wratil, C. (2015). Public opinion and the crisis: The dynamics of support for the euro. *Journal of European Public Policy, 22*(2), 238–256.

Ioannou, D., Jamet, J. F., Kleibl, J. (2015). Spillovers and euroscepticism. ECB Working Paper Series, No 1815/June.

Katsikas, D. (2017). *Public opinion in the Eurozone before and after the crisis:Core vs periphery; Based on an analysis of Eurobarometer surveys. Presentation at the International Seminar, Crises and Institutions in Latin America and Europe, October 17.* Brazil: University of São Paulo.

Nancy, J. (2016). Major changes in European public opinion regarding the European Union. Exploratory study, European Parliament Research Service. https://www.europarl.europa.eu/at-your-service/files/be-heard/eurobarometer/2016/major-changes-in-european-public-opinion-2016/report/en-report-exploratory-study-201611.pdf. Accessed 30 Oct 2019.

Roth, F., Jonung, L., & Nowak-Lehmann, D. F. (2016). Crisis and public support for the Euro, 1990–2014. *Journal of Common Market Studies, 54*(4), 944–960.

Serricchio, F., Tsakatika, M., & Quaglia, L. (2013). Euroscepticism and the global financial crisis. *Journal of Common Market Studies, 51*(1), 51–64.

Taggart, P. (1998). A touchstone of dissent: Euroscepticism in contemporary Western European party systems. *European Journal of Political Research, 33*(3), 363–388.

Van der Eijk, C., & Franklin, M. N. (2004). Potential for contestation on European matters at National Elections in Europe. In G. Marks & M. R. Steenbergen (Eds.), *European integration and political conflict*. Cambridge: Cambridge University Press.

17

Waves of Populism and Systemic Factors

Carolina Salgado and Paula Sandrin

Abstract This chapter gives a brief historical account of previous and current waves of populism in Latin America and their intermeshing with systemic factors, and discusses the historical relationship between populism, democracy and neoliberalism, giving particular focus to Bolivia, Chile and Brazil.

Introduction

A quick glance at Latin America's current political landscape could give us the impression that the "pink tide" of left-wing governments of the early twenty-first century, which brought to power Hugo Chávez in Venezuela, Evo Morales in Bolivia, Rafael Correa in Ecuador, Daniel Ortega in Nicaragua and Luís Inácio Lula da Silva in Brazil, has reached its limits, and the region is now experiencing a "turn to the right" evidenced by the election of Chile's Sebastián Piñera in 2017, Colombia's Iván Duque in 2018 and, most infamously, Brazil's Jair Bolsonaro, also in 2018. The ousting of Bolivia's Evo Morales could be read as the clearest signal of the pink tide's evanescence. Similar to the election of Donald Trump in the United States and the growth of the right-wing populism in Europe, Latin America would be experiencing a surge in support for right-wing populist parties and movements.

Notwithstanding such picture of the last round of Presidential elections, in this chapter, we argue that one cannot homogenize the turn to the right in Latin America. In order to develop the argument, theoretically and empirically, the chapter is divided in two parts: in the first part, we give a brief historical account of previous and current waves of populism in the region and their intermeshing with systemic factors, and discuss the historical relationship between populism, democracy and neoliberalism in the region, giving particular focus to the current political landscapes of Bolivia and Chile. In the second part, we explore the conditions of possibility of the extreme right's operationalization of political power in Latin America,

C. Salgado (✉) · P. Sandrin
Pontifical Catholic University of Rio de Janeiro (PUC-Rio), Rio de Janeiro, Brazil

drawing on Brazil as a case study. Through the distinction between access and exercise of power, we look at how the extreme right in Brazil managed to gather the necessary popular support to come to power, how it has been exercising power for the first year of Bolsonaro's term and outline why his government cannot be described as another version of right-wing populism.

Before we proceed, it is important to clarify the concept of populism we are using, since i. the term can acquire quite different meanings depending on context, political orientation and theoretical affiliation, and ii. a clarification is important for differentiating populism from extremism. For example, in Europe, the word populism seems to bring to mind nativism and xenophobia, whereas in Latin America, the word is more usually associated with clientelism and economic mismanagement (Mudde & Kaltwasser 2017:2). Indeed, two key features of populist discourses, "regardless of [their] specific political orientation, [are] the central role of the reference to the signifier 'the people' and its opposition to the dominant ideology" (Stavrakakis 2014:505). The framing of the political debate is dichotomous. Thus, the two operational criteria or discursive conditions necessary to identify a party or a movement as populist are the prominence of (or the privileged position occupied by) the core signifier "the people", around which other signifiers are articulated; and the division of the socio-political field between two opposing groups: the people and the elite (Stavrakakis 2017:4).

Populism, Democracy and Neoliberalism in Latin America: A Brief History

When discussing Latin America's history of populism, it is common to discern three waves of the phenomenon (Kaltwasser 2014a; Kaltwasser 2014b; Mudde & Kaltwasser 2017). The first, between the 1940s and 1960s, saw populist leaders taking office in Argentina (Juan Domingo Perón), Brazil (Getúlio Vargas) and Ecuador (Jose María Velasco Ibarra). In an era marked by migration to urban areas and industrialization, these leaders implemented social programs and corporatist projects designed to incorporate previously marginalized segments of the population into the citizenry. During this first wave, the state was expanded, the economy was partially nationalized and protectionist trade policies were implemented. In this context, "the people" was often depicted as a "virtuous and mestizo community composed essentially of peasants and workers, but not of inhabitants of indigenous and African descent" and "the elite" as "an oligarchy which, due to its alliance with foreign imperialist forces, was not qualified for promoting national sovereignty" (Kaltwasser 2014a:5). This first wave came to a halt with the military regimes of the 1960s and 1970s.

The second wave of populism, characterized by the support for neoliberal ideology and policies, began in the early 1990s and had as figureheads Carlos Menem in Argentina (1989–1999), Fernando Collor de Mello in Brazil (1990–1992) and

Alberto Fujimori in Peru (1990–2000). In a context marked by, on the one hand, Latin America's 1980s' debt crisis and hyperinflation, and, on the other hand, the end of the Cold War, transition to democracy and the Washington Consensus (on the merits of privatization, deregulation, liberalization and fiscal discipline), these leaders reproduced the consensual mantra of the time, that is, that liberal democracy and market economy were the only viable political and economic models. "The elite" was equated with defenders and supposed benefiters of state-led development, deemed responsible for catastrophic economic management, whereas "the people" were seen as "a passive mass of individuals whose ideas and interests could be inferred by employing opinion polls" (Kaltwasser 2014a:5).

These leaders presented themselves as political outsiders, forged alliances with business communities and had the support of foreign and domestic groups for the implementation of neoliberal reforms (Kaltwasser 2014b:159). At first, these leaders were able to garner popular support by solving problem of hyperinflation, restoring economic stability and effectively directing collective discontent with these countries' dire economic situation against political and state actors seen as the "establishment" (Kaltwasser 2014b:148). In addition, these second-wave populist actors appealed to the poor in the informal sectors, by promising to incorporate them into the market economy and by employing targeted spending programs (Kaltwasser 2014a:5). These free market policies, however, led to unemployment and a growth in inequality, generating further discontent and paving the way for the third wave of populism in Latin America.

The pink-tide governments in Latin America in the early twenty-first century, particularly those of Venezuela, Bolivia and Ecuador, presented "the people" as "all those who are excluded and discriminated against (such as indigenous groups and impoverished sectors)" and "the elite" as "as the defenders of neoliberalism and the political actors who support a Western model of democracy that is not suitable for Latin America" (Kaltwasser 2014a:6). By "Western model of democracy", these leaders meant deliberative and liberal conceptions of democracy, "in which citizens are treated as passive entities, mobilized periodically by elections, in which they do nothing more than select their representatives" (Mudde & Kaltwasser 2017:17), while they favored majoritarian and participatory conceptions of democracy (Kaltwasser 2014a:7). In this sense, they presented their populist platforms as democratic forces which, by mobilizing, giving voice, representing, incorporating and integrating excluded sections of society, increased democratic accountability and contributed to a more inclusive political system (Mudde & Kaltwasser 2017:83).

These left-of-center governments, as well as governments of other political orientations in Latin America during the first decade of this century, benefited greatly from the global natural resource boom caused by China's economic growth. As global suppliers of agrarian and mineral commodities, Colombia, Venezuela, Ecuador and Mexico reaped material benefits from growing Chinese demand as oil exporters; Chile and Peru as copper exporters; and Brazil and Argentina as iron ore and soybeans exporters (Kaltwasser 2014b:160).

Although presenting themselves as critics of neoliberalism and imperialism, pink-tide leaders did not differ from their neoliberal counterparts in Peru and

Colombia when it came to mining, oil and industrial agriculture, a contradiction that led to former Ecuadorian Minister of Energy and Mines, Alberto Acosta, to claim that Correa's government had "replaced Uncle Sam with Uncle Chen", relying on China "to sustain social programs and political position at the expense of real development" (Zaitchik 2019). In fact, the exploitation of natural resources led to disputes between populist leaders and indigenous communities they claimed to represent and include, particularly in Ecuador and Bolivia.

In spite of the social and environmental effects of these development projects based on the export of raw materials and commodities, socio-economic indicators improved during the boom years as a result of redistribution policies: between 2002 and 2012, some 70 million people were lifted out of poverty, according to the United Nations Economic Commission for Latin America and the Caribbean (ECLAC). Greater access to consumption and employment maintained support for these governments while the bonanza lasted. The Global Financial Crisis of 2008 began to have impact on Latin America a few years later, through the collapse of natural resources' prices. Growth slowed and many of those who had been lifted out of poverty saw the erosion of their gains.

This frustration and discontent eroded the support for pink-tide governments and, from 2015 onward, conservative politicians espousing a neoliberal ideology acceded to power once again in many Latin America countries: Mauricio Macri in Argentina in 2015, Michel Temer in Brazil in 2016, Sebastián Piñera in Chile in 2017 and Ivan Duque in Colombia in 2018. The election of Jair Bolsonaro in Brazil in 2018 and the ousting of President Morales in Bolivia in 2019 would signal the move toward the far right of the political spectrum, bringing a combination of neoliberal economic policies and more authoritarian and repressive forms of political rule.

Our argument in this chapter is that, although we can discern a growing support for far-right, anti-democratic currents in Latin America, these currents seem stronger only in a handful of countries (Brazil and Bolivia, in particular). In other places, the picture is more mixed, as the victory of leftist Andrés Manuel López Obrador in Mexico's 2018 presidential elections, the electoral defeat of center-right Mauricio Macri in Argentina to Alberto Fernández, from the left-wing faction of the Justicialist Party in 2019, and protests against the center-right government of Sebastián Piñera in Chile in 2019 testify. In order to clarify this complex political landscape, we propose now to analyze, in the next section, the cases of Bolivia and Chile and, in the following one, the case of Brazil in more detail, for the latter seems to be the extremist outlier in the region.

The Contradictory Cases of Mass Protests in Bolivia and Chile

The 2019 mass protests in Bolivia and Chile appeared to signal opposing tendencies in the region. In Bolivia, mass protests led to the downfall of one of the most prominent opponents of neoliberalism in Latin America, whereas in Chile, the protests indicated a general discontent with neoliberal policies implemented by center-rightist President Sebastián Piñera and some of his predecessors. Hence, governments from opposing ends of the political spectrum faced popular unrest.

Evo Morales' 14-year presidency collapsed amid accusations of election fraud and the President's disrespect for the 2016 constitutional referendum, in which the majority of the population voted for presidential term limits. Violent confrontations ensue between his supporters, who praised Morales for the reduction of poverty and inequality and the political and socio-economic inclusion of indigenous groups, and his opponents, who claim to be defending liberal democracy and fundamental freedoms. Hence, in the Bolivian case, different conceptions of democracy were at loggerheads.

It is important to note that those opposed to Morales included right-wing conservative politicians (such as interim President Jeanine Anez), part of the business community, urban unions, middle-class professional organizations, students and environmentalists (Iamamoto 2019). Therefore, even though his opposition indeed included right-wing groups, it also included sectors identified with the Left who distanced themselves from Morales due to his disrespect for the popular vote and his extractivist development model. In fact, some indigenous groups, whose socio-political marginalization and impoverishment were abated during Morales's term, had been criticizing and opposing Morales' extractivist policies and their socio-environmental impacts on their traditional modes of living since at least 2011. In that year, lowlands' indigenous groups organized a series of demonstrations to oppose the construction of a highway passing through a national park and indigenous ancestral territory (Iamamoto 2019).

If Bolivia in the 2010s was a "poster child" of pink-tide opposition to neoliberalism, Chile has long been considered a model of political stability and pro-market policies in Latin America, being lauded by conservative politicians such as Argentina's Mauricio Macri and Brazil's Jair Bolsonaro as an example to be followed. The country has been praised for its "responsible" monetary and fiscal policies, the strength of its financial and banking sectors, its economic growth and high-performing stock market, as well as for being one of the world's most open economies (Kowalczyk 2019).

Even Concertación and Nueva Mayoría, the center-left coalition that governed Chile for most of the post-dictatorship period (1990–2009; 2014–17), followed the general guidelines of the free market economic model, in spite of the implementation of gradual reforms aimed at alleviating the consequences of the economic model inherited from the Pinochet dictatorship (Meléndez & Kaltwasser 2017:524–525). During the periods governed by the center-left coalition, households in extreme poverty declined from 10.6% to 3% and those in poverty from 22.7 to 6.2. In addition, the coalition managed to slightly reduce the country's inequality, which had risen sharply during the Pinochet dictatorship (1973–1989) (Kowalczyk 2019).

Supporters of Chile's neoliberal model often point out to the extraordinary period of economic growth experienced by the country—between 1990 and 2019, Chile suffered only 2 years of recession; the 21% growth in average real income between

2000 and 2018; and the "very respectable" 65% increase in the real minimum wage over the same period (Saldías 2019) as proof that neoliberal policies can also generate inclusiveness.

Although incomes have risen, one of the highest inequality coefficients in the world has made Chile one of the most expensive countries of Latin America. Higher costs of living coupled with low social spending and the privatization of water and social services (including education, health care, transportation and pensions) have led to long working hours, lack of affordable social services and security, low pensions and growing household debts (Kowalczyk 2019). The downside of free-market policies has meant stress and desperation for most Chileans. While Chile's protests erupted as an immediate response to a raise in the Santiago Metro's subway fare and increased due to the government's use of disproportional police violence, they also signaled widespread dissatisfaction with the high cost of living, growing indebtedness, privatization and inequality brought about the neoliberal economic model.

With these two contradictory cases of mass protests as reactions to neoliberal policies enforced by populist governments in mind, the next section analyzes the case that can be considered the region's outlier. Because of its distance from the concept of populism we are employing in this chapter, and its subsequent closeness to right-wing extremism, we address the current political scenario of Brazil through a theoretical framework that distinguishes the access to from the exercise of political power.

Understanding Right-Wing Extremism Through the Access and Exercise of Political Power

This section brings about a twofold argument: Bolsonaro's government constitutes a right-wing or conservative strand of extremism, produced by an alliance between upper classes' neoliberal leanings, evangelical social conservatism and military authoritarianism (Goldstein 2019:258), which has an anti-democratic character, being more a child of right-wing dictatorships of the 1960–1980s than previous waves of populism in the region surveyed in the previous section. In this sense, we argue that Bolsonaro's far-right government is an outlier in the region and is not representative of a broader right-wing populist current in Latin America. In this section, we outline why this is so, exploring how the extreme right in Brazil operationalized such alliance in order to gather the necessary popular support to come to power and how it has been exercising power for the first year of term.

In Latin America, we have a shortage of studies within social and political sciences about the strategies and mechanisms of the extreme right. According to several analyses mainly concerning phenomena from the twentieth-century Europe like Fascism, Nazism, extremism, radicalism, totalitarianism and authoritarianism (Adorno 1951; Arendt 1951; Lipset & Raab 1978; Chomsky & Herman 1979; Bobbio 1996; Paxton 2004), the extreme right differs from the right-wing populism in at least one crucial, structural dimension: the ultimate refusal of democracy. In his chapter about the distinction between extremists and moderates, Bobbio says that:

> "it is hardly surprising that extremists of both the left and the right despise democracy for the virtues it fosters and requires for its survival. Their terminology agrees in defining 'mediocracy', meaning government both by the middle classes and by mediocrities. Democratic mediocrity was a typically Fascist theme, but it can be found in revolutionary radicalism of any form" (1996:25).

In line with such reasoning, the German political scientist Uwe Backes affirms that:

> "extremism thus aims at *"monism" and "monocracy"* in the sense of the enforcement of a bundled claim to power which – if at all possible – eliminates any competition, does not tolerate variety and opposition, seeks to render it harmless at the very least, stops political change, obstructs and suppresses the autonomous commitment of groups and individuals at least when this stands in the way of the ambitions of the rulers" (2004:249).

Significantly, these analyses present reasoning that account for the wave of right-wing dictatorships in Latin America between the 1960s and 1980s, and it is beyond the present scope to deepen the discussion of the left/right variants of extremism, conceived by Bobbio as antithetical terms. However, it seems useful for the present argument to inquire, at first: looking at the Brazilian 2018 presidential election, can we place Jair Bolsonaro at the extreme right of the political spectrum, and if so, on which bases? Secondly, looking at the first year of his mandate, can we say that Bolsonaro's government is extremist, and if so, what does it imply?

These questions shed light on an important aspect already identified as such in recent literature on the impact of the right on Latin American democracy: "on the one hand, the stabilization of democratic *access* to political power, and on the other hand, the development of institutions that seek to democratize the *exercise* of political power" (Luna & Kaltwasser 2014:16; Mazzuca 2010). The research agenda on the exercise of political power originates from the theoretical framework of Guillermo O'Donnell et al. (2004) entitled the quality of democracy, which expands Robert Dahl's definition of polyarchy (1971) toward a distinction between democratic *regime* and democratic *state*, and has been proved useful to better access the democratization processes in Latin America from the 1980s.

Whereas the Brazilian 2018 presidential election has developed within democratic rules, it seems that current interpretations about the first year of Bolsonaro's mandate that emphasize its anti-democratic character (Ballestrin 2019; Brum 2019; Chauí 2019; Goldstein 2019) are looking at the means to exercise political power. Then, to assume Brazil as an anti-democratic state is a natural development of a patrimonialist status of the current administration, embracing Mazzuca framework about the exercise of political power that says:

> "The qualitative component of the administration is the specific mechanism or set of mechanisms by which state resources are transformed into goods and distributed. Within a given state, these mechanisms may vary across sections of the territory, social groups, and policy realms, but a key distinction is whether goods and services are provided according to universal/general standards, like merit and need, or particularistic decisions based on personal connections and the ruler's discretion. Particularistic criteria are naturally associated with

> the portion of state resources that is appropriated by the rulers. (...) Following Weber again, extreme forms of appropriation and particularism in the exercise of state power define the patrimonial type of administration, or patrimonialism" (2010:343).

In those interpretations, we find terms such as post-democracy (Crouch 2004), de-democratization and democracy without demos (Rancière 2010) to set some sort of connections between the global phenomena of the far-right's rise in an attempt to derive a spatio-temporal understanding for the current political scenario of Brazil. They advance relevant features of the present generation of right-wing extremists, such as: to play on popular fear and ethnic tensions (Barber 2019); ideological polarization on topics like abortion, gender or immigration; cultural and artistic censorship; rejection to secular humanism or anti-intellectualism (Bobbio 1996:23); "monitory democracy" (Keane 2009; Stavrakakis 2016); "moralization of politics" (Rubim 2009); and anti-pluralism and tribalism (Galston 2018:106).

By contrast, we propose a reflection alternative to the debate around democracy and (anti)democratic means. Certainly, Brazilians have been experiencing a harsh cutback in the quality of democracy since January 2019 but, at the same time, we argue that so far it is not in the interest of upper economic classes to undertake regime change. Therefore, the proposal consists in switching the focus from political to psychological conditions of access and exercise of power resorted by Bolsonaro and his class coalition. The essence of their acts and discourses mainly propagated through social media consists in manipulating fearfulness, risk and threats in a way that directly hits the psychological structure precisely of the poor people. We call *the politics of social antagonism* (Nunes 2019) the whole project that has been undertaken in Brazil at least since September 2018, which will be further explored in the case study.

The Politics of Social Antagonism in Brazil

As analyzed in details in Chap. 12 in this volume by Guilherme and Ribeiro Hoffmann, Rousseff's impeachment, in August 2016, delimited the turn to the right through Michel Temer's neoliberal economic agenda and insensitivity to social issues. We see a clear distinction between Temer political personality and the overall agenda of his term, and Jair Bolsonaro exercise of political power. Therefore, accounting for what we call *the politics of social antagonism*, we look at the bases for Bolsonaro election and the means for governing over 2019.

Right-wing extremism is ostensibly related to anti-democracy for those reasons that have to do with the history of Europe during the 1930s. However, another crucial aspect to identify in right-wing extremism is the leadership rhetoric before coming to power. By the beginning of the presidential campaign, Bolsonaro had around 12% of voting intentions: how did he and his class coalition manage to get the necessary support of the mass to win the pool? It is important to bear in mind the evolving atmosphere of political, social and economic convulsion in Brazil since at least June 2013. Then, although being a phenomenon without a consensual day zero, "bolsonarism" is one among manifold causes and circumstances for the electoral victory. For this reason, we focus on the project of a given class coalition that is bigger than "bolsonarism" and Bolsonaro himself (Nunes 2019).

We argued that a radical triangle of fearfulness, risk and threats was manipulated through discourses of "lives are risky, caution is warranted", "the world is a dangerous place, we have terrorist threats, criminal violence, illness, immigration", and "the only source of reliable aid and support in difficult times is our own family. We must respect our elders´ religious and beliefs" (Barber 2019). Such existential insecurities that emerge in liberal democratic regimes, which "rest on a philosophy of individual freedom (...) can also induce people to seek psychic security through submission to external authority" (Galston 2018:108). Bolsonaro was named by a coalition consisted of landowners, military, Evangelicals and upper economic classes as the one with answers to wide existential insecurities—simple answers, like punishment, penalties, prison, gun bearing, reduction of criminal age, imposition of conservative values through censorship in culture and education and, above all, the suppression of minorities considered the opponents of the "traditional society" within an era of deteriorating conditions of social reproduction.

These conditions are the outcome of a triple crisis that Western liberal democracies are experiencing, gradually, since the 1980s, which are intrinsically connected with each other: financial, environmental and of representativeness. As explored in details in many chapters of this volume, the financial crisis of 2008 has highly contributed for the far-right pattern of "repressive egalitarianism", an expression coined by Theodor Adorno in 1951.[1] In Latin America, a continent with sharp inequalities, the repressive egalitarianism translates into both a reactionary politics of recognition and a regressive politics of redistribution (Nunes 2019).

The first is implemented through the suppression of minority rights, which were acquired by means of inclusion and meritocracy policies, undermining precisely such progressive feature of neoliberalism (Nunes 2019). The second is confirmed by the fact that Bolsonaro and his Minister of Economy, Paulo Guedes, have never proposed a structural change. Rather, they aim to preserve and expand the free market economy on the basis of attracting foreign capital in strategic sectors, deregulating labor relations, privatizing strategic and non-strategic state-owned companies, and putting regulatory agencies at the service of the free market.

Overall, in 2019, Brazilians saw several demonstrations of extremism in politics, economy, culture and public security "on behalf of the real yearnings of the conservative people in Brazil and other countries of Latin America" to recover the "traditional order", which is based on "the principles of God, homeland, family, property, individual freedom, and the right to self-defense", according to *Carta de Foz*, the final document launched in the occasion of the first Conservative Summit in the

[1] The logic of repressive egalitarianism, according to him, is when fascists "emphasize their being different from the outsider but play down such differences within their own group and tend to level out distinctive qualities among themselves with the exception of the hierarchical one" (Adorno 1991:146).

Americas, an event designed by the Bolsonaro family and their political party (PFL), held in Foz do Iguaçu on eighth December 2018.

The conservative yearnings, then, have materialized, for instance, through the censorship (resource cuts via public notices and show cancellations) of national agencies like ANCINE and FUNARTE to movies and performances with gender and LGBT themes,[2] the extinction of the Ministry of Culture,[3] prohibitions in the Book Biennial,[4] the attack to the feminist philosopher Judith Butler in São Paulo,[5] the proliferation of attacks on African-based religions,[6] and the deep funding cut of the public universities.[7] In parallel, the sustained version of neoliberalism is, according to Marilena Chauí, the new totalitarianism, in which "the society becomes the mirror for the State, defining all social and political spheres not only as organizations, but taking the market as a central reference, as a specific type of organization: *the company*" (2019).[8]

The conditions of possibility for the operationalization of political power by the extreme right in Latin America, such as those entrusted by Bolsonaro, can be clearly seen in Latinobarometer 2018, closing the crisis circle with the aspect of representativeness:

---

[2] https://www.nexojornal.com.br/expresso/2019/10/05/A-sombra-da-censura-nas-a%C3%A7%C3%B5es-do-governo-na-%C3%A1rea-cultural.

[3] https://blogs.oglobo.globo.com/afonso-borges/post/e-assim-em-janeiro-de-2019-foi-extinto-o-ministerio-da-cultura.html.

[4] https://g1.globo.com/rj/rio-de-janeiro/noticia/2019/09/08/autores-e-editores-fazem-manifesto-contra-censura-na-bienal-do-livro-do-rio.ghtml; https://www.nexojornal.com.br/expresso/2019/09/06/O-que-h%C3%A1-de-ilegal-na-censura-de-Crivella-na-Bienal-do-Rio.

[5] https://www1.folha.uol.com.br/ilustrissima/2017/11/1936103-judith-butler-escreve-sobre-o-fantasma-do-genero-e-o-ataque-sofrido-no-brasil.shtml; https://epoca.globo.com/cultura/noticia/2017/11/filosofa-judith-butler-e-agredida-em-congonhas-antes-de-deixar-sao-paulo.html.

[6] https://www1.folha.uol.com.br/ilustrissima/2019/09/relatos-apontam-proliferacao-de-ataques-as-religioes-afro-brasileiras.shtml; https://oglobo.globo.com/sociedade/denuncias-de-ataques-religioes-de-matriz-africana-sobem-47-no-pais-23400711.

[7] https://www.correiobraziliense.com.br/app/noticia/politica/2019/05/01/interna_politica,752508/corte-geral-de-30-nos-orcamentos-das-universidades-federais.shtml.

[8] It is worth mentioning that the market is also the engine of Bolsonaro's policies that affect the environment. Notwithstanding we affirm that left and right do not differ much in relation to the exploitation of natural resources (see page 4), in 2019, Brazilians witnessed an exacerbation of skepticism about climate change. While the "Green Economy" is growing worldwide, the Bolsonaro government was responsible for several square kilometers of fire in the Amazon. Discussions and accusations took place between scientists and the Minister of the Environment, Ricardo Salles, culminating in the exoneration of the former director of the National Institute for Space Research (Inpe), Ricardo Galvão. For more information, see: https://g1.globo.com/natureza/noticia/2019/08/11/nos-usamos-publicacao-cientifica-nao-balela-diz-ex-diretor-do-inpe-a-ministro-do-meio-ambiente.ghtml.

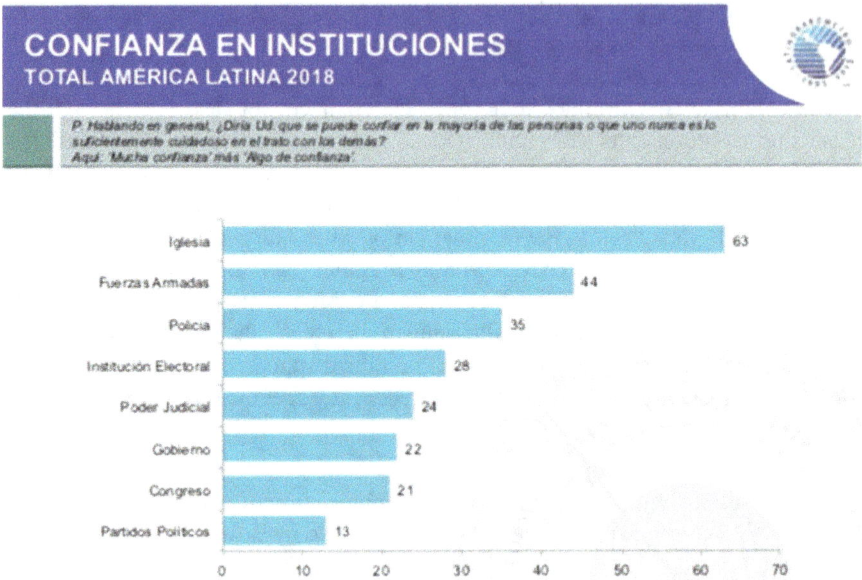

SOURCE: http://www.latinobarometro.org/lat.jsp

Among these eight institutions and the 18 countries surveyed, Brazilian respondents ranked the country in fifth place in trust in the Church[9] and third in trust in the Army. By contrast, they ranked Brazil in 16th position in confidence in Congress and the last position (along with El Salvador) in confidence in political parties. Marta Lagos, the Director of Latinobarometer in Chile, analyzed: "The fragmentation of the party system speaks of a high rate of leadership expiration and the emergence of new figures that increasingly represent small groups of citizens. (…) The second dimension is the elites. Corruption has deeply penetrated presidents, parliaments, members of the executive branch in many countries, undermining the image of democracy, confusing the population. A corrupt regime cannot be a democracy" (2018:5–6).

[9] There is a huge debate in Brazil with regard to the turning to politics of certain religious groups, as well as their power of influence and electoral decision. Notably, the Evangelical Neopentecostals, represented by the *Igreja Universal do Reino de Deus* and *Assembleia de Deus*, drove the growth of around 10% in the number of elected parliamentarians in 2018. For more information, see: http://agenciabrasil.ebc.com.br/politica/noticia/2018-10/em-crescimento-bancada-evangelica-tera-91-parlamentares-no-congresso; https://www.nexojornal.com.br/expresso/2019/07/13/O-fortalecimento-evang%C3%A9lico-no-Brasil-e-na-Am%C3%A9rica-Latina.

Conclusion

In this chapter, we advanced the argument that the turn to the right in Latin America mirrors, in some respects, global trends, although it is far from uniform, being stronger in some countries more than others. In a region known for a rich tradition of populist governments and movements, of both left and right variants, we argue that it is important to take into account systemic factors which have impacted on the region as a whole (such as Global Financial Crisis of 2008, commodities' prices boom and bust) and their differential political effects, while not losing sight of local specificities.

In our view, the three case studies, Bolivia, Chile and Brazil, allow us to see clearly the multiplicity of political struggles taking place in the region, since they concern the deposition of a left-wing populist leader (Bolivia), protests against a right-wing conservative government (Chile) and the election of a right-wing extremist (Brazil), all taking place within a year. We addressed a particular understanding that populists, left-wing or right-wing, in Europe or Latin America, mobilize the term "the people" in a variety of ways, delimiting the boundaries of who the people are, who is in and who is out (Fitzi et al. 2019). Populists say they represent "the people" (in Latin America, "el pueblo"/"o povo") against others, be they corrupt elites, transnational corporations, international finance institutions, globalists, leftists, migrants, refugees and so on.

Nonetheless, the question of why the poor vote for the right is not new, albeit still complex, for academic researchers within social and political sciences (Frank 2007; Huber & Stanig 2009; Suryanarayan 2019; Galston 2018). The majority of studies highlight strategies of conservative political parties, as well as non-electoral means of the right to broaden its influence and increase its scope of political action (Domínguez 1997; Middlebrook 2000; Payne 2000; Eaton 2011; Luna & Kaltwasser 2014). A mix of neoliberal ideology of individualism, competitiveness and personal responsibility, and evangelical social conservatism at the structural level have been generating support among the middle and lower classes in those three countries for less state intervention in the economy, more violent and punitive measures to maintain law and order, and freedom of speech to manifest racist, homophobic and sexist positions.

Against this background, we raised the questions of what identifies right-wing extremism as such, and how a move toward the far right could have taken place in Brazil. We drew on a theoretical framework that distinguishes the access to from the exercise of political power, and we claimed that more attention should be given to psychological rather than just to political conditions for the establishment of a far-right government. Applying the theoretical framework, we called the politics of social antagonism the project that encompasses a class coalition strategy to come to power, and the following measures to implement its economic, political, cultural and security agendas.

References

Adorno, T. (1951). Freudian theory and the pattern of fascist propaganda. http://www.freudians.org/wp-content/uploads/2014/09/Adorno_Freudian_Theory_Pattern_Fascist_Propaganda.pdf. Accessed on 10 Jan 2020.

Adorno, T. (1991). In J. M. Bernstein (Ed.), *The culture industry: Selected essays on mass culture*. Abingdon: Routledge.

Arendt, H. (1951). *As origens do totalitarismo*. São Paulo: Companhia das Letras.

Backes, U. (2004). *Meaning and forms of political extremism in past and present*. http://www.cepsr.com/dwnld/backesx20040401.pdf. Accessed on 10 Jan 2020.

Ballestrin, L. (2019). *Pós-democracias no sul global e a melancólica desdemocratização no Brasil contemporâneo*. https://jornalggn.com.br/artigos/pos-democracias-no-sul-global-e-a-melancolica-desdemocratizacao-no-brasil-contemporaneo-por-luciana-ballestrin/. Accessed on: 03 Jan 2020.

Barber, N. (2019). *Why do some poor people vote against their interests? If head and hearts are at odds, emotion often wins out*. https://www.psychologytoday.com/us/blog/the-human-beast/201903/why-do-some-poor-people-vote-against-their-interests. Accessed on: 15 Jan 2020.

Brum, E. (2019). *Doente de Brasil*. https://brasil.elpais.com/brasil/2019/08/01/opinion/1564661044_448590.html. Accessed on: 01 Sept 2019.

Bobbio, N. (1996). *Left and right. The significance of a political distinction*. Chicago: The University of Chicago Press.

Chauí, M. (2019). *O que é a nova ultradireita?* https://outraspalavras.net/outrasmidias/marilena-chaui-o-que-e-a-nova-ultradireita/. Accessed on: 03 Jan 2020.

Chomsky, N., & Herman, E. (1979). *The Nazi Parallel*. https://chomsky.info/washington03/. Accessed on: 15 Jan 2020.

Crouch, C. (2004). *Post-democracy*. Cambridge: Polity Press.

Dahl, R. (1971). *Polyarchy: Participation and opposition*. New Haven: Yale University Press.

Domínguez, J. I. (1997). *Technopols, freeing politics and Markets in Latin America in the 1990s*. Pennsylvania State University Press.

Eaton, K. (2011). Conservative autonomy movements: Territorial dimensions of ideological conflict in Bolivia and Ecuador. *Comparative Politics, 43*(3), 291–310.

Fitzi, G., Mackert, J., & Turner, B. (Eds.). (2019). *Populism and the crisis of democracy, Vol.II Politics, Social Movements, and Extremism*. London: Routledge.

Frank, T. (2007). *What's the matter with Kansas? How conservatives won the heart of America*. Palgrave Macmillan.

Galston, W. (2018). *Anti-pluralism. The populist threat to liberal democracy*. New Haven: Yale University Press.

Goldstein, A. A. (2019). The new far-right in Brazil and the construction of a right-wing order. *Latin American Perspectives, 46*(4), 245–262.

Huber, J. D., Stanig, P. (2009). *Why do the poor support right-wing parties? A cross-national analysis*. Prepared for the RSF Inequality Conference, UCLA, January 2007. http://leitner.yale.edu/sites/default/files/files/resources/docs/huber-stanig.pdf. Accessed 04 Mar 2020.

Iamamoto, S. (2019). Após eleição na Bolívia, campo e cidade se enfrentam com greves e bloqueios". https://blogdosakamoto.blogosfera.uol.com.br/2019/10/30/apos-eleicao-na-bolivia-campo-e-cidade-se-enfrentam-com-greves-e-bloqueios/. Accessed on 13 Jan 2020.

Lagos, M. (2018). El fin de la tercera ola de democracias. *Latinobarómetro*. http://www.justificando.com/2019/01/08/2018-ano-horrivel/. Accessed on: 15 Jan 2020.

Luna, J. P., & Kaltwasser, C. R. (2014). *The resilience of the Latin American right*. Baltimore: Johns Hopkins University Press.

Mudde, C., & Kaltwasser, C. R. (2017). *Populism: A very short introduction*. Oxford: Oxford University Press.

Nunes, R. (2019). *As origens do bolsonarismo*. https://www.youtube.com/watch?v=lWMb3W5_Puk&t=6363s. Accessed on: 10 Jan 2020.

Kaltwasser, C. R. (2014a). Latin American populism: Some conceptual and normative lessons. *Constellations*

Kaltwasser, C. R. (2014b). From right populism in the 1990s to left populism in the 2000s—And Back again? In J. P. Luna & C. R. Kaltwasser (Eds.), *The resilience of the Latin American right*. Baltimore: Johns Hopkins University Press.

Keane, J. (2009). *Monitory democracy and media-saturated societies*. http://www.johnkeane.net/wp-content/uploads/2009/01/Keane_griffith_review_ed24_monitory_democracy_media_saturised.pdf. Accessed on: 22 Jan 2020.

Kowalczyk, A. (2019). Neoliberalism created the crisis in Chile. *Jacobin*, 11 September 2019. https://www.jacobinmag.com/2019/11/neoliberalism-chile-uprising-austerity-protests-pinera. Accessed on: 22 Jan 2020.

Lipset, S., & Raab, E. (1978). *The politics of unreason: Right wing extremism in America, 1790–1977*. Chicago: University of Chicago Press.

Mazzuca, S. (2010). Access to power versus exercise of power reconceptualizing the quality of democracy in Latin America. *Studies in Comparative International Development, 45*, 334–357.

Meléndez, C., & Kaltwasser, C. R. (2017). Political identities: The missing link in the study of populism. *Party Politics, 25*(4), 520–533.

Middlebrook, K. (Org.) (2000). *Conservative parties, the right, and democracy in Latin America*. Baltimore: Johns Hopkins University Press.

O'Donnell, G., Vargas, C. J., & Iazzetta, O. M. (Eds.). (2004). *The quality of democracy. Theory and applications*. Notre Dame: University of Notre Dame Press.

Paxton, R. (2004). *The anatomy of fascism*. Penguin Books.

Payne (2000). "Uncivil Movements: The Armed Right Wing and Democracy in Latin America", by Leigh A. Payne. Baltimore, MD: Johns Hopkins University Press, 2000.

Rancière, J. (2010). *Dissensus. On politics and aesthetics*. New York: Continuum.

Rubim, A. (2009). Mídia, política e eleições de 2006, *Teoria e Debate* 69. https://teoriaedebate.org.br/2009/03/17/midia-politica-e-eleicoes-de-2006/. Accessed on: 17 Jan 2020.

Saldías, N. (2019). Chile's protests are a rejection of neoliberalism. *World Politics Review*, 04 November 2019. https://www.worldpoliticsreview.com/articles/28316/chile-s-protests-are-a-rejection-of-the-excesses-of-neoliberalism. Accessed on 22 Jan 2020.

Stavrakakis, Y. (2014). The Return of "the People": Populism and Anti-Populism in the Shadow of the European Crisis. Constellations, 21, 505–517. https://doi.org/10.1111/1467-8675.12127

Stavrakakis, Y. (2016). O triste espetáculo da "democracia sem demos. Yannis Stavrakakis, interviewed by Julia Goldenberg, on *Pagina12* | Translation: Inês Castilho. https://outraspalavras.net/sem-categoria/o-triste-espetaculo-da-democracia-sem-demos/. Accessed on: 05 Jan 2020.

Stavrakakis, Y. (2017). Discourse theory in populism research – three challenges and a dilemma. *Journal of Language and Politics, 16*(4), 523–534.

Suryanarayan, P. (2019). When do the poor vote for the right wing and why: Status hierarchy and vote choice in the Indian states. *Comparative Political Studies, 52*(2), 209–245.

Zaitchik, A. (2019). Under left- and right-wing leaders, the Amazon has burned. Can Latin America reject oil, ranching, and mining? *The Intercept*, 07 December 2019. https://theintercept.com/2019/12/07/amazon-latin-america-extractivism/. Accessed on: 21 Jan 2020.

18

Regional Organizations, Crisis and Latin American Regionalism

José Briceño-Ruiz and Andrea Ribeiro Hoffmann

Abstract This chapter analyses the crisis of Latin America regionalism focusing on the changes and continuities of regional organizations such as UNASUR, Mercosur, ALBA and Pacific Alliance and discusses future scenarios.

Introduction

The main objective of this chapter is to understand how the global crisis that started in 2008 in the USA and national crisis in countries such as Brazil and Venezuela have affected Latin American regionalism. The chapter also explores how Latin American regionalism could be reconfigured under the new conditions. The prevailing narrative about the impact of the crisis in Latin American regionalism is negative given the expected impact of the current trends on asymmetries among and within countries. The previous period of post-liberal and post-hegemonic regionalism, despite its fragilities, was one of diminishing poverty and inequalities, and increasing inclusion and participation of traditionally excluded sectors of the society in the political processes. The current turn to neoliberalism together with rise of democratic instability and extreme-right movements have not only uncovered the fragilities of the achievements of the last decade, but also put into question the strategies pursued by the previous governments, creating a paralysis, a vacuum of forward-looking alternatives.

In this chapter, we firstly assess the development of the Southern Common Market (Mercosur), the Union of South American Nations (UNASUR), The Bolivarian Alternative for the Peoples of the Americas (ALBA) and the Pacific

J. Briceño-Ruiz
National Autonomous University of México (UNAM), México City, Mexico
e-mail: bricenoruiz@unam.mx

A. Ribeiro Hoffmann (✉)
Pontifical Catholic University of Rio de Janeiro (PUC-Rio), Rio de Janeiro, Brazil

Coordinator of the second phase of the Jean Monnet Network "Crisis-Equity-Democracy for Europe and Latin America", Rio de Janeiro, Brazil
e-mail: a_ribeiro_hoffmann@puc-rio.br

Alliance during the last decade and how they have reacted and adapted differently to global and local level pressures. However, these organizations are also deeply intertwined, as they exist in a complex network of overlapping memberships and mandates, and therefore, we analyse these interconnections and common trends for Latin American regionalism as a whole in the last section of the chapter. We also reflect on the alternative future scenarios.

Mercosur: From Open Regionalism to Post-Liberal Regionalism and Back?

From the regional organizations analysed in this chapter, Mercosur is the only one that was created in the early 1990s, during the so-called second wave of regionalism. Its main objective, as stated in the constitutive Treaty of Asuncion, was to create a common market in order to accelerate economic development with social justice and achieve a better insertion in the global economy. Mercosur was conceived as part of a strategy of incorporation into the processes of globalization in line with the concept of open regionalism, as an intermediary stage for the expansion of domestic markets and internationalization of local firms, as well as a platform to negotiate the Free Trade Area of the Americas (FTAA) (Bianculli 2016). Other, implicit, objectives were to lock-in democracy and de-securitize relations after the end of the Cold War (Oelsner 2014).

For about a decade, Mercosur was considered successful in fulfilling these aims, until an economic crisis which led to the devaluation of Brazilian currency in 1999, and a generalized crisis in Argentina in 2001. Despite a brief period of 'soul searching' (Bouzas 2002) thereafter, Mercosur's project was renovated; its free-trade-oriented agenda was transformed, and a model of social development was implemented, in line with the centre-left leaning governments at the time. Over almost 30 years of existence, Mercosur promoted norms and regulations in several issue areas, with different record of success in terms of achieving agreements on common positions and implementation. Mercosur was considerably successful in promoting free mobility of goods and persons, health and education regulations, and human rights, for instance, but less successful in promoting the free mobility of services and capital, and the protection of democracy. It has not played an important role in security and defence, but, overall, Mercosur remained until recently a tacit agreement among its member-states governments and societies (Ribeiro Hoffmann 2020).

The declaration from Paulo Guedes, Minister of Economics of President Bolsonaro in Brazil criticizing Mercosur, has raised the suspicion about the fate of this organization.[1] The leadership, or at least strong support, of Brazil to Mercosur

[1] https://g1.globo.com/economia/noticia/2018/10/30/declaracoes-de-paulo-guedes-sobre-mercosul-surpreendem-membros-do-bloco.ghtml; https://g1.globo.com/economia/blog/joao-borges/post/2018/11/02/paulo-guedes-pretende-fortalecer-politica-de-comercio-exterior.ghtml.

is a key condition for its relevance as a regional organization in Latin America, even if Brazil cannot be defined as a regional hegemon in traditional terms, its size matters (Soares and Hirst 2006; Merke 2015). While other organizations in the region such as UNASUR include 'secondary powers' or 'middle powers' in addition to Argentina, such as Chile, Peru and Colombia (Ruvalcaba et al. 2016) that combined have leadership capacity to advance a common project, this is not the case of Mercosur. One way to analyse the impact of the crisis on Mercosur is, therefore, through the changes in Brazilian interests and foreign policy towards this organization.

Despite the traditional strength of the Brazilian Ministry of Foreign Affairs (Itamaraty), and its historical preference for continuity, Brazilian foreign policy has become more susceptible to changing governments during the last decade, with an increased role of presidents in the agenda setting, a phenomenon referred to as 'presidential diplomacy' (Burges and Chagas 2017, Malamud 2014). Brazil's activism in South America is strongly associated with the government of President Lula and his Foreign Ministry Celso Amorin, who advanced South–South relations at global level, and in South America, by strengthening of Mercosur and creating UNASUR, as will be discussed below. This activism declined under the government of President Dilma Rousseff and even further after her impeachment in 2016, as Mello (2018) summarizes:

> (…) since Rousseff's first administration (2011–2015), one could notice a continuous decline in Brazil's international image and projection, which had received a significant impulse during Lula da Silva's two mandates as president (2003–2010). Despite the fact that his successor preserved Lula's conceptual guidelines, foreign policy implementation progressively lost momentum and proactivity in the international front as well as centrality within the domestic political agenda. (…) The prolonged political crisis that led to the impeachment of President Dilma Rousseff in August of 2016, putting her vice-president Michel Temer at the head of the Executive, brought important repercussions for the conduction of Brazilian foreign policy. While still being sworn in as the interim minister of Foreign Relations, José Serra – a prominent politician connected to the opposition and former candidate in the presidential elections of 2002 and 2010 – pronounced a speech that seemed to indicate a profound reorientation in the strategies and priorities of Brazil's diplomacy (Mello 2018, p.1–2).

The new foreign policy orientation under President Temer included the alleged 'des-ideologization' of foreign policy (meaning the alignment of Party the Labour governments with other centre-left governments in the region); the promotion of free trade and the opening of markets for Brazilian exports; a strategic partnership with Argentina and efforts to revitalize and 'correct' Mercosur. Trade liberalization was a goal which meant a renewed relationship with traditional partners such as the USA and Europe; a focus on 'new partners' in Asia, particularly China and India; and a new approach to 'Modern Africa' focusing on commercial, investment and technology partnerships, correcting previous 'South-South strategy' (Mello 2018).

This new orientation, even if not abandoning Argentina, signalized a bilateralization of relations. The suspension of Venezuela from Mercosur and isolation of the country in other organizations, as discussed below for the case of UNASUR, reverted the previous approach of inducement change via engagement. Under

Bolsonaro's government, these trends were radicalized. His Minister of External Relations, Ernesto Araújo, equated 'globalism' and the 'global order' with socialism in his inauguration speech and criticized newspapers such as the *Foreign Affairs* and the *New York Times* as vehicles of this (undesired) global order. He also stated that despite being against 'globalism', Brazil is a universalist country that wants to build something 'good and productive' with each partner; among the partners he included Israel, USA, Latin-American countries 'which liberated themselves from the Foro de Sao Paulo', 'those who fight against tyranny in Venezuela', the 'new Italy', Hungary and Poland. As for the UN system, he proposes a reorientation to strengthen sovereignty instead of NGOs interests, and to revitalize trade negotiations.[2] Mercosur's future will depend on the reaction of its other member-states to this new situation, and the disposition to cooperate with a government which has a conservative socio-cultural platform, a discourse against human rights and the fight against climate change. The return of Kirchnerism to power in Argentina through Alberto Fernández in 2019 makes this scenario even more complicated due the deep ideological differences with Bolsonaro.

UNASUR: A Process in Deep Crisis

Despite the reiterated description in the media of UNASUR as a 'Chavist' or 'Bolivarian' initiative, the origins of UNASUR can in fact be traced back to the Brazilian project of creating a South American Free Trade Area that would be the result of the convergence between Mercosur and the Andean Community. This project was fostered by Minister Celso Amorim, during the government of President Itamar Franco, in 1994, in line with the '4 + 1' strategy advanced to negotiate the FTAA, that is, to engage with external markets from group positions and avoiding bilateral negotiations with the USA. Following President Fernando Henrique Cardoso convened, in 2000, a Summit of South American Head of States and Governments in Brasilia, in which he proposed the creation of a South American Community of Nations (SACN). This latter would be a minimalist project that aimed to promote a convergence between the Andean Community and Mercosur. The SACN also promoted cooperation in infrastructure, with the creation of the Initiative for the Integration of the Infrastructure of South America (known in Spanish as IIRSA), established South America as a zone of peace and combat cooperation to terrorism. This regional initiative was established in Cuzco, Peru, in December 2004 (Briceño-Ruiz, 2010).

However, with the election of left-wing governments in Argentina and Brazil, and the activism of Venezuelan foreign policy under Hugo Chávez, the scenario changed. Chávez rejected SACN for two reasons: firstly, he considered that a new South America bloc could not be the result of the convergence of the Andean

[2] http://www.itamaraty.gov.br/pt-BR/discursos-artigos-e-entrevistas-categoria/ministro-das-relacoes-exteriores-discursos/19907-discurso-do-ministro-ernesto-araujo-durante-cerimonia-de-posse-no-ministerio-das-relacoes-exteriores-brasilia-2-de-janeiro-de-2019

Community and Mercosur because of their underlying neoliberal principles. Secondly, he considered South America as a single nation, and not a 'community of nations'. This idea was accepted in a Summit of South American leaders held in Margarita Island, Venezuela, in 2007, and the denomination SACN was replaced for UNASUR, formally created in May 2008 (Briceño-Ruiz, 2010).

Despite the initial Brazilian influence, Venezuela and its ALBA allies (Bolivia and Ecuador), and to a lesser extent Argentina, played the main role in the transformation of the SACN into UNASUR. Other countries such as Peru and Chile were also important players. As Comini and Frenkel (2017, p. 189) argued, UNASUR was the minimum common denominator of two models: one giving priority to the international markets and the promotion of relations with the rest of the world, called by them 'polygamic'; and another privileging regional markets and further relations firstly with the neighbours and, after consolidating those relations, with the rest of the world, referred to as 'concentric circles'. Therefore, from a modest and minimalist project that aimed to achieve a limited number of goals, integration in South America became a maximalist scheme with multiple political, economic and social objectives. New institutions were created in order to exchange information and best practices and foster common approaches in a number of issue areas such as the 13 sectorial 'Councils', the most active being the South American Council of Defence and the South American Council for Health.

UNASUR was considerably successful in its early years. Firstly, it contributed to the resolution the domestic crises in Bolivia and Ecuador, and the conflict between Colombia, Ecuador and Venezuela in 2011. The South American Council of Defence (SACD) was perceived as an original regional space able to counterbalance the US influence in military affairs, including ambitious goals such as the creation of a South America School of Defence (Frenkel, 2016). After the demise of Inter-American Treaty of Defence (TIAR) in 1982, in the context of the Malvinas war, the Organization of Americas States (OAS) had lost its influence in the discussion of security and military affairs in the region. At least partially, the SADC was designed to fill the vacuum produced by the Malvinas War. UNASUR also advanced initiatives in the area of development and finance: the idea of creating a Bank of the South was part of a debate about a 'new financial architecture' for South America, able to mitigate the influence of International Monetary Fund in the region. IIRSA was perceived as a necessary instrument to improve the South American infrastructure and facilitate closer relations among the countries of the whole region (Palestini and Agostinis 2015). Cooperation in health became one of the most innovative in UNASUR (Ribeiro Hoffmann & Tabak 2016; Yeates & Riggirozzi 2017; Herrero & Loza 2018).

While UNASUR allowed a dialogue between governments with different ideologies and views on economic and social issues (Mace, 2018), government changes in countries such as Argentina and Brazil after 2015, and the domestic crisis in Venezuela evidenced the weakness and shortcomings of the organization. The crisis in Paraguay launched by the 'fast track' impeachment of President Fernando Lugo was the first main failure of UNASUR in its role as mediator. Contrary to the crisis in Bolivia and Ecuador, the constitutional order was not restored in Paraguay; President Rodriguez replaced Lugo, and even if Paraguay was suspended of

UNASUR, Asunción did not accept the regional intervention in the crisis. UNASUR also did not address the controversial impeachment of President Dilma Rousseff.

The case of Venezuela was even worst; this crisis was not only unsolved by UNASUR but triggered this bloc's decay. After the death of Chavez and contested elections in 2013, Venezuela entered in a spiral of conflict and violence. Manifestations in the streets demanded the end of Maduro's government in 2014. Led by the opposition leaders Leopoldo López, María Corina Machado and Antonio Ledezma, part of the Venezuelan opposition promoted *La Salida* (the exit) which meant the immediate resignation of the Maduro regime. The governmental response was military repression and the detention of Lopez accused of promoting violence and the death of 43 people. President Maduro initially accepted mediation by UNASUR, while rejecting the OAS, seen as dominated by US interests. Secretary General Ernesto Samper actively participated in the mediation efforts, but the political dialogue failed as Maduro's administration did not accept almost any of the opposition demands. In particular, the demand for a release of all political prisoners was rejected, and Lopez and Ledezma were both condemned to jail. Another attempt to mediate political dialogue in Dominican Republic in December 2017 was also unsuccessful. The failed UNASUR mediation transformed its image because the perception that it served the interest of the Venezuelan government increased.

Closa and Palestini (2015) argued that UNASUR was created to protect incumbent governments such as Morales, Correa and Lugo, and that the mechanism was never applied to a legitimate elected government that had decided to violate the democratic rules and practices, as was the case of Venezuela, or, one could add, Brazil under Bolsonaro. Riggirozzi and Grugel also noted that 'the fact that South American countries use UNASUR to defend democracy is not evidence...that UNASUR is part of a project of deep democratization or citizenship governance. UNASUR is willing to act to stop elected governments being overthrown, but it is not pushing for mechanisms to ensure citizen voice or representation' (Riggirozzi & Grugel 2015, p. 796). The modification of the institution of electoral observation at UNASUR and the creation of the concept of 'electoral following' (*acompañamiento electoral*), in which non-governmental organizations (NGOs) would observe the elections without elaborating reports about the quality of elections, were also signals of weakening democracy in the region (McConnel et al. 2015).

The political changes which took place after 2015 with the election of right-wing governments further weakened UNASUR. A key factor that deepened the crisis was the inability of member-states to appoint a new Secretary General in 2017. President Macri, who was holding the Pro tempore Presidency, proposed José Bordón, a known Argentinean diplomat, but he was rejected by Venezuela. As consensus is required to make decisions at UNASUR, the appointment of a new Secretary General was suspended, leading to further paralysis. Argentina, Brazil, Colombia, Chile, Paraguay and Peru suspended their participation in the meetings of UNASUR institutions in April 2018. Afterwards, Argentina, Brazil, Colombia, Ecuador and Peru withdrew from the organization. More recently, Chile and Colombia proposed the creation of a new organization to replace UNASUR, the Forum for the Progress of South America (PROSUR in Spanish), but it is too soon to include this organization in the analysis.

ALBA: When Domestic, Regional and Global Factors Matter

Closely related to Chávez and Venezuela, but also influenced by Cuba, ALBA was presented as an 'alternative model' of regional integration with some characteristics which differentiated it from other regional organizations: first, no geographical contiguity among its members; second, absence of free trade as a goal, instead, a narrative allegedly based on solidarity and 'concertation'; third, open intention of being a 'non-capitalist' model of regional integration; and four, emphasis on the role of society (the people) in the integration process.

Initially ALBA was a Venezuelan unilateral initiative, announced by Chávez in the Summit of Association of Caribbean States held in Margarita Island, in December 2001, aiming at presenting an alternative to the US proposal of the FTAA, more radical than the '4 + 1' strategy advanced by Brazil via Mercosur earlier. ALCA was the Spanish acronym for FTAA, and Chávez smartly opposed ALCA to ALBA, namely, the US interests to the Latin American ones. Norman Girvan summarized ALBA's goals:

Tariff protection for infant industries is allowed; public procurement as a tool of development is recognised; intellectual property rights are subordinated to the right to development and health; basic social services are, by implication, insulated from privatisation and commercialisation; special treatment for indigenous enterprises is assured there will be concessionary treatment of smaller and weaker economies; and the rights of labour and indigenous peoples are guaranteed (Girvan 2011, p. 164–165).

When Chávez met Fidel Castro in Havana, in December 2004, and ALBA became a bilateral initiative, opposition to ALCA was still the main (outward looking) goal; it did not have the clear-cut objectives in terms of projects to be implemented in the region beyond being linked by the Venezuelan government to the strategy of endogenous development furthered in those years by Chavez (Briceño-Ruiz 2011). The paradigmatic shift in ALBA took place after 2006, a year in which Chávez adopted the twenty-first century Socialism as the ideological fundament of the so-called Bolivarian Revolution. From that year onwards, the shape of ALBA as a project for the region gradually emerged.

In terms of member-states, ALBA was widened to include new countries led by left-wing governments such as Bolivia under Evo Morales, Nicaragua ruled by Daniel Ortega and Ecuador led by Rafael Correa. Later, eastern Caribbean Islands such as Dominica, Saint Vincent and Grenadines, Grenada, Saint Kitts and Nevis and Saint Lucia became ALBA's members. Even Honduras under the José Manuel Zelaya's government participated in the initiative. Thus, ALBA became the unique regional group in the continent that included Caribbean, Central American and South American members with no contiguity, but ideological similarity. In substantive terms, ALBA defined more clearly its activities. Initially, ALBA was centred on the Venezuelan–Cuban axis, and the initial strategy was to replicate at Latin American level what they were doing bilaterally. Thus, social programmes in the sectors of education and health, the 'Misiones', were incorporated into ALBA in order to be implemented in other Latin American and Caribbean countries. In 2006, Venezuela launched Petrocaribe, and Bolivia promoted the idea of the Peoples Trade Treaty (Tratado de Comercio de los Pueblos—TCP in Spanish) as an alternative to the free-trade agreements fostered in the framework of the open regionalism. In 2008, Ecuador proposed the Unitary System for the Regional compensation of Payments (known in Spanish as Sucre), and the proposal of creating Grand national projects and enterprises was announced. At the institutional level, despite being an intergovernmental organization, ALBA included a Social Movement Council, an innovation compared to other regional institutions where the social participation was included only as mechanisms of consultation (Muhr 2012).

These initiatives were initially successfully implemented led by Venezuela as a paymaster, favoured by the high prices of commodities, particularly, oil. Some Grand nationals were announced such as in the sector of medicaments. ALBA also played a political role, particularly in the crisis in Honduras in 2010 (De La Torre 2017) and, to a lesser extent, in Paraguay in 2013 after the coup d'état against Zelaya and Lugo. It also developed joint positions at global level, for example, in the United Nations Framework Convention on Climate Change's (UNFCCC) conference in Copenhagen in 2009 (Watts and Depledge 2018). ALBA became to be seen as an 'alternative model' of regional integration, as their political leaders argued; the literature refer to it as a model of counterhegemonic governance (Muhr 2012); a new strategic regionalism (Aponte García 2014), an alternative to general law of capitalist accumulation (Seabra and Gimenez 2014) or a manifestation of decolonial delinking (Al-Kassimi 2018). Under the leadership of Chávez, ALBA, even with internal contradictions and excessive rhetoric, became a player in the regional affairs.

Notwithstanding these initial successes, ALBA showed clear shortcomings. Firstly, the borders of ALBA were never clear; some initiatives that the Venezuelan government considered part of ALBA were something different from ALBA for other countries, the best example being Petrocaribe. Secondly, ALBA was always quite dependent of the Venezuelan financing. Thirdly, many projects were not implemented and others just partially, such as the 'Peoples Trade Treaties' or the Sucre (see Chap. 7). Only few Grand national projects announced from 2008 to 2016 were implemented such as ALBA-Cultura, ALBA Pesca and ALBATEL (Benzi 2017, p. 84). Strategic projects such as ALBA- Alimentos (ALBA food) and ALBAMED (ALBA medicaments) did not advance. Fourthly, the impact on civil society, in particular the role of the Social Movements Council, one of the innovations of ALBA, was limited.

Peter Birle (2018, p. 166) argued that although the participation of civil society actors was rhetorically emphasized repeatedly, there was no real communication or decision channels available to achieve that goal. Moreover, ALBA did not attract other countries in the region such as Brazil, Argentina, Uruguay, El Salvador or

Paraguay, when ruled by left-wing governments. Finally, as ALBA discarded free trade, the economic interdependence among the countries was weak, a factor pointed out in the literature as key or at least important to sustain processes of regional integration. Interdependence can also be achieved by promoting investments of the integration of production, for example through regional chain values, but these were not goals fostered. An Agreement of Economic Cooperation signed in 2013 by Bolivia, Cuba, Ecuador, Nicaragua and Venezuela in the framework of the Latin American Integration Association would be the basis to constitute the Economic Zone with Mercosur, but the lack of complementarity among the member of ALBA and Petrocaribe made a convergence difficult (Giacalone 2017, pp. 56–57). When right-wing governments took power in Argentina and Brazil in 2015 and 2016, the issue was excluded from the agenda of Mercosur.

To sum up, ALBA is a process in crisis as most of its goals have not been achieved, and as it suffered from the weakening of Venezuela, its paymaster. The global crisis that started in 2008 initially did not affect the agenda of ALBA because oil prices remained relatively high, and the demand for oil by China and India continued stable for some years; only in 2013, when the Chinese economic growth slowed down and when fracking became an important source of oil production that situation changed. The severe decline in oil prices to less than US$ 30 in 2014 had an impact on the Venezuelan economy, with important implications on the development of the Bolivarian revolution, but also on the Venezuelan regional integration policy and ALBA. Mostly important, the death of Chavez in 2013 and the domestic political crisis and lack of regional leadership which have only increased since then have practically sealed ALBA's fate; its survival is closely related to the survival of President Maduro in Venezuela.

Pacific Alliance: The Way Ahead?

The Pacific Alliance was advanced by the Peruvian President Alan Garcia and included Chile, Colombia and Mexico. It can be seen as a follow-up from the Pacific Rim Arc initiative from 2007 that included countries from South and Central America and aimed at fostering a common economic approach towards Asia, and engaging with the megaregional negotiations, but was undermined by different approaches among free trade and left-leaning governments at the time. The election of centre-right governments provided a new opportunity to the advance of free trade at the regional level. The Pacific Alliance was announced in the Lima Declaration, signed in 2011, and this was followed by the Framework Agreement of the Pacific Alliance signed in 2012 and by the Additional Protocol of the Framework Agreement of the Pacific Alliance, subscribed in 2014. Durán and Cracau (2016) argued that the entry into force of the Additional Protocol marked an important step towards the regional integration effort, immediately eliminating tariffs for nearly 95% of intra-regional imports and fostering economic integration through accumulation of origin and trade facilitation, and the formation of regional value chains.

Legler et al. (2018) discuss the 'actorness' of the Pacific Alliance and argue that the lack of formal institutions and international legal personality is compensated by the existence of a 'web of agency' constituted by a number of actors engaged in the process of regional integration, which have provided security regarding its continuity and consolidation. They also argue that the ideologically based identity of the Alliance, confirmed by the commitment with neoliberalism, representative democracy, human rights and rule of law, compensates for the lack of geographic continuity, appointed in the literature as a hindrance for regional integration. In fact, the Pacific Alliance has a clear focus on the free trade agenda, in line with open regionalism, differently from Mercosur, UNASUR and ALBA at the time of its creation.

Scholars disagree as to what extent the creation of the Pacific Alliance contributes to the consolidation, or the fragmentation of Latin American regionalism (Heine 2016, Bernal-Meza 2015, Briceño-Ruiz and Morales 2017, Aranda and Salinas 2015). For those governments favouring free trade, the convergence between the Pacific Alliance and Mercosur is seen as an alternative to reunite countries, as supported by the Economic Commission for Latin America and the Caribbean (CEPAL), and discussed further below. But the fact that the Pacific Alliance does not include security in its agenda does not mean that its member-states are not involved in (geo)political considerations in the region; they did take parallel stances in the situation in Venezuela, for instance, what could represent a challenge in case of further escalation of the crisis. The rise to power of Andres Obrador in Mexico in 2018 has also raised the question of the stability of the neoliberal consensus among Pacific Alliance member-states (Legler et al. 2018).

Concluding Remarks: Rising From the Ashes? South American Regionalism After the Crisis

This chapter shows that Latin American regionalism is experiencing a period of crisis and redefinition. The crisis is related to a large extent to the effects of global financial crisis, and the end of the commodities' boom in key countries such as Venezuela and Brazil, which have acted as leaders of regionalism. ALBA and UNASUR are in deep crisis. After being presented as a 'new model of integration' based on solidarity and cooperation, ALBA suffers from the increasing deterioration of the Venezuelan economy, and the negative image of President Maduro's government. Even if the treaty of UNASUR is still in force, it is paralysed after most of its member-states suspended their participation or denounced its treaty. The creation PROSUR is an attempt to replace UNASUR with a less political and more free trade agenda. Mercosur is in a process of redefinition, the convergence with Pacific Alliance is in discussion, but the anti-globalist approach of Bolsonaro's government foreign policy and its prioritization of the USA and sole partner rise doubts about the Brazilian commitment to Mercosur. The Pacific Alliance did not evolve much beyond a network hub for pro-free trader stakeholders.

Despite the uncertainties, possible scenarios are beginning to take shape. One way ahead would be the revival of UNASUR but, at least in the short term, this does not seem likely; the crisis in Venezuela has profoundly damaged its role in the region, and Brazil under President Bolsonaro's foreign policy of alignment with the USA and distance from South–South cooperation will not exert leadership. The protection of democracy has been key to UNASUR, but the recent crises, including Venezuela and Brazil, indicate that mechanisms developed are not robust enough to hold governments accountable. The worldwide crisis of democracy has further weakened the idea of democratic interference as countries become more zealous of sovereignty, and nationalist and extreme-right populism is on the rise. Sectorial cooperation in key areas such as security and defence, and health, key to UNASUR, were dismantled.

An alternative scenario would be a minimalist project based on the convergence in trade and the creation of regional value chains between a rolled-back Mercosur and the Pacific Alliance, but there are limitations regarding the complementarity of its member-states and the political disposition of Mexico under President López Obrador. PROSUR could evolve from this principle, but it is too early to assess this initiative.

We argue that the revitalization of Latin American regionalism could find a supportive pillar in the advancement of free trade, an agenda which could counterbalance protectionist trends, including the policies promoted by President Trump. However, the return of free trade should not be made at expenses of weakening the social and productive dimensions of regionalism. Both Mercosur and UNASUR have developed important social dimensions aiming at reducing asymmetries within and among their member-states in the last decades. Similarly, the integration of the production is still a goal to be achieved as Latin American countries must diversify their economies and become less dependent on the export of commodities in order to achieve sustainable development. To sum up, despite the uncertainties about the future institutional framework, a multidimensional integration that includes trade, the productive sector and infrastructure, as well as political and social areas is the way to deepen Latin American regionalism.

References

Al-Kassimi, K. (2018). ALBA: A decolonial delinking performance towards (western) modernity – An alternative to development project. *Cogent Social Sciences, 4*(1), 1546418.

Aponte García, M. (2014). *El nuevo regionalismo estratégico. Los primero diez años del ALBA-TCP*. Buenos Aires: CLACSO.

Aranda, G., & Salinas, S. (2015). ALBA y Alianza del Pacífico: ¿Choque de integraciones? *Universum (Talca), 30*(1), 17–38.

Benzi, D. (2017). *ALBA - TCP. Anatomía de la integración que no fue*. Buenos Aires: Ediciones Imago Mundi – Universidad Andina Simón Bolívar.

Bernal-Meza, R. (2015). Alianza del Pacífico versus ALBA y MERCOSUR: Entre el desafío de la convergencia y el riesgo de la fragmentación de Sudamérica. Pesquisa & Debate. *Revista do Programa de Estudos Pós-Graduados em Economia Política, 26*, 47.

Bianculli, A. C. (2016). Latin America. In T. A. Börzel & T. Risse (Eds.), *The Oxford handbook of comparative regionalism*. Oxford: Oxford University Press.

Birle, P. (2018). Führungskrise oder unvereinbare Zielsetzungen? Über die Schwierigkeiten und Herausforderungen regionaler Integration in Lateinamerika. In M. Koschkar & C. Ruvituso (Eds.), *Politische Führung im Spiegel regionaler politischer Kultur* (pp. 159–178). Wiesbaden: Springer.

Bouzas, R. (2002). Mercosur:¿ Crisis económica o crisis de la integración?, Notas preparadas para el Grupo de Reflexión Prospectiva sobre el Mercosur, FLACSO-Universidad de San Andrés, 2002.

Briceño-Ruiz, J. (2010). From the south American Community of Nations to the Union of South American Nations. *Latin American Policy*.

Briceño-Ruiz, J. (2011). El ALBA como propuesta de integración. In J. Altmann (Ed.), *América Latina y el Caribe. ALBA: ¿una nueva forma de integración regional?* (pp. 19–84). Buenos Aires: Teseo – FLACSO.

Briceño-Ruiz, J., & Morales, I. (Eds.). (2017). *Post-hegemonic regionalism in the Americas: toward a Pacific–Atlantic divide?* Abingdon: Routledge.

Burges, S. W., & Chagas Bastos, F. H. (2017). The importance of presidential leadership for Brazilian foreign policy. *Policy Studies, 38*(3), 277–290.

Closa, C., & Palestini, S. (2015). *Between democratic protection and self-defense: The case of UNASUR and Venezuela*. Florence: RSCAS 2015/93.

Comini, N., & Frenkel, A. (2017). UNASUR. De proyecto refundacional al fantasma del Sudamexit. *Anuario de la Integración Regional de América Latina y el Caribe, 13*, 181–207.

De La Torre, C. (2017). A Populist International? ALBA's Democratic and Autocratic Promotion. SAIS Review of International Affairs, 37(1), 83–93.

Durán Lima, J. E., & Cracau, D. (2016). The Pacific Alliance and its economic impact on regional trade and investment: Evaluation and perspectives. *ECLAC International Trade Series nr.128.*

Frenkel, A. (2016). Entre promesas y realidades: La UNASUR y la creación de la Escuela Suramericana de Defensa. *Relaciones Internacionales, 31*, 33–52.

Giacalone, R. A. (2017). Principios económicos y narrativas políticas de las propuestas de reconfguración del orden regional latinoamericano. En N. Mellado, & J. C. Fernández Saca, *Desafíos para el regionalismo latinoamericano en el contexto internacional del siglo XXI* (pp. 51–76). Antiguo Cuscatlán, La Libertad, El Salvador: Editorial Delgado.

Girvan, N. (2011). Is ALBA a new model of integration? reflections on the Caricom experience. *International Journal of Cuban Studies, 3*(2–3), 157–180.

Heine, J. (2016). Sigla nueva en sopa de letras: raíces y ramificaciones de la Alianza del Pacífico. *Revista Mexicana de Política Exterior, 106*, 35–48.

Herrero, M. B., & Loza, J. (2018). Building a regional health agenda: a rights-based approach to health in South America. *Global Public Health, 13*(9), 1179–1191.

Legler, T. F., Garelli Rios, O., & González, P. A. (2018). La Alianza del Pacífico: un actor regional en construcción). In E. Pastrana Buelvas & H. Blomeier (Eds.), *La Alianza del Pacífico: ¿atrapada en el péndulo del regionalismo y del interregionalismo?* (pp. 143–172). Bogotá: Konrad Adenauer Stiftung.

Mace, G. (2018). *Fracture de l'UNASUR? Crise du régionalisme sud-américain?*. https://doi.org/10.13140/RG.2.2.16321.66407.

Malamud, A. (2014). Presidentialist decision making in Latin American foreign policy: examples from regional integration processes. In Routledge handbook of Latin America in the world (pp. 124–136). Routledge.

McConnel, S., McCoy, J., & McCarthy, M. (2015). ¿Desafiando a norma? Acompañamiento electoral internacional en Nicaragua y Venezuela. *América Latina Hoy, 70*, 109–132.

Mello e Silva, A. (2018) From Euphoria to Inertia: Brazil's International Rise and Decline, *E-International Relations*. Apr 29.

Merke, F. (2015). Neither balance nor bandwagon: South American international society meets Brazil's rising power. *International Politics, 52*(2), 178–192.

Muhr, T. (2012). (Re) constructing Popular Power in Our America: Venezuela and the regionalisation of 'revolutionary democracy'in the ALBA–TCP space. *Third World Quarterly, 33*(2), 225–241.

Oelsner, A. (2014). Articulating Mercosur's security conceptions and practices. In *Regional organisations and security: Conceptions and practices*. London: Routledge.

Palestini, S., & Agostinis, G. (2015). Constructing regionalism in South America: The cases of sectoral cooperation on transport infrastructure and energy. *Journal of International Relations and Development*, 1–29.

Ribeiro Hoffmann, A. (2020). Mercosur between resilience and disintegration. In Weiffen B. and Nolte, D. *Regionalism under stress: between disintegration and resilience. Europe and Latin America in comparative perspective.* Abingdon: Routledge.

Ribeiro Hoffmann, J.Tabak (2016) Discussing Global Health and Access to Medicines in the UN System: The Case of the Union of South American Nations (UNASUR), *The Hague Journal of Diplomacy, 12.2* (2016):178–196.

Riggirozzi, P., & Grugel, J. (2015). Regional governance and legitimacy in South America: the meaning of UNASUR. *International Affairs, 91*(4), 781–797.

Ruvalcaba, D. M., Rocha Valencia, A., & Durán González, T. (2016). Las potencias subregionales en el sistema internacional de posguerra fría: ¿nuevos actores en la política internacional? *Geopolítica(s). Revista de estudios sobre espacio y poder., 7*(1), 71–107.

Seabra, R. L., & Gimenez, H. M. (2014). Contra o "vazio teórico" da ALBA, uma análise propositiva a partir da lei do valor. Revista de Estudos e Pesquisas sobre as Américas, 1.

Soares de Lima, M. R., & Hirst, M. (2006). Brazil as an intermediate state and regional power: Action, choice and responsibilities. *International Affairs, 82*(1), 21–40.

Watts, J., & Depledge, J. (2018). Latin America in the climate change negotiations: Exploring the AILAC and ALBA coalitions. *Wiley Interdisciplinary Reviews: Climate Change, 9*(6), e533.

Yeates, N., & Riggirozzi, P. (2017). Global Social Regionalism: the case of the Union of South American Nations' health policy. PRARI Working Paper 15–10, Milton Keynes, The Open University.

Part V
Results of the Research

19

Crises in Europe and Latin America: Conclusion

Andrea Ribeiro Hoffmann and Bettina De Souza Guilherme

Abstract This chapter summarizes the findings of the theoretical and analytical chapters, and comparatively assesses the causes of the crises, the crisis management strategies, and their impact in a selection of case studies from the national level – Greece, Portugal and Italy in Europe; and Argentina, Mexico, Brazil and Venezuela in Latin America; and the regional level – the European Union, and regional organizations and regional governance structures in Latin America such as CELAC, Unasur, Mercosur and Alba.

Introduction

This edited volume analyzes the crises in Europe and Latin America, starting from the debt crisis in the 1980s in Latin America and its lost decade, covering the 2008 global financial crisis impact on the European Union (EU), and the resulting lost decade for Europe, and the current crisis in Latin America, which started by 2012. At the theoretical and analytical level, it aimed to understand the causes of these crises, to what extent we can find common systemic causes, and to what extent each region faced (additional) particular processes derived from their local socio-economic specificities and the way they managed the crises both at the

A. Ribeiro Hoffmann (✉)
Pontifical Catholic University of Rio de Janeiro (PUC-Rio), Rio de Janeiro, Brazil

Coordinator of the second phase of the Jean Monnet Network "Crisis-Equity-Democracy for Europe and Latin America", Rio de Janeiro, Brazil
e-mail: a_ribeiro_hoffmann@puc-rio.br

B. De Souza Guilherme
Founder and Co-coordinator of the Jean Monnet Network "Crisis-Equity-Democracy for Europe and Latin America", IRELAC, Rio de Janeiro, Brazil

European Parliament, Brussels, Belgium
e-mail: bettina.desouza@europarl.europa.eu

regional and domestic/country levels. Another objective was to address the impact and consequences of the crises, both in their economic and political aspects. In particular, we aimed to understand the relation between the financial crisis and the democratic backlash with the rise of populism and extreme-right movements and parties in Europe and Latin America.

This chapter summarizes the findings of the theoretical and analytical chapters, and comparatively assesses the causes of the crises, the crisis management strategies and their impact in a selection of case studies from the national level (Greece, Portugal and Italy in Europe; and Argentina, Mexico, Brazil and Venezuela in Latin America) and the regional level: the European Union, and regional organizations and regional governance structures in Latin America such as CELAC, Unasur, Mercosur and Alba.

The following chapters draw on these findings and advance policy recommendations about possible ways out of the crises, focusing on measures at the regional level, and political cooperation between the EU and Latin America at the interregional level, especially the EU–CELAC dialogue.

Financial Crises in Global Historical Context: Exploring the Common Systemic Causes of the Current Situation

The authors of this edited volume have come to share the understanding that the financial crises in Europe and Latin America have common systemic causes, even if each region and each country had additional particular local economic and political dynamics. Schulmeister (Chap. 2) and Ghymers (Chap. 3) analyze the systemic causes of the crises in detail. Schulmeister contextualizes historically the current global financial governance structures and traces the origins of the asymmetries and imbalances to the end of the Bretton Woods system and the processes of deregulation in the 1970s/1980s. He argues that this unregulated system has caused a sequence of "bull and bear" markets which led to the global financial crisis of the 1970s, 1980s, the end of 1990s, early 2000s and, in a more radical way, 2008. He also shows that the successions of bull and bear markets shape commodity price dynamics, especially over the past 15 years, when financial investors became increasingly active in commodities' derivatives trading, and that this has created high levels of volatility. By differentiating between "real capitalism" and "finance capitalism", and between the US and European models of capitalism, Schulmeister traces the conditions under which financial crises burst and diffuse around the globe.

Ghymers also argues that the current global macroeconomic crisis, the weakening of democracy and, in addition, climate change are all expressions of the incoherence of the present global economic system, which operates on the basis of biased relative prices, relative returns for financial activities which are too high with respect to productive activities, prices for safe assets in the US dollar which are too high, and costs for carbon emissions which are too low. In particular, the use of one national currency (US dollar) as the main vehicle of international payments (Triffin dilemma) created distortions in the capital flows, with the US economy absorbing the net world savings in a way which impedes the huge resource transfers necessary for financing the energy transition in emerging and developing countries committed in the Paris Agreement.

Guilherme (Chap. 4) and Lins (Chap. 11) discuss further the differences in the position of Europe and Latin America in the global finance system, the interconnections between both regions and the similarities of the patterns of the 2008 crisis with those of the 1980s and 1990s. Lins highlights that the 1980s' Latin American foreign debt crisis reflected the priority of military dictatorships to maintain high levels of growth despite rising inflation in several countries of the region. High liquidity in international financial markets in the wake of the oil crisis ("petro dollars") granted these countries access to credit at initially low—though floating—interest rates, allowing them to postpone necessary reforms and preserve growth. As Schulmeister argues, the effect of the depreciation of the dollar with the oil crisis also raised the attractiveness of debts denominated in dollar. The enlargement of the EC/EU to the Southern countries, Greece, Spain and Portugal, and their rapid membership to the Economic and Monetary Union had been a political decision to stabilize their economies and democracies after coming out of dictatorships. Their economic development, however, was not sufficient to form an Optimum Currency Union, and as a consequence, they became a source of internal imbalances within the European Monetary Union (EMU). Being part of EMU and sharing the Euro directed the inflow of liquidity to Europe's periphery and created major (housing) bubbles. Greece, in particularly, was demonstrating growth rates twice the EU average, and for this reason, the EU showed more leniency with its current account deficits and public debts. This boom was (mistakenly) perceived as a sound process of convergence and took from them the pressure to undertake necessary reforms to increase competitiveness and real convergence.

The trigger for the eurocrisis was the announcement of the actual dimension of the public deficit by the Greek Prime Minister Giorgos Papandreou in late 2009. The bursting of housing bubbles, in particular in Spain, the disparity of interest rates and the escape of financial funds to the safe havens such as Germany and the USA, together with the lack of solidarity of the other EMU member-states, deepened the eurocrisis. At the same time, financial funds flew to emerging economies including in Latin America, which supported, together with the countercyclical policies, a jump in their growth rates. The global financial crisis of 2008 supported the rise of the emerging countries with the creation of the BRICS and the G20, which demanded for reforms of the Bretton Woods institutions to represent them more proportionally. The influence of the European Union at the international level diminished correspondingly. The EU was busy with its own problems, and in particularly, EMU showed neither unity nor solidarity and struggled with several simultaneous crises at the same time (eurocrisis, foreign political crisis with the Ukraine and the refugee crisis).

Additionally, the fact that the EMU followed the same path and recipes of the Washington Consensus and integrated the International Monetary Fund (IMF) within its TROIKA, benefiting from its ample experience in crisis management (much of it with little success and high social costs in Latin America), led to the loss of attraction of the EU as a model of regional integration and its social model. Indeed, the EMU crisis countries found themselves in a similar situation as Latin America, without any control over the currency in which their debt had been denominated and suddenly affected by the increase of interest rates which made their debts unsustainable. Additionally, the fiscal framework and its reinforcement and the adjustment programs proved to be largely pro-cyclical, suppressing investment and growth and constraining the functioning of the automatic stabilizers leading to a deepening and prolongation of the crisis with dramatic social and employment consequences in some of the crisis countries. The Eurogroup invited the IMF for its experiences, however, not its experiences and usual praxis of debt restructuring, but mainly its focus on adjustment programs in line with policies of the Washington Consensus. Latin America, likewise, did not receive support on debt restructuring in the 1980s' crisis. The European Social Model was not protected and did not make any difference to the design of the policies which had been implemented in the Latin America, partly under military regimes and partly under political forces supporting neoliberalism. Interestingly, as highlighted by former ECB President Draghi in his farewell speech, the USA did not apply the same kind of Washington Consensus austerity policies after the global financial crisis, but engaged into countercyclical fiscal policies which allowed a quicker recovery and return to price stability than Europe.

Regional and Country-Based Causes and Management of the Crisis

A key difference between the reaction and management of the crisis in Europe and Latin America was the role that regional-level institutions played. Despite all the problems and lack of democratic accountability, which were discussed in several chapters, the European Union had the Eurogroup, an informal intergovernmental coordination body which was actually strengthened during the crisis, and established new mechanisms such as the Banking Union, still ongoing, while most regional organizations in Latin America did not develop any relevant collective mechanism to deal with financial crisis.

Guilherme (Chap. 4), Katsikas (Chap. 5) and Schulmeister (Chap. 6) analyze several aspects of the EU reaction and attempt to manage the crisis. Schulmeister shows how instruments such as the financial transactions tax (FTT), which could have contributed to buffer the negative impact, ended up being rejected by the Commission, which was captured by the interests of big financial players and surplus countries, mainly Germany and France. Katsikas argues that the European EMU was actually the biggest victim of the 2008 global financial crisis given its incomplete nature and lack of supranational mechanism, which led to the creation of ad hoc intergovernmental political handling of the crisis with the creation of further treaties (Fiscal Compact) and intergovernmental institutions (ESM) outside of the legal framework of the EU and as a consequence, not accountable to EU citizens. The intergovernmental crisis management style favored the rise of the hegemons and the division of Europe in creditor and debtor countries, instead of a strong solidary reaction to the eurocrisis, which could have put the speculation on hold. The lack of solidarity and joint risk-sharing in an EMU, in which member-states have given up their tradition tools to smoothen asymmetric shocks, weakened Europe, the euro and EMU. Additionally, the publically exposed animosity stirred nationalism and populism which will make future solutions to jointly counteract any eurocrisis much more difficult. It legitimized attitudes of an extreme right-wing party which in the past would not have been considered politically acceptable. The rise of this party (the "Alternative für Detschland", AfD) put a stress on the political predictability of German's politics. The strategies adopted by the EU ended up leaving the costs of the adjustment to the crisis-hit countries, which had to implement individual bailout programs. The strategy was not anti-cyclical and accentuated the crises especially in countries such as Greece and Italy. Germany prevented an early involvement of the IMF and with it the usual debt restructuring which would have affected their own banking sector but insisted in its involvement once the private (financial market) debts had already been rolled over to the public debts in Greece. Worst, Ghymers (Chap. 22) reminds that the eurosystem then was the only monetary area of the world operating without a Lender-of-Last-Resort (LOLR), giving so to financial markets the power to precipitate non-necessary liquidity crisis in a one-bet speculation in case of doubts on sovereign debts.

Guilherme (Chap. 4) discusses in details what she calls the "double democratic deficit" of the EMU, and how it failed to protect the EU and its citizens from the financial crisis and to manage the crisis in a credible, equitable and democratic way. She argues that a key underlying cause of this failure is the monetarist and neoliberal/ordoliberal approach of the project agreed at Maastricht and vis-a-vis the alternative Werner Plan which had Keynesian and federal elements, such as pointed out by Schulmeister (Chap. 2) when he discusses the design of the global financial system. Guilherme argues that the Maastricht Treaty deliberately eliminated fundamental building stones from the Werner blueprint which would have made EMU more crisis resistant, resilient and allowed a more efficient, equitable and democratic crisis management. The omissions include regulation and supervision of financial markets, monitoring and counteracting of internal imbalances, including policies to support the competitiveness of the weaker economies and regions, stabilization functions such as a euro area budget and a European Monetary Fund and political decision taking institutions which are fully democratically accountable and within the EU legal framework. She shows how the ordo/neoliberal and intergovernmental design of the EMU led to choices made during the crisis by creditor countries, especially Germany, which favored the banks and not crisis-hit countries and EU citizens. Furthermore, the austerity bias of its approach—especially but not only in crisis-hit countries—had negative effects on overall EU growth and a deflationary impact on the rest of the world. On the other hand, there were positive collective responses at the EU level, such as via EFSI, better known as the Juncker Plan, aimed at stimulating investment in EU countries via an expansion of the role of the European Investment Bank (Griffith-Jones, Chap. 21).

Latin America did not have regional governance institutions to deal with macroeconomic and financial matters equivalent to the EU, despite the shortcomings of the latter. Lins and Ribeiro Hoffmann (Chap. 7) show that most Latin American countries dealt with the crisis individually; very few collective initiatives were attempted, such as via the Development Bank of Latin America (CAF) and the Latin American Fund of Reserves (FLAR). Regional integration organizations such as Unasur, Mercosur or ALBA did not have mechanisms to deal with the crisis, and at the multilateral level, the Inter-American Development Bank (IADB) provided important support too.

Impact and Consequences of the Crisis at the Domestic and Regional Levels: Challenges to Equity, Democracy and Regionalism

The impact and consequences of the crisis at the domestic level were analyzed in selected case studies in Europe (Greece, Portugal and Italy) and in Latin America (Brazil, Venezuela, Argentina and Mexico). Katzikas and Bazoti (Chap. 8) analyze the main traits of the Greek politico-economic system and argue that the EU policy program failed to take into account these characteristics and therefore accentuated the negative impact of the crisis on the Greek people. He argues that even if the fiscal balance had been restored, and some progress was done in public administration and regulations, structural problems remain unresolved, and the population still suffers from the decline of GDP and increase of poverty levels. These have fed left- and right-wing populism and anti-EU feelings. Romano (Chap. 10) also explores the domestic structural problems of Italian economic and political system and shows how they have contributed to the lack of resilience when the crisis hit the country following the Greek crisis and the lack of appropriated response at the EU level to that crisis and the risk of contagion. He analyzes the economic and political legacy of the crisis and shows that not only were the social and economic structural problems, such as unemployment, low productivity and high public debt, not resolved, but they also paved the way for populism.

Sandrin (Chap. 14) and Poli (Chap. 15) focus on the political impact of the crisis in Europe and show how most countries saw a surge in polarization, populism and extreme-right movements and parties during this period. Sandrin argues that economic crisis and the "left behind" are not enough to explain the current democratic crisis, and explores the role of identity and effects, and how they have been mobilized by the extreme right against various "others". Poli discusses the concept sovranism to make sense of the right-wing populist parties in Europe. She differentiates this concept from nationalism or fascism given the lack of a deep ideological backing and the vertical collusive relationship between "the people" and "the elite", instead of focusing only on the external others and/or anti-pluralism. Therefore, sovranist parties such as Golden Dawn in Greece (even though it has remained comparatively small), Alternative for Germany, Brexit Party in the UK, Lega Nord in Italy and Vox in Spain do not develop coherent policies and are normally led by charismatic leaders. Portugal followed different trends as argued by Lehmann (Chap. 9); despite being hit hard by the crisis, populism did not thrive and had a relatively successful economic recovery due to particularities and the capacity of the country's domestic society to avoid political rupture and a broad informal alliance of the center-left and left, pursuing Keynesian policies.

Despite the differences in timing and the role of the regional level, the impact of the crisis in countries such as Brazil and Venezuela was as drastic as in Europe, especially when considering the political impact. Venezuela has a different trajectory as the country was in crisis for some years before the financial crisis hit the region. As Briceno-Ruiz and Lehmann (Chap. 13) discuss, the problematic economic policies of former President Chavez and his successor Maduro (after Chavez's death in 2013) increased the vulnerability of the country to external shocks, especially given the overreliance on oil exports. Moreover, their anti-US and anti-Western geopolitical foreign policy led to the rejection of traditional institutions such as the IMF support to handle the crisis. Instead, Venezuela increased cooperation with Russia and China, a country which owns most of its external debt. The socio-economic situation in Venezuela is dramatic with levels of poverty and mass emigration unseen in the region, defined as a humanitarian crisis by the UN Refugee Agency. The political situation is even worse as political repression and lack of an effective opposition have progressively isolated the country.

Brazil has gone through radical changes since 2012–2013. Lins (Chap. 11) analyzes how the government deals with the financial crisis; she shows that by 2008 the Brazilian economy was undergoing a prosperous phase and adopted an expansionary policy under the governments of the Workers´ Party (Partido dos Trabalhadores—PT), to stimulate domestic consumption and investment. When the crisis hit, it continued this approach, and the countercyclical policies were initially successful. By 2011, however, the policy adopted in the USA and Europe reduced capital flows to emerging economies, and in addition, demand for primary goods decreased, as the world economy slowed down. Brazil used taxes to control capital outflows, but by 2013, the political crisis evolved and mass protests hit the streets, and culminated with the impeachment of President Dilma in 2016, as analyzed in detail by Guilherme and Ribeiro Hoffmann (Chap. 12). Former Vice-President Temer assumed the presidency, enforced a neoliberal U-turn in economic policy, initiating the dismantlement of social policies created under the PT governments, which has led to a fast increase of unemployment and poverty. The following elections were marked by polarization and fake news, and led to the election of right-wing President Bolsonaro. The challenges to democracy of his government are explored by Salgado and Sandrin (Chap. 17). They contextualize the Brazilian crisis in the waves of populism in Latin America and argue that the frustration and discontent with the pink-tide governments such as Chavez/Maduro in Venezuela and Lula/Dilma in

Brazil led to increased opposition and popular manifestations and a turn to neoliberal and right-wing governments in most countries. As seen above, Venezuela and Brazil had particularities, Venezuela for the continuity of the radical left government which became increasingly more repressive, and Brazil for the "impeachment" of the more socio-democratic PT governments by initially a neoliberal coalition which paved the way for the election of the extreme-right President Bolsonaro, and what they call the "politics of social antagonism". In both cases, Venezuela and Brazil exhibit a clear trend of militarization of politics, and the political system is ongoing, with Brazilian government leading in the proportional number of military as Ministers.

The cases of Brazil and Venezuela are complemented by a discussion of Argentina and Mexico by Lins. She argues that such as in the crises of the 1980s and 1990s, the IMF was the main multilateral institution involved in the financial crisis management in Latin America, especially Argentina, but differently from the previous crisis, domestic political choices prevailed over international pressures on crisis management and policy making. Lins´ analyses contribute to the reflection about the different location of Europe and Latin America in the global financial system, and about the similarities of the Latin American crisis in the 1980s and 1990s and the Euro crisis and their interconnections.

Finally, Katsikas (Chap. 16) and Briceño-Ruiz and Ribeiro Hoffmann (Chap. 18) analyze the impact of the crisis and of the way how the regional governance institutions reacted to the crisis on these institutions themselves. Verney and Katsikas (Chap. 16) show how the EU has been criticized for the lack of efficiency and democratic accountability, and how their role was questioned by political parties and the public in general. EU's image, and trust in the EU, especially in crisis-hit periphery countries decreased dramatically by 2012, and even though they recovered since then, they have remained at lower levels than before the crisis. They raise the risk that future policy failures might undermine the viability of the system as a whole, therefore calling the EU to positive action. And, as pointed out by Sandrin and Poli, the damage to democracy at the national level is not yet reversed.

Briceño-Ruiz and Ribeiro Hoffmann (Chap. 18) discuss the crisis of regionalism and the disintegration of the region, with the abandonment or formal renunciation of the founding treaties of organizations such as Unasur by several countries, and CELAC by Brazil. Countries which have played leadership role fostering regionalism such as Brazil and Venezuela became inward looking since then and adopted more nationalist foreign policies.

Final Remarks

The chapters of this edited volume show that despite the common systemic causes, the timing and nature of the crises in Europe and Latin America following the 2008 financial crash in the USA were and are very different. The Euro crisis hit Europe in 2010, and the existence of the European Union and the Euro made regional level actors, especially the Eurogroup, the key actors in managing the crisis, despite the legitimacy problems.

Latin America faced severe debt crisis already in the 1980s, following a continuous number of crises prior and since. However, by 2010 most countries were enjoying stability and growth led by among others, external investments and Chinese demand for primary goods; the impact of the crisis began to be felt by 2012–2013. These developments coincided with the decline of commodity and in particularly oil prices, and the price pressure from fracking, which had major consequences for the oil-exporting countries. The economic slowdown and rise of inequalities led to discontent, which were expressed in mass protests and the rise of new social movements.

Local specificities at the regional and country level explain the differences of the impact of the financial crisis in Europe and Latin America, including their place in the global financial system, and local social, cultural and political characteristics. Despite these differences, the consequences for European and Latin American societies were equally dramatic, challenging social cohesion and democracy, and contributing to political polarization and the election of populist and extreme-right parties in several countries.

The USA and the UK were not analyzed in this volume, but the election of Donald Trump and of Boris Johnson, implying not just Brexit but likely a hard Brexit, have also to be assessed in light of the management of the 2008 crisis and strengthens the argument of the Jean Monnet Network Crisis-Equity-Democracy for Europe and Latin America that these phenomena are interrelated and have reinforced each other given their common systemic sources, and transnational and interregional relations.

Recent events, especially in Chile with its so-called "social explosion" but also in other Latin American and even European countries, show that even in economically successful and politically stable countries, challenges such as a slowdown of growth and an increasingly unequal distribution of income as well as of wealth can produce major tensions in societies. They might lead to significant violence, which can potentially undermine future economic development and contribute to political polarization and instability. Only with more progressive policies, such as those which mitigate inequality—via increased social spending in key sectors such as health and education, as well as increased pensions and salaries for the poorer segments of society, funded by increased taxation on the wealthy, as well as policies that will encourage more dynamic, sustainable and inclusive growth—can such "social explosions" be followed by positive economic and political developments that improve both social coherence as well as democratic legitimacy.

Disclaimer The opinions expressed in this introduction/volume are the sole responsibility of the authors and do not necessarily represent the official position of the European Parliament or of any other EU institution.

Part VI
Proposals for Potential Reforms

20

Unconventional Policy Proposals

Stephan Schulmeister

Abstract This chapter addresses the three main challenges by sketching three types of policy proposals. First, measures for repression of "finance alchemy" as precondition for a sustained recovery of the real economy and for a "renaissance" of the European Social Model; second, measures for fighting climate change and for promoting ("green") economic growth over a transition period; and third, measures for overcoming the "digital colonization" of Europe by US providers of operation systems, standard software and online platforms.

Key Challenges for Overcoming the Present Crisis

The transition from finance capitalism to real capitalism—the trough phase in the long cycle triggered by financial crises as in 1873, 1929 or 2008—usually takes many years since governance according to the old "navigation map" makes things only worse, but a new map has not yet been developed. Such a transition phase calls for fundamental changes in the direction of the course even without guidance by a new theory (like Roosevelt's New Deal).[1] The new direction of economic and social policy can be derived from a comparison of the framework conditions shaping the post-war prosperity phase on the one hand and the subsequent crisis phase on the other hand.

[1] It is no coincidence that the new EU Commission calls its ecological growth strategy "European Green Deal". Climate change is only the most evident example of the basic problem of systemic crises, typical for the trough phase of the long cycle: the paths followed so far led into a dead end (on the long cycle as sequence of real-capitalist and finance-capitalist regimes, see *Schulmeister*, Chap. 2 of this book).

S. Schulmeister (✉)
University or Vienna, Wien, Austria
e-mail: stephan.schulmeister@wifo-pens.at

Until the 1970s, strict regulation of financial markets focused on striving for profits on activities in the real economy, production and income expanded over 20 years without major recessions. Social coherence was strengthened, in particular through building up the welfare state. At the same time, public debt declined relative to GDP. The guidelines of economic policy were derived from a simplified version of the theory of Keynes. Over the past decades, by contrast, neoliberal guidelines have been shaping the course of economic policy: financial markets were deregulated, the welfare state was weakened and climate change vastly ignored. The wide fluctuations of exchange rates, commodities prices, stock prices and interest rates had two types of effects. First, the emergence of "shocks" like the two "oil price shocks" of the 1970s (triggered by two preceding dollar depreciations), the 1982 debt crisis of Latin America or the great financial crisis of 2008. Second, the "structural" shifting of striving for profits from activities in the real economy to financial investment/speculation. Both effects caused unemployment, atypical employment and the public debt to rise. As a consequence, labour protection as well as the welfare state in general was weakened. Widening inequality and the growing number of people feeling "left behind" promoted the rise of nationalist-populist movements and politicians.

The dominance of neoliberal thinking in economics, in the media and in politics had not only specifically weakened the European Social Model but has also become the most important ideological reason for the failure to fight climate change—in spite of the growing evidence that global warming was caused by men. Even though standard economic theory acknowledges externalities as "market failures" (and climate change is the most threatening example), policy has remained unwilling to take serious collective actions. Those actions ran counter to the "Zeitgeist" which was (and still is) biased in favour of "market solutions".

The third "mega-trend" of last decades besides growing financial instability and continuing climate change has become digitalization in all its forms, from computer hardware and software, the internet, social media and the platform economy. In all these fields, innovative US corporations acquired global (quasi-)monopoly positions: Microsoft in operating systems and standard software, Apple in hardware and operating systems, Google in both fields as well as in search engines and online advertising, Facebook, Twitter and Instagram in social media, amazon in online commerce, Airbnb in arranging lodging and Uber in ride-hailing. The main reason for this success lies in the combination of "first-mover advantages", continuing globalization and—most important—"network externalities". The latter arise from the fact that all these activities are based on networks (including using the same standard software). For network economies, standard rules of market competition do not hold as the network gets the more attractive to "newcomers" the greater it has become ("the winner takes it all"). In this way, US corporations became "digital colonial masters" of the rest of the world (except—in part—for China), and the latter has to pay "tributes" in the form of money and data and remains technologically dependent. As market forces rather deepen than mitigate this relationship, overcoming the "digital colonization" of Europe constitutes a crucial challenge for European Union (EU) policy in the years to come.

This chapter addresses the three main challenges by sketching three types of policy proposals. First, measures for repression of "finance alchemy" as precondition for a sustained recovery of the real economy and for a "renaissance" of the European Social Model; second, measures for fighting climate change and for promoting ("green") economic growth over a transition period; and third, measures for overcoming the "digital colonization" of Europe by US providers of operation systems, standard software and online platforms. Even though the chapter deals only with these three challenges, one should be aware that a long-term economic, social and ecological renovation programme for Europe should also include the following components: first, the modernization and enlargement of the welfare state as probably the most important fundament of a new/renewed "European identity"; second, the implementation of infrastructure projects as part of development cooperation, in particular in Africa, but also in Latin America; and third, the development of new labour time models as prerequisite for combining low economic growth (once climate-neutrality and "true" full employment are achieved) with continuous implementation of technical progress (raising labour productivity) and sustained full employment. The following proposals are designed for the EU, but they could also be implemented in other countries and regions albeit with some modifications.

Promotion of Activities in the Real Economy Through Restricting "Finance Alchemy"

Fostering entrepreneurial activities in the real economy is the most important precondition for prosperity. It can only be achieved if "finance alchemy" is repressed and if exchange rates, commodities prices, interest rates and stock prices are stabilized. The reason is simple: Capital is a greedy, yet flexible, "animal", and it invests where profits are highest. If short-term speculation is unprofitable, then long-term investment in the real economy predominates—as over the 1950s and 1960s in industrial countries or since the reforms in China in the early 1980s.

Foundation of the European Monetary Fund

In a monetary union, interest rates on government bonds have to be stabilized at a common and sustainable level—otherwise speculators can play euro countries off against each other (as in the euro crisis). Hence, the European Stability Mechanism (ESM) should be transformed into the European Monetary Fund (EMF) as the common financing agency of all euro states. The EMF is financed by selling Eurobonds in capital markets as well as by deposits, which are open to any investor (not only banks) as a longer-term financial investment. Unlike Eurobonds, the EMF deposits would not be tradable and can therefore not be used to speculate on changes in interest rates (they are similar to the former German "Schatzbriefe", which allowed private individuals to finance the state directly). As EMF liabilities are guaranteed by the ECB, they are even safer than German government bonds (a central bank cannot go bankrupt).

The (long-term) EMF interest rate is set at a level below the level of medium-term economic growth (in nominal terms). In addition, the EMF stabilizes the interest rate at the target level by intervening in the secondary market. Under these conditions, speculation on the bankruptcy of an EMU member state becomes useless. At the same time, guarantees for the liabilities of the EMF by euro member states are superfluous. Loans are granted to euro states under certain conditions ("conditionality" as with the IMF). They need not be restrictive and are differentiated according to project and country. The loans should in particular support economically weaker countries and focus generally on projects in the environmental and social sectors. In this way, one could also enforce fiscal discipline of euro countries: If the latter fail to meet the EMF conditions, they are no longer eligible for EMF loans and have to finance themselves through national government bonds.

Transition from Continuous Trading to Electronic Auctions

The overwhelming majority of financial transactions are triggered by computer-based speculation systems. They exploit the phenomenon of "runs" (i.e., "mini-trends") of exchange rates, stock and bond prices and commodity prices, and reinforce them at the same time (e.g., through the "clustered" trading signals of trend-following systems). The sequence of "runs" accumulates into bull or bear markets lasting several years (see Chap. 2). The most efficient means of breaking the feedback between technical speculation and the trending of the key prices in the global economy would consist in moving from continuous trading in microseconds to electronic auctions, for example, every 3 hours. The auctions shall be conducted on electronic trading platforms in the same manner as the opening price is determined already today: The computer calculates the equilibrium price based on all buy and sell orders, valid for the following 3 hours (to stick to the example).

Auction trading would radically reduce the "finance alchemy", stabilize prices and thus make activities in the real economy more attractive. For everybody who buys or sells stocks, bonds, foreign exchange or commodities futures for investing, trading or hedging purposes, it is sufficient when he/she can do so every 3 hours. At the same time, the technical trading systems cut off their "food", that is, high-frequency data. As a consequence, trends would occur less frequently and would be less pronounced so that speculation on the direction of imminent price *movements* on the basis of algorithm becomes less unprofitable. At the same time, focusing on market fundamentals would pay off more than is the case nowadays: In order to give buy/sell orders, traders are forced to form expectations about the *level* of the fundamental value of an asset. This is not the case in continuous trading: High-frequency trading is done automatically by computers and a technical trader will often buy (sell) an asset which he considers over(under)valued just because a short-term trend has taken off and his trading system produces buy (sell) signals.

Auction trading in asset markets would fundamentally change trading practices: "Automated trading systems" (including high-frequency trading) would no longer work as they are deprived of "fast" price data. For the same reason, traders no longer need to watch so many monitors. Instead, reflecting about the fundamental value of the respective asset and its determinants would become more profitable. Finally, one should keep in mind that electronic auction as means of approximating the equilibrium price is perfectly in line with mainstream economic theory. In fact, the founder of general equilibrium theory, Leon Walras, considered this method as the optimum possible.

General Financial Transactions Tax

Even though moving to electronic auctions would be most efficient in curbing short-term speculation, it is very improbable that such a move would take place in all countries with important financial markets. This will limit the stabilizing effect, for example, if only the "Post-Brexit-EU" makes this step. It would nevertheless be useful, if "finance alchemy" emigrates from this area. In order to prevent banks and corporations resident in the EU to engage in (very) short-term speculation elsewhere (e.g., in London), one should introduce a financial transactions tax based on the "residence principle" as proposed by the European Commission (see Chap. 6).

Towards a Supranational Monetary System

The double role of the dollar as the national currency of the US and as a (substitute) world currency is a major cause of fluctuations in dollar-denominated commodity prices (including "oil price shocks"), of the financial crises of dollar-indebted emerging market economies and of the excessive external debt of the US (see Chaps. 2 and 3). At the same time, the dollar is the most unstable of all major currencies because it is the "vehicle currency" in foreign exchange markets. Since the creation of the euro, there are only four major currencies in the global economy, the dollar, the euro, the renminbi and the yen. By setting target rates with small fluctuation margins (about 2%), the exchange rates between these currencies could be stabilized. Such an agreement would also be important as a prevention against "devaluation races", as this danger could sharply increase in the next financial crisis. At the same time, this agreement would be a first step towards the long-term goal of a genuine global currency ("globo"), which would act as a unit of payment and account for global economic "flows" (commodity trading) and "stocks" (transnational financial assets and liabilities) and consist of a bundle of the most important national currencies.

Improving the Environment as (Transitory) "Growth Engine"

Many (very) great investment programmes (in the spirit of the New Deal) would improve the environment over the long run, in particular by reducing CO_2 emissions, and would strengthen economic growth during the implementation phase at the same time ("green growth"). Examples of such projects are the thermic isolation of the whole stock of buildings in the EU, the construction of a (super-)high-speed railways net across Europe as alternative to air travel, and the transition from fossil energy to emission-free cars in individual mobility and to hydrogen technologies in industrial production. However, the potential of a (temporary) "green growth" can only be efficiently utilized if the price of CO_2 emissions and, hence, the price of crude oil, coal and natural gas as the most important polluters, rises steadily and faster than the general price level—simply because the profits from investments in energy efficiency consist of the saved energy costs ("opportunity profits").

Fixing the Long-Term Price Path of Crude Oil, Coal and Natural Gas in the EU

Recently, the renowned Harvard professor Jeffrey Frankel (2020) summed up the problem of how to motivate everybody to avoiding greenhouse gas emissions: "(….) the policy that will move us closest to achieving global environmental targets (….) is to raise the price of emitting carbon dioxide and other greenhouse gases. (….) it would be great if policymakers could commit to a century-long rising path for the carbon price. People could then plan far ahead. Firms would know with certainty the penalty for building long-lasting coal-fired power plants. (….) What is critical, though, is quickly to establish the expectation that the price of carbon will follow a generally rising path in the future". The crucial point is *fixing the expectations of all actors* that the price of CO_2-emission will *never again become cheaper*, but will permanently rise somewhat faster than the general price level. As long as there is uncertainty about the future price development of oil, coal and natural gas, even temporarily high prices will not sufficiently motivate households and companies to invest in emission-free technologies.

A concrete example: between 2004 and 2008 and between 2009 and 2012, the price of crude oil rose dramatically and with it the price of fuels, heating oil and natural gas (Fig. 20.2 shows the price of Brent crude oil and diesel in Germany in €—the latter rose to more than 1.50€). However, the oil bull market was followed by a bear market, and the diesel price fell again to only about 1€ in 2009 as well as in 2016. As a consequence, the demand for SUVs picked up again and investments in CO_2 reductions, which were profitable at an oil price of 70€ (and more), turned into "sunk investments". The following fact massively exacerbates the problem: Investments in energy efficiency or in renewable energy only pay for themselves after many years (energetic renovation of buildings, spread of e-cars including supply networks, etc.) or even decades (development of hydrogen technology in industry and—possibly—also in (heavy) traffic, trans-European network of high-speed trains as a prerequisite for a radical restriction of air traffic, etc.). An ecological investment offensive therefore requires *maximum planning security*.

Even under the extremely restrictive conditions of (general) equilibrium theory, market prices cannot take into account the "external costs" caused through production and consumption. It is up to policymakers to "internalise" these costs (directly through environmental taxes, indirectly through emissions trading, in which the quantity of permits is gradually reduced). This market failure is exacerbated by a second market failure typical for all asset prices, including not only stock prices and exchange rates, but also the prices of fossil energy or of CO_2 permits: They fluctuate in a sequence of bull and bear markets, that is, they deviate widely from their "fundamentals". The development of the oil price (and thus indirectly also of the prices of natural gas and coal) is a particularly pronounced example of the "manic-depressive" dynamics of speculative prices (see Figs. 2.3, 2.5, 2.6, 2.7, 2.8, and 2.9 in Chap. 2).

By combining both types of market failure in those goods whose consumption is mainly responsible for global warming, this problem reached a life-threatening dimension. Climate researchers recognized the extent of the problem in recent decades, and most economists, however, did not as they disregarded the importance of the two types of market failures in times of neoliberal thinking. In particular, the idea that the "freest" markets, the financial markets, systematically create false prices (through "bulls" and "bears") is unthinkable within the paradigm of general equilibrium economics.

Economic policy has been focused on the two standard instruments for pricing CO_2 emissions, carbon taxes or emission trading schemes. Unfortunately, neither of them can achieve a path of continuously rising CO_2 prices. Let's begin with carbon taxes. In all EU countries, there has long been a tax on fuels. It is equivalent to a tax on CO_2 emissions caused by fuel consumption since there prevails a fixed relationship between the quantity of fuel consumed and the related CO_2 emissions. In Germany, for example, the tax on diesel is 47 cents per litre. Since the burning of 1 litre diesel produces 2.65 kg CO_2, the diesel tax burdens the emission of 1 ton of CO_2 by roughly 180€ (= 0.47/2.65 per kg). This is much more than in most planned or—like in Sweden or Switzerland—already implemented (general) carbon taxes. Due to the extent of fluctuations in the world market price of crude oil, phases of marked price reductions for petrol, diesel and heating oil are inevitable despite a CO_2 tax (even as high as 180€ per ton). This also applies if—as planned—the CO_2 tax is raised gradually. In the last 10 years alone, for example, the price of oil fell twice to such an extent that the price of diesel declined by about 50% (Fig. 20.2). As long as the oil price is determined on the derivative markets, where short-term speculative transactions dominate (the trading volume of "paper barrels" is many times greater than global oil production), CO_2 taxes cannot anchor the expectations of a steadily rising price of CO_2 emissions. Rather the opposite: the more the EU (and other countries) succeed in reducing the consumption of fossil energy, the more likely it is that world oil prices will fall, which in turn will counteract the increase in the price of fossil energy through CO_2 taxes.

Regardless of this "rebound effect", renewed drops in oil prices are likely because both supply and demand are not price elastic. Even small increases in global oil supply (e.g., due to "undisciplined" OPEC countries or other oil producers such as Brazil, Guyana, Norway and Canada) or a slight weakening of demand (e.g., due to a further deterioration of the global economy or even a new financial crisis) triggers significant price declines. The basic structural problem is as follows: the global reserves of fossil energy are much larger than the global "CO_2 budget"—if a climate catastrophe is to be avoided, the reserves must not be exhausted. This over-supply will exert a permanent downward pressure on fossil energy prices.

The problem of setting an upward price path of CO_2 through emissions trading schemes can be illustrated using the EU trading scheme (EUETS) as example: It was introduced in 2005 and covers only the main CO_2 emitters from industry such as iron and steel, paper, chemicals, power generation and (EU internal) flights, which together account for about 45% of all CO_2 emissions. In theory, emission trading is the optimal control instrument: the amount of CO_2 is limited by the volume of permits and the cap is gradually reduced. A uniform price is formed on the permit exchanges, which ensures that the emissions occur where their benefit is greatest: A company that needs more certificates because of a good business situation buys them via the exchange from another company that has a surplus. These transactions constitute compliance transactions.

In order for emissions trading to create incentives to invest in the CO_2 reduction, the permit price would have to rise steadily. However, this is precisely what is not the case. In fact, the price for the emission of 1 tonne of CO_2 fluctuated between €32.3 and €3.1 (Fig. 20.1). Moreover, between 2011 and 2017, it was at such a low level that it did not create an incentive to invest in CO_2 avoidance.

This disaster has two main causes. First, the certificates for a longer period must be fixed in advance (almost 12,000 operating sites need planning security). This organizational necessity must lead to misallocations and thus "wrong" CO_2 prices due to the fundamental uncertainty about the medium-term economic development. For example, the financial crisis was—of course—not foreseen, resulting in an oversupply of emission permits so that their price fell to below €10 in 2009 and to below €5 by 2013 (Fig. 20.1). The fact that the EU had to introduce a "Market Stability Reserve" to reduce the (over)supply of allowances illustrates the issue. Second, financial actors on the CO_2 permit exchanges "interpose" themselves between companies with a surplus or deficit of permits and use the derivatives based on permit price as speculative vehicles. Thus, since 2010, 99% of all transactions have been based on derivatives and only 1% on genuine certificates (hedging can therefore only play a minor role). Already in 2012, the total CO_2 transaction volume (including derivatives) was more than 33 times higher than the companies' "compliance needs" (Berta et al. 2017). Moreover, the CO_2 price dynamics shows the pattern typical for speculative price in general: Short-term trends, which are exploited by algorithmic trading, accumulate into longer-term bull or bear markets (Figs. 20.1 and 20.2).[2]

[2]The properties common to speculative assets are: They can easily and almost permanently be traded, at least in derivatives markets (as in the case of commodities), the supply is fixed over the short run and might be shrinking over the long run (as with Bitcoins or CO_2 permits). In the respective markets, professional players trade with amateurs. In some cases, the latter buy or sell the respective asset for reasons of their business in the real economy (e.g., exporters/importers or tourists in the foreign exchange market or industrial or energy companies in the CO_2 emission market).

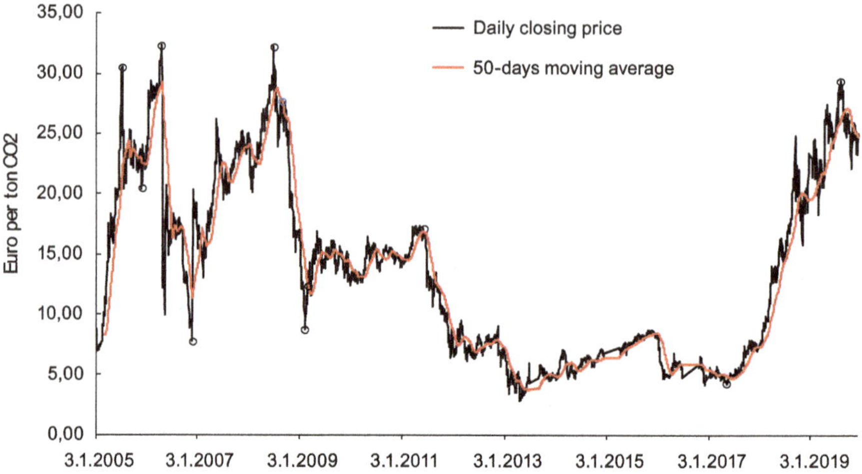

Fig. 20.1 Fluctuations of the price of EU CO_2 emission allowances

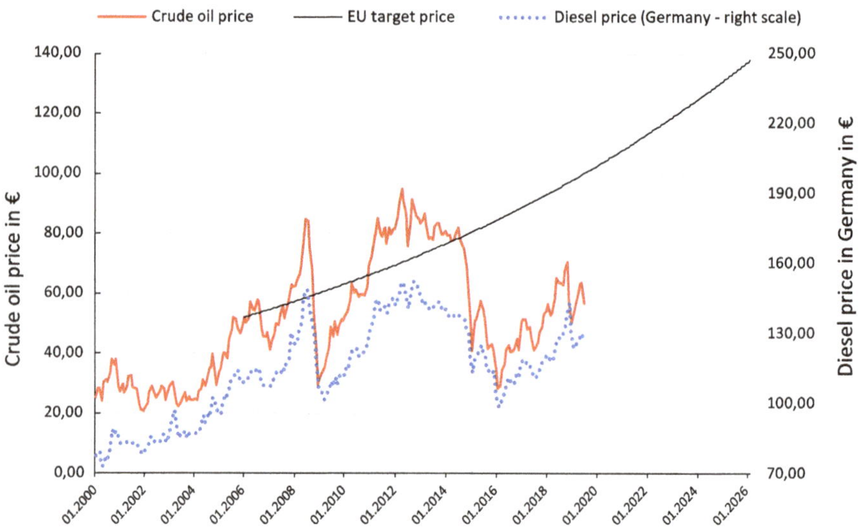

Fig. 20.2 Price incentives for CO_2-reduction—market or target prices

The participating industrial and energy companies, whose CO_2 emissions should be optimally allocated by the system, have to accept permit prices resulting from speculative derivative transactions of "financial investors" (traders). They of course also take into account "news" about the fundamentals, but mainly as a trigger for short-term price movements, which are exploited and reinforced at the same time by technical trading systems (Figs. 20.1 and 20.2 show a particularly simple system: buy or sell when the price intersects the line of the moving average of the last 50 prices from below or above—the "trading systems" used today are much more complex, but all of them aim at exploiting the "trending" of asset prices).

To summarize, the fluctuation of crude oil, coal and natural gas prices as well as of carbon emissions prices is almost systematically preventing ecologically necessary investments, since the profit of the latter lies in the avoided energy costs. Such investments will only be made to a sufficient extent if fossil energy becomes steadily and predictably more expensive. How could this be achieved? Instead of taxing the CO_2 content of oil, coal and natural gas, the EU should set a path with steadily rising prices for these energy sources (initially for about 20 years) and skim off the difference between the EU target price and the respective world market price by means of a monthly adjusted quantity tax—instead of the prices of fossil raw materials and the products made from them, the (implicit) quantity tax should fluctuate.

Here is a thought experiment using the example of crude oil to illustrate the working of such a price and tax regime. On 1 January 2006, the following regulation came into force in the EU: Starting from the (then) current oil price (Brent) of 52.0€, the price valid within the EU would rise along a predetermined path by 5% per year (just 3 percentage points higher than target inflation). This rate of change would be much smaller than the fluctuations realized since then, but it is always positive—and everybody knows it in advance. As a result of a second "bear market", the price of oil fell from €95.0 to €28.3 between March 2012 and January 2016, while the price of diesel in Germany fell from €1.52 to €0.99 (Fig. 20.2). However, the EU guideline price for oil would be €84.8 in January 2016. For February 2016, the EU oil tax would thus amount to 56.5€ (84.8 minus 28.3) per barrel, about twice the oil bill (the figures are for illustrative purposes only; if an EU price path had actually been introduced, the world market price of oil would have developed differently, most probably, it would have been further dampened).

If one considers that the EU had to pay a total of €414.5 billion in 2016 for energy imports—almost exclusively fossil—it becomes clear that the return on an EU tax on fossil energy would be well over €500 billion (even without the UK). In the long term, it would increase at an above-average rate: On the one hand, the EU target price is rising, while on the other hand, the EU's climate policy is curbing its energy imports and thus world market prices. This would also bring about a lasting change in the distribution of oil and natural gas income: These are mostly "rentier income" of the owners of the great oil and gas reservoirs. Whenever oil prices rose in the past, the producing countries, but also the oil companies, made extra ("windfall") profits. By constantly increasing the price *itself*, the EU is dampening world market prices and thus diverting part of the "rents" into the budgets of the Member States.

Technically, the implementation of such a flexible quantity tax would be very simple in the "digital age": Based on the difference between the EU target price and the world market price, the tax per unit of quantity of oil, coal and natural gas valid in the following month is determined at the end of each month by the EU Commission and paid in the Member States by producers and importers of fossil energy in the EU.

What would be the most important price and investment effects of EU target prices for fossil energies (because of the different "CO_2 intensity", the price path for coal should be steeper and that for natural gas flatter than the oil price path)? All goods and services would become more expensive within the EU to the extent that fossil fuels are used in their production (from fuels including kerosene to plastic products). Products produced with renewable energy or less energy would become relatively cheaper. Goods imported into the EU would be subject to an analogous energy tax (border carbon adjustment tax). Since EU price paths "internalise" the environmental costs of fossil fuel consumption, such a levy would not contradict the rules of the World Trade Organization (WTO). As long as no comparable CO_2 taxes exist in the EU's trading partners, EU exports would have to be relieved from the EU tax paid (analogous to VAT).

The investment effects would be most significant: Since owners of single-family homes, housing cooperatives and so on *know* how much heating costs they could save by renovating buildings to make them more energy-efficient, they would expand their investments accordingly. The mandatory price paths would relieve the car companies of a large part of the risk of long-term and expensive investments in the development of electric vehicles. Of course, the "pace" of the price paths should be adapted to developments at greater intervals, but since a reduction in the price of fossil energy is ruled out, the following holds: the earlier an investment is made, the greater is its profit. Such a system of pricing fossil energy would therefore trigger a sustainable investment boom. This could be promoted by using part of the (enormous) returns from the energy tax for long-term large-scale projects (another part should offset the burden of energy price increases on low-income groups). These projects include the energetic restoration of the entire building stock in the EU, the creation of a trans-European network for high-speed trains, the switch to electric cars and to hydrogen technology, especially in the most energy-intensive industries (steel, paper, basic chemicals, building materials) and finally investment in public transport.

Such a Green New Deal would rise and—more important—stabilize economic growth in the EU while at the same time improving long-term environmental conditions. Such a (temporary) "green growth" would reduce unemployment and atypical employment, and with it the (fear of) poverty and declassing of more and more people. Technically, it would be far easier to implement just three flexible quantity taxes on oil, coal and natural gas than managing the complex and bureaucratic EU emissions trading scheme (not to speak about extending it to transport and housing) or taxing the CO_2 equivalent of all primary production inputs.

Thermic Renovation of the Stock of Buildings in the EU

The energy requirement of (residential) buildings for heating, air-conditioning and warming water can technically be reduced by almost 100% in most cases. Even if one would reach only the "low energy standard", one could save roughly 80% in energy and, hence, in CO_2 emissions. At the same time, however, the renovation rate per year is less than 1% in the EU. This situation calls for initiating and implementing a mega-project in the spirit of the New Deal: The thermic renovation of the overall stock of existing—primarily residential—buildings in all EU countries over a period of 15–20 years. This project should be promoted at all levels—from the EU down to the communities—by linking together business, banking, public administration, house owner and residents in "concerted actions". The project needs to be promoted through campaigns in TV, print and social media, documentation of best practices (in particular with respect to the insulation material), engagement of local banks taking over the management of single projects ("one-stop-shop") in exchange for secure investment/credit opportunities in real capital, etc. The macroeconomic effects of this project would be very substantial for several reasons: It consists of millions of single projects and, hence, stimulates the economy on a large-area basis, that is, EU-wide. The production is labour-intensive and requires in particular not "too" highly qualified workers. For both reasons, the multiplier effects will be above average. Very rough estimates indicate that the annual GDP growth in the EU could be raised by up to 3 percentage points through such a "mega project" (Schulmeister 2018, p. 334).

Trans-European Network of High-Speed Railways

If the price of fossil energy would steadily increase in the EU, using airplanes as means of transport would become particularly more expensive. At the same time, air traffic accounts for a substantial part of CO_2 emissions. To steadily reduce them, one needs alternatives for transportation, in particular over distances below 1000 km, for example, a net of high-speed railways.

Nowadays, high-speed trains already reach more than 500 km/hour in tests. It is therefore not unrealistic that it might take roughly 3 hours to get by train from Berlin to Paris. If, at the same time, an air ticket for the same trip cost several hundred euros, more and more people would prefer the train (as is already the case today for the trip from Milan to Rome as the train takes less than 4 hours). Constructing such a railway network will take several decades, it would create a great number of jobs and it would "move" the countries at the EU periphery like Romania, Bulgaria, the Baltic states and also—in the future—the Western Balkans closer to the centre, not only as regards travel distance, but also the social–psychological and political distance.

Overcoming Europe's "Digital Colonization"

Wherever exchange, transportation and communication links are to be extended, uniform networks and standards offer the most efficient solutions. This holds for physical networks as "natural monopolies" (railways, power and water lines, etc.), for information networks as "quasi-natural monopolies" (Facebook, Twitter, etc.), for search engines like Google, for operating systems (Windows of Microsoft, OS of Apple), for standard software like Microsoft Office as well as for internet platforms for services exchange (Airbnb, Uber, etc.). As efficient as such "universal solutions" are, they give private (US) corporations (quasi-) monopoly positions in the global economy. As a result, Facebook, Google, Apple, Microsoft, Airbnb, Uber or Amazon not only receives billions of euros as monopoly rents, but also an incredible amount of information about the lifestyles, values and preferences of every single user in the world. This information is linked and used for commercial and political advertising. Whoever has these data at his disposal can also manipulate democratic processes.

This situation poses a challenge for the EU in several respects. First, the EU has no chance to obtain any control or even substantial information on the use of the data collected by the giants of the Silicon Valley. Second, households and companies in the EU will have to pay monopoly rents to the USA which can be increased at will—for at least the next decades. Third, Europe remains technologically dependent on US companies in a field which is extremely important and vulnerable at the same time—in particular in times of crises (e.g., all government agencies in the EU use Microsoft Office).

The only viable way out of the dilemma: Europe must develop its own operation system, standard software, networks and search engines. Just as with the "natural" monopolies of rail, electricity or water supply networks, the "quasi-natural" IT monopolies should be operated by enterprises in the public interest. To this end, a European Software Consortium (ESC) should be created, in which the best IT companies, university departments and research institutes from the entire EU work together. After all, there are hundreds of thousands of highly qualified computer scientists and engineers, most of whom are highly motivated to work on such a European emancipation project.

The best historical example of such a strategy was the creation of Airbus in 1970, when Europe was lagging behind the US in the aircraft industry more than it is today in information technology. The formation of a trans-European consortium, massive subsidies and the political consensus on the importance of this project made it possible to catch up within 20 years. The realization of this Pan-European mega-project requires close cooperation between research policy and companies (at the EU level as well as within the member states) and massive financial support for the ESC. For example, the number of ESC employees could well reach the size of Airbus (about 60,000). An annual budget of 15 billion euros may seem gigantic at first glance, but it would still only be 0.1% of the EU GDP (without the UK). Finally, implementing this project also requires a sustained campaign to educate the public that Europe's information technology dependence will not only force tribute payments to the USA for decades, but will also threaten freedom of opinion, democracy and human rights. If all these conditions were fulfilled, Europe could overcome its "digital colonization" in 10–20 years.

References

Berta, N., Gautherat, E., & Gun, O. (2017). Transactions in the European carbon market: A bubble of compliance in a whirlpool of speculation. *Cambridge Journal of Economics, 41*(2017), 575–593.

Frankel, J. (2020). The best tool to fight climate change. Project Syndicate. https://www.project-syndicate.org/commentary/higher-carbon-price-best-tool-to-fight-climate-change-by-jeffrey-frankel-2020-01. Accessed 1 Mar 2020.

Schulmeister, S. (2018). *Der Weg zur Prosperität*. Salzburg: Ecowin.

21

Investment in the EU and the Role of EFSI

Stephany Griffith-Jones

Abstract This chapter analyzes the Juncker Plan, in particular, the European Fund for Strategic Investment (EFSI), highlighting its achievements in expanding investment in the European Union and challenges in mitigating future risks to the European Investment Bank, as well as maximizing the development impact of its activities.

Introduction

Economic growth and specifically investment levels in the European Union (EU) recovered far more slowly after the financial crisis than, for example, in the United States or even more in Asia (Klein 2019). Total investment is too low in the European Union. For some time before the crisis, the EU had relatively low levels of investment, reaching 22.5% of GDP in 2006. In emerging and developing economies, it reached 26.7% in the same year. But the 2007–2009 financial crisis and the Eurozone debt crisis dragged it sharply downward. By 2016, total EU investment had fallen to 19.9% of GDP, even as emerging and developing countries were at 24.5%. The fall in public investment has been striking in the Eurozone—over 20% between 2007 and 2016. The trend was most notable in the crisis-hit countries. For example, gross public investment in Greece fell from a high 4.9% of GDP in 2006 to 3.1% in 2016—and that of a far smaller GDP due to a major contraction. In Spain, the same ratio declined even more dramatically, from 4.3% in 2006 to 1.4% in 2016. Net public investment—gross investment minus depreciation—was actually negative in the Eurozone in 2016. Some member states were, of course, affected more, but this decrease in public investment represented a worrying trend common across most of the Eurozone. Even in Germany, gross public investment was low and below the Eurozone average.

S. Griffith-Jones (✉)
Initiative for Policy Dialogue, Columbia University, New York, USA

Institute of Development Studies, Sussex University Brighton, Brighton, UK
e-mail: sgj2108@columbia.edu

The reasons for the decline in public investment across Europe were clear. In crisis-wracked countries, austerity forced on countries including Greece, Spain, Portugal and Ireland compelled large cuts in government expenditures. It was impossible to cut the lifelines on which so many depend, for instance, assistance in housing. The consequences of these cutbacks are felt immediately; it will be years before the consequences of cutbacks in public investment are noted. Therefore, politicians focus cutbacks disproportionately on investment. But even in countries with public finances that would have permitted greater investment, notably Germany, ideology prevented higher public investment, that would have both increased aggregate demand and immediate growth, as well as future growth.

In 2015, the European Commission acknowledged the Growth and Stability Pact served the Eurozone badly and published a framework allowing countries to deviate from the anti-deficit rules to promote investment. Though the flexibility introduced was welcome, the problem that the Pact curtails productive investment at precisely the time it is needed most remained. Even worse, it curtails productive investment at precisely the time when the social benefit cost ratio is highest, and when the opportunity cost of these investments is low. Public investments are not crowding out (displacing) either private investments or consumption, because it can use resources that otherwise would be idle. On the contrary, public investments crowd in private investment.

Even in financial terms, economic downturns are the time to make investment. With long-term government bond yields close to zero, it would have been easy to find public investment projects that generate a much higher return. By failing to increase government investments in this period, Europe missed an opportunity, which was reflected in the far lower growth rate it had than for example the United States, even though the financial crisis originally came from the United States. During and after the Eurozone debt crisis, problems with low aggregate demand, economic uncertainty and a weakened private banking system contributed also to low levels of private investment. The reduction was sharpest in the southern Eurozone countries, with private investment decreasing from 22% of GDP in 2007 to 14% in 2014—but the picture was almost uniformly grim across Europe.

After the Eurozone debt crisis started, creditor Governments (especially Germany, but also Holland, and Finland) were unwilling to modify in a significant way the so-called Growth and Stability Pact, so as to allow countries to increase their national fiscal deficits to fund higher public investment; this was argued would have been a desirable path forward by many academics, such as Peter Bofinger and Gustav Horn in Germany, as well as Paul Krugman and Joseph Stiglitz internationally (e.g. for the latter see Stiglitz 2019), as well as of course the governments and academics of crisis countries and France. At the same time, it was difficult formally to expand EU level of investment (e.g. via Structural Funds), because the European Union budget had been approved until 2020; of course supplementary funds could have been made available if member states were willing, again, this was blocked especially by creditor countries. Simultaneously, in the wake of the financial crisis of 2007–2009, and the Eurozone debt crisis of 2009–2010, there had been renewed support for public regional and national development banks, as the limitations and problems of a purely private financial sector became more evident to different strands of economic thinking (Griffith-Jones and Ocampo 2018).

In this context, the European Investment Bank Group (EIB), with its long track record of successfully playing a key and large role in funding intra-European infrastructure, including renewable energy, Small and medium enterprises (SMEs) and innovation, took on renewed importance. Thus, an indirect route, using the European Investment Bank, was chosen to encourage investment, especially private one, in the European Union. A first step was the doubling of paid-in capital of EIB by all member states in 2012, which allowed EIB to expand its lending (Griffith-Jones and Kollatz 2012). The public contribution by member states was limited, but was reported to generate far higher finance and investment via leverage with private resources.

Furthermore, as a more traditional Keynesian response (at both national and Eurozone levels) was not deemed acceptable, EFSI was created, as a sort of Keynesian mechanism "sans dire", and with no or little additional public money, but a large potential impact, due to the effect of leverage. Indeed, the EIB is implementing the European Fund for Strategic Investment (EFSI), which is the core of the Investment Plan for Europe (the "Juncker Plan"), and aims to fund much needed investment for Europe, especially in the wake of devastating austerity (phase 1) as well as to facilitate much needed structural change to a greener, more dynamic and more inclusive economy (phase 2). Emphasis was placed on financing riskier investment, for example in the crisis-hit countries, as well as in the newer member countries. In this context, the Juncker Plan seems broadly highly successful (Fig. 21.1).

The EFSI is a EUR 26 billion guarantee from the EU budget, which comes mainly from existing research and innovation and transport budget lines, complemented by a EUR 7.5 billion allocation of the EIB's own capital, given EU budget limitations. The total amount of EUR 33.5 billion aims to leverage additional investment of at least EUR 500 billion between 2015 and 2020. Essentially a small fraction of the EU budget is used as a guarantee for EIB projects that have a higher risk profile than the usual ones. The aim is to push the EIB to finance valuable but risky projects that could not secure funding on their own, to adopt a junior position with respect to co-financiers, to reduce the risks taken by private investors and to increase the chances of attracting their investment (interview material). EFSI has two components, the innovation and infrastructure window managed by the EIB, and the SME window implemented by the EIF (European Investment Fund).[1]

It is interesting that about a fourth of the transactions of EFSI are estimated to have been channeled through national development banks (NDBs), thus increasing the role these banks play in the EU. They will play an even larger role in InvestEU. Indeed, in InvestEU, the EU guarantee can be granted directly to NDBs, up to a certain proportion. If properly done, increasing the loan volume through leverage is a positive thing, as it should facilitate higher levels of investment. However, there is a risk that the greater the loan volume achieved through involving

[1] https://www.eif.org/what_we_do/efsi/index.htm. Accessed 08 March 2020.

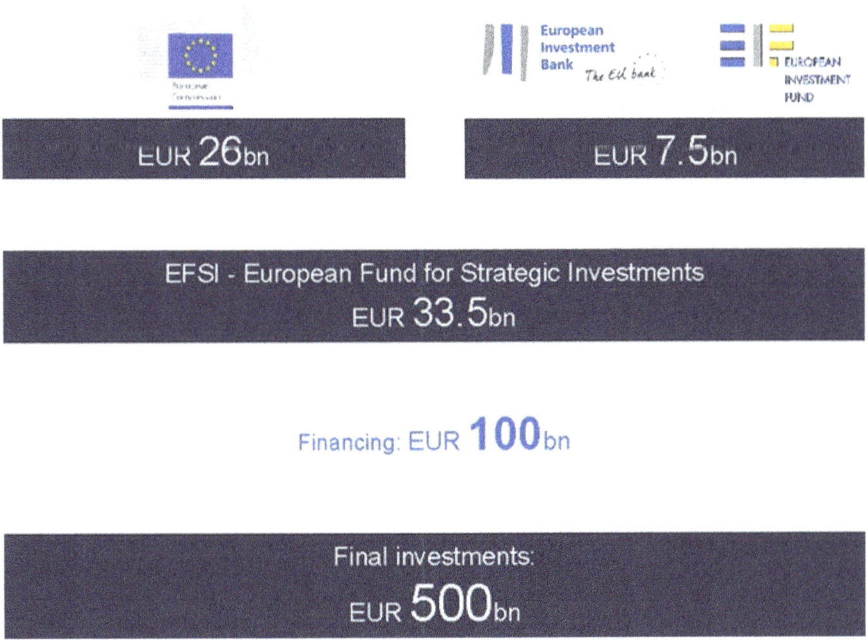

Fig. 21.1 Structure of EFSI. (Source: Interview material)

private intermediaries, the more indirect the operations become, and the less strategic direction the European institutions are able to exert over projects. In this sense, there is some trade-off between loan volume and policy steer.

For the next EU budget (2021–2027), the Commission is developing the continuation of EFSI, with some modifications as the InvestEU Fund. The InvestEU Fund will consolidate various EU financing programs and instruments into one, which should lead to economic efficiency gains, and politically may be more desirable, due to greater decentralization; InvestEU will follow the Juncker Plan model of mobilizing additional private funds for additional investment. This is expected to allow the EU budget to provide a €30 billion guarantee, expected to crowd in an additional total of €650 billion of mainly private investments over the 7-year period. It is argued this will result in investment far greater than is possible via for example public investment, in the context of member states' budget real and perceived constraints, or via conventional EIB activities, as happened before EFSI.

One of the continuous challenges to move beyond the crisis is to restore growth in the European Union, but this should not just be more dynamic but both more sustainable and inclusive growth. Particular priority has rightly been given by the EU to measures and instruments to facilitate a speedy and significant transition to a low carbon economy.

Indeed, the European Commission's Green Deal released in December 2019, and the accompanying Investment Plan (EGDIP), which aims to make the EU into the first climate neutral bloc in the world by 2050, will be key. The European Investment

Bank (EIB) as well as the European countries' national development banks (NDBs)—which have been expanding in scale and extension to practically all EU countries—are expected to play a key role, both in funding key investments for the green transformation directly, as well as in catalyzing significant additional private finance (both lending and equity) to low carbon projects.

It is important that the EU as a whole as well as individual EU countries deploy broader policy measures to facilitate finance (both public and private) is redirected and channeled to low carbon or carbon neutral activities. These broader policy measures could, for example, include financial regulatory and fiscal policies that would supplement and support the activity of EIB and NDBs in the green transformation.

In this sense, it is important to have an ambitious design of structural transformation for the EU economies (e.g. in sectors like electro-mobility and renewable energy, and the infrastructure that supports them), with a large impact on lowering carbon emissions to meet the challenges of the climate emergency.

A Bit of History

The EIB was established in 1958 by the Treaty of Rome, and historically provided infrastructure financing, usually through long-term fixed interest rate loans, backed by member state guarantees. The EIB then broadened its activities and currently focuses on: innovation, SMEs, infrastructure and environment.

The EIB essentially took little risks on its activities and had an AAA credit rating, which it could use to cheaply finance its activities on international financial markets, and then on-lend very cheaply to its customers. It is interesting that even though several member countries were downgraded from AAA (some dramatically like Greece), after the Eurozone debt crisis, the EIB maintained its AAA status, though using lower leverage than in the past (Interview material). The fact that EIB maintains AAA status is very positive from the perspective of the borrowers, as well as its strength as a major EU institution. From the late 1980s/early 1990s, the EIB began changing its business model to take on more risk, as its statute was amended to manage the new European Investment Fund (EIF). The EIF has a unique capital structure, with most of its capital contributed by the European Commission and the EIB, 11.6% of its capital is owned by public and private financial institutions; most of these are national development banks, but also some large private banks, like Barclays (Interview material). The instruments evolved. The EIB and EIF began giving loan guarantees, relaxing requirements for member state guarantees and using equity instruments. Though guarantees can be problematic, especially if badly structured, or if a big financial crisis happens (where uncorrelated risks become correlated), they have important advantages. Furthermore, it is argued by some that "the biggest risk are grants", because there is in that case certainty the funds will not be paid back. So guarantees have two advantages: firstly, they provide leverage, and secondly, they are like a revolving fund and resources can be used again if there are no major losses. On the other hand, if major losses occur, the provisions are not sufficient and guarantees have not been fully priced, then governments (taxpayers) have to pay in the future. Furthermore, there is evidence that, though the EIB and EIF pay fully the price of the European Commission guarantee, it is likely that an important part of EFSI guarantees granted to commercial banks do not price fully their cost. Above all, the pricing of guarantees seems opaque. This is reportedly in contrast with loans, where products are more fully standardized and transparent (Interview material).

The EIB's approach to innovation also changed. Until 2007, innovation was only funded through grants. In 2007, the EC and the EIB set up the Risk Sharing Finance Facility (RSFF) with the stated aim of improving access to finance for activities in the field of R&D and innovation. It was built on the principle of *pari passu* (equal) credit risk sharing between the EC and the EIB, which was designed to give the EIB capital relief, and therefore allow it to take more risk by providing loans or guarantees with a sub-investment grade risk profile. This could be said to be the first time EU institutions used financial engineering to make risk-sharing agreements, and became the blueprint for EFSI (interview material).

The Working of EFSI

EFSI has a high overall multiplier target of 15×. The first step is the internal multiplier of 3×, where the EFSI guarantee of 33.5 billion Euros from the European budget is expected to generate 100 billion Euros of EIB financing on international financial markets. The second step is the external multiplier of 5×, where the internal funds of 100 billion are expected to catalyze additional private and public financing to reach a total mobilized investment volume of 500 billion. The external multiplier varies across financial products, so the 5× target applies to the entire portfolio of operations. The overall multiplier target of 15× is the relation between expected total investment mobilized (500 billion) and the initial EFSI guarantee (33.5 billion) (EIB 2019) (Fig. 21.2).

The EFSI has taken a number of steps including the creation and use of new financial instruments (financial innovation), especially in EIB operations, while EIF operations for SMEs relied mainly on existing instruments; both encourage greater involvement of public and private actors, in particular national development banks (NDBs) and institutional investors. The mobilization of private capital brings potential benefits (achieving higher levels of investment, by "doing more with less fiscal resources"), but also generates potential risks, via contingent liabilities, that need to be properly accounted and provisioned for. In 2014, the RSFF was turned into InnovFin, and both the size of the funds as well as the range of financial products were increased.[2] COSME, the EU program for Competitiveness of Enterprises and SMEs, operated by EIF, was also set up during 2014–2020, with a budget of €2.3

[2] https://www.eib.org/en/products/blending/innovfin/index.htm. Accessed 08 March 2020.

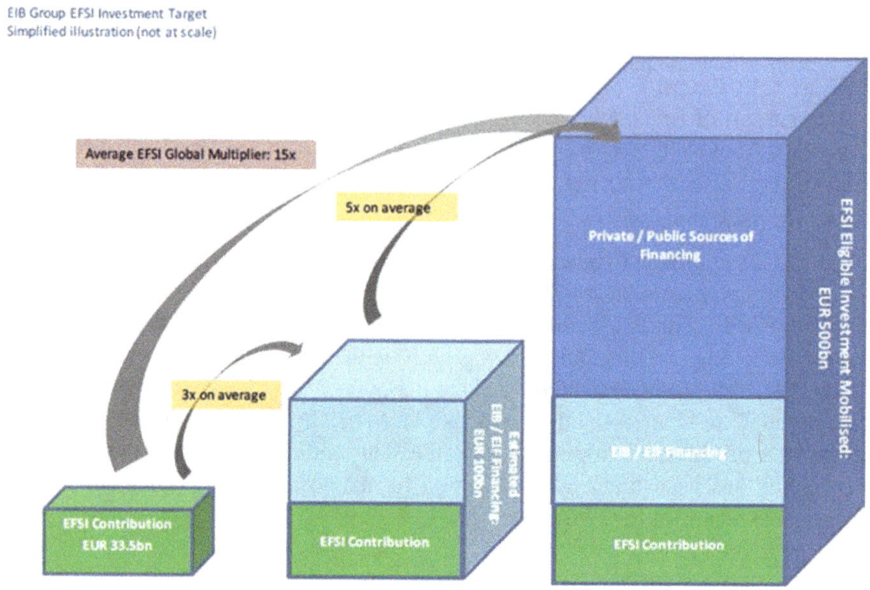

Fig. 21.2 Overall multiplier for EFSI. (Source: EIB 2019a)

billion, in order to provide financing support for SMEs.[3] COSME has a Loan Guarantee Facility that aims to enable financial institutions to increase loan and lease finance to SMEs, as well as an Equity Facility for Growth that provides risk capital to equity funds that invest in SMEs.

Financial Products

The EFSI has widened its range of financial products to include not only its traditional loans and guarantees, but also credit enhancement products, using the RSFF blueprint and equity type products (for more details, see Griffith-Jones and Naqvi Forthcoming). Equity type products imply more risk than loans, but have the advantage of also being able to "capture the upside" if projects are more profitable than expected. One such instrument being currently applied is venture debt. The EFSI operational strategy further specifies the different products that the EIB Group can use to deploy EFSI. These include senior and junior loans, risk-sharing instruments and capital market instruments including equity or quasi-equity participations (European Court of Auditors 2019, p. 18).

Under the SME window, EIF continues to rely on existing products already used under COSME, InnovFin and other mandates. It was reportedly an advantage for

[3] https://ec.europa.eu/docsroom/documents/9783. Accessed 08 March 2020.

the SME window, EFSI, especially initially, used existing, well-tested product lines. This seemed a wise decision. It may have contributed to the more rapid deployment of EFSI finance for SMEs, especially initially seen as more successful. The EIF's volume of operations has been increased very significantly thanks to EFSI, growing from EUR 3.3 billion in 2014 to EUR 10 billion in 2018, that is more than tripling in 4 years (interview material). EIF's focus is to enhance access to finance for SMEs as part of its EU mandate, but also provides ecosystem support like development of the European venture capital market, as well as the market for business angels, via a fund to co-finance with angels, that helps develop fintech, crowd funding, etc. EIF covers the whole financing chain, starting with funding for seed capital to later-stage growth to mid-cap market, but also is active in more mature markers with guaranteed products. EIF does not finance SMEs directly, but always goes through intermediaries—the guarantee is provided to banks or counter guarantees are provided to guarantee institutions (NDBs mainly like BPI France, KfW). The counterparty has to do riskier business than they would do normally if they get EIF guarantees.

Because COSME was focused on smaller transactions, over one million SMEs have been supported. EFSI support has also not just increased number of SMEs served, but also riskier SMEs, in more countries. Start-ups are often neglected on the side of debt, some sectors are neglected, for example, creative, but even traditional sectors have niches of sectors not well served. Under the infrastructure window, in addition to relying on traditional long-term senior loans (about 60% of the total), the EIB expanded the use of existing higher-risk products and developed new ones. The EIB has conducted securitized transactions under the infrastructure window in partnership with the EIF. One of the interesting new products is venture debt where EIB provides debt, but there is an equity kicker—if business does well, EIB also gets part of that higher profit, as compensation for taking higher risk, implying this is an instrument where EIB captures the upside, which is clearly desirable, as EIB is not just sharing risks but also profits with private company.

Analytical Framework for Different Risks

There is a key distinction on the nature of risk that is essential to clarify, both from an analytical point of view and a policy perspective. This should be important to evaluate initiatives like EFSI and InvestEU. There is first the "economic" type of risks; these are basically related to the natural uncertainty related to projects or sectors. These are typically: (1) in infrastructure projects (e.g. risks of construction difficulties and delays, especially in engineering ambitious projects, see for example, Griffith-Jones 1993); (2) "Economic" risks are also very prevalent in the funding of innovative companies, such as start-ups, often based on potentially excellent ideas, but lacking assets for guarantees, and/or track record; (3) Financing SMEs is generally considered riskier in most countries, except in countries like Germany, with decentralized banking systems, which allow for greater knowledge of companies. SME financing becomes riskier if financial crisis happens, when the benefits of diversification are reduced; (4) Very importantly, "economic" risks can also relate to sectorial or cross-sectorial innovation that may lead to major increases in productivity and/or significant structural transformation, for example to a greener economy (Mazzucato 2013); (5) Also assuming "economic" risk implies lending to or investing in countries that are (usually temporarily) seen as less creditworthy by financial markets, especially, during, and in the long aftermath of, financial crises or other major shocks.

These "economic" types of risks are in sharp contrast with "financial engineering" risks, created by financial actors, often partly hidden by opaque and complex structures, and whose impact only often emerges ex post in crises' situations. The alleged, and sometimes legitimate, aim may in some cases partly be to increase leverage of public resources, and for this reason may be backed also by policy-makers, with the aim of doing "more with less", as in the case of the European Union. However, the main general aim of creating instruments with "financial engineering" risk is to increase profitability for private financial actors, while minimizing their risk of losses. The financial sector, however, must serve the real economy, and financial objectives, for example, the development of capital markets, must never be an end in itself. EFSI and InvestEU must have a greater focus on the final beneficiaries of projects rather than on the private financial intermediaries.

The distinction between "economic" and "financial" risk was less important in the aftermath of the 2008 and Eurozone debt crisis, as there was a great need to counter-cyclically increase lending volume to maintain investment as the private financial sector became risk averse. However, now the private financial sector has become more willing to lend, and even does so at very low margins, there is not much benefit in most countries and sectors to de-risking them further. Indeed, they may even need to be held back from causing a bubble in certain sectors (interview material). However, there remains a need to take "economic risk", especially for sectors important for industrial policy/structural transformation, or developmental objectives, such as green energy, innovative companies or riskier less developed EU countries. Financial risk on the other hand needs to be limited in scale, very carefully evaluated ex-ante, to avoid large contingent liabilities and possible significant losses.

One of the main aims of the Juncker plan and EFSI is to provide finance to valuable projects that would not get financed on private markets, or through normal EIB channels due to their high risk. Although these risky projects might not be bankable in the sense of resulting in short-term profits, they are vital for long-run growth and structural transformation. The Juncker plan envisions doing this by getting the EIB to take on more risk than it normally would. While EFSI (in its phase 1) initially had a counter-cyclical focus in the postcrisis environment, EFSI 2 and InvestEU have more of a structural transformation objective.

The EU institution's matrix for assessing whether this developmental role is being played is to take into account the risk profile of the EIB's financial products, rather than on the beneficiaries. This can be problematic in some cases, as economic and financial risks can at times diverge, and projects that the EIB classified as "high risk" according to the EFSI objectives may in fact only be risky in the financial sense. In some cases, the same project was classified as a riskier EFSI project rather than a normal EIB project, purely because the financial products changed to riskier ones (interview material).

While funding projects with economic risk is good, taking excessive financial risk through complex financial products or through too high risk sharing with the private sector creates the danger that the public entities (and ultimately the taxpayers) will bear the risks, while the private sector reaps all the rewards. It could also have negative long-term budgetary implications via contingent liabilities. This leads us to the third issue, which is that of the distribution of risks of losses and profits, between the public actors (in this case, EIB and European Commission funds, for example deployed as guarantees) and the private financial actors (lenders and investors). If with the aim to attract additional private lending or investing, financial products are created that generate too much additional financial risk and transfer too high a proportion of that risk to the public sector (especially without transferring any of the potential upside of profits to the public sector), then this is highly undesirable from a welfare and public policy perspective. This is particularly the case if these instruments lead to high losses, which can only be known ex-post in the future; such losses could be costly to the public sector, if the instruments are not properly priced, and can generate future problems if there are no adequate provisions against such potential future losses. Because many of the projects have long maturities, it is harder to know what the longer term possible losses and thus budgetary implications of the risk-sharing agreements are before loans become due (interview material).

Collaboration with National Development Banks

The EIB's cooperation with member states' national development banks (NDBs) has been strongly enhanced as part of EFSI, including its leverage strategy. As discussed above, participation of an NDB as a financial intermediary increases EFSI's leverage due to the catalytic effect. NDB participation also helps with overcoming fiscal constraints. Although NDB activities do count as contingent liabilities, they do not count toward the Maastricht criteria (EC 2015). Cooperation between the EIB and NDBs can take four forms: (1) Co-investment, at the project level; (2) Intermediated financing where the EIB provides loans or guarantees to NDBs for on-lending; (3) Risk-sharing instruments where the EIB makes an agreement to cover up to a certain percentage of credit risk associated with a portfolio of loans. This reduces the exposure of the NDB to certain sectors or client segments, and frees up capital and other resources to grant new loans; (4) Collaborative investment platforms that involve joint cooperation among the EIB Group, several NDBs and potentially other IFIs, the latter especially in the context of InvestEU (EIB 2016).

Distribution of EFSI Resources Between Countries

Is EFSI a tool that can benefit all Member States? Because the EFSI has been designed to allocate financial support without so-called "political interference" in the selection of projects, it is more prone to support those economies where greater investment opportunities already exist. Since the very beginning of the program, the uneven geographical distribution of its support has been criticized. Larger and richer economies have more experience to develop a greater number of viable projects. By mid-2016, almost all financing granted under the EFSI (92%) had been allocated to the initial member countries, the EU-15, among which the largest beneficiaries were Italy, Spain and the UK. This is in stark contrast with the "new" EU-13 (mainly the Central and Eastern European countries that joined later), which accounted for a mere 8% of disbursements.

Although less developed EU countries were initially excluded, the situation seemed to be improving, as special efforts were made in this. Data from the European Parliament shows that while the more advanced Western European countries are the main beneficiaries in terms of absolute investment, once size of the economy and population are accounted for, the distribution is much less concentrated (European Parliament 2017, pp. 13–15). Countries harmed by austerity, including Spain, Portugal, Italy and Greece, now rank among the highest receivers of EFSI investment as a percentage of GDP, which is to be praised. In investment per capita terms, they also remain high, but Central and Eastern European countries, in particular, Romania, Croatia and Hungary, remain lagging behind. Capacity building to overcome discrepancies like these must become one of the key objectives for both the European Investment Bank as an institution and EFSI as a mechanism (Griffith-Jones and Naqvi Forthcoming).

Conclusion

Relying on a budgetary allocation of EUR 33.5 billion, EFSI aims to leverage additional investment of at least EUR 500 billion between 2015 and 2020. The plan seems to be broadly on track, with EUR 70.4 billion of financing approved, from which EFSI claims to have mobilized a total of EUR 375.5 billion, as of July 2018.[4] One important achievement of EFSI is that of the clients it has served, 75% are new ones, who had never borrowed before from the EIB. This is encouraging, in terms of additionality achieved and new clients. Furthermore, before EFSI, the EIB is reported to have had among its operations only 5% of risky business; however, by 2018, 20% of EIB operations are reportedly risky business (interview material). This is a positive achievement, particularly to the extent that increased risk means increased economic risk and not purely financial risk.

[4] https://www.eib.org/en/efsi/. Accessed 08 March 2020.

In the context of supporting innovative technologies, with climate mitigation aspects, it is impressive that the EIB has funded 40% of offshore wind installed capacity in Europe; it often moved to support the more innovative aspects of offshore (larger scale of blades, and even floating offshore wind farms). The EFSI thus has important achievements, including the significant leverage it is providing on scarce EU budget resources, to help provide lending and guarantees to important innovative projects and provide additional resources to countries that have suffered from the Eurozone crisis, or who are new EU members, as well as supporting increased investment in the EU more broadly. It has also allowed the EIF to significantly increase its operations in its important role of catalyzing financing for SMEs.

While the mobilization of private capital brings potential benefits (achieving higher levels of investment, by "doing more with less fiscal resources"), it also generates potential risks, via contingent liabilities, that need to be properly accounted for and provisioned for. The use of opaque new financial instruments can further increase unnecessary "financial" risk, of the type that resulted in the 2007 subprime mortgage crisis, without increasing necessary and valuable "economic" risks. There is also a risk that the greater the loan volume achieved through involving private intermediaries, the more indirect the operations become, and the less strategic direction the European institutions are able to exert over projects.

While funding projects with economic risk is valuable, taking excessive financial risk through complex financial products or through excessive risk sharing with the private sector creates the danger that public entities (and ultimately the taxpayers) will bear the risks, while the private sector reaps all the rewards. This is highly undesirable from a welfare and public policy perspective. If the EIB wants to take more risk, it is key it identifies higher risk projects/sectors/countries, as opposed to higher risk financial products.

References

EIB (2016). Rules applicable to operations with investment platforms and national promotional banks or institutions. Available at https://www.eib.org/attachments/strategies/efsi_steering_board_rules_applicable_to_operations_with_investment_platforms_and_npbs_or_institutions_en.pdf.

EIB (2019). A. EIB EFSI multiplier methodology calculation. Available at https://www.eib.org/attachments/strategies/efsi_steering_board_efsi_multiplier_methodology_calculation_en.pdf.

European Commission (2015). 'Working together for jobs and growth: The role of National Promotional Banks (NPBs) in supporting the Investment Plan for Europe'. Communication from the Commission to the European Parliament and the Council. Available at: http://europeanmemoranda.cabinetoffice.gov.uk/files/2015/07/11283-15.pdf.

Griffith-Jones, S. (1993). *Loan guarantees for large infrastructure projects: The issues and possible lessons for a European facility*. Office for official publications of the European communities. https://stephanygj.net/papers/LoanGuaranteesforLargeInfrastructureProjects1993.pdf. Accessed 1 Mar 2020.

Griffith-Jones, S., & Kollatz-Ahnen. (2012). Stimulating Europe. Financial Times, 18 June 2012. http://policydialogue.org/files/publications/papers/Stimulating_Europe_061812.pdf. Accessed 1 Mar 2020.

Griffith-Jones, S., & Naqvi, N. (Forthcoming). Leveraging policy steer? Industrial policy, risk-sharing and the European Investment Bank. In D. Mertens, M. Thiemann, & P. Volberding (Eds.), *The reinvention of development banking in the EU*. OUP.

Griffith-Jones, S., & Ocampo, J. A. (Eds.). (2018). *The future of national development banks*. Oxford: Oxford University Press.

Klein, M. (2019). Italy embraces China and Europe's elites have only themselves to blame. Barron's 5 April 2019. https://www.barrons.com/articles/europes-elites-have-only-themselves-to-blame-for-italys-embrace-of-china-51554481025. Accessed 1 Mar 2020.

Mazzucato, M. (2013). Financing innovation: Creative destruction vs. destructive creation. *Industrial and Corporate Change, 22*(4), 851–867.

Stiglitz, J. (2019). *People, power, and profits: Progressive capitalism for an age of discontent*. Penguin UK.

22

EU and Solidarity Financing

Christian Ghymers

Abstract This Chapter shows that there still exist urgent actions possible with existing tools and procedures for breaking the prisoner dilemma through modalities of solidarity leading to more responsibility. These feasible solutions are simple recipes based upon past experiences for opening again the European Union (EU) win–win game by activating conditional incentives able to enhance channelled financial market reactions favourable to adjusting countries, preventing self-fulfilling speculation and benefiting the whole EU.

Introduction

Northern European Union (EU) member states (MS) fear that solidarity financing could weaken national responsibility and postpone the necessary budgetary consolidation in the South. However, this position has made more difficult any adjustment and increased the gravity of the crisis, with Southern economies falling in deeper depression, worsening their fiscal position but also leading to depressing spillovers to the North. This "loss-loss" game illustrates the "*prisoner dilemma*" impeding solidarity and responsibility in the euro-area: the European Central Bank (ECB) cannot give liquidity without guarantee of effective fiscal sustainability while fiscal sustainability is impossible without a liquidity safety net for preventing contagion and rescuing treasuries in liquidity trouble even when they try to adjust. A significant part of this deadlock comes from the overwhelming dogmatic ideas relative to spontaneous efficiency of free markets—especially for financial markets—combined with the rent-seeking interests of incumbent authorities whatever left or right.

In a nutshell, this general dogmatic belief has led to combine two big "technical" mistakes of the Economic and Monetary Union (EMU) architecture:

C. Ghymers (✉)
Founder and Co-coordinator of the Jean Monnet Network "Crisis-Equity-Democracy for Europe and Latin America", IRELAC, Brussels, Belgium

(i) The euro-area remains especially exposed to the destabilizing power of wild financial markets because it is the only monetary area in the world without a genuine Lender-of-Last-Resort (LOLR) and without credible mechanisms of solidarity among its members. In the EMU, this gives financial markets the power to precipitate a liquidity crisis (and even to turn it into a solvency crisis cfr. Spain) in a one-bet speculation in case of doubts on sovereign debts because national treasuries cannot control, by definition, the currency and the exchange rate in which they issue their debt, like Argentina during its currency board with the dollar.

(ii) This fatal caveat was combined with a surveillance process of national policies, which remained excessively intergovernmental and imbalanced, with ministers playing as "*Judges and Parts*". It focused almost exclusively upon fiscal policies (Stability and Growth Pact—SGP) and adopted a benign neglect about the divergences and current account disequilibrium that the single currency inevitably had to imply.[1] The argument of financial efficiency was used for presenting these results as sound because they are the inner advantage of the single currency, which eradicates saving constraints, allowing both left and right governments to satisfy their respective electorates in such an EMU regime spurring consumption, indebtedness and speculation, but accumulating unsustainable disequilibrium within the euro-area.

The same dogmatism explains the refuse to care about the credit-boom and the unproductive uses of these huge free capital flows in the Southern economies, even in the surveillance exercises of the Commission/ECOFIN! Such degree of incompetence had inevitably to be sanctioned by citizen reactions once the artificial benefits of the single currency vanished, increasing unfair inequalities, insecurity feelings among EU citizens and distrust among MS, trapping them into a typical "prisoner dilemma". Unfortunately, but logically, the euro and the EU became the easiest scapegoat for the failure to bring a visible value added.

Although these mistakes must be corrected anyway through a new EU architecture with a new EMU Treaty, the necessary consensus needs too much time before being ready for facing the new coming difficulties and crisis. Therefore, this Chapter shows that there still exist urgent actions possible with existing tools and procedures for breaking the prisoner dilemma through modalities of solidarity leading to more responsibility. These feasible solutions are simple recipes based upon past experiences for opening again the EU win–win game by activating conditional incentives able to enhance channelled financial market reactions favourable to

[1] With a single nominal interest rate and inflation rates higher in the South than in the North (price level convergence and growth differentials), inevitably real interest rates are too low in the South and too high in the North, creating credit-boom in the South amplified by huge capital movements from the North to the South but in speculative investment spurring consumption. This is basic economics and would have required special policy measures with other tools yet available (bank reserve requirements, capital ratio, prudential regulations) at national level, but dogmatism was used by politicians and even in the Commission the answer given to the current account imbalances in the South financed by capital inflows was that "*markets know better that civil servants*".

adjusting countries, preventing self-fulfilling speculation and benefiting the whole EU.

The Basic Principles for Breaking Out the EMU Prisoner Dilemma Blocking EMU Governance

Solving the present prisoner dilemma relies upon correcting the two caveats of the present EMU by linking visibly national responsibility to the access to cheap conditional EU solidarity funds. As demonstrated in the last decade by the disasters of the over indebtedness cases (Greek, Spain, Portugal and Ireland), the way the budgetary consolidations were imposed became very counterproductive and damaging for all EU partners. Making available adequate conditional EU solidarity could give immediate positive results through their powerful impacts on the spreads of sovereign bonds and the positive growth spillovers for both debtors and creditors.

Analyses of the facts and the history of the EU integration tends to show that integration progress depends upon the degree of mutual confidence among member states, which is fragile but reversible as shown by past episodes of European integration. Observation of four decades of monitoring economic policy coordination and of EMU process permits to draw three intertwined lessons:

(i) Confidence among Member States as well as citizens with respect to EU requires a clear deal between solidarity and responsibility;
(ii) This deal needs a credible process of collegial monitoring based upon factual indicators allowing for national policymakers to work together for building trust and consensus on common interests and making citizens more aware of the convergence between national self-interests and the shared euro interests, that is, to make explicit and tangible the win–win game at stake and the cost/benefit challenge of national responsibility giving right to solidarity.
(iii) All the attempts since the very beginning of the EU to coordinate national policies failed as far as they were conceived as a central coordination, while they succeeded when they resulted from the progressive awareness of the self-interest at stake for each Member State to respect by their own sovereign decisions the common discipline and interests (Ghymers 2015).

These lessons explain that coordination among sovereign states never works for the sake of "general interest" but only for the selfish interests of governments and their electorates. Therefore, it is possible to use this basic principle for activating specific tools revealing the self-interests of each sovereign government to converge. This explains the success of the European Monetary System (EMS) with its exchange-rate mechanism (ERM) which "internalized" visibly the consequences of policy choices and the degree of solidarity (Ghymers 1995) and allowed for forging (progressively) a consensus thanks to a clever procedure combining:

(i) The collegial monitoring of the ERM imposed automatically by the European Currency Unit (ECU) which effectively "multilaterialized" all bilateral parities, because any exchange-rate adjustments had to be bargained collegially[2] through a peer review of sovereign policies at EU level, and;
(ii) Monitoring the impacts of these sovereign policies upon the exchange rates and the spreads of interest rates.

The following proposals are based upon these ERM lessons transposed to the single currency for internalizing national policies by influencing financial markets through two linked key tools correcting the two major failures of EMU:

(i) A less discretionary and more powerful system of solidarity (in the ERM, the solidarity was used very selectively by the monetary hegemon, Germany and the Bundesbank);
(ii) A more objective and less intergovernmental monitoring of all national policies.

These two instruments could be made quickly available inside the present imperfect treaty by using current procedures and instruments.

The Proposed Recipes for Redeeming the Two Major Failures of the Euro-Governance

The idea is to incentivize national responsibility by providing to adjusting MSs cheap but conditional EU financial assistance proposed by an independent monitoring, that is, exactly what the present EMU does not provide. Such a reconciliation between EU solidarity and MS responsibility results from two complementary initiatives:

1. To transform the European Stability Mechanism (EMS[3])—which is not a solidarity tool (no concessional loans but castigating loans with very high spread) and too limited size for compensating credibly the inhibition of the LOLR function of the ECB into an effective LOLR by changing it into an "*European Debt Agency – EDA*" offering conditional incentives for increasing national responsibility. EDA would use the Treaty as an EU public Bank (Art. 123, §2 see following section) for getting conditional access to ECB overdraft facilities for short-term liquidity assistance and, by ECOFIN decision, could also issue—

---

[2] Because the ECU basket was a fixed number of national currencies, any change in the parity of one member implies arithmetically that all the other central parities also do change, therefore requiring a collegial agreement, thus opening a discussion on the policy adjustments for making sustainable the new parities as a formal condition imposed by the partners for accepting the demand for realignment from one of the MS.

[3] Created in 2012 with a special Treaty for replacing the temporary European Financial Stability Facility (EFSF) and the European Financial Stabilisation Mechanism (EFSM) created in 2010.

under strict conditions—euro-bonds for supporting medium-to-long-run assistance to Member States under consensual structural adjustment.
2. To make attractive for MSs the respect of the conditions for access to the EDA loans by channelling financial markets reactions (spreads) with credible assessments and objective surveillance communiqués issued by a more independent monitoring body than the Commission/ECOFIN; this means to outsource to independent experts with the mandate to formulate public recommendations for preventing liquidity crisis without creating moral hazard situations. Commission/ ECOFIN decision procedures would still enact, amend or oppose to, but being fully accountable of any discrepancy with this new independent European Monitoring Board – EMB by "reversing the charge of the proofs", Commission/ ECOFIN having to demonstrate to public opinions their reasons for not following the independent surveillance exercise and its technical proposals.

The combination of these two simple ECOFIN decisions would reduce the inner myopia of financial markets by ensuring a credible guidance for preventing any self-fulfilling speculation and turning them in a powerful support to sustainable and responsible national policies. The idea is to incentivize governments and get citizens' support for respecting strict conditions by organizing clear, simple, reduction in the interest-rate spreads when sovereign policies are credibly sustainable according to technical assessments issued by independent experts, validated by Commission/ECOFIN under the scrutiny of a broad, trans-European public debate. This means to stop the present bias of a too intergovernmental surveillance by the "judges & parts" composing the ECOFIN.

Concrete Modalities for Implementing the Two Proposed Recipes

Art. 123 §2 of the present Treaty provides the simple legal way for giving to the EMS a potential direct access to the ECB cash facilities, thus allowing this EMS to fulfil de-facto the role of an EU missing LOLR. Indeed, Article 123 in its §1 prohibits (correctly) any ECB loan or overdraft to any government or public institutions, but §2 precisely sets (correctly too) that: "*§1 shall not apply to publicly owned credit institutions which, in the context of the supply of reserves by central banks, shall be given the same treatment by national central banks and the European Central Bank as private credit institutions*". Thus, the Commission/ECOFIN decision process could—instantaneously—make the EMS a public bank of EU Member States—calling it "European Debt Agency - EDA"—for giving a clear signal to the financial markets that the euro-area has instantaneously the capacity to get unlimited liquidity in case of justified needs (under conditions) for giving emergency liquidity loans, stopping thus any one-bet speculation like what occurred in the worrying episode of the Euro sovereign-debt crisis, which would not have happened if the euro-area has had such an LOLR or a genuine Central Bank.

Furthermore, in order to provide medium-to-long-run support to adjusting MSs, this EMS/EDA could issue its own euro-bonds under strict conditions imposed by ECOFIN. The purpose of this measure is triple: (i) to create an operational lever upon the spreads on sovereign bonds for supporting—always under conditions—convergent policies by buying them (or swapping them) with euro-bonds, (ii) to develop the euro-bond market for accelerating the financial integration in the euro-area by improving liquidity conditions for euro-bonds, and (iii) to provide additional safe-assets which are the too-narrow base of the reversed pyramid of private liquidity which is pro-cyclical and exposed to run for safe assets once global activity turns negative. This would create a mechanism for "internalizing" the effects of respecting—or not—the common discipline: rewarding approved adjustment policies by reducing the interest-rate spreads imposed by myopic financial markets, that is, giving visible incentives to any member of the euro-area to respect the common rules, especially the fiscal discipline, while preventing wild overshooting resulting from the financial market excessive reactions.

More technically, the mechanism consists in three articulated successive steps:

(i) First, the introduction of a system of "*blue-bonds versus red-bonds*". Bonds getting the EU label of conformity of national fiscal policy with the common discipline become "*Blue-bonds*" and enjoy seniority and full guarantee from the EU MS, and all other sovereign bonds become "subordinated" (i.e. neither priority nor solidarity guarantee) and become "*red-bonds*" paying a higher spread in exchange for free sovereign issuance. Therefore, once an economy would not respect the fiscal discipline, all its bonds issued would be castigated automatically by a spread with respect to its past warranted blue-bonds. Such a spread permits to internalize very visibly the costs of the non-respect of the common rules or interests of the euro-area. The collegial assessment proposing the blue label and the conditionality relies upon an independent technical surveillance process (see following section).

(ii) Second, a solidarity arm with the possibility for *EDA to conditionally buy or to swap red-bonds* with its own EU bonds, improving liquidity conditions and reducing the spreads; even an adjusting economy like Greece could demand through the technical surveillance exercise (see below) to upgrade as blue-bonds its new issuances when a formal stability programme is agreed upon with ECOFIN and duly implemented. This tool would give—immediate and costless—budgetary advantages to sustainable reforms/policies credibly committed with ECOFIN and monitored along a medium-term programme of reforms. It could also be possible to use the amount of swaps as a lever for influencing the spreads on sovereign red-bonds according to the speed of implementation of reforms or adjustments. EDA would make profits with the resulting appreciation of the red-bonds of adjusting economies, allowing to assess its efficiency and to build up free EDA reserves.

(iii) The next step would be to consider *swapping all the sovereign blue-bonds by single EU-blue bonds issued by EDA*. Indeed, all the euro-area members would be already solidary linked by their mutual guarantee given to the labelled sovereign blue-bonds. Therefore, additional liquidity advantages could result for all members (but especially to small/medium economies) and by the technical progress to get a genuine benchmark for the euro assets opening interesting perspectives of an additional coordination tool. The purpose of this proposed experimental new tool would be to unify progressively the euro-bond markets while respecting the no-bailing clause and increasing the enforcement power of the SGP through the self-interest of Member States to coordinate budgetary stances. This tool could be an attractive way to enforce the policy discipline without having to take financial sanctions in case of damaging policy divergences.

The whole philosophy behind a pact between more EU solidarity for more national responsibility relies entirely upon objective and credible technical conditionality. This has not been convincingly the case in the EMU governance. Therefore, for breaking the prisoner dilemma, the inseparable complementary initiative is to improve the transparency of the monitoring in charge of ECOFIN. Although a significant progress was made in 2015 with the creation of the European Fiscal Board (EFB)—an independent advisory committee of fiscal experts—the past period shows clearly several failures: intergovernmental bias with national Ministers behaving in the ECOFIN as "judge & parts", lack of independence and courage of the Commission, lack of transparency and open public debates, and—most grave—insufficient coverage of the surveillance limited de facto to the SGP. No effective monitoring was possible before the crisis, and incumbent governments benefited electorally from the short-term advantages of the single currency. In the present situation, they try to benefit from their opposition to EU solidarity, demonstrating so that MSs behave as free riders with the EU, which indicates so an incoherence in the present Treaty and an abuse by the MSs in the EU decision-making.

This is why the recipe needs two components: (i) the scope of the "Independent European Monitoring Board – EMB" covers all the policies; (ii) the "charge of the proof" is reversed by giving the main role to the independent experts for assessing policies and proposing measures and conditionality, the Commission/ECOFIN being able to change or to oppose but being publicly accountable of their decisions in a special procedure of trans-European public debate among professionals organized by the European Parliament.

The purpose is to separate explicitly technical analysis from political decisions, preventing the damages from too dogmatic positions as this has been the case since the euro creation. Politics must remain in its own realm with political choices being transparently decided by elected power after previous technical assessments providing the cost/benefits of any action. This split makes authorities more accountable to public opinion. Both technicians and politicians will become more accountable of critical political decisions (like the use of EDA solidarity and its conditionality) as a result of professional debates, Parliaments' hearings (European and national) and trans-European debates.

Concretely, the existing EFB would be strengthened and included in the broader EMB as a specialized department in charge of fiscal policies, proposing to simplify the SGP. A full team of independent economists would cover the other economic policies relevant for EMU. Operationally, this would be easy to do by moving some experts from DG ECFIN of the Commission to the EMB plus acknowledged experts proposed by the European Parliament together with the Commission and approved by the ECOFIN. This EMB would issue and publish regular technical reports assessing the macroeconomic development and the policy-mix stances. In addition, EMB would be responsible for issuing the technical assessments and conditionality proposed to Commission/ECOFIN decisions for getting access to the solidarity facilities or for being rated as blue-bonds or red-bonds. Then, Commission would formally—but publicly—report to the ECOFIN, taking position on the EMB proposals. Any discrepancy with the EMB report would be intensively scrutinized by the EP, the financial press, the think-tanks, International Financial Institutions and the international economist community, creating some "cooperative competition" between Commission and EMB, stimulating a broad public debate across the EU before ECOFIN final decisions. In case of significant discrepancies between final decisions and EMB, a special hearing with additional experts would be organized by the European Parliament and published.

The purpose is to restore the spirit of the Treaty by increasing transparency and accountability and creating horizontal debates across the whole EU reducing the democratic gap and improving the existing decision making of ECOFIN and EP, ultimate legitimate actors.

References

Ghymers, C. (1995). La coordination des politiques économiques dans la Communauté européenne: Une évaluation en vue de la Conférence Intergouvernementale. *Revue du Marché Commun* n 385, February 1995.

Ghymers, C. (2015). Une relecture du Plan Werner par rapport à ses antécédents et à ses successeurs. In E. Danescu & S. Muñoz (Eds.), *Pierre Werner and Europe: His approach, action and legacy*. Brussels, New York: OIE-Peter Lang.

23

EMU Architecture: Flaws and Reforms

Bettina De Souza Guilherme

Abstract In this part of the book, we discuss proposals to improve architectural and crisis management lacunas. While other partners of the network present own proposals, this chapter has the objective to sketch out proposals, which have been discussed or are still in the pipeline at the top level of European Union (EU) decision-takers and institutions to remedy lacunas, errors and omissions of the Economic and Monetary Union (EMU) architecture. A main argument advanced is that the reforms with a focus on "risk-avoidance" and stronger "surveillance" and "monitoring" had more success, while any reforms based on the principle of "risk-sharing have encountered major resistance, both for the financial market regulation and for the fiscal framework.

EMU Design Flaws and Ongoing Reforms

Design flaws of the Economic and Monetary Union (EMU) have been extensively discussed in the first part of the joint volume. EMU's imbalances and instability have their origin within its asymmetric construction both in terms of a fully fletched supranational monetary union and a largely intergovernmental fiscal policy coordination and in terms of risk avoidance and risk-sharing mechanisms. The focus of the surveillance before the crisis was on the fiscal deficits, while both public and private debt, and the rise and risks of macroeconomic imbalances and of deregulated financial markets were largely disregarded. EMU did not have the institutions, finances, tools and rules in place to deal with the crisis in an efficient, adequate and equitable way. Informal bodies outside of the EU legal framework rose to be the top decision-making institutions taking decision with major impact on the lives and work of EU citizens, while democratic accountability was eroded both at EU and at national levels.

B. De Souza Guilherme (✉)
Founder and Co-coordinator of the Jean Monnet Network "Crisis-Equity-Democracy for Europe and Latin America", IRELAC, Rio de Janeiro, Brazil

European Parliament, Brussels, Belgium
e-mail: bettina.desouza@europarl.europa.eu

The reform of the financial market regulation has advanced considerably in the aftermath of the Lehmann's bank default, leading to the establishment of the "Banking Union," with a strengthening of financial service regulation and the introduction a supranational supervision by the European Central Bank for systemically relevant banks as the first pillar. This can be considered a major achievement, which prior to the crisis would have been difficult to envisage. The second pillar of the Banking Union deals with a single resolution mechanism (SRM), regulating the orderly restructuring of a bank by a resolution authority when the bank is failing or at risk to fail for the banks covered by the single supervisory mechanism to avoid that tax payers have to pay once again for a failing bank sector. This is why it has at its heart the Single Resolution Fund (SRF), financed by contributions of the banking sector. In case that the SRF does not have sufficient means, the Member States decided in 2013 the establishment of a "common backstop," which would serve as a safety net in case that, after a bailing in or haircut of the banks' shareholders and creditors, the Single Resolution Fund would temporarily not have sufficient resources for an orderly resolution of the distressed banks. The Commission proposed to make the backstop part of a future European Monetary Fund (EMF), to be established within the EU legal framework, but the Eurogroup preferred to keep the intergovernmental European Stability Mechanism (ESM) in place and decided in December 2019 to establish the common backstop in the ESM at the latest by 1 January 2024. "The size of the credit line(s) will be aligned with the target level of the SRF, which is 1% of covered deposits in the Banking Union (currently estimated at around €55 billion). If the credit line is used, the SRF will pay back the ESM loan with money from bank contributions within three years, although this period can be extended by up to another two years. As a result, it will be fiscally neutral over the medium term."[1]

In terms of increasing financial stability and the resilience of EMU, the common backstop represents indeed a major step forward and a precious contribution. In terms of democratic accountability on the other hand, the fact that the ESM was entrusted with the common backstop could eventually signify the perpetuation or at least the prolongation for a considerable time of an intergovernmental crisis management void of proper democratic accountability. A solution could be to transform the ESM into the EMF through co-decision, however duly allowing the European Parliament to make an input in the shaping of this important crisis management tool after all the failures and policy errors in the crisis management and, second, to ensure its accountability.

However, it is clear that even given the common backstop, the missing part of the regulation and improved resilience as part of the consolidation of the crisis management in the financial markets sector is the risk-sharing element, the third pillar of the Banking Union, which is the European Deposit Insurance Scheme (EDIS). In November 2015, the Commission presented a proposal on the European deposit

---

[1] Explainer on ESM reform and revisions to the ESM Treaty, ESM website: https://www.esm.europa.eu/about-esm/esm-treaty-reform-explainer. Accessed 01 March 2020.

insurance scheme (EDIS) for bank deposits in the euro area, building on the system of national deposit guarantee schemes, which guarantees the deposit of up to 100,000 euros in the case that a bank fails in all EU member states and is funded entirely by banks. EDIS would provide a stronger and more uniform degree of insurance cover in the entire euro area and thus provide a strong protection against speculation. The Commission proposal foresees a gradual introduction of EDIS with first a "reinsurance phase" in which EDIS would provide liquidity to national Deposit Guarantee Schemes (DGS) in case of a bank failure, which would then have to be paid back by the national DGS. In a later phase, the principle of "coinsurance" would apply and EDIS could also cover losses, without that national DGS would repay them (European Commission 2020). EDIS would on the one hand reduce the vulnerability of national DGS with limited financial means to large local shocks and on the other hand move against the sovereign-bank nexus by significantly reducing the link between banks and their national sovereign ensuring that the level of depositor confidence in a bank would not depend on the bank's location. This could signify an important stepping stone in the direction of a genuine European financial and capital market. However, negotiations were blocked by both the European Parliament and even more in the Council, until late 2019, when the German finance minister Scholz presented a proposal on EDIS. However, his proposal restricts EDIS to the reinsurance phase and request at the same time more stringent conditions such as a concrete target for nonperforming loans (NPLs). According to the IMF's Compilation Guide on Financial Soundness Indicators 2004 "a loan is nonperforming when payments of interest and/or principal are past due by 90 days or more, or interest payments equal to 90 days or more have been capitalized, refinanced, or delayed by agreement, or payments are less than 90 days overdue, but there are other good reasons5 —such as a debtor filing for bankruptcy—to doubt that payments will be made in full. After a loan is classified as nonperforming, it (and/or any replacement loans(s)) should remain classified as such until written off or payments of interest and/or principal are received on this or subsequent loans that replace the original." Scholz's proposal envisages a NPL ratio of below 5% gross and 2.5% net, country by country and to introduce non-zero credit risk weights and a concentration charge on government debt which would increase capital cost for large exposures to individual countries. Both conditions are detrimental to high-debt countries like Italy, Portugal and Greece, and the most recent German proposal might fail for this reason. The German proposal is a clear attempt to transform a proposal, which was meant to be the strongest risk-sharing element of the Banking Union, into another element of risk reduction and at the same time falls short of the aim of EDIS to give to same feeling of security to avoid a bank run or the distinction of the rating of the security of deposits according to the location of the deposit.

Risk avoidance had already been the main characteristic of the Maastricht original design of the fiscal framework. Following the crisis, it was further strengthened with the 2 and 6 packs, the Fiscal Compact, the institutionalization of the so-called European semester, which is the coordination process of economic policies, the establishment of the Macroeconomic Imbalance Procedure (MIP) to monitor any developments which could lead to new imbalances. At the same time, the crisis management and the reforms widened the democratic deficit brought about by the increase of intergovernmentalism with the rise of the informal Eurogroup together with the Eurosummit to the most important decision-taking bodies of the EMU, and the creation of further intergovernmental institutions such as the ESM and intergovernmental treaties such as the Fiscal Compact, all outside of the legal framework of the EU and bypassing the democratic accountability of the European Parliament and in many cases of national parliaments. These developments have induced a process of erosion of democratic legitimacy and accountability both at national and at EU levels and successively led to a loss of trust in traditional political institutions at EU level but even to a stronger extent at national level with the rise of protest movements, mushrooming of new parties and movements, an increasing polarization of society and politics. Neither of the previously mentioned democratic erosions has so far been remedied.

First, the asymmetric construction of EMU hampered its resilience and proved ineffective to avoid or shield from a crisis, and the reforms in the aftermath of the crisis have at best shown mixed results. The further tightened fiscal rules showed success in imposing discipline in regard to the fiscal deficits, which led to a slow reduction of the public debt level towards the pre-crisis level over a timespan of more than 10 years (however not yet reached). On the other hand, the fiscal framework, even more with the reforms and the imposed adjustment programmes, proved to be largely pro-cyclical, inefficient to protect the quality of public expenditure—in other words growth-enhancing investment—with negative impacts on productivity, competitivity and growth, and inefficient to lead to a reduction of the debt level of highly indebted countries, as has been reported by the president of the European Fiscal Board (EFB) to the European Parliament (European Fiscal Board 2019). The European Fiscal Board, an independent advisory body to the European Commission with the objective to improve the current economic governance framework of the Economic and Monetary Union, criticized the multiple sources of unnecessary complexity in the current framework and proposed its simplification with a focus rather on debt reduction than on the public deficit. The EFB proposals rely on "a simple medium-term debt ceiling and one operational target, namely, a ceiling on the growth rate of primary expenditure net of discretionary revenue measures, and an escape clause triggered on the basis of independent economic judgement. This proposal would focus more clearly on underpinning sustainability, improve observability, simplify the rules and reduce pro-cyclicality." Additionally, the European Fiscal Board proposes the introduction of a limited Golden rule to protect public investment. The EFB proposes to exclude some "specific growth enhancing expenditure from the net primary expenditure growth ceiling" and "national fiscal council institutions could monitor the classification of growth-enhancing expenditure" (European Fiscal Board 2019).

In the meantime, climate change had proven to be a major threat to human survival and requires a change of paradigm which will affect all fields of policy, including economic and financial policies. The last elections to the European Parliament increased both its legitimacy and the pressure to address the climate crisis with serious action. As a consequence, the newly invigorated European Commission adopted the European Green Deal as part of which the Commission announced that it will refocus the European Semester process of macroeconomic coordination to integrate the United Nations' Sustainable Development (SDGs) goals, to put sustainability and the well-being of citizens at the centre of economic policy, and the sustainable development goals at the heart of the EU's policymaking and action. With the refocusing of the European Semester, the Commission changed the Annual Growth Survey into the Annual Sustainable Growth Strategy 2020 and with it the content: "Environmental sustainability, productivity gains, fairness and macroeconomic stability will be the four dimensions of our economic policy in the years to come. These dimensions, which are closely interrelated and mutually reinforcing, should guide structural reforms, investments and responsible fiscal policies across all Member States" (European Commission 2019, p. 3).

The Climate Change Agenda goes beyond fiscal policies, and the Council and European Parliament negotiated a list of investment (taxonomy) which should serve as guidelines for the ECB, EIB and financial markets, which investments should be considered environmentally friendly and should be favoured. With the coinciding of the Climate Change Agenda and outstanding reforms of the fiscal framework, the coming years will be decisive for implementing reforms which will render the EU more resilient for financial, economic and climate crisis. However, one cannot close the eyes to the fact that there is a lot of resistance to changes and efforts to water down or limit reforms as was the case with the Financial Transaction Tax (FTT) to make the financial markets pay taxes in general (as any other business sector) and compensate for the enormous costs the financial crisis had caused but also taking into account the resistance against a common fiscal capacity to counteract against asymmetric shocks. Indeed, the crisis gave rise to various concepts of fiscal capacities which remained not only at the academic level but entered the deliberation at the highest level of the EU institutions.

The European Parliament was indeed the first EU institution, which in 2011, after a nearly 2 years of extensive hearings with experts, fact finding missions and deliberation—within its Special Committee on the Financial, Economic and Social Crisis—founded with the purpose to evaluate the causes and make proposal for a better crisis resilience of EMU, voted in favour of a euro-area budget and of "the development of the concept of a European Treasury to strengthen the economic pillar of EMU." (European Parliament 2011) According to the European Parliament, the euro-area budget should be "a budget of sufficient size to accommodate the euro in a sustainable way, providing the currency with a relevant budget space on the level of political organisation at which it is issued." Concerning the details on a euro-area budget, the European Parliament referred in its resolution to the McDougall report (European Commission 1977), which had analysed the conditions necessary for the implementation of the Werner plan for an Economic and Monetary Union in the 1970s and affirmed that: (1) *the volume of such a budget would have to be between 2,5 and 10 percent of Union GNI, depending on whether and which reallocation functions would be assumed by the Union budget (...)*; (2) *the budget would need to be financed on the basis of own resources, (...) and;* (3) *national budgets would be reduced correspondingly in order to achieve tax neutrality for citizens and businesses.*

The president of the European Council together with the Presidents of the Commission, the Euro-group and the European Central Bank published the "Four Presidents Report" (Van Rompuy 2012), which underlined that "while the degree of centralization of budgetary instruments and the arrangements for fiscal solidarity against adverse shocks differ, all other currency unions are endowed with a central fiscal capacity." The report defines a specific and time-bound road map for the achievement of a genuine Economic and Monetary Union with the objective to improve the resilience of EMU. The Four Presidents envisaged "the creation of a shock-absorption function at the central level," as the "culmination of the process" of achieving a fully fledged EMU in its stage 3 (post 2014). In their report, they stress that the establishment of "a well-defined and limited fiscal capacity to improve the absorption of country specific economic shocks, through an insurance system set up at the central level" accompanied by "a built-in incentives-based system (which) would encourage euro area Member States eligible for participation in the shock absorption function to continue to pursue sound fiscal and structural policies in accordance with their contractual obligations."

The envisaged proposal should thus link "the two objectives of asymmetric shock absorption and the promotion of sound economic policies" with the intention to render them "complementary and mutually reinforcing." Additionally, it emphasizes the importance of an "increasing degree of common decision-making on national budgets and an enhanced coordination of economic policies," in particular in the field of taxation and employment, to prepare for this stage.

The European Commission published its Reflection Paper on Deepening the EMU in May 2017 and announced that it will look into different options for a macroeconomic stabilization function for the euro area such as: (1) a European Investment Protection Scheme; (2) a European Unemployment Reinsurance Scheme; (3) a rainy day fund that could accumulate funds on a regular basis; (4) a dedicated euro-area budget; (5) the conversion of the ESM into a European Monetary Fund integrated in the EU legal framework.

In addition to these stabilization facilities, the Commission announced an instrument or budget line to support (administrative) capacity building and/or structural reforms, which should also support convergence and cohesion to counteract internal imbalances, and proposed a regulation establishing the Structural Reform Support Programme. An interesting feature of the Reform Support Programmes as well as of the Commission Proposals on the Common Provision Regulation (CPR) for all the Structural and Cohesion funds is the idea to rather work with incentives to better implement the Country-Specific Recommendations (CSR) of the European Semester as a conditionality. This approach should be the carrot to incentivize adherence to the Country-Specific Recommendations (CSR) of the European Semester additionally to the enhanced surveillance of the European Commission with the possibility of sanctions, which represents the whip.

In 2018, the Commission presented its proposal on the establishment of a European Investment Stabilization Function (EISF) building on the Five Presidents' report (Juncker 2015) and on the Commission Reflection Papers on Deepening the EMU and on the future of EU finances of 28 June 2017. The proposal has the objective to protect investment in the event of a downturn, by supporting well-identified priorities and already planned projects or activities at national level, such as infrastructure or skills development. As experienced in the Great Recession, public investment was the first to be cut in the national budget, which actually deepened the economic crisis and had detrimental effects on growth, employment and productivity. The proposal is based on Article 175(3) of Treaty on the Functioning of the European Union (TFEU), which allows for the creation of an instrument supporting eligible public investment in Member States that are confronted with a large asymmetric shock with a view to strengthen cohesion. It would empower the Commission to grant financial assistance to Member States, which are faced with a large asymmetric shock, by contracting borrowings on the financial markets or with financial actors and lending them on to the Member State concerned to maintain eligible public investment, specified in an Annex. Additionally, the proposal included the possibility that the interest rate costs incurred on the loan could be subsidized. With the purpose to link both the risk reduction and risk-sharing approach, access to the Stabilization function is conditional on compliance with decisions and recommendations under the fiscal and macroeconomic surveillance framework.

The criterion to activate the support is a double unemployment trigger, because strong increases in national unemployment rates are a relevant indicator of the impact of a large asymmetric shock. Additionally, it includes an obligation to use the support received for investment in policy objectives under the Common Provisions Regulation and to maintain the average level of public investment of the last 5 years. The proposal was both long awaited but also encountered strong criticism on the one hand from those who are in principle against any risk sharing and on the other hand for the rather modest volume of €30 billion earmarked for it.

The European Parliament (2015) having already expressed its support for a fiscal capacity, and stabilization function took up the challenge to deliberate on the bases of the draft report of the co-rapporteurs Beres-Boege within a joint committee of Budget and ECON members among the following lines: First of all, the report proposes that activation trigger should be "automatic," still based on both the level of national unemployment rate compared to its past average and the change in unemployment compared to a certain threshold. The rapporteurs intended to avoid delays for the activation and the repetition of the previously witnessed political conflicts around financial assistance. Furthermore, with the intention to avoid any revival of debtor and creditor conflicts on the financial means, the European Parliament's draft report additionally proposed to feed the fund with Member States' contributions of 10% of monetary income allocated to the national central banks of the Eurosystem pursuant to Article 32 of Protocol No 4 on the Statute of the European System of Central Banks and the European Central Bank[1a] and that it should not be less than billion euros. In this way, the Parliament intended to increase the budget for the EISF to at least €55 billion. Additionally, to the conditionality proposed by the Commission, the EP asked for compliance with "a convergence code" focusing on a few decisive criteria allowing for better national ownership and for a special clause ensuring that EISF support should be conditional on respect for Union values, and Member States subject to a procedure pursuant to Article 7(1) or (2) of the Treaty on the European Union should not be eligible.

The Parliament (2017) preferred the EISF to be independent from, and in parallel to the ESM and his successor and to ensure a much greater accountability than the non-existing accountability of an institution founded outside of the EU legal framework with a yearly exchange of view with the relevant committee and immediately, whenever the EISF becomes operational. However, given that the report fell into the last year of the legislature, it became victim to the increased political polarization in the European Parliament ahead of elections and was not put to vote. It remains a pending file to be picked up once one of the future presidencies, possibly the Portuguese, in the first half of 2021, intends to push for it again.

In the Council, the proposal had encountered major resistance and did not advance much. Indeed, the proposal can also be seen as a fruit of the strong push for a Eurozone budget by the newly elected French president Emanuel Macron. In his speech of 26 September 2017 at the University of Sorbonne, the newly elected president presented his clearly pro-European stance and highlighted the importance of a euro-area budget to provide public goods and stability when confronted with economic shocks: "We need convergence and stability through national reforms, but also by coordinating our economic policies and a common budget. If we want to reduce our differences and develop our common goods – everything I have just mentioned, security, protection in the context of migration, digital transition, ecological transition, a genuine development and partnership policy – these common goods, foremost among which is our currency, must be financed. And we therefore need more investment, we need the means to provide stability in the face of economic shocks, as no state can tackle an economic crisis alone when it no longer controls its monetary policy. So for all these reasons, yes we need a stronger budget within Europe, at the heart of the eurozone."

To achieve a euro-area budget, the German support is essential, and in June 2018, Macron achieved an agreement with Merkel, which was a compromise and spelled out in the Meseberg Declaration, in which they proposed "establishing a Eurozone budget within the framework of the European Union to promote competitiveness, convergence and stabilization in the euro area, starting in 2021. Decisions on the funding should take into account the negotiations on the next Multiannual financial framework. Resources would come from both national contributions, allocation of tax revenues and European resources" (Macron and Merkel 2018). However, in the text, it no longer defined the purpose of the eurozone budget to be for stabilization but rather to increase "competitiveness and convergence, which would be delivered through investment in innovation and human capital. It could finance new investments and come in substitution of national spending." Instead of the European Investment Stabilization Function, the Meseberg Declaration proposed a European Unemployment Stabilization Fund, for the purpose of stabilization in case of severe economic crises, without transfers. This idea was promoted by the German Finance Minister Olaf Scholz, but found strong opposition both within the German parliament and among the Nordic countries of the European Union.

The Unemployment Re-Insurance Scheme has the aim to provide counter-cyclical stabilization in case of large labour market shocks and could be funded by national contributions and then grant loans to national unemployment insurance schemes in times of severe economic crises. The objective of the loans would be to avoid cuts in unemployment benefits or increases in social insurance contributions in recessions and thereby would allow the role of domestic unemployment insurance schemes to act as an automatic stabilizer (which had been restrained by the adjustment programmes). Additionally, it would help to support income in a recession or stagnation and in particularly the social strata which bears a large part of the social costs in a recession, which in term would increase the trust in European institutions (Beblavý et al. 2015). According to an impact assessment by the Bertelsmann Foundation (Dolls 2018), the re-insurance scheme would have cushioned on average 15–25% of the income losses following large labour market shocks in the period 2000–2016 through the interregional smoothing channel of the re-insurance and would have been revenue-neutral at EA19 and not led to permanent transfers across member states. On average, the member states would have paid less than 0.1% of their gross domestic product (GDP) annually.

Some of the proposals of the European Commission's Reflection Paper go beyond a funding mechanism and don't have the target to mitigate economic shocks. While the newly elected Commission president, Ursula Von der Leyen, announced a proposal for a European Unemployment Reinsurance Scheme to be presented by the end of 2020, the only proposal following up Macron's call for a euro-area budget, which is currently being negotiated in the Council and the European Parliament, is the budgetary instrument for convergence and competitiveness for the euro area (BICC). It is a new version of the Reform Support Programme+. In practice, it extends the programme from its previous focus on structural reforms to investment relevant for convergence and competitiveness. It will not fulfil the purpose of a stabilization of the eurozone in asymmetric shocks, but, if designed in an appropriate way, it could help to improve the competitiveness and the convergence of the weaker regions and countries and thus counteract the internal imbalances. However, given the strong conditionality to the adherence to the fiscal framework and the country-specific recommendations, some of the peripheral countries fear that it will rather lead to a kind of "rebate" because the countries which are meeting these preconditions might in fact be the strongest economies.

One of the objectives is to offer a carrot to a greater adherence to the country-specific recommendations within the European semester. However, the budget foreseen in it is also limited to €30 billion, which raises the same criticism as the proposal of the EISF and the reform support programme. The former ECB president M. Draghi considered the agreement on "the Budgetary Instrument for Convergence and Competitiveness a step in the right direction, but it does not yet meet the necessary criteria in terms of size or design." According to him, "The most effective response, however, would be an investment-led stimulus at the euro area level. This would be the best way to achieve an efficient distribution of spending among euro area countries – and is a further reason why I have called for a euro area fiscal instrument."

Another instrument which has better chances to be achieved because it tries to avoid any mutualization of debts or permanent transfer is the idea of the Rainy Day Fund. A rainy day fund has however the handicap that it would normally limit its payments to the accumulated contributions and would probably be too small in case of a large shock. Lenarčič and Korhonen (2018) published a saving-loans proposal of the Rainy Day Fund (RDF), which would avoid (permanent) transfers between member-states in the form of a "non-mutualised European RDF, composed of national compartments. In good times, countries would accumulate savings in their compartments, accruing self-insurance. In bad times, they would be entitled to use the savings in their own compartment, and – if needed – could access limited borrowing from the rest of the fund. Further, the rules for national contributions, payouts, and repayment of any loans would be based on changes in unemployment rates, rather than on levels," and would "follow the Carnot et al. (2017) 'double condition' rule which assumes payments to the fund when unemployment is low and decreasing and disbursements when it is high and increasing. Countries would repay their loans according to rules similar to those for fund contributions, while observing a final maturity linked to the average length of the business cycle" (Lenarčič and Korhonen 2018).

In addition to the Euro-area budget and treasury, the European Parliament had already in 2011 supported the possible mutual issuance of sovereign debt, Eurobonds stimulating fiscal discipline and the EU's borrowing capacity. The European Parliament's concept on the Eurobonds was largely based on a proposal by Delpla and Von Weizsaecker (2011) on the blue bond (2010) and foresaw "that when Eurobonds are to be issued, their issuance should be limited to a debt ratio of 60% of GDP under joint and several liability as senior sovereign debt, and should be linked to incentives to reduce sovereign debt to that level" and that "the overarching aim of Eurobonds should be to reduce sovereign debt and to avoid moral hazard and prevent speculation against the euro." At the same time "access to such Eurobonds would require agreement on, and implementation of, measurable programmes of debt reduction."

The appealing feature of the Delpla and Von Weizsaecker proposal was that the blue bonds would constitute "a liquid and safe asset on par with the US Treasury bond. This should help the rise of the euro as a major reserve currency, enabling the entire euro area to borrow part of the sovereign debt at interest rates comparable to, or hopefully even below, the benchmark German bond" (Delpha and Von Weizsaecker 2011). Von Weizsaecker continued his commitment to the Eurobonds as a member and rapporteur on the subject "Sovereign bond-backed securities (SBBS)" in the European Parliament. The creation of European Safe Bonds (ESBies) should help to resolve the 'diabolic loop' between sovereign and bank risk, coupled with cross-border 'flight-to-safety' capital flows by serving as securities issued by a European Debt Agency (EDA)." ESBies should be composed of the senior tranche on a portfolio of sovereign bonds issued by EU Member States, held by a European Debt Agency or the ESM and potentially further guaranteed through a credit enhancement. The European Commission's legislative proposal foresaw that the SBBS would consist of a diversified pool of euro-area sovereign bonds, according to their economic weight. Advantages of the SBBS are that they would be considered save and not require any form of fiscal solidarity among euro-area governments.

Concerning a possible European Debt Agency, the European Parliament had already in 2011 requested to transform the temporary European Financial Stability Fund (EFSF) into a European Debt Agency and the Parliament to be given a consistent role in this modification of the Treaty. However, the European Parliament had no say in the establishment of the European Stability Mechanism (ESM), whose objective is to provide financial assistance to the euro-area Member States, which undergo a balance of payment crisis, which risks to endanger the financial stability of the euro area or of its MS. The EMS remained up to this day a purely intergovernmental organization outside of the legal framework of the EU, which has been condemned by the European Parliament as a "setback in the development of the Union, essentially at the expense of Parliament, the Court of Auditors and the Court of Justice."

During the Euro crisis, the Eurogroup set up the co-called "Troika," consisting of the European Commission (DG Ecfin), the European Central Bank and the International Monetary Fund (IMF) to set up the adjustment programmes for the debtor countries and to monitor their implementation. Since the Eurogroup is not a formal institution within the EU legal framework, the entire set-up of the financial assistance was exposing a blatant void of democratic legitimacy and accountability. EU institutions were "instrumentalized" to implement and monitor the political guidelines decided within the Eurogroup in "consensus." Given that no procedures and rules for any case of "risk of sovereign default" had been foreseen, the debtor countries were absolutely dependent on the "good" or "bad" will of the creditor countries, which resulted that the costs of the adjustment of the internal imbalances and the bailing out of financial institutions (mainly from the creditor countries) fell entirely on the debt countries. It is obvious that the set-up of the decision-making process resulted in a number of conflicts of interest of this crisis management process given the involvement of their national banks in the creditor countries. The European Parliament established the so-called Troika Inquiry Committee to analyse how these financial assistances had been handled. It exposed further conflict of interest of the European Central Bank—being responsible for the supervision of the biggest financial institutions and its role as the central bank (and normally lender of last resort) of all EU Member States, which lead the ECB to prevent the bailing in of the banks—at least in the first years of the crisis and thus insisting in rolling over the costs of the bank failures to citizens and tax payers. At the same time, it seems contradictory that an "independent" central bank imposes on Member States to change their traditional, equally "autonomous" collective bargaining structures by social partner to the detriment of labour. The current irony of history is that the ECB is not able to fulfil its primary objective to maintain price stability with the aim at inflation rates of below, but close to, 2% over the medium term. The inflation rate for 2019 has been 1.3%, and one of the main reasons is that in spite of the improved employment situation wage growth does not pick up given wage bargaining shocks and the increased number of involuntary part-time, both a consequence of structural reforms as recommended or imposed. The European Commission was as well acting in obvious conflict of interest as it is the institution which should be the guardian of the EU treaties, including the Charter of Fundamental Rights and all the objectives of Europe 2020.

Some might argue that the imposed austerity programmes were a necessary evil to lead the crisis countries to a situation of sound public finance and to calm the financial markets. However, in retrospect, it is clear that the policy recommendations had not sufficiently taken into account the criteria of debt sustainability at the beginning of the financial assistance (as is usually a precondition of the involvement of the IMF), had been based on overoptimistic forecasts which were unrealistic to achieve, had ignored the functioning of fiscal multipliers and thus led—as had been admitted both by the IMF and the Commission—to a largely pro-cyclical policies which deepened and prolonged the crisis and finally even led to an increase of the debts of the debtor countries. Here I would like to introduce a crucial question: Would anybody in retrospect consider these policy recommendations in such an economic situation and within the given fiscal framework of the EMU as "sound budgetary policies" and will they be the same policies again? Were the underlying reasons behind these draconian but economically nonsensical measures at the given time not rather meant as a deterrent for any future fiscal lenience? Indeed, this is the Achilles heel of any future assistance programme design. ECB's Draghi resumed in his farewell remarks that "in other regions where fiscal policy has played a greater role since the crisis, we have seen that the recovery began sooner and the return to price stability has been faster. The US had a deficit of 3.6% on average from 2009 to 2018, while the euro area had a surplus of 0.5%. In other words, the US has had both a capital markets union and a counter-cyclical fiscal policy. The euro area had no capital markets union and a pro-cyclical fiscal policy." However, his quotation exposes the fact that according to the standards of the EU fiscal framework, the surplus of 0.5% would certainly be considered the sounder budgetary policy and would be reapplied again. It might be worthwhile to empower the European Fiscal Board to have a role in the definition of the adjustment programmes, as recommended by Christian Ghymers (Chap. 22), however, after the European Parliament has defined a framework of (human) and social rights, which must not be undermined again.

The European Court of Justice has clearly explained the conditions for financial assistance in the EU: *Article 125 TFEU does not prohibit the granting of financial assistance by one or more Member States to a Member State which remains responsible for its commitments to its creditors provided that the conditions attached to such assistance are such as to prompt that Member State to implement a sound budgetary policy.* Based on this article, the ESM financial assistance is strictly conditional on the implementation of policy measures. As previously with the Troika, measures are specified in a Memorandum of Understanding (MoU), but will be negotiated by the European Commission on behalf of the ESM, the European Central Bank (ECB), the International Monetary Fund (IMF) (where applicable) and the beneficiary Member State. The lending instrument and the attached conditions are approved by the ESM Board of Governors, which is composed of the Euro

Area Finance Ministers. In other words, the ESM is once again the prolonged arm of the Eurogroup, instrumentalizing both the European Commission and the ECB for the purpose of elaborating Memorandum of Understandings in line with their guidelines, by taking decisions in consensus, risking to repeat the same kind of conflicts as experienced in the past crisis. Additionally, although both institutions participate regularly in exchange of views in the European Parliament, neither the Eurogroup nor the ESM is legally democratically accountable to the European Parliament (Zoppe et al. 2019).

Addressing the Erosion of Democratic Legitimacy and Accountability of the EMU

In order to correct the architectural omissions, which led to an erosion of democratic legitimacy and accountability both at EU and at national levels, it would thus be urgent to either abolish the Eurogroup altogether again given that the UK has left the European Union which had been one of the main reasons to establish it anyway. Otherwise, the best alternative would be to integrate it within the EU legal framework and thus correct the democratic deficit by making it fully accountable to the European Parliament. To avoid also a conflict of interest of president of the Eurogroup which is at the same time a full-time finance minister of a member-state, it would be better to introduce a full-time president of the Eurogroup, in whose nomination procedure the European Parliament would be involved. One possibility which has been proposed in the Commission' Reflection Paper on EMU was to merge this function with the Commissioner on economics and to make him Vice President of the European Commission. The European Parliament in turn could create a subcommittee on EMU and limit the voting rights to members of the European Parliament from EMU Member States in plenary.

Concerning the democratization of the financial assistance, be it within a European Monetary Fund (EMF) to be created, or by transforming the already existing European Stability Mechanism into an EMF, the important element is to give the European Parliament the right to co-decision on its architecture and to propose the changes necessary to take into account the lessons learnt from the assistance programmes of the last decade. It is clear that the policy recommendations within the financial assistance programmes cannot be a one-size-fits-all, but need to take into account the specific economic situation, crisis and circumstances of each country at a given time and respect democratic preferences of policies to achieve certain economic objectives. However, it would be extremely useful for the European Parliament to already define a certain framework and conditions and (human)rights which must be guaranteed.

Resuming the reforms undertaken or being discussed at EU level in the aftermath of the crisis, we can clearly identify that there is a persistent resistance to any measures of risk sharing both in the area of financial markets, but even more concerning fiscal policies. Yet, if we consider the most successful crisis management undertaken at EU level, we can clearly see that the ECB was the one institution which put on hold financial market speculation by demonstrating that they will do "whatever it takes" in a common monetary policy. Had there been a Eurozone budget or any other form of fiscal capacity in place, alone its existence would already have calmed down the eurocrisis, or it might even never have come about.

Changes of the treaties are a risky endeavour in the European Union. However, Fabbrini (2019) states that "the current EU constitutional framework already allows taking important steps towards the creation of a fiscal capacity, and Brexit –the decision of the United Kingdom (UK) to withdraw from the EU – actually opens a window of opportunity to this end. Nevertheless, as the in-depth analysis suggests in light of comparative insights, the proper design of a Eurozone budget is a precondition for its success: in particular, it is crucial that such a fiscal capacity be funded by real own resources, rather than state transfers, and subjected to mechanisms of democratic legitimation." Indeed, the UK departure represents a window of opportunity for treaty changes and a chance to move towards a more solidary and united European Union. Europe's resilience and role in the world actually depend on its capacity to grow together not only in the form of an internal market but truly towards a real Economic and Monetary Union, and on whether Europe can regain its influence by sharing sovereignty: "In a globalized world, sharing sovereignty is a way to regain sovereignty" (Draghi 2019).

Disclaimer The opinions expressed in this introduction/volume are the sole responsibility of the authors and do not necessarily represent the official position of the European Parliament or of any other EU institution.

References

Beblavý, M., Marconi, G., & Maselli, I. (2015). A European unemployment benefits scheme: The rationale and the challenges ahead. *CEPS Special Report, 19*. https://www.ceps.eu/ceps-publications/european-unemployment-benefits-scheme-rationale-and-challenges-ahead/. Accessed 1 Mar 2020.

Delpla, J., & Von Weizsaecker, J. (2011). Eurobonds: The blue bond concept and its implications. *Bruegel Policy Contribution*, Issue 2011/02 March 2011. https://bruegel.org/wp-content/uploads/imported/publications/110322_pc_blue_bonds.pdf. Accessed 1 Mar 2020.

Dolls, M. (2018). *An unemployment re-insurance scheme for the Eurozone? Stabilizing and redistribute effects*. Bertelsmann Stiftung 2018. https://www.bertelsmann-stiftung.de/fileadmin/files/BSt/Publikationen/GrauePublikationen/EZ_Study_Re-Insurance_2018_ENG.pdf. Accessed 1 Mar 2020.

Draghi, M. (2019). Farewell speech, at the ECB, Frankfurt, 29 Oct 2019.

European Commission. (1977). *The MacDougall report — Volume I. Study group on the role of public finance in European integration*. http://ec.europa.eu/economy_finance/emu_history/documentation/chapter8/19770401en73macdougallrepvol1.pdf. Accessed 1 Mar 2020.

European Commission. (2019). *Commission communication on the European Green Deal, COM (2019) 640 final, 11.12.2019*. https://ec.europa.eu/info/sites/info/files/european-green-deal-communication_en.pdf. Accessed 1 Mar 2020.

European Commission. (2020). *European commission 2020 work programme: An ambitious roadmap for a union that strives for more*. https://ec.europa.eu/commission/presscorner/detail/en/IP_20_124. Accessed 1 Mar 2020.

European Fiscal Board. (2019). *Assessment of the EU fiscal rules with a focus on the six-pack and two-pack legislation, August 2019*. https://ec.europa.eu/info/publications/assessment-eu-fiscal-rules-focus-six-and-two-pack-legislation_en. Accessed 1 Mar 2020.

European Parliament. (2011). *Resolution of 6 July 2011 on the financial, economic and social crisis: Recommendations concerning the measures and initiatives to be taken (2010/2242(INI))*. https://www.europarl.europa.eu/sides/getDoc.do?reference=P7-TA-2011-0331&type=TA&language=EN&redirect. Accessed 1 Mar 2020.

European Parliament. (2015). *Resolution on the review of the economic governance framework: Stocktaking and challenges of 2015*. https://www.europarl.europa.eu/doceo/document/TA-8-2015-0238_EN.html. Accessed 1 Mar 2020.

European Parliament. (2017). *Resolution on the budgetary capacity for the euro area in 2017*. https://www.europarl.europa.eu/doceo/document/TA-8-2017-0050_EN.html. Accessed 1 Mar 2020.

European Commission. (2017). Reflection paper on the future of EU finances, 28 June 2017, https://ec.europa.eu/commission/sites/beta-political/files/reflection-paper-eu-finances_en.pdf

European Parliament. (2018). Draft report on the proposal for a regulation of the European Parliament and of the Council on the establishment o1f a European Investment Stabilisation Function (COM(2018)0387 - C8-0241/2018 - 2018/0212(COD)), Committee on Budgets and Committee on Economic and Monetary Affairs, Rapporteurs: Reimer Böge, Pervenche Berès, https://www.europarl.europa.eu/doceo/document/CJ16-PR-628556_EN.htm. 4 October 2018.

Fabbrini, F. (2019). A fiscal capacity for the Eurozone: Constitutional perspectives. In *depth analysis. European Parliament, February 2019*. https://www.europarl.europa.eu/RegData/etudes/IDAN/2019/608862/IPOL_IDA(2019)608862_EN.pdf. Accessed 1 Mar 2020.

IMF Compilation Guide on Financial Soundness Indicators 2004, paragraphs 4.84-4.85, (https://www.imf.org/external/np/sta/fsi/eng/2004/guide/index.htm)

Juncker, C. (2015). Completing Europe's economic and monetary union ("Five Presidents report"). Report by Jean-Claude Juncker, in close cooperation with Donald Tusk, J. Disselbloem, M. Draghi, & M. Schultz. https://ec.europa.eu/commission/sites/beta-political/files/5-presidents-report_en.pdf. Accessed 1 Mar 2020.

Lenarčič, A., & Korhonen, K. (2018). *A case for a European rainy day fund. European stability mechanism*. https://www.esm.europa.eu/sites/default/files/dp5.pdf. Accessed 1 Mar 2020.

Macron, E., & Merkel, A. (2018). *Meseberg declaration: Renewing Europe's promises of security and prosperity*. 19 June 2018. https://archiv.bundesregierung.de/archiv-de/meta/startseite/meseberg-declaration-1140806. Accessed 1 Mar 2020.

Van Rompuy H. (2012). Towards a genuine economic and monetary union/"Four Presidents report", Report by President of the European Council Herman Van Rompuy, EUCO 120/12, 26 June 2012. https://www.consilium.europa.eu/media/33785/131201.pdf

Zoppe, A., & Dias, C. (2019). *The European stability mechanism: main features, instruments and accountability*. European Parliament. Economic Governance Support Unit. https://www.europarl.europa.eu/RegData/etudes/BRIE/2014/497755/IPOL-ECON_NT(2014)497755_EN.pdf. Accessed 1 Mar 2020.

24

Strengthening of Bi-Regional Cooperation between EU and LAC

Christian Ghymers

Abstract This chapter proposes the strengthening of the bi-regional cooperation EU-Latin America and the Caribbean (LAC) based upon a bottom-up exchanges across experts and officials through an innovative two-leg strategy of bi-regional dialogues.

Introduction

The European Union (EU) economies and other regions of the world are affected by the Global Financial Crisis (GFC) and its continuation and prolonged effects. Starting from the identification of the unsustainable character of the present economic system for intertwined macrofinancial and environmental reasons (see Chaps. 2 and 3 in this volume), the purpose of this chapter is to propose a costless formula of bi-regional cooperation between the EU and the Latin America and the Caribbean (LAC) region for tackling the unsustainable aspects of their economies. The basic assumption upon which relies our Network "Crisis – Democracy – Equity" is that in spite of huge differences between the EU and LAC regions from a structural and socio-institutional point of view, the GFC and its consequences deserve to be analysed in a comparative way in order to identify not only common elements and interests but also differences with the view to formulate concrete proposals for resolving the systemic crisis in a cooperative way.

Economic growth in the LAC area as in the EU is not sustainable. In particular productivity growth is very low in the EU and even negative in LAC. The solution is to recover a higher sustainable path of growth for productivity in both regions. The argument advanced in this chapter is that this urgent requirement could be better satisfied by an acceleration of the bi-regional cooperation EU-LAC especially

---

President of Interdisciplinary Institute for the Relations between Europe, Latin America and the Caribbean (IRELAC), Brussels, Belgium.

C. Ghymers (✉)
Founder and Co-coordinator of the Jean Monnet Network "Crisis-Equity-Democracy for Europe and Latin America", IRELAC, Brussels, Belgium

based upon an innovative two-leg strategy of bi-regional dialogues among stakeholders and experts: (i) one between stakeholders from academic, scientific and firms cooperation in order to reduce their gaps with the SMEs and accelerate the diffusion of innovation and technologies in the whole economies, and (ii) a complementary one for interconnecting experts dedicated to macroeconomic aspects for anchoring stability through a mutual scrutiny of policy mixes in a macroeconomic mutual monitoring spurring regional and bi-regional cohesion and increasing the common EU-LAC voice on financial markets and inside multilateral organizations.

The Method: Fostering a Dynamic Bi-regional Cooperation with a Bottom-Up Exchanges Across Experts and Officials Through a Two-Tier System of NetworksIntra- and Inter-regions

We propose a Plan with simple mechanisms for triggering new dynamics in the bi-regional relations. The proposal consists in a set of two complementary exchange initiatives able to change the routine and to free innovation capacities, and is based upon the concrete experiments of the EU,[1] of REDIMA[2] - Red de Dialogos Macroeconomico, ECLAC-CEPAL (Ghymers 2005), for Latin America as well as equivalent cases in other regions:[3]

1. To propose to all Bi-regional Summit participants the development of a "bottom-up method" for broadening the process of defining the content of the Strategic Alliance and the inputs for selecting cooperative ideas and projects to the Summit agenda. This "peer pressure" method consists in launching a two-leg (macroeconomic and industrial dialogue networks), two-sector (public policies and private firms) and two-tier (regional and bi-regional levels) system of broad informal networks (internet) gathering basic actors for expressing their views and needs of regional and bi-regional cooperation:

   1.1. First, to create (with incentives) in CELAC and EU civil-servant networks between national administrations and experts, one network per technical

[1] Not for importing the EU model, but only the method which proved to be useful for stimulating regional cooperation by breaking the prisoner dilemma between national governments (see Ghymers 2005).

[2] Although conceived for macroeconomic policy monitoring, the REDIMA experiment is valid for spurring regional cooperation in any key area since it tackles the obstacles due to situation of prisoner's dilemma (see Ghymers 2005).

[3] The move from West African Monetary Union (UMOA) to West African Economic and Monetary Union (UEMOA) in the Western CFA Franc monetary Union and the move from the Monetary Union (UMAC) to Central African Economic and Monetary Community (CEMAC) in the Equatorial CFA Franc monetary union. See: Ghymers (1997).

issue or policy; each participant acts on his own, without committing his administration or minister in confidential exchanges under "Chatham rule";

1.2. Second, to do the same for the business sectors, using the national Chambers of Commerce and SMEs' associations as well as company or sector representations;

1.3. Third, to connect each regional network (public policies and private firms) for developing at bi-regional level a direct mean of free exchanges and cooperation, giving so a direct voice channel to the peers in charge of policies and Trade/investment/production/employment;

1.4. Fourth step is to collect the results at official level for processing them with transparency at ministerial level for bringing them in the Summit agenda and taking actions in bi-regional cooperation programmes.

These autonomous networks managed by the basic actors allow for direct trans-regional consultations first, followed by extending consultations and exchanges to the bi-regional level between these basic actors from each regions. Autonomous networks permit a genuine technical democratization which gives a voice and stimulate initiative and innovation from civil servant experts and private firms. Experiences in Africa and Latin America show that encouraging and warranting the informal and free nature (open competition between participants speaking on their own and not in the name of their institution) of the exchanges ensure a powerful dynamics and an endogenous development of structured networks beneficial for the policymakers. An emulation among technicians spurs the use of this tool in the own interest of the participants and their hierarchies, with a mechanism of self-selection from them to the EU/CELAC procedures, through incentives created by each country (and/or sub-region) in favour of the people in charge of each national administration (regional rewards, scholarships, missions, etc.).

By organizing incentives for making each separated technical network to report systematically to the decision-maker levels (ministers of both regions and Summit participants), they provide them with a spontaneous generation of ideas and projects which offer an extraordinary flow of innovations and efficient contributions to regional integration and bi-regional cooperation. In exchange, the participants can express their voice and transmit their views and advices to policymakers for reaching consensual positions successively at regional and bi-regional levels, about the main issues for which these actors consider that regional cooperation would be beneficial for them.

The need to maximize the interests of basic actors in the bi-regional cooperation moves them in favour of cooperative actions, both among peers in the public sector and for SMEs or for other interested firms. Thus, these networks—if sufficiently autonomous—have the potential to decentralize and to trigger a competition among actors which stimulates the efforts for identifying and selecting concrete bi-regional cooperation in their own interests in their area of technical responsibilities but limited by the scrutiny of their peers. Not for taking decisions but just for emulating regional and bi-regional cooperation at technical levels of public policies and firms. This "peer selection" mechanism is very powerful when it enjoys sufficient autonomy for freeing technical competences in a competitive run for identifying common interests according to pure technical or scientific criteria by the technicians who participate in each network. The role of governments is only active at the two ends of the networks: at the starting point by deciding their administrations to launch the networks allowing civil servants to participate actively on their own (not as their delegates) since national administrations and ministers are the direct beneficiaries of the works of the networks, and at the end of the works for decision making after collecting the results with conclusions, proposals, ideas or merely information on what the partners think, are doing or planning to do (exchanges of best practices or failures).

The final step of this "REDIMA[4] recipe" for renewing the bi-regional agenda and working methods is to organize at official level (Ministers and Heads of State or Government) a decision-making process. It would merely consist in creating "Bi-regional Minister Councils" for deciding the ranking of priorities for common action and cooperation, as well as the organization and monitoring of the implementation of the Summit decisions. This method should be applied for dealing with four different issues by exchanging best practices and analysis on: (i) policies for restoring a sustainable growth path for productivity, (ii) social policies, (iii) decarbonization and environmental policies, and (iv) implementing a Mutual Macroeconomic Monitoring for anchoring macroeconomic stability and mutual confidence.

Restoring Sustainable Productivity Growth

Most of the lagging productivity in both regions comes from the insufficient diffusion of technology (mainly in the service and logistic sectors) rather than at the technological frontier, and adopting a bi-regional approach allows for exploiting differences and triggering fast synergies to close the gap between the frontier firms and most other firms and sectors inside each economy, a much easier task if an adequate EU cooperation allows for wrapping together the productivity increases. Contrary to superficial views, EU and LAC respective productivity weaknesses are additional reasons for spurring a deeper Strategic Alliance between the two regions. This chapter advocates for using the existing Bi-regional Summit Diplomacy as a catalytic tool for generating a new dynamic in these EU-LAC relations by formulating an operational method for decentralizing the preparation of the Summits and taking charge of dynamizing the follow-up with cooperation tools. This broadening of the bi-regional Summit is presented as an "EU-LAC Monnet Plan" for defining and executing the "Strategic Alliance" which was declared in 1999 in Rio by the EU and the LAC countries but with a too timid content and few realizations in two decades.

[4] See footnote 2, the purpose is to extend the REDIMA approach to key aspects of the EU-LAC cooperation.

The Economic Deadlock of the LAC Economies According to Their Productivity Performance (TFP)

It is an amazing phenomenon that productivity progress—the driving engine of socio-economic prosperity—is in trouble and about to stop in the advanced economies—especially in EU economies—and has even turned negative in LACs ones. The adequate concept to use is that of "total factor productivity" (TFP) (or multifactor productivity), i.e. the difference between the rate of growth of output and the rate of growth of the factors and inputs used for producing that output. It therefore provides a simple but powerful indicator of economic efficiency or "cost reduction" for an economy as a whole. It is the only sustainable source of long-term economic growth and social progress. Without productivity growth, an economy will slowly grind to a halt and to social and financial troubles. It is the only growth factor that does not suffer from diminishing returns as homogeneous inputs typically do. TFP growth represents the so-called "positive externalities" which arise from technological progress, innovation and the socio-institutional framework in which production is organized. If sustained, low productivity growth would have profound adverse implications for progress in global living standards, the sustainability of private and public debts, social protection systems, and the ability of macroeconomic policies to respond to future shocks and to the ageing costs. The LACs' economies are affected by the same disease as other regions but at a higher degree of toxicity. During the same long-term period as shown in Fig. 24.1, the TFP growth for the CELAC economies is even worst since it is negative (−0.11% per year), and only the very poor region of Sub-Saharan Africa registers a worse performance (−0.5%) (Fig. 24.2).

This very poor performance of long-run TFP growth translates or "explains" statistically the impossibility for LAC economies, as a whole, to catch up with the advanced economies and to follow the emerging ones. The observed growth rate for the GDP of LAC area is the result of an improvement of labour absorption (demographic dividend and women inclusion, i.e. more productive workers) and human

Fig. 24.1 CELAC region, long-term annual growth rate of Total Factor Productivity Growth, 1960–2014 (Source: IDB 2018)

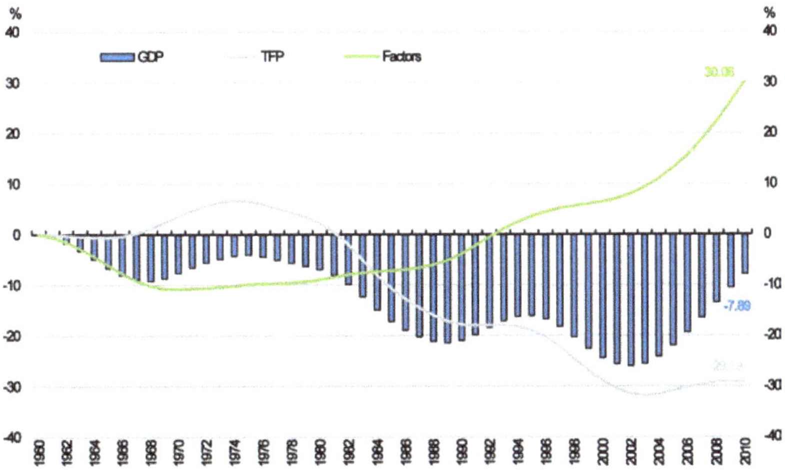

Fig. 24.2 LAC region, relative evolutions of GDP, TFP and Factors accumulation with respect to the US economy 1960–2010. (Source: OECD 2019)

capital (better education) combined with an investment increase. However, these efforts were more than compensated by a loss in efficiency, i.e. the bad TFP performance (30% less than the US). Alternatively, this appears also in the fact that in the LAC region, any additional investment yields less than in the advanced economies or the emerging ones. For example, in South Korea, the capital stock increased two times faster than GDP between 1960 and 2017, while in Brazil, the capital stock increased three times faster than GDP for the same period. But this gap in "capital deepening" is not due to a better effort of investment in Brazil with respect to Korea, but to a lower growth of GDP for the same effort of investment, i.e. to a lower efficiency of Brazilian economy, and apart from that in Brazil, labour inputs also contributed positively to output increases. IDB (2018) calculated that if the LAC would have invested at the same rate than that in Emerging Asia (+7% in LAC investment ratio) and if the efficiency of the investment would have been the same (capital output ratio of 3.5 versus 5 in LAC), the level of LAC GDP would be six times higher in 2017 than the observed GDP for the same year.

The diagnostic appears to be clear: the LAC economies as a whole are less efficient than the advanced and emerging economies, their scarce resources dedicated to investment are more wasted than elsewhere, and in the next future, the demographic dividend as well as the environment's deterioration are about to turn into additional negative factors for growth. A radical change is needed both for reversing the general slowdown in TFP and for solving the specific inefficiency of the LAC economies.

The Common Features Between the EU and LAC Performances in TFP

The EU and LAC regions share the same TFP disease as the rest of advanced economies, but with a common distinctive feature with respect to the US economy. When comparing the EU to the US TFP growth, the main part of the European lag comes from the lower productivity performance in European service sectors, as a result of low competitive pressures and heterogeneous regulations which blunt the incentives to adopt best practices. When comparing the LAC economies with the US and the EU ones, this disadvantage is even bigger and constitutes a major obstacle to the catching-up process and the necessary improvement in their competitiveness for facing the global and social challenges their economies are condemned to solve quickly. Inefficiencies come mainly from services but are also affecting manufacturing since in globalization the competition in tasks (not any more in products) makes efficient services the key for participation to Global Value Chains (GVCs). Inefficiencies in services result from distortions in incentives for innovation and protection rules favourable to inefficient firms, both in the LAC and the EU, but with big differences between the EU and the LAC. These differences offer a wonderful opportunity for bi-regional alliances and cooperation, mutually beneficial. TFP potential growth is enormous for both regions by organizing technological transfer between the EU and the LAC in a strategy for SMEs' joint competitiveness on GVCs.

This handicap in services is really the key of the needed productive transformation the LAC economies (as well as the EU ones) require. Services, in the broadest sense, including logistic and infrastructure, are the basic determinants of a fruitful and dynamic participation to Global Value Chains (GVCs) which would allow the increase of TFP and so putting both regions on a higher growth path. In fact, this common feature to the EU and the LAC economies is *linked to the* weakening diffusion mechanism of innovation to the whole economy. The reasons are very complex and very different from one region (or country) to the other; however, it is interesting to try to apply to them the same analytical scheme in order to identify common issues from idiosyncratic specificities. The lagging TFP in the LAC should not be a surprise as the diffusion mechanism is precisely what characterized an emerging economy while the so-called "under-development trap" impedes this diffusion and maintains dualistic features inside the same economy with a big difference in productivity across sectors. This "internal gap" in productivity reflects the social exclusion in the LAC economies and generates a "vicious circles" typical of poorer countries. In fact, as shown by ECLAC studies, the internal productivity gap between the modern export sector and the rest of the economy reveals a sectoral strong heterogeneity which generates social inequalities, which in turn slows down progress in productivity and innovation, leading to the so-called "external gap", or lack of structural competitiveness, due to exports with low impact on growth and social progress (less inclusive exports and international insertion). Large internal gaps reinforce the external gap and partially feed on it. Thus, vicious circles are created, not only in terms of poverty and low growth, but also slow in learning and weak structural changes, all of which hinder regional integration and reinforce their handicap in competitiveness, to be able to insert themselves to value chains under good conditions. Since low productivity sectors have great difficulties for improving human capital, innovating, adopting technology and driving learning processes, the internal heterogeneity worsens systemic competitiveness issues, poor international insertion and social exclusion.

In the EU, although the breakdown of the diffusion mechanism cannot be explained in the same way by under-development, there are yet similar processes through the increasing social inequalities linked to rent-seeking attitudes which lead to social exclusion too with a negative impact upon growth. In addition, the impact of the global crisis has played the same role in both regions for dampening the TFP progress through less investment and less innovation. The remedies are very similar, but in the EU, they deal more with the technological frontier firms and sectors. Since the LAC economies are much less present at the frontier (top technological firms and sectors), the priority for the LAC economies is merely to concentrate efforts where the results on TFP should be the highest and the cheapest, i.e. to focus their efforts towards the third mechanism: to raise the productivity of laggard firms and to accelerate the technological diffusion to the whole economy, to SMEs and to the labour force, something that necessarily involves universities. The technological gap is not only much easier and faster to close for the followers than for the leaders, but it is a prerequisite for climbing the production chains up to acquiring leading roles. Indeed, the spillovers across firms and sectors are increasing with the catching-up process and are two ways: modernization by importing leader technology opens the road to local innovation and diversification of technology, creating specific "niches" inside the Global Value Chains (GVCs) and improving also profitability for both partners.

This general predicament is of course easy to say, but it takes its attractive operational sense by considering the higher returns the bi-regional cooperation could bring inside the strategic alliance that both regions intended to build together. The major objective should be to dedicate this alliance for improving their joint competitiveness in the globalized world by cooperating to increase the diffusion mechanism for reducing their respective productivity gaps with the technological frontier and the top firms.

Some Key Weaknesses in LAC Economies Which Explain the Lagging TFP

Considering the most important causes for the lagging TFP in the LAC economies, a simple activation and extension of the existing tools for bi-regional cooperation could do most of the tasks for meeting the challenges both regions are facing. First, economic openness in the LAC economies remains insufficient, despite some clear progress. Without getting into details or countries, Fig. 24.3 speaks for itself showing the LAC economies are the less opened of the regions. Empirical results demonstrate that trade openness is an important factor of TFP through several channels (competition, investments, specialization, technological information and spillovers). International Monetary Fund (IMF) research shows that reduction in input tariffs and non-tariff barriers is found to raise strongly TFP levels (Ahn et al. 2016; Dabla-Norris and Duval 2016), especially where protection is still high. Trade appears to be closely correlated to foreign direct investment (FDI) to which the region is not sufficiently open for benefitting from knowledge spillovers of FDI which spur TFP. Figure 24.4 shows this strong correlation.

The kind of strategic alliance both regions are trying to implement points precisely to increase mutually their respective markets and their reciprocal flows of investment, one of the keys to TFP improvements. Second, Fig. 24.5 shows that the region is also the less integrated into *Global Value Chains*. Globalization produced this fragmentation of the production processes, allowing for firms from less developed economies to join the global production network by specializing in specific activities within the value chain, focusing on those core tasks they are most efficient at without being obliged to create their own whole cluster and network as mature economies were obliged to do in their past stages of development. Recent empirical studies established a direct impact upon TFP and higher participation in GVCs (effects of specialization and scale economies, access to frontier technologies and markets, higher technology inputs, knowledge spillovers through cooperation with providers and suppliers). Economies can participate in GVCs by using imported inputs in their exports (so-called backward linkages) or by supplying intermediates to third country exports (forward linkages). GVC participation varies substantially

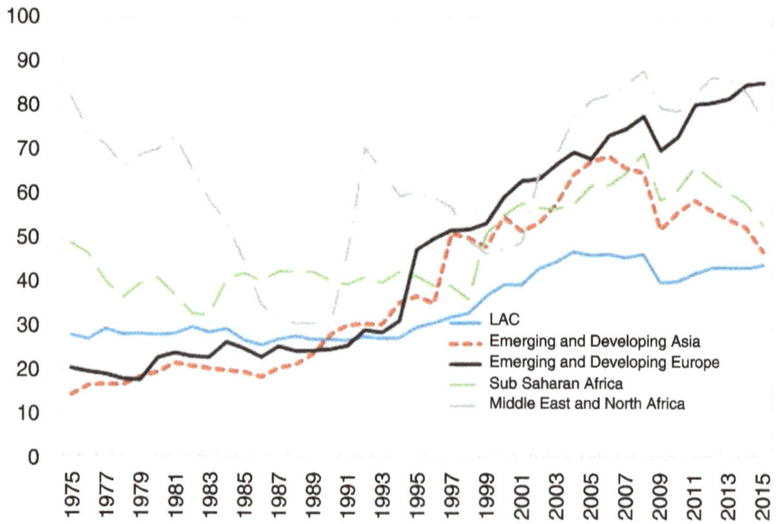

Fig. 24.3 Regional comparison of trade openness of LAC economies 1975–2016 (trade flows measured as % of GDP). (Source: Morgan 2017)

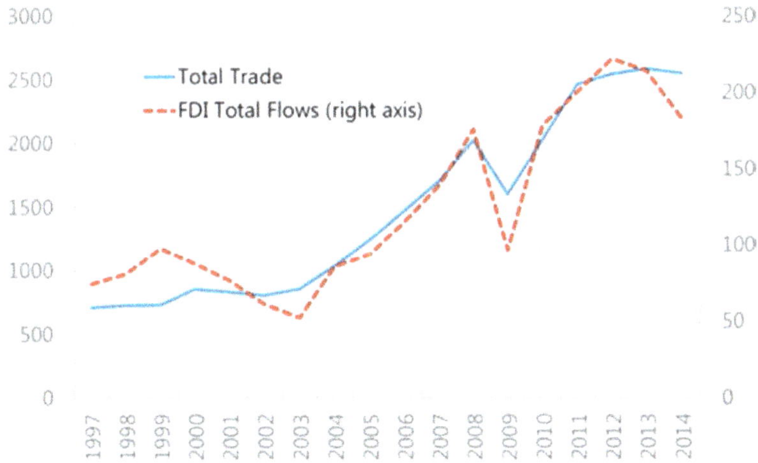

Fig. 24.4 Correlation between Trade and FDI for LAC (billions of US $). (Source: Morgan 2017)

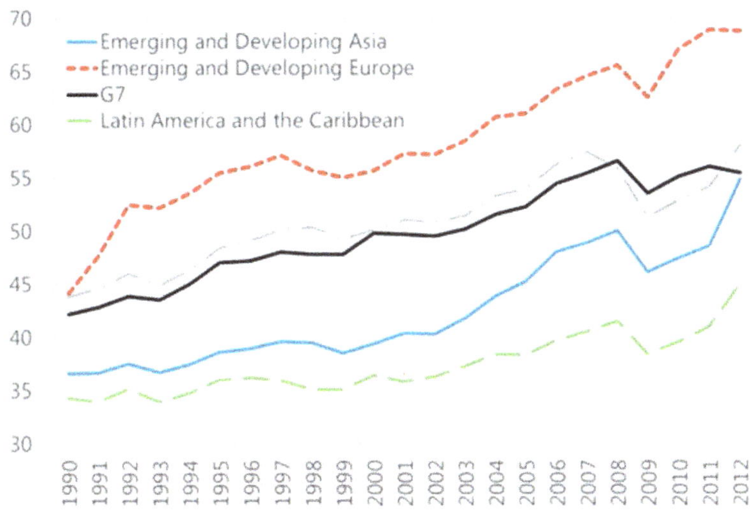

Fig. 24.5 Global Value Chain participation index by region (share of domestic and foreign value added in gross exports). (Source: Morgan 2017)

across different Latin American countries. According to OECD (2019) database, Chile has the highest level of total GVC participation of the Latin American economies, accounting for 52% of gross exports (which is mainly driven by forward participation because of its copper exports). However, many other Latin American economies are not well integrated within GVCs compared to other developing Asian and Eastern European economies. For example, the total GVC participation represents only 31% of gross exports in Argentina and 35% in Brazil.

More importantly, regional value chains within Latin America are also much less developed than in Europe, South-East Asia or North America. Intra-regional links are very low: out of the total foreign value added used for producing exports, only 9% was sourced from within the region against 50% in the EU and 40% in Asia (Cadestin et al. 2016). Latin American economies are more integrated with external actors (e.g. China) than intra-regionally but with less transmission to the national economies. Also, firms in Latin America show a very low propensity to innovate through international collaborations, with 21% of Brazilian and 8% of Chilean large firms and only 2% of Brazilian and 3% of Chilean small firms doing so. These figures are much lower than in the OECD and Asian economies. For example, the share of SMEs collaborating on innovation with higher education or research institutions in the OECD economies is 14.5%, and for large firms, it is 37% (OECD 2019). On these aspects too, a bi-regional approach would inevitably bring more regional cooperation, and also a more inclusive development through the explicit cooperation orientation and tools that are available.

Third, regional integration is lower than in other regions, and even Africa has now a higher share of intra-regional trade than the LAC area. This feature is a major handicap for productivity increase and for competitiveness and incorporation to dynamic GVCs. One of the constant guidelines of the EU agreements is to incentivize regional integration with specific methods and tools (Fig. 24.6).

Although not the only weaknesses that affect negatively the TFP growth in the LAC, these three categories are precisely those that could be solved through a strategic alliance with the EU along the lines exposed in the next section.

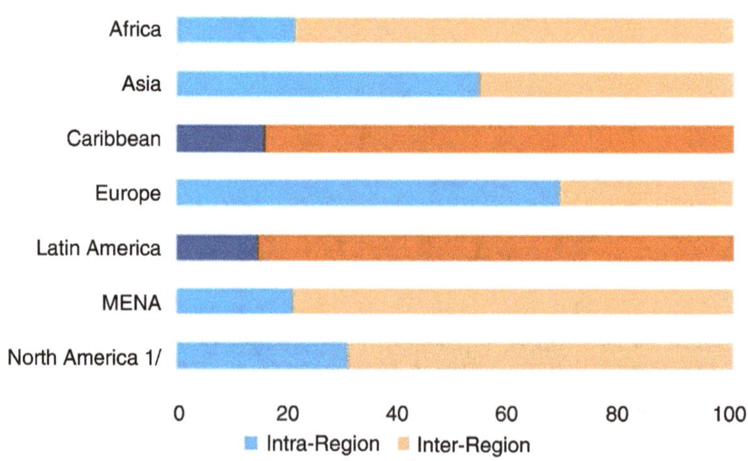

Fig. 24.6 Intra-regional exports versus inter-regional by region (in % of total exports 2015). (Sources: IMF 2017)

The Win-Win Game of an EU-LAC Cooperation Addressing the Laggard TFP

According to our analysis, the priority for both the EU and the LAC economies should be to deal with the weakening in the technological diffusion mechanism. Indeed, in the EU, the TFP issue relies mostly in the too low productivity in the service sectors. In the LAC, the issue is much deeper because the gap is higher and more generalized to the whole economy: the rising gap between frontier firms and the rest of the economy dominated by inefficient SMEs is bigger. The positive appealing aspect is that focusing the efforts upon the pace at which the innovations spread throughout the economy by dealing with SMEs could yield much more TFP jumps than to try to develop new technologies for the frontier firms. Furthermore—and more importantly—the easiest way to do it is through a mutually profitable bi-regional cooperation between academics and SMEs, since it is based upon technological exchanges, regional benchmarking, joint researches and joint ventures, which are powerful ways to spur catching-up and innovation.

Our argument is structured as follows:

- Based upon the big change induced by globalization provoking the acceleration of the law of comparative advantages, a systematic fragmentation of tasks and outsourcing has resulted worldwide of the whole production chain, including the part R&D (knowledge).
- Exchanges of experiences between the EU and the LAC allow for making more visible common interests to strengthen the GVCs to which both producers belong:
    1. Weakest/smallest producers benefit more from being brought into a GVC for technological transfer and access to market which is fast, cheap and with a lever effect in the local environment,
    2. Wide productivity gaps allow for complementarity opportunities to be exploited in mutual interests along the GVC in a double dynamic: lower costs for inputs for the most advanced partner, opportunities for outsourcing beneficial to both partners (new jobs in both regions as competitiveness increases along the GVC, cfr. Germany case with Eastern European economies) and broader field of differences spurring innovation.

Indeed, the actual way to spur productivity simultaneously in both regions is by using the profit-seeking drive of firms (and also in some cases with the cooperation of academics) looking at differences and complementarities that the respective GVCs' participation of these regions offers: the EU needs anyway more competitive inputs for remaining competitive in its specialties, and it could find them in the LAC economies by contributing to adjust the technological know-how necessary for reducing the costs, while the LAC needs more incorporation to dynamic GVCs on which its members could develop new specialties, become more innovative and benefit from better access to more sophisticated technologies and markets. A closer bi-regional cooperation—focusing on applied research and helping SMEs to internationalize—could speed up the technological catching-up in both regions (moving towards the production frontiers) and even provide the resources for innovating and feeding the creation of new technological leadership (moving-up the production frontier).

Figure 24.7 presents a dynamic synthesis of what the EU-LAC Strategic Alliance should do. The red frontier is the local best technology, but most local firms are far from this frontier. Improving their effective use of technologies would move them upwards (red arrow of TFP jumps). The green frontier represents the top productivity performers trying to displace upwards the technological frontier. The incorporation of more SMEs from both regions into GVCs would allow a double upwards movement: increasing efficiency with existing technologies with an improvement in competitiveness of the whole GVC which could therefore benefit from more resources for R&D able to displace upwards the technological frontier with positive feedbacks for the whole chain and for both regions. The recipe consists in focusing SMEs' reciprocal contacts and ventures through universities' bi-regional cooperation on local grounds for improving their operational efficiencies and technological catching-up, increasing their ability to integrate GVCs. The increased profits from acceding jointly to cheaper and better inputs for the joint GVC (upwards movement of red arrow) should allow for accelerating R&D dedicated to pushing upwards the joint technological frontier (upwards move of green arrow).

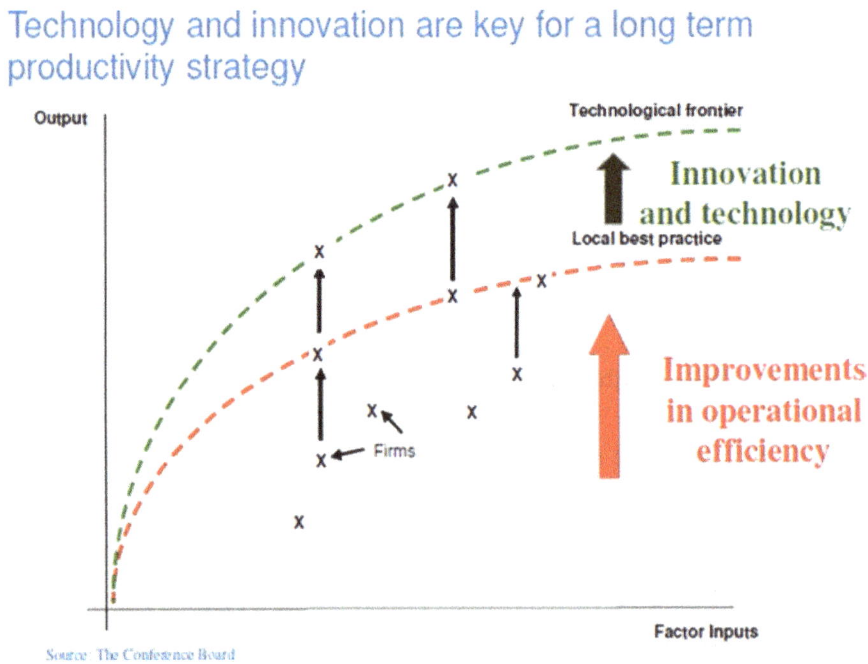

Fig. 24.7 Dynamic upwards moves of TFP through Bi-regional University-SMEs cooperation along joint GVCs (Source: Conference Board)

The Complementary Win-Win Game of EU-LAC Cooperation on Social and Environment Issues by Extending the REDIMA Method

The failure of both regions to cushion the social impacts of globalization, although to different degrees, provides another important application for the proposed REDIMA method because it would spur the exchanges of best practices across the Atlantic for improving the social consensus and fighting populism. The dynamics of improving productivity thanks to the kind of bi-regional cooperation exposed above require a parallel cooperation on social aspects because social consensus is a necessary component for productivity progress. The same analytic reasoning added by the absolute urgency to curb global climate changes justifies the necessity to create also a REDIMA network on de-carbonization. Furthermore, these two additional networks would lead "*to realize that a true ecological approach always becomes a social approach*" (Pope Francis 2015).

Conclusions

Bi-regional cooperation initiatives should give a special priority to match European Universities with that of the LAC, and simultaneously to organize the connection of SMEs from both regions for spurring their mutual internationalization and their technological and managerial evolution. Academic Summits have opened the way, but they should now be strengthened both at policy and company levels.

The basic idea justifying such a stronger cooperation of academics, governments and private firms from the EU and the LAC relies upon the very fact that the patterns of technology adoption, reallocation and productivity growth within and between firms in both advanced regions and lagging ones of these two regions are directly complementary for strengthening respective competitiveness on world markets. The successful integration of the Central and Eastern European countries into the EU economy in more advanced countries' production networks (especially through the German/Austrian firms' strategies) shows the ideal road to follow and to apply for the relations between the EU and the LAC economies. Ideal conditions of such a "win-win game" for both regional partners (the EU and the LAC) could be organized along the same lines and would lead to a significant improvement in Total Factor Productivity as a combined result of more global competition pressures but inside a more cooperative scheme at bi-regional and regional levels.

The EU and the LAC share the same values and socio-economic objectives more than with any other regions, making the LAC area the best candidate for a successful alliance with the EU. This is not just a political discourse argument, but a strategic reality: the LAC countries offer sufficient differences and divergences for creating attractive synergies as any other LDCs or emerging countries, but at the same time, they offer simultaneously the closest similarities between social objectives and the kind of societies in which citizens want to live which are necessary for mutual trust into a binding strategic alliance for the long run.

The concrete proposal: a set of bi-regional networks applying the REDIMA recipe to monitor four key areas of cooperation:

1. *Macroeconomic Monitoring: MMM*

   The purpose is triple: (i) to stimulate each region to organize a previous mutual monitoring across national peers at regional level, improving intra-regional mutual communication and building trust, therefore reducing uncertainties and promoting regional consensus; (ii) the group dynamics and the resulting emulation process among national participants in face of their peers from the other region contribute to improve national governance, making-up for respective institutional weaknesses at national level (external scrutiny equivalent to checks and balances); (iii) to identify common interests in order to build consensual views and credibility in front of third partners, financial markets as well as inside multilateral organizations (IMF, WB, WTO, ILO, UN, etc.).

   Concretely, the importance and interest to establish such a dialogue with the EU should motivate the LACs to put in place their own scheme of *Mutual Macroeconomic Monitoring schemes (MMM)* (by sub-regions and for the LAC area as a whole), in order to level up to EU working method. This technique allows for generating individual incentives for the national players to use the mutual surveillance in their own interests through the credibility building brought by the MMM and the scrutiny of competing partners. The best example is the possibility to influence the "spreads" (interest rate risk premium) by winning credibility and being supported by the technical peer review involving experts of both regions.

   How? By focusing attention of markets (and national public opinion) upon national policy performance and commitments, creating market and creditors' reactions which reward sound policies (effects on credibility), that makes more identifiable the gains of regional integration and macroeconomic cooperation (making it self-rewarding and conciliating national and regional interests). In terms of game theory, this dynamic process leads to "dominant strategies" that coincide with regional optimum, making possible a process of visible "win-win" game in which the positive outcome increases as the game is repeated, and incentives to defect tend to diminish with time as effective regional cooperation develops, as the game is repeated and seen as becoming an outgoing process (endogenous nature of the gains from Regional integration, seen in Axelrod's work showing that expectations can speed-up cooperation). The MMM delivers a mix of competition and cooperation: the bi-regional level creates a more effective way to create quickly the "checks-and-balances" and to spur regional integration that LACs would otherwise have spent too much years and efforts to win alone by their own.

2. *Social Policy Mutual Monitoring: SPMM*
   Extending the scope of the mutual monitoring to social issues would spur the awareness of the importance for productivity to go along with improving the social consensus.
3. *Mutual Monitoring of Environment: MME,*
   Complementary dimension of both social and economic policies, especially for making aware that GDP measures do not yet take on board the negative value added of environment destruction and CO2 emissions which correspond to lower effective productivity.
4. *Mutual Monitoring of Productivity: MMP*
   This monitoring would focus the university-firm gap, especially for SMEs, as well as the issue of negative externalities not included in national accounts.

References

Ahn, J., Dabla-Norris, E., Duval, R., Hu, B., & Njie, L. (2016). Reassessing the productivity gains from trade liberalization. *IMF Working Paper No*. 16/77. https://www.imf.org/external/pubs/ft/wp/2016/wp1677.pdf. Accessed 2 Mar 2020.

Cadestin, C., Gourdon, J., & Kowalski, P. (2016). Participation in global value chains in Latin America: Implications for trade and trade-related policy. *OECD Trade Policy Papers, No*. 192. https://www.oecd-ilibrary.org/docserver/5jlpq80ts8f2-en.pdf?expires=1583163295&id=id&accname=guest&checksum=3C61860F4157F6A928FA4649C6C486BD. Accessed 2 Mar 2020.

Dabla-Norris, E., & Duval, R. (2016). How lowering trade barriers can revive global productivity and growth. IMF Blog, 20 June 2016. https://blogs.imf.org/2016/06/20/how-lowering-trade-barriers-can-revive-global-productivity-and-growth/. Accessed 2 Mar 2020.

Francis (Pope), Encyclical Letter "Laudato Si" of The Holy Father Francis on "Care For Our Common Home". Rome: Vatican Press, 2015, §49.

Ghymers, C. (1997). Piste pour une initiative communautaire envers l'Afrique Sub-Saharienne. *Revue De Pecunia*, ICHEC, Bruxelles, *8*(1).

Ghymers, C. (2005). *Fostering economic policy coordination in Latin America: The REDIMA Approach to escaping the prisoner's dilemma*. Santiago: Libros de la CEPAL, n 82.

IDB. (2018). Informe macroeconómico de América Latina y el Caribe de 2018. https://publications.iadb.org/publications/english/document/2018-Latin-American-and-Caribbean-Macroeconomic-Report-A-Mandate-to-Grow.pdf. Accessed 2 Mar 2020.

IMF. (2017). Cluster report – Trade integration in Latin America and the Caribbean. *IMF Country Report No*. 17/66, March 2017. file:///C:/Users/IRI/Downloads/cr1766.pdf. Accessed 2 Mar 2020.

Morgan, D. E. (2017). Trade developments in Latin America and the Caribbean. International Monetary Fund, March 2017. file:///C:/Users/IRI/Downloads/cr1766-ap-5.pdf. Accessed 2 Mar 2020.

OECD. (2019). Boosting productivity and inclusive growth in Latin America. http://www.oecd.org/publications/boosting-productivity-and-inclusive-growth-in-latin-america-9789264269415-en.htm. Accessed 2 Mar 2020.

Afterword

Financial Crises, Regionalism and Domestic Adjustment

Loukas Tsoukalis

I have compared elsewhere[1] the international financial crisis that began in 2007 in the US sub-prime market and soon turned into an existential crisis for Europe's common currency the euro, to a set of Russian dolls, the *matryoshkas*. You opened one and found another one inside, one uglier than the other.

The international financial crisis, the biggest since 1929, marked a huge failure of markets, institutions and democratic politics. Capital liberalization and financial deregulation had been meant to operate in the context of efficient markets with rational actors armed with perfect information. Instead, when the big bubble burst, we all discovered—the more innocent among us with utter dismay—that there was greed, wrong incentives and herd instinct, all operating in conditions of high uncertainty and imperfect information, together with political capture. The process of financialization had set the stage for casino capitalism, and when things turned bad, governments were called upon to save the system from implosion. They were forced to use taxpayers' money in order to bail out those who had made large profits and paid themselves exorbitant bonuses while the going was good. The alternative of doing nothing was clearly much worse. But it was all bound to have long-lasting effects: the economy suffered a heavy blow and the victims (so many of them) were justifiably angry. Big economic crises always leave scars on the body of democratic polities, and they take long time to heal.

In the European Union (EU), we had built a monetary union which remains today the most daring act of integration. But the decision to create the euro back in the early 1990s had not been matched by a collective will to endow the common

[1] Loukas Tsoukalis (2016), *In Defence of Europe: Can the European Project Be Saved?* (Oxford: Oxford University Press),

currency with the institutions and policy instruments to ensure its long-term viability. As so often in the past with earlier initiatives of European integration, the euro was an incomplete construction to which new pieces were expected to be added as we went along. Thus, when the international financial crisis reached the European shores, it exposed the vulnerability of the regional monetary construction.

The Europeans were unlucky because big bang crises are only supposed to happen once in a lifetime, if that, although in a world of global capital markets such crises may prove to be much more frequent than in the past. The Europeans were unlucky and totally unprepared because they lacked the instruments to defend their currency. They were also mentally unprepared, because the prevalent view (that of the strongest country, Germany) allowed little margin of manoeuvre in the use of monetary and fiscal policy to deal with the crisis.

Hence, adjustment in Europe took longer and was much more painful than in the United States. The burden of adjustment fell almost entirely on deficit/debtor countries. They were forced to resort to internal devaluations, because national currencies were no longer there to be devalued nor was monetary policy available since responsibility for it had been transferred to the European central bank. To many people's surprise, the International Monetary Fund (IMF) became directly involved in the domestic adjustment programmes of euro members, thus further undermining the political credibility of Europe's monetary union. We all then discovered that Greece and Ireland were still very different from Louisiana and Nebraska as members of the European and the US monetary unions, respectively. We had been told otherwise until then.

The last set of *matryoshkas* consisted of individual members of the Eurozone, namely those most exposed to the crisis. They had been wild revellers in the party having enjoyed a long boom with borrowed money under the protection of the common currency. Banks in Ireland and Spain had been for years on a borrowing spree feeding the local versions of the big bubble. In Greece, the state had done the same acting as the main vehicle for borrowing, instead of the banks. Yet, when the crisis hit, all of them faced the same problem: their sources of finance, being mostly other European financial institutions, suddenly run dry—and debts could no longer be serviced. Other Eurozone governments felt obliged then to come to the rescue and brought the IMF along in order to avoid a generalized financial meltdown.

Was the crisis entirely the fault of debtors who had borrowed as if there was no tomorrow, or were creditors also to blame? This is the perennial question being asked when debt crises occur, although the answer given in real life is usually the same. It is mostly a matter of balance of power.

Even today, it is difficult to tell which one of the *matryoshkas* was the ugliest. Back then at the peak of the crisis, Europeans spent an inordinate amount of time fighting it out in a toxic blame game—and European politics turned ugly. The official verdict finally pronounced by the creditors was that the ugliest was Greece, and this provided the legitimization for austerity policies in the Eurozone. Austerity in turn prolonged the crisis. Had it been Ireland or Spain, instead of Greece, the main culprit, it would have constituted an explicit or otherwise recognition that the main problem behind the crisis was bank debt and not government deficits. After all, the latter were the result and not the cause of the crisis, with the notable exception of Greece. Narratives usually shape policies. This was also true in the way in which Europeans (mis)handled the financial crisis in the early 2010s with major negative effects in economic, political and social terms, although very unevenly distributed between and within countries.

Financial crises in Latin America in the 1980s had provided a foretaste of what was to follow on a much bigger scale in other parts of the world few decades later. In terms of adjustment programmes that debtor countries had to go through, there is close similarity between Argentina in her recurring financial crises and Greece in the early 2010s. After all, the IMF was directly involved in all adjustment programmes, and the main recipe has hardly changed over time. Both countries discovered in their own painful way that on the verge of bankruptcy they could afford only small portions of sovereignty and democracy. This has been true of other countries as well in similar circumstances except for the few, lucky enough who fall into the category of too big to fail. In such cases, bargaining power changes dramatically: Keynes had told us about this long time ago.

Latin American countries have other similarities especially with countries in southern Europe which found themselves in the eye of the latest financial storm. Corruption and low trust in public institutions are among them. We now know that the rise in populism caused by debt crises can have either a left- or a right-wing orientation; it does not only go in one direction. But populism is always closely associated with policy failures: difficult to admit when you are part of the system.

Greece's democracy has proved to be remarkably resilient given what the country had to go through during the crisis. Surely, being part of the European political order also made a difference. And being a member of the European monetary union ultimately prevented Greece's official bankruptcy, although the price the country was asked to pay was very high indeed.

The regional factor played virtually no role in Latin America's financial crises, as was to be expected. Regionalism is after all still at an early stage in that part of the world. And in Latin America's financial crises, the creditors always came from outside the region as did and still does the big power with heavy political clout in the Western hemisphere. Things were supposed to be different in Europe where regional integration is much more advanced than anywhere else. However, the international financial crisis of 2007–2008 soon morphed into a crisis that threatened both the euro and European integration in general, thus revealing the inherent weaknesses and limitations of the regional construction. True, much has changed in Eurozone governance since and because of the crisis. Thus, European integration has shown its capacity to adjust, although never enough and usually at the last minute.

Have we learned the lessons from the latest big crisis of the international financial system? Have we introduced mechanisms to prevent similar crises from occurring in the future? If only we could give unqualified positive answers to such questions. If not, will the euro prove to be robust enough when the next crisis hits? We keep going, unable or unwilling to think out of the box and hoping we will be lucky enough when it happens. However, I must confess to a late bout of optimism concerning Europe's capacity to handle crises since the pandemic struck. Some 'unthinkables' do indeed happen under extreme conditions. Even the IMF is changing.

Permissions

All chapters in this book were first published by Springer; hereby published with permission under the Creative Commons Attribution License or equivalent. Every chapter published in this book has been scrutinized by our experts. Their significance has been extensively debated. The topics covered herein carry significant information for a comprehensive understanding. They may even be implemented as practical applications or may be referred to as a beginning point for further studies.

The contributors of this book come from diverse backgrounds, making this book a truly international effort. We would like to thank all the contributing authors for lending their expertise to make the book truly unique. They have played a crucial role in the development of this book. Without their invaluable contributions this book wouldn't have been possible. They have made vital efforts to compile up to date information on the varied aspects of this subject to make this book a valuable addition to the collection of many professionals and students.

This book was conceptualized with the vision of imparting up-to-date and integrated information in this field. To ensure the same, a matchless editorial board was set up. Every individual on the board went through rigorous rounds of assessment to prove their worth. After which they invested a large part of their time researching and compiling the most relevant data for our readers.

The editorial board has been involved in producing this book since its inception. They have spent rigorous hours researching and exploring the diverse topics which have resulted in the successful publishing of this book. They have passed on their knowledge of decades through this book. To expedite this challenging task, the publisher supported the team at every step. A small team of assistant editors was also appointed to further simplify the editing procedure and attain best results for the readers.

Apart from the editorial board, the designing team has also invested a significant amount of their time in understanding the subject and creating the most relevant covers. They scrutinized every image to scout for the most suitable representation of the subject and create an appropriate cover for the book.

The publishing team has been an ardent support to the editorial, designing and production team. Their endless efforts to recruit the best for this project, has resulted in the accomplishment of this book. They are a veteran in the field of academics and their pool of knowledge is as vast as their experience in printing. Their expertise and guidance has proved useful at every step. Their uncompromising quality standards have made this book an exceptional effort. Their encouragement from time to time has been an inspiration for everyone.

The publisher and the editorial board hope that this book will prove to be a valuable piece of knowledge for students, practitioners and scholars across the globe.

Index

www.ingramcontent.com/pod-product-compliance
Lightning Source LLC
LaVergne TN
LVHW011517200926
848484LV00001B/57

* 9 7 8 1 6 4 7 2 5 4 5 1 3 *